D1546307

Showbiz **Politics**

Showbiz
Politics

HOLLYWOOD IN AMERICAN
POLITICAL LIFE

Kathryn Cramer Brownell

The University of North Carolina Press CHAPEL HILL

© 2014 The University of North Carolina Press
All rights reserved
Set in Utopia by codeMantra
Manufactured in the United States of America
The paper in this book meets the guidelines for permanence and durability
of the Committee on Production Guidelines for Book Longevity of the Council on
Library Resources. The University of North Carolina Press has been a member
of the Green Press Initiative since 2003.

Jacket illustration: John F. Kennedy campaigning in Los Angeles, September 1960. Photograph
by Cornell Capa, © International Center of Photography, courtesy of Magnum Photos.

Library of Congress Cataloging-in-Publication Data
Brownell, Kathryn Cramer.
Showbiz politics : Hollywood in American political life / Kathryn Cramer Brownell.
    pages cm
Includes bibliographical references and index.
ISBN 978-1-4696-1791-6 (cloth : alk. paper) — ISBN 978-1-4696-1792-3 (ebook)
1. Motion picture industry—Political aspects—United States—History—20th century.
2. Politics and culture—United States—History—20th century. 3. Motion picture
producers and directors—Political activity—United States. 4. Motion picture actors and
actresses—Political activity—United States. 5. United States—Politics and government—
20th century. I. Title.
PN1993.5.U6B758 2014
302.23'43097309045—dc23
2014021665

Portions of this work appeared earlier, in somewhat different form,
in "'Movietime U.S.A.': The Motion Picture Industry Council and the Politicization of
Hollywood in Postwar America," *Journal of Policy History* 24, no. 3 (July 2012): 518–42,
copyright © 2012 copyright © Donald Critchlow and Cambridge University Press,
reprinted with permission; and "'It Is Entertainment and It Will Sell Bonds!': 16mm
Film and the World War II War Bond Campaign," *The Moving Image* 10, no. 2 (Fall 2010):
60–82, reprinted with permission of the University of Minnesota Press.

18 17 16 15 14   5 4 3 2 1

To Grandma and Grandpa Rohde

Contents

Acknowledgments, xi

Abbreviations, xv

INTRODUCTION / Put on a Show!, 1

1 / California-Made Spectacles, 12

2 / The Hollywood Dream Machine Goes to War, 42

3 / The Glittering Robes of Entertainment, 75

4 / Defending the American Way of Life, 102

5 / Building a Star System in Politics, 129

6 / Asserting the Sixth Estate, 158

7 / The Razzle Dazzle Strategy, 188

CONCLUSION / The Washington Dream Machine, 225

Notes, 233

Bibliography, 279

Index, 293

Illustrations

Eleanor Roosevelt leads the Birthday Ball celebration in Washington, with Hollywood celebrities, January, 1944, 31

Eleanor Roosevelt converses with Shirley Temple, July 1938, 39

A small community joins together to welcome Bette Davis on her war bond tour, 1942, 66

Bette Davis delivers a speech during her war bond tour, 1942, 80

Live performance by the Armed Forces Radio Service, 1950, 125

President Dwight D. Eisenhower with Robert Montgomery preparing to address to the nation regarding the integration of schools in Little Rock, Arkansas, September 24, 1957, 132

Robert Montgomery advising President Eisenhower before Eisenhower declared his intention to seek a second term as president, February 29, 1956, 142

John F. Kennedy shaking hands with "Jack Kennedy fans" on the California campaign trail, 1960, 159

John F. Kennedy addresses both delegates at the Democratic National Convention in Los Angeles and television viewers, July 15, 1960, 167

Sammy Davis Jr. spontaneously hugs Richard Nixon at a youth rally in Miami after Nixon accepted the Republican presidential nomination, August 22, 1972, 208

Sammy Davis Jr. and Richard Nixon in the Oval Office, March 4, 1973, 214

Acknowledgments

After many years of working on this project, I owe many thanks for the patience, support, and encouragement of individuals who have made this book possible. First and foremost, I would like to thank my teachers. Many years ago, in Angell Hall, Matthew Lassiter awakened my passion for history, and he has encouraged my scholarly development since these undergraduate days at the University of Michigan. Moreover, I will forever be grateful for his recommendation to study at Boston University with Bruce Schulman. As my mentor, Bruce has patiently read countless drafts of articles, chapters, and conference papers and always offers amazing insights with his incredible range of expertise. Moreover, Bruce has taught me important lessons about both history and life, and I am incredibly grateful for having the privilege of being his advisee and now having the honor of calling him a friend. His eleventh-hour reading of the book manuscript with painstaking care proved once again his personal and scholarly generosity.

At Boston University, I learned how to study and teach history from an extraordinary faculty. From my first days of graduate school to my first days teaching in the department, Charles Dellheim, Nina Silber, Jon Roberts, Arianne Chernock, Sarah Phillips, Louis Ferleger, Phillip Haberkern, and Brendon McConville provided incredible support, generosity of time and knowledge, and constant encouragement in my development as a scholar and teacher. Brooke Blower has especially been a constant source of support and a wonderful role model. As a teacher, she has encouraged me to consider innovative and untraditional ways of exploring American history. She has also inspired me personally and professionally with her drive, attitude, and accomplishments. She, along with Bruce Schulman, Sarah Phillips, Stephen Whitfield, Ian Scott, and Julian Zelizer, provided invaluable insights and expertise, and their keen critiques and observations shaped my revisions in substantial ways. The terrific scholars from the Boston University graduate program are now some of my closest colleagues and friends, and their critical eyes have shaped this project from its inception. A special thanks to Francois Lalonde, Audrey Giarouard, Scott Marr, David Mislin, Zack Smith, D. J. Cash, and Kate Jewell for all of their encouragement, good humor, and frequent commiseration during the research and writing stages of the project. Anne Blaschke and Lily Geismer both read multiple chapters, articles, and conference papers, and their comments, critiques, and insights have made me a better scholar and writer. Moreover, as close friends, they have helped to keep me sane and grounded in the process. From Boston to West Lafayette, David Atkinson and Charity Tabol have been a constant source of support, encouragement, and laughter. I feel so fortunate to have had David as a friend as we navigated the challenges and exciting possibilities of graduate school and now as a colleague as we embark on new opportunities together at Purdue. He has read multiple chapters, brainstormed various ideas and writing strategies with me, helped me adjust to life in Indiana, and provided much-needed comic relief along the way.

I also benefited from the support of scholars beyond Boston who have shown generosity in sharing wisdom and time in support of my work. Steven Ross has not only produced landmark scholarship on Hollywood's influence in American politics that has defined the field, but he has also taken the time to help me grow as a scholar through conversations and diligent and insightful comments on the book manuscript in its various stages. I am truly inspired by his accomplishments and touched by his kindness, and he has helped to make this a far better book. Likewise, I have shared many terrific conversations with Donald Critchlow about nuances in the relationship between Hollywood and politics. His penetrating questions pushed me to deepen my analysis and think critically about political history. David Greenberg and Brian Balogh have also shaped my understanding of twentieth-century political history and the role of the media in ushering in political changes. I am grateful that they have taken the time to share their new research with me and to provide comments on my work along the way. Jennifer Frost, Lary May, Emilie Raymond, and Clayton Koppes have read and commented on various stages of this work and have shared their expertise and archival insights in an always encouraging, constructive, and positive way.

I would also like to thank my new colleagues at Purdue University, who have welcomed me so warmly to the history department and West Lafayette. With the leadership and support of Doug Hurt, the department has provided an incredible work environment and generous resources to finish the book. I received terrific feedback from faculty and graduate students through a Works in Progress session. For always taking the time to chat and share his incredible expertise, I would like to thank Randy Roberts, who has been welcoming and encouraging since my arrival in West Lafayette. Along with constantly providing honesty, humor, and reassurance, Jennifer Foray also helped me conceptualize and frame the broader project.

Caroline Janney has been an incredible department mentor and friend, and her insight and feedback have helped me navigate the final stages of the manuscript and my new professional environment at Purdue.

I have also benefited from the work of the outstanding editorial staff at the University of North Carolina Press. As a first-time author, I could not have had a better experience in all phases of the editorial process. Ron Maner and Dorothea Anderson provide exceptional copyediting support. Alison Shay has responded to all of my many emails and tedious requests quickly and with constant enthusiasm. I am especially indebted to the keen insights and skills of my editor, Joe Parsons. He has made my experience at UNC Press truly exceptional. Without his encouragement and commitment to the project, I would still be revising my first draft and would have to experience Michigan athletic triumphs and failures alone.

The American Political History Institute and Boston University Humanities Foundation have given me financial support and professional opportunities during my time at Boston University. Archivists at the Franklin D. Roosevelt Presidential Library, Dwight D. Eisenhower Presidential Library, and Richard Nixon Presidential Library in particular shared their extensive knowledge of the collections with me as I combed through boxes of newly released archival materials. Jenny Romero at the Academy of Motion Picture Arts and Sciences was always helpful, patient, and speedy with my many research requests. When traveling to the Wisconsin Center for Film and Theater Research, Stephen Vaughn shared his sources and archival knowledge of the collection and his expertise more broadly about Ronald Reagan, the Motion Picture Industry Council, and the Screen Actors Guild. During my weeks out in Los Angeles, Jay Janelle, Lori Thompson, and Chris Holmes made me feel at home at "Jay's Place" and always helped me navigate the complexities of the Los Angeles highways.

Finally, I wish to thank my friends and family for their unwavering support and faith over the years. I have my brother, Chris, to thank for convincing me to take a history course at Michigan and generously affording me my first opportunity to "teach" history during our exam preparations. Julia Weiss, Brandi Phillips, and Justine Derry have always known how to fulfill the dual role of supporter and necessary distractor, as has my "Chicken Box family." Meredith Reilly, Sarah Uhran, and Katie Moore have not only provided guest rooms on my research visits across the country but have driven me to ask new research questions and take into consideration alternative perspectives that have vastly improved the book. Judy Brownell has encouraged my professional goals without question, despite all the challenges of living on Nantucket, and in the process we have bonded over our shared love of the history of wine and of politics. Gary Klingsporn has been an incredible blessing, and his constant encouragement, understanding, and empathy have helped me pursue challenging and exciting opportunities over the past few years.

My parents, Fred and Terri Dunham and Doug and Dianna Cramer, have also provided an unfaltering source of support and have always encouraged me to achieve academic excellence. My mom has endured (and professed to enjoy!) long-winded conversations about archival finds, academic challenges, and career possibilities with constant enthusiasm and optimism.

In gratitude for the lessons they have taught me through their words and actions all my life, this book is dedicated to my extraordinary grandparents, Robert and Patricia Rohde. With their unconditional love, their unfaltering support, and their own amazing achievements, they have encouraged me to dream big, work hard, and always love the Michigan Wolverines, lessons for which I will be forever grateful. Lastly, I reserve the greatest gratitude for my husband and partner, Jason Brownell. His perspectives and unique insights have made me a better scholar, and his support and understanding have made long-distance commutes to Nantucket from Boston, the U.K., and now West Lafayette possible. Words cannot express the impact of his love, patience, encouragement, and understanding on my life. He has given me the motivation, drive, means, and ability to pursue my passion and make it my profession, and he makes me always remember to take time to put down my books, laugh, and enjoy life in the present.

Abbreviations

BBD&O	Batten, Barton, Durstine & Osborn Advertising Agency
CREEP	Committee to Re-elect the President
CSU	Conference of Studio Unions
DNC	Democratic National Committee
FBI	Federal Bureau of Investigation
GOP	Grand Old Party (Republican Party)
HDC	Hollywood Democratic Committee
HFWA	Hollywood Free World Association
HICCASP	Hollywood Independent Citizens Committee of the Arts, Sciences, and Professions
HUAC	House Un-American Activities Committee
IATSE	International Alliance of Theatrical Stage Employees
ICCASP	Independent Citizens Committee of the Arts, Sciences, and Professions
MGM	Metro-Goldwyn-Mayer Studios
MPA	Motion Picture Alliance for the Preservation of American Ideals
MPIC	Motion Picture Industry Council
MPPDA	Motion Picture Producers and Distributors of America
NAACP	National Association for the Advancement of Colored People
NC&K	Norman, Craig & Kummel Advertising Agency
OWI	Office of War Information
RA	Republican Associates
RNC	Republican National Committee
SAG	Screen Actors Guild
SCLC	Southern Christian Leadership Conference
USO	United Service Organization
Y&R	Young & Rubicam Advertising Agency

Put on a Show!

Almost seventy years before the movie star Arnold Schwarzenegger launched a successful 2003 campaign for the California governorship on the *Tonight Show* and used famous movie phrases like *"Hasta la vista, baby"* as his political slogans, another California gubernatorial drama played out over the airwaves, on newsreels, and in the printed press to captivate the nation for its entertainment value and political novelty.[1] Long before advertising budgets for electoral campaigns soared past $400 million, the *New York Times* followed a California race that stood out as "the costliest campaign in the state's history."[2] Decades before Ronald Reagan's 1980 election to the presidency showcased how acting skills and political networks honed in Southern California could pave the path to the White House, journalists penned the "fantastic" and shocking story of how a political campaign on the West Coast had "turn[ed] into a movie set."[3] This California electoral battle in 1934 showed the political potential of the so-called Hollywood Dream Machine and displayed strategies, assumptions, and tactics that Ronald Reagan and then Arnold Schwarzenegger would deploy to win high political office decades later. Long ago in California, the American public saw traditional political mudslinging meet a new media politics, and journalists and politicians alike watched with unease and concern as Hollywood spectacle transformed political life in Southern California.

Pitted against one another in this 1934 gubernatorial election were show business professionals with celebrity appeal and an intimate knowledge of how to sell a particular message through the silver screen. During the political conflict that unfolded, the players involved understood that success depended on media perceptions of who was the villain and who was the hero. On one side stood the internationally known author Upton Sinclair. With an artfully crafted message designed for mass appeal to the

1

unemployed across California, the United States, and even the world, Sinclair promised to "End Poverty in California," a catchy slogan that quickly became known simply as EPIC. Having risen to fame through a series of muckraking exposés on the malpractices and greed of corporations across the country—from the meatpacking industry to the motion picture industry, which frequently employed him—Sinclair focused his energies on reforming political corruption in the machine-dominated Democratic Party. Using his literary skills, Sinclair wrote a fictional booklet that imagined the success of his proposed policies—cooperative farms that would put California's 700,000 unemployed residents to work and a graduated income tax system that would redistribute money more equitably across the state.[4] The socialist Sinclair sold the story, *I, Governor of California: And How I Ended Poverty: A True Story of the Future*, to struggling voters not just in print but also with radio productions and staged performances.[5] The brilliant showman captured the support of voters across the state during the Democratic primary elections through his bold media message of political change and economic salvation.

On the other side assembled Hollywood studio executives, the Lord & Thomas advertising agency headed by adman extraordinary Albert Lasker, and the public relations firm Whitaker & Baxter.[6] Lord & Thomas produced a compelling soap opera radio show, *The Bennetts*, to discuss the threat of Sinclairism to middle-class goals of college education and church participation. Clem Whitaker and his wife, Leone, combed Sinclair's writing for "incendiary quotations" about marriage, religion, sex, communism, and patriotism and flooded news outlets with a "blot of Sinclairism" series that used the writer's own words and ideas against him. The chairman of the California Republican Party and head of Metro-Goldwyn-Mayer Studios (MGM), Louis B. Mayer, took the lead in joining with his motion picture rivals in this "United for California" campaign to support the incumbent Republican governor, Frank Merriam.[7] Sinclair's proposed tax and economic system would dramatically affect the motion picture industry, which had moved to the West Coast during the past fifteen years for the abundance of sunshine and the lack of government regulation of studio productions. Mayer united Republicans with prominent supporters of the recently elected Democratic president Franklin Roosevelt, including the pro–New Deal studio executive Jack L. Warner and the newspaper mogul William Randolph Hearst. To counter Sinclair's fictional vision of the future, the executives used the tools at their disposal, the production studios, to paint a very different picture of life under Sinclair's rule. Using the theaters as a battlefield, the anti-Sinclair forces produced short films that interviewed

hired actors posing as ordinary citizens to dramatize the widespread re-
jection of Sinclair and EPIC. The films used powerful images of "tramps"
overwhelming California to convince audience members that the reality
behind the EPIC plan was "devious."[8]

The campaign aroused national attention because it shocked outside
observers that an electoral battle could so closely emulate a Hollywood
production. Little did anyone anticipate that over the next forty years politicians and voters would come to accept and depend on these very same
carefully crafted political productions to win elections, pass legislation,
and defend democracy abroad. Scholars frequently point to the anti-Sinclair mobilization, and the role of the professional consulting company
Whitaker & Baxter, as the beginning of modern media politics and its de-
pendence on advertising firms and political consultants. Historians, journalists, advertisers, and consultants themselves have pointed to the 1934
election as a time when "for better or worse, the democratic process was
transformed."[9] This narrative, however, overlooks the controversy aroused
by the anti-Sinclair campaign and the contentious process by which this
style of mass-mediated politics became a part of national politics. In doing
so, this narrative advances the idea of what media scholars have called
"technological determinism"—the belief that technology, like radio, motion pictures, and then television, had inherent features that shaped how
the medium would transform social, cultural, and political structures, a
theory Marshall McLuhan articulated in his 1964 book, *Understanding
Media*.[10] Media scholars have dismissed this theory by studying how individuals, cultural values, political decisions, and social structures actually
shape and are shaped by the incorporation of new technology into American society. And yet political scientists and historians continue to advance
this assumption, particularly when explaining the twentieth-century shift
from a political system controlled by parties and urban machines to one
dominated by the mass media.[11]

Moreover, political scholarship focuses overwhelmingly on the triumph
of the consultant and advertising in American politics, without seriously
considering the third essential element of the mass-mediated environment: entertainment. From the 1920s through the 1970s, interest groups
became purveyors of public opinion and consultants replaced party machines, creating a "mass-mediated politics" in which political communication and electoral battles occur principally through events staged for television or the silver screen.[12] Throughout this process, entertainment became
integral to political communication. It was not a by-product of the shift
toward advertising and consultants but a driving force in this historical

development. This book tells the story of how the media mobilization and use of professional entertainment tools that appeared as "fantastic" in 1934 came to dominate American politics. While it explains why programs like *Saturday Night Live* and *The Daily Show* have assumed such prominence in twenty-first-century campaigns, this book reveals how the turn toward entertainment in political communication reflected a conscious and contentious development rooted in over forty years of collaboration among politicians, advertisers, political consultants, and the Hollywood entertainment industry. This book argues that Hollywood as an industry, a value set, and a production philosophy played an instrumental role in the triumph of not simply the age of the political consultant, but even the age of "showbiz politics"—a political environment shaped by the marriage of advertising, consulting, and entertainment and reliant on the active construction of politicians as celebrities to gain political legitimacy and success.

Political historians have turned to California to understand how social movements and local institutions have driven national ideological shifts and political realignment in twentieth-century American politics. Fueled by the post–World War II military-industrial complex, the growth of the suburban landscape combined with the migration of southern evangelicals to make Southern California a vibrant place in which ideas of individualism, the free market, traditional family values, and anticommunism flourished in local communities to challenge the New Deal state and give birth to the modern conservative movement.[13] At the same time and in the same state, modern liberalism has evolved, and recent scholarship has chronicled how Democratic organizations actively linked sexual, gender, and racial equality to economic rights that expanded the "social democratic politics" of the New Deal state.[14] References to advertising, "media-driven performative politics" and "cultural engagement" appear in passing during these narratives, which chronicle the impact of grassroots mobilizations that shaped California, and then national, politics over the course of the twentieth century.[15] Celebrity political activism, negotiations over media strategies, and popular attitudes about changes begot by a mass-mediated politics are eclipsed in favor of a story that uses advertisements or entertainment events as illustrative of a political movement or ideology, but not a political negotiation or development itself. But, in California, a system of popular governance, which allowed for the growth of movement politics on the Left and the Right, relied on mass media strategies for engagement and communication to form alternative political networks and challenge the political establishment. Historians have bypassed a consideration of the ways in which this California-rooted celebrity political style developed and how the state's media institutions fundamentally altered the way people related to and understood their broader political system.

Showbiz Politics fills this historiographical void by placing this rise of a "media-driven performative politics" at the center of modern American political development. Strategies of mass-mediated politics that surfaced during the 1934 California campaign originated during the 1920s in Los Angeles, a sprawling city shaped by the expansion of the motion picture industry and its studio executives, who crafted and sold the "Hollywood ideal" through a seemingly systematic "Dream Machine." The Hollywood ideal, more than the ethos of any other community or industry, vividly reflected how the consumption-driven economy and culture of modern America transformed the American dream into something drastically different than the Horatio Alger narrative of hard work and thrift. In Hollywood, publicity derived from the mass media determined success. Integral to the studio system were the publicity departments, which carefully monitored public opinion and popular tastes about films and actors. These offices cultivated relationships with reporters, reviewers, and editors across the country to create positive coverage about upcoming films. Meanwhile, publicity focused on the personal lives of actors—from their romantic adventures to their preferences for lotion or toothpaste—to help propel them to fame, while also generating ticket sales. The Hollywood Dream Machine denoted a well-oiled media exploitation operation that saturated newspapers, magazines, radio, and newsreels with exciting stories about a new star. Image mattered. Careers—as an actor, producer, director, or studio executive—depended not merely on education, background, or work ethic, but rather on the right information being successfully transmitted to the public through the mass media.[16]

In 1934, Frank Merriam deployed the Hollywood Dream Machine to win the California governorship. All the major studios took advantage of the strict contracts governing their stars' behaviors to force donations and public support for Merriam. The anti-Sinclair forces worked closely with professional publicists to ensure that a constant flood of negative messages dominated theater screens, airwaves, and newspapers. While both Sinclair and his opponents took to the mass media to spread their campaign messages, corporate studios aligned with consultants and advertisers to use their expertise and resources to triumph over the underfunded and disorganized EPIC forces. The anti-Sinclair effort showcased the power of a new politics that would fundamentally change American elections and the broader political system over the next forty years.

While Hollywood studio executives were divided in party loyalties and had previously avoided potentially divisive and alienating political activism on their studio lots, they came together to advance their business interests. Fearful that Sinclair's message could appeal to a majority of voters during the general election, executives used all of their political and economic clout to convince Californians of the dismal future that would take shape under Sinclair. Jack Warner postponed his $350,000 building project at the Warner Bros. lot until the end of November.[17] Joseph Schenck, head of United Artists, publicly traveled to Florida to explore alternative warm weather options for studios in case Sinclair did win.[18] For both Democrats and Republicans, the growing economic strength and cultural appeal of the motion picture industry combined with the weakness of partisan identification and party organizations in California to facilitate the flourishing of a "showbiz politics"—a political process that valued advertising, showmanship, and media spectacles over the traditional politics of party loyalty, patronage, and urban machines.

The founders of Whitaker & Baxter, Clem Whitaker and Leone Baxter, used their success working alongside studio executives during the campaign to launch a political consulting firm that would become a major player in California politics over the next two decades. Similarly to what Louis B. Mayer had told a dismissive Republican Party several years earlier, the husband-and-wife public relations business held firm in their basic philosophy: "Every American likes to be entertained. . . . So if you can't fight it, PUT ON A SHOW! And if you put on a good show, Mr. and Mrs. America will turn out to see it."[19] Understanding the appeal of entertainment, the Lord & Thomas agency not only hired actors for its radio soap opera, *The Bennetts*, but it also produced another successful radio spot about two hoboes and their trek across the country to the land of EPIC.[20] Whitaker & Baxter, Albert Lasker's advertising company, and Hollywood professionals understood the potential of showbiz politics. They worked together to reshape California politics by "putting on a show" to bring political messages to voters and win elections.

In 1934, however, this new political style that studio executives and public relations firms celebrated triumphed only in California, and not all observers lauded these distinctly Hollywood-based strategies of political advocacy. During the same year, Catholic bishops mobilized in a national Catholic Legion of Decency campaign to intensify their calls for federal censorship of the industry they felt corrupted the morals of the nation. To prevent a boycott by millions of Catholic moviegoers, studio executives agreed to adhere to the strict self-censorship code enforced by the recently formed

Production Code Administration, but this regulated commercial films, not politically motivated creations.[21] Angry letters appeared at the White House asking for Roosevelt to explore the tactics used to defeat Sinclair. Liberals in Southern California protested against the "dirty" tricks devised by the studio executives. Screenwriter Phillip Dunne joined with actors Melvyn Douglas and Fredric March to vow "never again," ultimately beginning a progressive political mobilization that would also rely on entertainment to influence a national election on the opposite end of the political spectrum a decade later.[22] Immediately following the election that he "conceded had been stolen" from him, Sinclair sought to expose the malicious and manipulative actions behind Hollywood's political offensive.[23] In *I, Candidate for Governor: And How I Got Licked*, Sinclair lamented "what money can do in American politics," but even more than the influence of money, he pointed to the negative influence of the studio system.[24] Seeking to show the evil nature behind "one of the great institutions of California," Sinclair condemned the entrance of studios into politics as antithetical to their place as purveyors of entertainment.[25]

Public outcry over the studio executives' manipulation of the political campaign in 1934 tapped into the broader debates about Hollywood's role in corrupting American values. Despite having grown into a major national industry over the previous twenty years, motion pictures and their prominent place in American society continued to stir controversy. During the 1920s and 1930s, Hollywood had attracted intense suspicion from middle-class reformers and religious leaders for its business practices and the public behavior of its star personalities.[26] The debate surrounding the 1934 election illuminated how Hollywood, as a business, a mind-set, and a new conveyor of cultural values, remained on the periphery of American life. Moreover, this criticism revealed the deep misgivings stirred by the inclusion of Hollywood structures, styles, and entertainment tactics in the American political process. Far from a natural development, the spread of a showbiz politics was immensely feared and actively thwarted.

Over the next forty years, the controversy surrounding the 1934 election would fade, and the press, politicians, and the public would accept, and ultimately depend on, the power of entertainment in American politics. If putting on a show constituted an exception to the rule, a "fantastic" tale to those on the East Coast in the 1930s, by the 1970s the dirty tricks of "fake newsreels" would be renamed "advertising spots," actors would serve as campaign managers and even win national office, and public relations and advertising firms like Whitaker & Baxter and Lord & Thomas would assemble lists of clients for local, state, and national campaigns.

The Upton Sinclair mobilization, however, demonstrates that before television, before motion pictures assumed an overtly political role, and even before the potential of radio was realized, professional showmen in California saw that outside of a machine-dominated party system, their skills in entertainment production could be used to reshape the political process in ways that would depend on the expertise (and frequently pad the pocketbooks) of those in "showbiz." Historians and political scientists frequently point to the 1950s as ushering in the "age of the public relations professional" with the popularization of television.[27] Overwhelmingly, this scholarship focuses on political consultants and advertisers who came on the scene in the 1950s and dominated the political process by the 1970s.[28] But overlooked in these assessments is how during the 1950s these public relations professionals looked to California politics for lessons on how to tackle the challenges and opportunities that television presented. Stanley Kelley's classic 1956 account, *Professional Public Relations and Political Power*, focuses extensively on how California's open party system and the influence of the entertainment industry created a political culture in which the philosophy of Whitaker & Baxter to "put on a show" resonated. Californians, observed Kelley, had a "proclivity for direct legislation," and its political system, which had undergone extensive reforms from the progressive era, limited the role of political parties in electoral campaigns. The result: individuals and organizations, from studio executives like Louis B. Mayer to the husband-and-wife team that went on to form Whitaker & Baxter's Campaigns Inc., had an opportunity to shape dramatically the electoral process by using their particular skills that were honed in Hollywood lots or at local advertising agencies.[29]

By the 1980s, the Hollywood Dream Machine would become the staple of American politics, so much so that Ronald Reagan would wonder how anyone could be president without having a background as an actor.[30] And yet, this acceptance of "showbiz politics" emerged from shifting political conceptions of the "public" and a growing political belief in the power of the media. Dwight Eisenhower's television campaigns in the 1950s, the electoral successes of John F. Kennedy and Ronald Reagan, and the media struggles of Richard Nixon convinced other politicians that an embrace of showbiz politics won elections and facilitated political communication with the electorate. The inroads Hollywood had made into the political process since the 1920s made this perception of the power of entertainment a political reality.

By exploring the institutionalization of Hollywood styles, structures, and personalities in the American political process, this book traces the key personal relationships, institutions, and government policies that established the foundation for a celebrity political culture and made entertainment a central feature of American political life. With an examination of both the liberal and the conservative elements in Hollywood, this book shows how, despite popular perceptions, neither the Republican Party nor the Democratic Party dominated the political loyalties of the entertainment industry and how figures on each side of the political spectrum contributed to the rise of the contemporary form of showbiz politics. Investigating philanthropic efforts such as benefit performances, collaboration with the government on wartime propaganda, advertising strategies, and the financial pressures of a candidate-centered primary campaign, this study demonstrates how Hollywood, as an industry and a mind-set, contributed to the embrace of mass-mediated politics.

During the nineteenth century, party machines organized spectacles—from torchlight parades to marching bands to picnics—to encourage political participation. School textbooks, families, and local party activities shaped civic culture and taught public behavior.[31] In the twentieth century, through public relations campaigns, propaganda efforts, and public and private collaborations between Hollywood and presidential administrations, Hollywood entertainment began to shape civic culture, giving celebrities a more prominent political voice and transforming politicians into celebrities. *Showbiz Politics* traces the transformation from party spectacle to professional Hollywood production as parties turned toward the mass media to communicate information about candidates, ideologies, and policies. This development was hardly inevitable and never uncontested. Studio executives and their publicity departments worked diligently to recraft the meaning of "celebrity" to sell tickets at the box office and make Hollywood entertainment morally acceptable to a white, Christian establishment. Driven by economic concerns for professional advancement and personal desires for social prestige, these executives, who overwhelmingly had poor, immigrant, and Jewish backgrounds, understood the importance of asserting their places in California politics during the 1920s and 1930s but struggled to find a place in the national political landscape.

This book begins by examining the polarizing, divisive, and costly debates over the meaning of entertainment, the public role of celebrity, and the fears of "silver screen propaganda" that permeated the years between the 1934 California gubernatorial campaign and the national embrace of advertising and television in the presidential election of 1952. To combat moral and political panics about the corrupting power of "entertainment," Hollywood activists engaged in a variety of types of political activity that ultimately built institutional connections with the federal government. By engaging in different types of political activism—"industry politics," "patriotic politics," and "ideological politics"—Hollywood activists made entertainment an integral component of public life. In the process, celebrities and studio executives showed national politicians how valuable entertainment could be in generating funds for philanthropic campaigns and shifting public opinion during an international crisis and, ultimately, in spreading democracy across the world during the Cold War.

The second part of this book explains how presidential administrations adapted to the growth of a celebrity political culture that came out of these institutional collaborations and wartime propaganda campaigns. Actors George Murphy and Robert Montgomery and studio executive Jack Warner engaged in presidential "electoral politics" during the 1950s as they advised Dwight Eisenhower on how to construct his television appearances and approach his advertising campaign. By accepting their advice, Eisenhower validated the electoral expertise of these professional showmen, who had transformed the California landscape twenty years earlier with similar "media-driven performative strategies."[32] Veering away from patronage and urban machines to win elections, Eisenhower worked with show business professionals to attract independent voters across party lines through the language of entertainment, a language that television viewers understood.

On January 19, 1961, Bette Davis joined a parade of stars at a glamorous inaugural gala in the Washington Armory to celebrate the election of John F. Kennedy to the presidency. As she looked out at the president-elect and the famous faces that filled the audience, she declared, "The world of entertainment, show biz if you please, has become the sixth estate. . . . There is no better proof than here tonight."[33] By 1960, celebrities had become an integral part of American politics, as patriotic propagandists, technical advisers, smooth electoral salesmen, essential fund-raising attractions, and even as potential candidates running for office themselves. Kennedy recognized this and took advantage of his intimate knowledge of Hollywood studio structures to create his own Hollywood Dream Machine to win the Democratic presidential nomination and ultimately the presidency. In doing so, Kennedy replicated the strategies employed by the anti-Sinclair forces in the 1934 election. During the 1960s, actors like George Murphy and Ronald Reagan won political office because voters recognized that as entertainers they had the skills necessary to govern in a political culture where power and authority came from publicity generated through the mass media, not through the party establishment.

Perhaps nobody grasped the growing importance of entertainment in the political process during the 1960s quite like Richard M. Nixon. Nixon's political rise, failures, and successes showcased how politicians, entertainers, and the American people grappled with the possibilities and limitations of a "showbiz politics" during a dramatically changing media landscape. A native of Southern California, Richard Millhouse Nixon was born in 1913, the same year that Jewish filmmakers started to arrive in search of prosperity from the new moving picture industry.[34] How both changed American politics is the story of this book.

CHAPTER ONE

California-Made Spectacles

On March 12, 1929, Louis B. Mayer, a poor Jewish boy turned movie mogul, did not "sleep a wink." Overjoyed after accepting Herbert Hoover's invitation to spend the night in the Lincoln Bedroom at the White House, Mayer reveled in his rise from a penniless Russian immigrant to the guest of the president of the United States. He had worked diligently for the Hoover campaign and the Republican Party over the past few years, delivering speeches to businesses and voters across Southern California, and had emerged as a notable Republican figure in local circles. As he worked the local Republican activist popularly known as "Mrs. Hollywood," Ida Koverman, Mayer established himself within the California Republican Party during the 1920s.[1] Using the glamour of his stars and the production power at MGM, the studio executive cleverly researched the movie interests of notable figures visiting Los Angeles and arranged meetings and photography opportunities that generated national publicity for the stars, his studio, and the Republican Party.[2]

But in 1928, as his presence at 1600 Pennsylvania Avenue the following year demonstrated, Mayer elevated his status in the Republican Party. At the national convention in June, Mayer not only added more glamour and enthusiasm with staged performances and a talking film of Hoover, but he also convinced his powerful friend and colleague, William Randolph Hearst, to throw his support behind Hoover's candidacy. Mayer orchestrated political rallies for Hoover during the national campaign and recruited famous stars like Ethel and Lionel Barrymore and Al Jolson to appear at the events. And yet, while Herbert Hoover and the Republican Party certainly appreciated Mayer's support, Hoover dismissed the notion of making Mayer's entertainment strategies a priority within the national campaign.[3] The White House dinner invitation in the aftermath of his victory came only after Koverman pressured Hoover to give the studio executive an opportunity for national attention so he could "strut around like a proud pigeon" over the campaign work he had done.[4]

Although Mayer organized star-studded events for Hoover, a general disdain for the use of motion pictures and professional showmanship permeated the national Republican Party, something Will Irwin, a journalist veteran of the World War I Committee of Public Information, encountered as well.[5] A former muckraking journalist, Irwin had immersed himself in studying Hollywood's recent history as he wrote a biography of studio executive Adolph Zukor.[6] After overseeing the production of a film that chronicled Hoover's career, *Master of Emergencies*, Irwin assured Hoover that it was "a better vote getter than any local politician." Hoover, however, was not impressed with the medium and told Irwin that "it would only get votes from the morons."[7] Irwin reminded Hoover that "at least three-fourths of the voters, in my opinion, are moronic enough to be persuaded by their eyes and their emotions." The exchange, however, showed the tendency to look with disdain at entertainment and emotional appeals through the mass media.

While Hoover hoped that Mayer could deliver California for him, using Hollywood publicity strategies in the national campaign remained suspect. Even Irwin himself, following his work with Hoover, asked the candidate to promise him that if he won, he would "never offer me a political job!"[8] In 1928, showbiz politics had emerged as a mere afterthought, perhaps a cute spectacle, but not a serious political tool to communicate to voters, raise money, generate publicity, or win elections. Mayer imagined how the power of celebrity might transform the political process, but national politicians, along with the American public, saw Hollywood as the land of the lotus, characterized by leisure, sexuality, frivolous consumption, and excess.[9] The office of the presidency stood out in stark contrast.

Lying in the Lincoln Bedroom, Mayer may have himself felt accepted by Herbert Hoover and the national political elite, but the industry he represented struggled to find social respectability, cultural acceptance, and political power. Mayer's ideas for how to use entertainment, celebrity, and showmanship frequently fell on unreceptive ears. More broadly, his involvement with the Republican Party had emerged as an exception to the dominant political activity in the movie colony, which centered primarily on the pursuit of economic prosperity and security, not party influence. For example, seven years earlier, a prominent Indiana Republican who had previously assumed leadership of the Republican National Committee (RNC) and then the position of postmaster general in Warren Harding's administration, Will H. Hays, took up a lucrative position as president of the Motion Picture Producers and Distributors of America (MPPDA). While his Republican connections helped secure meetings on Capitol Hill, he focused his efforts not on influencing party decisions or structures but rather on lobbying Washington legislators about censorship policies, ensuring access to international box offices through favorable trade rates, and halting antitrust investigations.[10]

Mayer may not have convinced the national Republican Party to realize fully the political potential of Hollywood strategies, but he did begin a tradition of "wheeling and dealing" behind the scenes with presidential administrations and national campaigns. Jack Warner would build on this to generate votes for the Democratic challenger, Franklin D. Roosevelt, four years later. This political activity, however, centered on promoting the industry: defending its economic structures, lobbying for favorable policies, and promoting its civic role and the public responsibilities of celebrities. While "industry politics" at time brought partisan rewards and connections (particularly in the California Republican Party), the promotion of the industry—its business interests behind the scenes and its respectable image in the public eye—trumped partisanship.

Driven to protect their studios, Warner and Mayer found opportunities in the open California social and political structures not only to "strut like peacocks" around their local communities, but also to exercise their publicity muscle to shape state politics, as they both eagerly did to protect their economic interests in the 1934 gubernatorial campaign. Over the next decade, in an effort to enhance box office receipts, studio executives and their publicity departments remade the image of Hollywood entertainment as "pure family fun" and its celebrity spokesmen as clean, respectable, and charitable citizens.[11] By pursuing a national campaign to expand public goodwill toward the industry, executives' careful promotion of "Hollywood's heart" proved an effective way to gain national leverage in policy debates and shape civic culture around entertainment in ways that increased box office returns and transformed celebrities into public servants on and off the screen.

Politics in the "Land of the Lotus"

In 1930, New York congressman Hamilton Fish Jr. traveled across the country to assess the danger of communist political activities. He focused on educational programs designed to influence youth through summer camps, labor union pamphlets, and the writing contained within the *Daily Worker*, the Communist Party organ. During this national research tour,

Fish stopped in Los Angeles and had a conversation about the potential use of the silver screen to disseminate communist propaganda with a prominent anticommunist, Major Frank Pease, the head of the Hollywood Technical Directors League. While Pease feared the potential for propaganda by known communist producer Sergei Eisenstein, Fish concluded that while communists might potentially produce Russian propaganda to spread throughout the United States, Eisenstein's subversive potential remained limited. In his final report, of almost ninety pages, Fish dedicated only four sentences to the role of the cinema in the propaganda effort and mentioned nothing about motion picture productions from Hollywood. Propaganda, according to Fish, meant educational programs, union literature, or efforts to undermine American industrial credibility and banking institutions—not messages spread through entertainment. Fish's dismissive attitude toward cinema reflected the national political view of the motion picture industry at the time. Progressive reformers feared that the consumer culture promoted by celebrities on the screen could undermine the morals of the nation's children, and local politicians grappled with the questions of censorship raised by these middle-class crusaders. Fish did not entirely dismiss the idea that the cinema could be used as a political tool, but he did not see it as a priority, and he ultimately concluded that its power "yet remains to be seen."[12]

Fish's assessment reflected the broader tendency to view Hollywood as part of a lower- and working-class world of leisure that lacked a political authority. During the 1920s, Republican presidents—from Harding through Hoover—began relying on media advice from advertising executives and journalists, but players in the entertainment industry, like Louis B. Mayer, remained firmly outside national politics.[13] But on the local level, the motion picture industry's growing economic power opened doors for political advancement. Mayer took advantage of progressive reforms and the open primary system in California to show exactly how media messages and celebrity power could be channeled into political authority in local and state politics. By 1934, studio executives joined together to show Californians, and national observers, how the entertainment industry could transform the nature of political campaigns. Both the Democratic and the Republican parties in California realized the "political potential" that Fish and Hoover had dismissed just a few years earlier. This potential, however, was bound by concerns about shifting moral and cultural values, which weighed heavily on those who feared a society in which "image" and personality mattered more than hard work, thrift, and climbing the party ladder. Political authority during the 1920s remained in the hands of party bosses, corporations, and growing interest groups that claimed to represent the people. Hollywood as an industry, ideal, and spokesman of the "people" remained far away from this source of power.[14]

Since the introduction of the "moving picture" at the turn of the twentieth century, Hollywood as a community, business, and idea had occupied an outsider's role in American life, which was centered intellectually, culturally, and financially in the Northeast. During the first decade of its existence, the industry lacked centralization and a strong economic structure of production, distribution, and exhibition. Frequently played during vaudeville acts or in dingy nickel theaters, movies attracted immigrants and poor workers and their families. As a leisure industry for the "masses," which at times radical labor leaders attempted to use to spread a class consciousness to unorganized workers, nickelodeons constituted a threat to the dominant social, political, and economic order. As for saloons, middle-class reformers and the corporate establishment worked to regulate and control the theaters and their patrons.[15]

If the working Left experimented with film's potential to galvanize audiences early on, immigrant entrepreneurs, like Louis B. Mayer, took advantage of the new medium's business potential. Trained to read the public desires and fashion tastes in the garment industries, innovative Jewish immigrants also had a deep desire to remake themselves into "Americans." A consummate performer with a flair for the dramatic, Mayer frequently told his "rags to riches" version of the American dream as he, a young Jewish immigrant, staked his future on the idea that motion pictures could be more than distasteful, cheap, and rowdy entertainment. At the age of nineteen, Mayer moved to Boston and worked to renovate a burlesque house, which the middle- and upper-class people of Haverhill, Massachusetts, derogatively called the "Garlic Box," in reference to the lower-class Italian customers it attracted. Mayer bought the building and remodeled the structure and the content of the silver screen to attract the town's elite. Renaming it the Orpheneum, Mayer promised that the theater would be devoted to "high class films" and "refined amusement," and he relentlessly pursued local public relations campaigns with civic leaders to clean up the image of the popular entertainment.[16]

The Russian immigrant stood determined to transform the early motion picture industry into a socially respectable business, an extremely ambitious goal at the time.[17] Both the content on the silver screen and the more democratic and egalitarian space of theaters forced the middle class and the ruling elite to deal concretely with the rising political and cultural power of the working class.[18] Traditional businessmen, who hailed from socially respectable families with ties in manufacturing and banking, ran early motion picture companies like Vitagraph and Biograph. But penniless Jewish immigrants like Louis B. Mayer, Adolph Zukor, and William Fox, who had an "adoration of America" and a respect rather than a disdain for the masses, constructed "Hollywood" as a distinctly new business, place, and ideal that challenged the dominant class and religious hierarchies.[19]

Over the next decade, as consumer dreams, mass production, and an urban leisure culture found a national audience, so too did motion pictures. Moving out to Los Angeles in search of a hospitable climate and low taxes, motion picture pioneers embraced and further advanced the corporate consumer ethos of the 1920s. Once in Los Angeles, Mayer emulated the production tactics of Henry Ford in producing Model T's in Detroit.[20] But he dealt in talent, and he needed not just an efficient production model, like Ford's assembly line, but also a publicity department that promoted his stars. Hollywood celebrities did not just sell movies; they embodied a new version of the American dream in which heroes achieved fame and fortune overnight rather than through years of hard work and thrift. Studios built on this belief that anybody could be transformed into a glamorous movie star with just a little bit of luck by publicizing accounts of how Dorothy Lamour was operating elevators in a Chicago department store and how Frances Farmer was ushering at a Seattle theater when they caught the eyes of casting directors. Valuing youth, beauty, and personality over character, diligence, and patience, this "Waitress-to-Movie-Queen pattern" inspired hopes and dreams of immediate wealth and fame in millions of young men and women.[21]

The motion picture industry in the 1920s, though spreading in popularity, faced an uncertain future. Despite the growing appeal of movies, highly publicized scandals ignited rumors about the throngs of young women who had fallen into traps of money, drugs, and power-hungry studio men. The popular perception of the industry as a promiscuous and dangerous social scene motivated legislators in thirty-two states to discuss censorship laws in 1921.[22] Hoping to curb such negative publicity and keep the screen free from government control, the successful newspaper editor with an investment in the new media industry, William Randolph Hearst, worked with Mayer, Samuel Goldwyn, Carl Laemmle, and William Fox to develop a liaison between the federal government and the industry to meet the threat of censorship and reassure East Coast investors nervous about the stability of the morally suspect industry. When Will Hays accepted the industry's offer to move from his cabinet position in Washington to the presidency of the MPPDA, he gave the industry a concrete link to a dominant political party and its businessmen members.

Under the eye of Will Hays, whom insiders quickly nicknamed the "movie czar," Hollywood studio executives focused primarily on economic concerns about how to grow the production, distribution, and exhibition facets of the industry. Their central concerns lay not in getting influence in national political parties but rather in using any type of clout to negotiate economic growth in ways that skirted around antitrust laws. After Adolph Zukor acquired the Paramount theater and distribution networks and formed Paramount Pictures in 1916, William Fox, Carl Laemmle, Louis B. Mayer, and Samuel Goldwyn followed this successful model of vertical integration.[23] The business-friendly policies of the GOP in the 1920s, which ushered in a decade of corporate growth and market consumption, helped build Hollywood into an "industrial-financial colossus," making it one of the country's most lucrative industries, with a gross income of over $1 billion a year.[24] In return, during the 1920s, industry leaders like Mayer aligned their political interests with the Republican Party in California, which not only advocated for economic growth but also, because of progressive reforms, was receptive to extrapartisan organizations and individuals with skill in constructing personalities and media appeals to win popular elections. Hollywood entrepreneurs had these skills and used them to gain political recognition, defend their economic interests, and elevate their social status as individuals and as an industry in California.

Just as in national politics, Republicans dominated the California political scene in the 1920s; however, the progressive wing of the party triumphed on the West Coast. By 1920, Republican progressive reformers had successfully dismantled the political machine run by the Southern Pacific Railroad in California. Since 1910, under the leadership of reformer Hiram W. Johnson, California voters had changed the rules of the political game, with the implementation of the initiative, the referendum, recall procedures, and the system of cross-filing. During Governor Johnson's administration, from 1911 to 1917, the rhetoric of antipartyism combined with new voting systems to create a unique system for popular governance.[25] While Johnson's reforms took political control away from railroad machines, returning political power "to the people" meant that political hopefuls had new hoops to jump through to attain political office—the most controversial being the system of cross-filing, the ability of candidates to file candidacy simultaneously in both parties' primary campaigns. This reform aimed to broaden California democracy by making popular voting in primaries matter more than partisan affiliation. But, while it did dismantle the power of the railroads, it also introduced an electoral system that re-warded candidate-centered campaigns and emotionally charged, nonpartisan messages. While candidates could submit their names to both the Democratic and the Republican primary ballots, progressive laws forbade official party organizations from endorsing one candidate over another in the primary election. As a result, bitter primary campaigns ensued, as candidates had to find alternative organizations to aid their campaigns to win the nomination.[26]

Cross-filing encouraged candidates to mobilize early through the primary campaign with extrapartisan resources that crafted emotional media spectacles to engage voters, strategies and principles that would eventually become staples of the modern "long campaign."[27] This electoral system demanded a different style of organization and voter mobilization that took image seriously, something Hollywood had also done over the past decade. The 1934 governor's race between Frank Merriam and Upton Sinclair proved how influential the production world could be in this open party structure of California politics. Both sides of the gubernatorial campaign showed how advertising companies and showmanship professionals— from public relations professionals to the motion picture publicity agents, actors, and executives themselves—could replace formal party structures in supplying the money, manpower, and media messages to help candidates win elections.[28]

Electoral innovations in California stood out in stark contrast to public relations developments in national politics at the time. During the 1920s, President Calvin Coolidge and his successor, Herbert Hoover, exploited aspects of Hollywood publicity and implemented its media strategies at various points during their presidencies, and yet they did so while creating a public image as conservative traditionalists.[29] Coolidge listened to his public relations adviser, Edward Bernays, who suggested he invite movie stars to the White House for breakfast during the 1924 campaign. Cameras captured the vibrant scene on the White House lawn that followed Al Jolson leading a group of celebrities in singing the campaign song "Keep Coolidge." In a combination of the old and the new, Coolidge appeared in a short campaign film, *Visitin' Round at Coolidge Corner*, which celebrated his New England, small-town roots and showed the incumbent as an ordinary, thrifty, hardworking, and religious man.[30] In explicit and hidden ways, Coolidge saw the importance of image and public relations in advancing his political agenda. He also realized the benefits that could be derived from a cooperative relationship between Hollywood and his administration. Thus, he worked diligently to thwart federal censorship initiatives and in return had frequent access to studio production lots and its celebrity workers, especially in the case of MGM.[31] Coolidge's successor, Herbert Hoover, also worked with advertisers, journalists, and, as the 1928 election showed, Louis B. Mayer, to bring innovative publicity tactics to his campaign and, later, to combat the hardships of the Great Depression. Like Coolidge, Hoover maintained his friendship with Mayer and worked to help the studio chief when he could.[32]

Hoover's view of film audiences as "morons," however, underscored the tendency of intellectuals, reformers, national politicians, and upper-class businessmen to view the "masses"—immigrants and the working class—in derogatory terms, thus showing a major difference between California political structures, which valued popular democracy and the voices of the "masses," and national political institutions, which sought to subdue the passions of the people. The propaganda effort waged from the Committee of Public Information during World War I spearheaded concerns of media's manipulative potential during the 1920s.[33] Jaded by the success of the "German Hun" campaign to arouse an irrational support for the war through images of German bestiality, George Creel, the head of the Committee of Public Information, and many former muckrakers who worked with him, lost faith in the rationality of the mass public.[34] Another Committee of Public Information organizer, journalist, and leading intellectual, Walter Lippmann, wrote in his seminal book *Public Opinion* (1922) about how media images and political propaganda manipulated and misinformed the "average citizen."[35] The shift toward the "politics of personality" and the flourishing of "celebrity" threatened to undermine democracy, claimed Lippmann. As Herbert Hoover responded to the dramatic technological and business changes in mass communications during the 1920s, he turned to professional and interest groups, like the Chamber of Commerce, for advice. Like Lippmann, Hoover advocated an "associative state" run by experts, managers, and trade groups, all of whom would represent the interests of the "people" without becoming susceptible to their emotional whims.[36]

In this view, the movie star, who achieved fame based solely on personality and media image, advanced the same two products of modern culture that could potentially threaten enlightened, educated government. Though Jewish entrepreneurs had built lucrative corporations, they had yet to achieve the national social and political prestige that they sought, both personally and professionally. Studio executives, many of whom had risen in less than a decade from penniless immigrants to millionaires, constantly worried that their newly acquired wealth would slip away as quickly as it had appeared. Even by 1940, when Hollywood had become firmly entrenched in American culture and had gained the respectability it yearned for during the 1920s, sociologist Leo Rosten observed that the industry, dependent on youth, carefully constructed media attention, and wealth derived from public opinion, was simultaneously outwardly optimistic and inwardly insecure. The gambles taken by entrepreneurs like Mayer paid out millions, generating wealth and fame for executives and their stars. But the beneficiaries of this "first-generation" wealth—earned not by thrift or heritage but by talent or "luck"—looked and acted very different from political and social notables outside Hollywood. Rosten observed that "the people of the movie colony are characterized by showmanship, not breeding; glibness, not wisdom; audacity, not poise," and the achievements of these entertainers came with a constant fear of "can it last?"[37] Will Hays worked to assuage this fear as he lobbied legislators during the 1920s to ensure the economic vitality of the industry. But the market crash in 1929 intensified this anxiety as industry leaders worried about diminishing box office returns, a new Federal Trade Commission investigation, and heated calls for censorship from Catholic leaders.[38] Political favor and social prestige to protect industry interests was needed more than ever, and Jack Warner would follow in Louis B. Mayer's footsteps to advance industry politics during the Great Depression.

A New Deal for Entertainment

In 1932, Mayer and Warner saw the only hope for the future of the nation in general and their studios in particular in their presidential candidates of choice. Despite the facts of the Depression, Mayer maintained confidence in Hoover and staged an elaborate evening to welcome his friend to Los Angeles during Hoover's reelection campaign.[39] But, hoping to outdo the work Mayer had done with Hoover over the past four years, Warner stole the Hollywood spotlight in September 1932 for the incumbent's opposition. Warner promised that his upcoming Motion Picture Electrical Parade and Sports Pageant would be "the spectacle of spectacles, the show of shows."[40] To surpass all previous stage and screen events, Warner invested substantial personal and company funds, bringing together studio executives, actors, writers, directors, technical operators, and prop men to produce an unforgettable evening.

The pageant began promptly at 8:00 P.M. with "a fanfare of trumpets," a "salute of colored lights," a motorcade of Los Angeles police officers, and a brass band to introduce the motion picture community to its guest of honor, Governor Franklin Roosevelt, the Democratic presidential nominee.[41] Warner and internationally known comedian Will Rogers welcomed Roosevelt to Southern California with a performance that fused vaudeville-style entertainment with Hollywood glamour. Beginning with a Western Film Stars Cowboy Circus and a celebrity polo match, the evening climaxed with the parade, which featured a float titled "The Spirit of Hollywood."[42] Featuring young women dressed as Lady Liberty amid dazzling lights, the float celebrated the nominee with the sparkling words "Hollywood" and "Gov. Franklin D. Roosevelt."[43]

Warner and Roosevelt both outperformed their Republican rivals that year, and the election marked the beginning of significant changes for the entertainment industry and for the Democratic Party. The explicit political advocacy of studio executives was the exception in the early 1930s, but Roosevelt's administration would change this into a rule. As Warner's spectacle revealed, the industry, not just an individual, jumped onto the Roosevelt bandwagon. While during the 1920s Mayer had made his studio a key player in the California Republican Party, Roosevelt's election inspired a New Deal coalition to take shape in Southern California and lay the roots for the Democratic Party to slowly establish political networks in the state. Moreover, the politicization of the entire industry—controlled by studio executives for the promotion of the industry's interests first and of politics second—made the Democratic Party recognize how Hollywood could be more than an outside interest group. Its personalities could be a resource for communicating to the average citizen, on whom Franklin Roosevelt relied for political success.

With his New Deal, Roosevelt not only dissolved the traditional boundaries between government and the American people, but he also reshaped the national party system by making the executive branch a key source of employment, hope, and inspiration during the stressful years of depression and war.[44] Driven by concerns over public criticisms of lavish Hollywood practices during an era of economic distress, studio executives also aimed to lift the morale of the whole family through its productions sold as "pure entertainment." To achieve these dual campaigns, both Roosevelt and Hollywood studios relied on public relations operations that frequently overlapped. Just as Hollywood studios carefully prepared what information the public received about films and personalities through the media, so too did the Roosevelt administration purposefully select phrases, images, and carefully coordinated public events to convey a specific message to the American people. By establishing showmanship, a key quality in film production, as an essential element of politics, Roosevelt actively blurred the line between entertainment and politics. As moviegoers saw their president as a celebrity—through his starring role in newsreels and over the radio waves—Roosevelt also began to see his constituents as movie audiences.[45] In this changing political milieu, Roosevelt increasingly recognized how producers, writers, directors, and actors had unique assets that could sell his political agenda.

Before the 1932 election, *Variety* celebrated how Louis B. Mayer had become an "international statesman" with his contacts within the Hoover administration, claiming that Mayer stood as the "only American" to hold the "dual honor" of being a "national figure of politics and show business."[46] But after the election, Jack Warner quickly seized the opportunity to challenge the stature of his rival executive and assert his own connections to the president-elect's administration. The eager and ostentatious Warner constructed an elaborate event that embodied the motto of the Warner Bros. Studio: "Combining good picture-making with good citizenship."[47] In movie theaters across the country, as audiences watched newsreels of Roosevelt's bold inauguration proclamation that "we have nothing to fear but fear itself," they may have also had an opportunity to see a short film report that chronicled the journey of the 42nd Street Special.[48] This gold and silver train carried seven cars overflowing with stars, including Bette Davis, Leo Carrillo, and Claire Dodd, across the country to celebrate "A New Deal in Entertainment." "It looks like another Hollywood premiere," the studio-produced newsreel told audiences. "But, it is just Hollywood's acceptance of President Roosevelt's invitation to be his guests at his inauguration in Washington." As the 42nd Street Special toured the country with stopovers in more than one hundred cities, the actors and actresses stayed in character while Jack Warner made sure that they displayed their excitement about both the movie and the new president.[49] This cross-country trip publicly connected the stars of the silver screen with the president-elect. The report relayed the sense that Hollywood had arrived to overwhelm the East Coast. "Well Mr. Roosevelt," concluded the newscaster, "you invited them, but what will Mrs. Roosevelt say when the guests arrive by the carload?"

With costly efforts like the campaign spectacle and the 42nd Street Special, Harry and Jack Warner were frequently excessive in their support of Roosevelt and his New Deal programs, revealing an anxious desire for validation, nationally and within the industry itself. The Warner Bros. Studio had only recently established itself as a major studio with its 1927 hit *The Jazz Singer*, the first successful entrée into sound production. Two years earlier, the brothers had bought Vitagraph, the early production giant that had failed to compete with showmen like Louis B. Mayer and Adolph Zukor and had faltered by the 1920s. With studios on both coasts and a distribution circuit, Vitagraph gave the two brothers the opportunity to follow other Jewish entrepreneurs like Mayer and Zukor, who had started to build elaborate studio lots in Los Angeles. Jack and Harry Warner traced their roots to Poland, where their father had lived until 1883. The family had run a theater in New Castle, Pennsylvania, before attempting to cash in on the potentially lucrative and growing industry. Following *The Jazz Singer*'s success, the brothers attracted investors and strengthened the production and distribution system to become a major studio by the early 1930s. While the serious and sober Harry Warner spent most of his time in New York focusing on the business aspects of the studio, the younger brother, Jack, a self-aggrandizing performer known for his loud jackets, flashy smile, and tasteless jokes, honed his showmanship talents as the creative producer in the Hollywood studios.[50] Both brothers, however, felt the effects of the market crash, and they, like millions across the nation, turned to Franklin Roosevelt for an opportunity to gain social prestige and promote films that celebrated the worker, social justice, and New Deal programs. Through its theatrical and New Deal promotional films, Warner Bros. Studio promoted programs like the National Industrial Recovery Act and the icon of the "forgotten man," whom Roosevelt himself pledged to protect.[51]

During the 1930s, a New Deal ideology and coalition flourished in Hollywood, as a result of personal loyalty to Roosevelt (as in the case of the Warner brothers) and also because of the strenuous conditions of the studio systems themselves. Dominant images of happy, wealthy, and beautiful stars obscured the reality of the studio system, which controlled the lives of its employees and forced hard labor in the grueling production process. For example, the 42nd Street Special obliged contracted stars to travel the country in support of the new president, thus revealing the power of studio executives over their employees and their ability to use contracted publicity events to force actors to promote a particular political viewpoint. The standard contract for the cast of *42nd Street* included a provision for them to appear on the 42nd Street Special and explicitly warned that employment termination would result if any member of the tour brought about "public hatred, contempt, scorn or ridicule, or [anything to] tend to shock, insult or offend public morals or decency, or prejudice the Producer or the motion picture industry in general."[52] With long-term contracts, studios had complete control over the public images of their actors and actresses, and they determined which products and causes a particular star could promote.

Furthermore, while the studio system propelled some into fame, in reality, most workers in Hollywood did not achieve glamour and stardom. Humphrey Bogart's career emerges as an example of the struggles that actors endured under this system and the triumphs of which they dreamed. While disappointing his parents by dropping out of school and abandoning hopes of a medical career, Bogart, like many other ordinary Americans, looked to the theater for excitement. Working first as an office boy and then as a nameless background actor, Bogart gained acting experience in New York during the 1920s. Looking to Hollywood for fame and fortune, Bogart signed a contract for his first movie in 1930 and five years later began a fifteen-year contract with Warner Bros. that frequently left him unhappy. Throughout the 1930s, although he appeared in many movies, he did grunt work, mass-producing mediocre films without any special attention. Work, perseverance, and hopes for celebrity characterized the typical life of an actor or actress in Hollywood.[53]

The arrival of exiled European Jews and the transcontinental migration of New York cultural radicals added to the vibrant political climate taking shape in Los Angeles as newly arrived artists and writers on the Left eagerly participated in discussions of political philosophies, from the New Deal to communism.[54] Labor unions, which sprang up across the country, also became a force in the motion picture industry for workers hoping to change the demanding, exploitative, and frequently unrewarding working conditions under the studio system structures. In 1933, prominent actors such as Robert Montgomery, Will Rogers, Bette Davis, and Joan Crawford organized the Screen Actors Guild (SAG) to protect movie stars and unknown actors alike from the attempt of studios to slash wages and terminate employment at a whim. Each talent group formed its own guild to target the specific concerns of its trade: the Screen Writers Guild, the Screen Directors Guild, the Screen Producers Guild, and so on. The SAG, however, remained one of the most influential organizations because its membership roll included names that stimulated box office success. When looking back on the founding of the SAG, its former president, Ronald Reagan, praised its role in using star power to better the working conditions for all actors. "People started it who didn't need it themselves, but were willing to lend their individual bargaining power as stars to get benefits for players who needed collective strength," he explained.[55] Despite the range of income in the industry, Hollywood became one of the most unionized industries in the country. During the 1930s, celebrities aligned with stage extras in demands against the corporate studios, ultimately improving the working environment of actors, unifying the industry around the pro-labor president, and opening an opportunity for actors to hone skills in political negotiation, organization, and leadership through the guild itself.[56]

Roosevelt's California New Deal coalition joined laborers with radicals, intellectuals, and even studio executives like Jack Warner because of the common commitment to Franklin Roosevelt as a person and to the inspirational rhetoric that coincided with the rosy picture that motion pictures sold to millions of Americans. Roosevelt's New Deal shared a similar mission with Hollywood as a business: both wanted to inspire and uplift emotionally and economically depressed Americans.[57] Jack Warner, Douglas Fairbanks Jr., Samuel Goldwyn, Humphrey Bogart, and many more saw an opportunity to use their skills and knowledge to assert their public roles and the broader image of the industry in a way that filled their pocketbooks, warded off federal censors, and advanced their personal beliefs and causes. At a time when Americans faced an unprecedented economic crisis, executives knew it was good business to highlight how Hollywood "gives back" to its audience through charitable work to enhance its image among fans. Through this work, Hollywood personalities became the face of community activism across the nation and also made key social connections with politicians and learned organizational skills that eased their entrance into the political realm.

Along with defusing boycott threats for allegedly immoral behavior and productions, civic service also provided Jewish executives an opportunity to ward off anti-Semitism and gain social prestige previously garnered by the philanthropic efforts of established wealthy families like the Rockefellers and the Carnegies. And yet Hollywood philanthropy was different. By relying on public performances to generate awareness, raise money, and encourage participation, celebrity civic activism encouraged citizens to participate in community, national, and international causes as fans first and citizens second. Moreover, philanthropic activities paved an essential path for political awareness and organization among celebrities in Hollywood at a time when public expectations and studio contracts limited partisan opportunities. The steep financial returns of marquee benefit events quickly proved their worth to political leaders as well as captured the attention of political hopefuls—from socialists like Upton Sinclair to communists like motion picture writer John Howard Lawson.

The Great Depression hit Hollywood as hard as it did other communities throughout the nation, despite its status as a symbol of wealth and glamour. As the advertisements for the 1932 Warner Bros. "spectacle of all spectacles" revealed, the majority of motion picture employees worked behind the scenes in unrecognized, often unrewarding jobs as writers, directors, lyricists, cameramen, and engineers. The promotion of the pageant as a philanthropic event to benefit both the Motion Picture Relief Fund and the Marion Davies Foundation—charities for struggling entertainment industry workers—reminded all who read and watched the coverage of the event that Hollywood too was struggling economically. Similarly to many Warner Bros. Depression films, which showed glamour and beauty as false pretenses amid the economic crisis of show business, the evening emphasized that "EVERY DOLLAR" would be donated to charity. As one advertisement in a motion picture trade magazine emphasized, "Once more, don't forget that the big benefit for the needy and destitute in YOUR OWN BUSINESS is being held Saturday night in the Olympic Stadium. There should be a 100 per cent attendance. A real show is promised, and our Motion Picture Relief Fund needs the money urgently."[58]

While the evening provided an opportunity for FDR to gain electoral points with film industry workers, Los Angeles voters, and national movie aficionados who watched newsreels recounting the event, Jack Warner carefully structured advertisements and media announcements to focus attention on the fact that the "motion picture industry goes on parade for charity's sake."[59] The whole evening, explained Jack in a letter to his brother, "depends on the ability to be able to have Governor Roosevelt and [John Nance] Garner here as honor[ed] guests," for without them as exemplars of relief for suffering Americans, "it would be useless to go on with the program."[60] Although his desire to promote Roosevelt's candidacy drove the event, Warner understood the fragile boundaries that existed at the time between Hollywood and politics. "While it will be a complete smash for Roosevelt and Garner," Jack continued in the letter, "we will present it under the auspices of the three charity organizations named above."

Local Republicans saw through the "auspices of charity," and one motion picture paper editorial discussed how these political opponents "were rather burned at J.L.'s bringing Governor Roosevelt into the picture; said it was a political move first and charity second." But the article stressed that a charity event with a political purpose was justifiable because of the pressing need for money to help those in need. "We hope they are right and we hope they are burned sufficiently to get their candidate to Los Angeles and stage a greater pageant for their party, as long as the money goes into the coffers of the M.P. Relief Fund and Miss Davies' charity." In 1932, local charity efforts justified partisan activity in an industry expected to entertain audiences, not influence electoral politics. At the end of the day, the parade aided those in need in the local community, regardless of the candidate it promoted. As the editorial concluded, "Let's make the thing a political issue, let's taunt some of our best Republicans, reminding them of the march Jack Warner stole on them. Maybe we can uncover another function that will buy food, clothing, pay rents and hospital bills for the hundreds who require it IN THIS INDUSTRY."[61]

Throughout the 1930s, support for charity organizations emerged as an essential mainstay of the motion picture industry, and as with other public appearances, such as those on the 42nd Street Special train, studio publicity departments carefully made sure their employees participated. Studio executives wrote their top-earning employees constant letters urging them to donate their time and money to organizations like the Motion Picture Relief Fund, the Community Chest, and the Red Cross. Motivated by beliefs in civic responsibility and patriotic duty and by business sense, Jack Warner pressured his top-earning employees to do their part for charity by donating time, talent, and money. Warner "thrashed" director William Wyler for withholding donations to the Community Chest Drive of Los Angeles. "I don't know of nothing that will breed more discontent—more resentment among those unfortunately who must be helped, than the knowledge that people with heaven blessed incomes refuse to extend a helping hand," Warner cautioned Wyler.[62] "It is of such stuff that Communism is born." Then, to emphasize the business stake of the industry in charity activity, Warner continued: "I'd rather thrash this out between ourselves than have the public learn that the 'fantastically wealthy' movies people are too self-centered and too selfish to give a thought to their unfortunate neighbors. That would be disastrous to the popularity upon which our entire success depends." Warner's words reveal the importance of volunteerism, of both time and money, in maintaining favor with the public on whom they depended for success.

During the Great Depression, studio executives, publicity departments, and even gossip columnists such as Hedda Hopper and Louella Parsons worked tirelessly to depict celebrities not only as glamorous, beautiful, youthful, and fun, but also as dedicated community activists, concerned about the social problems of hunger, sickness, and homelessness.[63] Economic and political incentives undoubtedly drove this image as the industry sought to attract an audience and minimize censorship. However, promoting the image of a "civic Hollywood" gave many entertainers experience in raising funds and publicity that they would later use during electoral campaigns for underfunded candidates like Upton Sinclair, or for promoting and financing controversial issues of civil rights and the heightening awareness of the conflict with fascism in Europe.

Birthday Balls: Hollywood Philanthropy and
Roosevelt's New Deal Unite

Hollywood involvement with one charity in particular would ultimately demonstrate the extent to which volunteerism could reap political benefits with the highest office of the land. In 1934, a philanthropic tradition began that eventually succeeded in officially joining entertainment and presidential politics, all in the name of infantile paralysis. In the common bond of volunteerism, friends of President Roosevelt and his colleagues on the Warm Springs Foundation for Infantile Paralysis decided to throw a nationwide "surprise" celebration on FDR's birthday, January 30.[64] Mobilizing the country to nationally honor and recognize the newly elected president, the National Committee for the Birthday Ball for the President inspired over 5,000 local communities and businesses to organize celebrations, with profits benefiting the Warm Springs Foundation. Initially only one of thousands of communities that mobilized for the birthday event, Hollywood celebrities would eventually dominate the annual "birthday balls," effectively bridging the local and national scenes each January. As Janet Gaynor, Mickey Rooney, Robert Taylor, Dorothy Lamour, and many other famous faces publicly graced the White House each winter, the birthday balls provided an opportunity to improve the image of the industry, while also introducing its stars to elite governing officials and bringing them closer to the Roosevelt administration in the public eye. The prominent White House appearance of staunch Republicans like Robert Taylor showed how strict studio contracts ensured that the promotion of the industry image trumped the personal political sentiments of individuals, which studio executives feared could hurt box office returns.

The stars of the silver screen were among millions of Americans throughout the country who quickly jumped at the chance to join in the birthday celebrations in 1934. Washington, D.C., joined other cities and towns in throwing the president a "rousing" birthday ball, which brought together businesses, civic organizations, and local musicians in a celebration of their president. At the midnight "gala" in Washington, the Catholic University Glee Club sang, and numerous "players" throughout the city also joined in the entertainment.[65] The birthday balls spread from coast to coast, allowing high school bands and local communities to join the national purpose of honoring the president and contributing to an important charity. At 11:20 P.M. on January 30, 1934, officially celebrating his fifty-second birthday, President Roosevelt addressed the nation in a radio speech, "on behalf of the crippled children of the nation," acknowledging the efforts of over a million people gathered at 5,000 parties to honor his birthday and support the charity nearest to his heart.[66]

The birthday balls created a public image that was good business for studios and good politics for the Roosevelt administration. Although advertised as strictly "non-political," the birthday ball celebrations emerged as another avenue for the president to promote goodwill and forge a national social network of support in the same way that Hollywood studios worked to gain the goodwill of moviegoers. President Roosevelt had drastically altered the relationship between the federal government, the market, and the individual through New Deal programs, which employed individuals, protected investments, and provided a "safety net" during tough times. But by making the national government an integral component in the well-being of Americans—whether through direct employment or with promises of a secure future through Social Security—the New Deal destabilized local patronage structures at the same time it made the Democratic Party depend on entitlement programs to sustain its constituency. Advances in radio communication allowed Roosevelt to communicate and implement these national programs. The promotion of the New Deal and the imagery of the "common man" in documentary films, radio programs, photography, and theatrical releases sold principles of the New Deal through popular consumer culture, and, in doing so, used basic principles honed in the entertainment industries to communicate to the people, not as uneducated or uninterested "masses" but as audiences, eager for both information and entertainment.[67]

The birthday balls emerged as an effective way to advance a specific image of Roosevelt that reinforced his broader New Deal agenda and created a more personal bond between the president and his constituents. The 1936 program cover of the Waldorf Astoria's birthday ball depicted Roosevelt as a caring, gracious politician and a father to those in need. Surrounded by needy children, Roosevelt, dressed in suit and tie, sat at a desk with pen in hand and firm resolve on his face, which looked to the future. A woman depicted as a saint kneeled next to the president, with head bowed, and presented a birthday cake to the "savior" of the children. In the chorus of a new birthday song, James A. Mundy wrote a political tribute to the president that also implicitly connected to the message of Roosevelt as the way to national salvation, a theme that would permeate his broader reelection campaign that year. "More birthdays for Roosevelt, More mirth days for Roosevelt! May he ever wear the smile, that success abundant brings; So let our prayers mingle and let our monies jingle in our nation's great drive, for the aid of Warm Springs."[68]

In January 1944, Eleanor Roosevelt leads the Birthday Ball celebration in Washington with Hollywood celebrities (left to right) Red Skelton, William Douglas, Lucille Ball, and John Garfield. The first lady served as President Roosevelt's "ambassador" to Hollywood in the public eye during the annual Birthday Balls. Courtesy of the Franklin D. Roosevelt Presidential Library and Museum, Hyde Park, New York.

This image of Roosevelt on the birthday ball programs and in songs connected his charity efforts to his role as deliverer of the nation and thus became a powerful way to gain national political leverage in an election year. Undoubtedly, Roosevelt won the votes and loyalty of immigrant workers and northern African Americans through Works Progress Administration jobs and of small businesses through the Federal Deposit Insurance Corporation.[69] But, although the benefits of patronage formed the basis for this political coalition, entertainment events like the birthday balls strengthened Roosevelt's personal connection to the American people and allowed him to present an artfully crafted image of himself as the "savior" of the country to create an emotional bond with his public personality.

Hollywood emerged as one of many local communities that voted for Roosevelt's programs and governance style in the 1936 election. A local trade paper poll declared the industry to be "6 to 1 for Roosevelt."[70] The industry's electoral support of the president translated into increased volunteer efforts for the birthday balls over the next four years by offering not just the time and money of individual stars but also the resources of the studio system. With the leadership of the movie industry, California contributed over 25 percent of the total money raised in the nation for infantile paralysis.[71] Movie theaters became collection centers for donations to the charity, and actresses like Norma Shearer made public promises—in her case, to contribute her life's radio earnings to the cause. Each January, the balls became more and more "glamorous" and the media increasingly focused attention on the "galaxy of motion picture stars" in Washington, D.C., rather than on local celebrations and glee club performances.[72] In a *Washington Post* account of the festivities, public appearances and itineraries of famous names reigned supreme, with only one line dedicated to the fact that the "same benefit performances will be in progress throughout the country."[73] Not only did the role of local communities fall to the wayside in the wake of the national prominence of Hollywood, but also the charity mission of the balls emerged as only an offhand remark: "As always, the proceeds will aid the sufferers from infantile paralysis throughout the United States."

Despite this noticeable shift in celebrating the "galaxy of stars" that the birthday balls attracted to the capital, President Roosevelt was still reluctant to place himself directly in the spotlight with these entertainment figures. He welcomed the support and publicity Jack Warner offered with the Motion Picture Electrical Parade and Sports Pageant, but his administration distanced itself from the industry that, while able to generate box office profits, still stirred public controversy with prominent censorship debates.[74] Just as Roosevelt used his wife as his eyes and ears of public opinion throughout the Great Depression, she served as his ambassador to the Hollywood community. Eleanor Roosevelt's courtship of Hollywood during the birthday balls revealed at once the president's desire to bring the powerful and popular entertainment medium and its public figures into his administration and his caution against too intimate an association. Filled with memories of the recent heated censorship battles and the bitterness from the use of "manipulative entertainment" and "propaganda" in the Sinclair race, Roosevelt also remembered the backlash following his friend and Democratic presidential predecessor Woodrow Wilson's attempt to incorporate popular stars like Mary Pickford and Douglas Fairbanks into the Committee of Public Information to sell liberty bonds for the World War I war effort.[75] Moreover, reporters in the *New York Times* frequently reminded readers of the dangers of Adolf Hitler's propaganda machine in Germany. Characterizing German control of all forms of media as the "black magic of mass suggestions," the *Times* reminded the public that in a world "where heroes can be made to order," the president faced the challenge of proving the sincerity and benevolence of his publicity events and media messages.[76]

The birthday ball celebrations benefited all parties involved, both in the public eye and behind the scenes. They shaped perceptions of entertainment as clean and family oriented and popularized images of Hollywood's heart while also promoting the role of the president as the "savior" of the nation at a time when he faced immense political criticism for efforts to pack the Supreme Court and lend support to the French and English efforts to stop the spread of fascism abroad. The American public saw Roosevelt hobnobbing each year with famous guests. Crowds came to Washington each January and packed the streets in efforts to secure admission into the birthday ball celebrations and catch a glimpse of celebrities.[77] Those who did not make the trek to Washington read stories about the events that played out during the celebration. For example, Roosevelt's remark to actress Janet Gaynor in 1939, calling her "cute as a button," made national headlines.[78] Upon returning to the West Coast, Gaynor cashed in on this public presidential praise by using it as the title for her upcoming film with Selznick International Studio.[79] The following year, the *Washington Post* paid particular attention to the fact that "Hollywood furnished the stars and Washington recruited the supporting cast of 20,000 last night in a gay climax to the celebration of President Roosevelt."[80] The names and faces of the nation's beloved stars, Mickey Rooney, Gene Autry, Dorothy Lamour, and many more, headlined the media's coverage of the 1940 event.[81] At times, the excitement of the crowds left out prominent politicians. As the *New York Times* noted, "A Presidential prospect scarcely rated a second glance in the Capitol's corridors unless accompanied by a Southern California glamour girl."[82] Entertainers had emerged at the forefront of a prominent celebration with the Roosevelt administration each year in ways that promoted the power of entertainment to enhance the public good.

Publicity surrounding the birthday ball celebrations, however, coincided with important behind-the-scenes collaborations between powerbrokers in Hollywood and the Roosevelt administration that brought economic benefits to studios and political benefits to the president and his family. In the closing months of 1938, Roosevelt's own son and close political adviser, James (Jimmy), accepted a job offer to work with Academy Award–winning producer Samuel Goldwyn.[83] When Jimmy Roosevelt moved to the West Coast, he joined his sister, Anna, who had married one of Will Hays's employees, John Boettiger, two years earlier.[84] Personal and professional connections cultivated with the Roosevelt administration over the past six years paid off for the industry economically that same year. After Assistant Attorney General Thurman Arnold filed a 118-page petition of antitrust violations against the industry, Will Hays responded by forming a commission to negotiate with government prosecutors, and he reached out to Roosevelt for support as he defended the industry's system of vertical integration and its block-buying policies. "These are times that call for increased cooperative endeavor not only within the industry, but between industry and government," announced Will Hays, offering a "quid pro quo" of industry efforts to move forward in dramatizing the evils of the Nazi regime in exchange for administration efforts to drop the charges of monopoly.[85] Harry Warner, likewise, reminded Secretary of Commerce Harry Hopkins of Hollywood's vital role in selling American goods to international markets, as well as the "good-will and propaganda function of motion pictures" that might be needed in an environment of increasing international tension.[86] Two years later, as the electoral climate intensified and the president sought an unprecedented third term, the film trade press publicized the ability of studios to make movies "dealing with Roosevelt policies" in ways that "might be effective in turning public sentiment to the administration."[87] After winning the election with the help of an active "Hollywood for Roosevelt" mobilization, the president had an opportunity to reward the efforts of his studio friends in Hollywood by intervening in the legal negotiations between Assistant Attorney General Arnold and the major studios. Working with Secretary of Commerce Hopkins, Roosevelt pressured the Justice Department to negotiate with producers, ultimately resulting in an agreement that altered aspects of the distribution process but allowed studios to keep their theaters. As Jack Warner penned his gratitude to his friend in the White House, he understood that the relationships he had built over the last eight years had saved his studio from economic collapse and he pledged his willingness to make any film the administration wanted in the future.[88]

Discarding the "Auspices of Charity"

Industry-driven political activism motivated studio executives to revamp the civic image of Hollywood celebrities and create public links between the White House and the industry as a whole, despite the partisan divides within studios. The 1940 election, however, illuminated the partisan potential created by these public collaborations, and liberal entertainers eagerly took advantage of the civic role that Hollywood had crafted for itself over the course of the 1930s to aid the Democratic ticket. With Jimmy Roosevelt and Melvyn Douglas leading the way, newly awakened liberal activists eagerly prepared for the 1940 campaign, the first presidential campaign in which they aspired to a national role in motivating the electorate to vote for the incumbent. While many wealthier executives and producers with Republican loyalties quietly sided with Wendell Willkie, Roosevelt supporters used the contacts and skills they had developed in fund-raising and in their studio work to mobilize prominent national media attention and support for the president. Over 200 well-known actors, producers, writers, and studio executives joined Hollywood for Roosevelt, a political group "representing the motion picture industry."[89] Complete with official stationery and membership certificates declaring loyalty to Roosevelt and vice presidential candidate Henry Wallace, the committee produced advertisements and media events celebrating the Democratic ticket. Chairs Pat O'Brien and Joan Bennett led the various branches of the committee, which focused on getting out the vote for Roosevelt through membership drives and speaking tours, on which key personalities like Douglas Fairbanks Jr. and Melvyn Douglas traveled around the state and country making speeches for FDR.[90] The committee also sponsored public meetings and worked with local civic organizations to greet visiting senators and vice presidential candidate Henry Wallace.

During these electoral events, the Hollywood for Roosevelt organization contributed important screen personalities and financial aid. Radio broadcasts sponsored by the committee not only brought Roosevelt's words to Southern California voters but also funded nationwide broadcasts, which fused musical composition with the talents of top motion picture stars, including Douglas Fairbanks Jr., Lucille Ball, Humphrey Bogart, Henry Fonda, and Groucho Marx. On October 31, these personalities came together in a national radio event, "Salute to Roosevelt," and several days later a huge collection of celebrities performed an "Election Eve" radio special. Newspaper and billboard endorsements rounded out the media efforts. Two attractive billboards cleverly stated "Hollywood for Roosevelt"—one with a cartoon design and the other with replications of celebrity autographs—which drew national attention.

Spending $1,600, the committee placed an ad in the *New York Times* with the headline: "Why We of Hollywood Will Vote for Roosevelt."[91] This advertisement stressed that Hollywood knew "how to make a star overnight" and asserted that Wendell L. Willkie, the Republican nominee, had engaged in false advertisement and make-believe. "Experience has taught the people of Hollywood that sound entertainment, no matter how imaginative, must be based upon recognizable truth; otherwise it is phony. Vast amounts of money and months of secret preparation have been lovingly spent in polishing Mr. Willkie's script. We have read the script. It is phoney." In the weeks leading up to the Republican National Convention, Willkie had collaborated with powerful businessmen and influential figures from the *Saturday Evening Post* and the *New York Herald Tribune* to create a publicity "build up" for the relatively obscure Wall Street industrialist.[92] As a former Democrat who had never served in public office, Willkie had little support within the party and very few delegates to support his nomination, so he embarked on a publicity campaign, backed by his wealthy friends. Opponents, first in the Republican Party and then during the national election, played on popular suspicion of "propaganda" in American politics to attack Willkie's candidacy. Interestingly, Hollywood liberals asserted their expertise in show business as justification for political involvement. Professionally trained to understand the deceptive potential of publicity, Hollywood professionals asserted that it was their responsibility to expose Willkie's attempts to manipulate public opinion. As a letter from the secretary of the committee to President Roosevelt frankly stated: "The Hollywood committee was composed chiefly of political amateurs. But they do not lack political sense."[93]

Perhaps amateur in the traditional sense, the Hollywood for Roosevelt committee heralded a new style of political organization. Mobilizing key lessons from the entertainment industry for the Roosevelt campaign, Hollywood for Roosevelt demonstrated its effectiveness in getting publicity, funds, and votes. While the *New York Times* advertisement criticized Willkie for his use of "make-believe" and "phony scripts" to create a false public persona, this committee unabashedly deployed the Hollywood Dream Machine to promote FDR's reelection. As Leo Rosten observed, while the lineup of Willkie supporters in Hollywood was "formidable," the Hollywood for Roosevelt organization produced a "remarkable radio campaign," which made it a "powerful" asset for the president.[94] The constant advertising of Roosevelt over airwaves, in star-studded public events, and through direct advertising and editorial support brought established techniques of film promotion into the political process.

Moreover, the 1940 Democratic mobilization inspired activists to think about how to strengthen the Democratic Party in California. Though various liberals had come together in 1938 because of what they considered the "infamous" gubernatorial election, which they saw as stolen from Upton Sinclair, four years earlier, the nature of Democratic mobilization remained scattered and unorganized. Civic involvement and international events had turned Los Angeles into a city of "causes" by 1940, and yet this politicized environment lacked organization and focus. But the Hollywood for Roosevelt committee members quickly aimed to remedy this as they wrote to the Democratic National Committee (DNC) with questions on how to develop long-term structures and strong leadership to ensure both the vitality of the Democratic Party in Southern California and the leadership role of its motion picture activists. Secretary Ralph Block appealed directly to the president for advice on how the Hollywood committee could hone its identity and organize itself and the California Democratic Party.[95] Roosevelt responded with encouragement, emphasizing how this particular committee's activities "might well be very effective in bringing the facts before the public."[96]

Spurred on by the 1940 election and events abroad as Hitler's army conquered France in less than six weeks, industry politics paved the way for engagement in "patriotic politics." Roosevelt supporters like Jack Warner framed political activities, on the domestic front and in raising awareness for the Allied war effort, in patriotic rhetoric, as they reminded the president that entertainment and motion pictures could shape public opinion and help dramatize international affairs in ways that portrayed Hitler as the villain and the Allied powers as the hero. In the wake of the antitrust settlement, all the major studios, regardless of party affiliation, worked to establish connections with the State Department and the Department of Defense to make their production centers available for administrative or defense training needs. As controversial movies, like the Warner Bros. film *Confessions of a Nazi* (1939), provided a powerful on-screen critique of Nazism, the behind-the-scenes discussion of the role that motion pictures could play in the Allied effort foreshadowed the intense collaboration that wartime measures would bring. But it also demonstrated a shift in the meaning of celebrity in the eyes of national politicians. No longer was Hollywood merely the "land of the lotus"—it had shown its potential to influence public discourse through entertainment.

The inauguration in January 1941 demonstrated a national political appreciation of the talents and activism of Hollywood celebrities. Rather than coming to Washington, D.C., as bystanders watching the festivities, as they had done in 1932, celebrities became participants. Charlie Chaplin, Raymond Massey, Irving Berlin, and Douglas Fairbanks Jr. performed a historical and patriotic show that fused the political history of the nation with contemporary entertainment. For the first time, President Roosevelt actually named the concert performed on the eve of the inaugural the

Inaugural Gala, emphasizing the new presence of his glamorous friends and performers in the concert. Conveniently, the theme of the gala was "anti-propaganda," in order to emphasize that this association with Hollywood celebrities did not constitute the type of manipulation used by fascist dictators abroad.

A month after the inauguration, New York senator James M. Mead proclaimed to the Senate the positive impact of Hollywood's and Broadway's political appearances in Washington, D.C., as they had added "color and glamour to the historic third-term inaugural, and to the more recent celebration of President Roosevelt's fifty-ninth birthday."[97] In this speech, Mead highlighted the "potency of marquee names that spell box-office power" for politicians seeking an audience. Furthermore, he emphasized the need for Washington to experience the happiness and hope that Hollywood brought to the capital every January. "I think I speak for the people of Washington when I say that they are grateful for this annual influx of glamour," declared Mead. "We are grateful not only because it helps a humanitarian cause, but for more selfish reasons: We like these personal appearances and these close-up glances of those who give us such an abundance of fun and diversion through the year." Color, glamour, fun, diversion: Senator Mead's remarks reflected a growing desire to receive more emotional fulfillment from political events and personalities in ways that Louis B. Mayer had envisioned in 1928. And yet, although Hollywood political mobilization had gained leverage in local California politics and entertainers had made an appearance on the national stage, they still stood on its periphery.

While Roosevelt and Mead emphasized the "glamour and fun" that entertainment brought to national politics, conservative critics of the New Deal and the incumbent's administration feared that this glitz served as a dangerous, not a delightful, distraction. A *Washington Post* columnist who frequently criticized Roosevelt's New Deal, Mark Sullivan, raised concern about the broader implications of the political need for "oomph" in the upcoming presidential election.[98] In language reflecting Walter Lippmann's criticism in 1922 and the Hoover campaign's wariness of the silver screen in 1928, Sullivan declared that he was "very, very tired of glamour in politics, tired of political adroitness, tired of showmanship. To assume that glamour and wisdom go hand in hand is a serious fallacy—the two qualities are more often divided than together."[99]

A conservative Texan, Martin Dies, had already started to take action against this "fallacy" with the investigation into the political activities of liberal celebrities that he had begun two years earlier. In a conversation

At Hyde Park in July 1938, Eleanor Roosevelt converses with Shirley Temple in the year of what Representative Martin Dies called the "Shirley Temple fabrication." The young actress visited the Roosevelts in both Hyde Park and Washington. Along with establishing a friendship with the First Family, she shared lessons about "waving to the camera" with the first lady. Courtesy of the Franklin D. Roosevelt Presidential Library, Hyde Park, New York.

with a former Communist Party organizer who had become an investigator for the House Un-American Activities Committee, J. B. Matthews, Dies learned about what he considered a very dangerous development in Hollywood: the rise of communist-front organizations and the use of unsuspecting celebrities to raise money and publicity for the communist agenda. Matthews explained to him how the Communist Party pulled the strings behind organizations like the League of Women Shoppers, which boasted the place of Miriam Hopkins and Bette Davis on its membership list, or how the communist paper in France, *Ce Soir*, "featured greetings from Clark Gable, Robert Taylor, James Cagney, and even Shirley Temple." Matthews discussed the rise of anti-Nazi organizations in Hollywood and how these ultimately provided support for the Communist Party by taking advantage of the deep pocketbooks and political naïveté of Hollywood's heart. While Matthews quickly added that "no one, I hope is going to claim any one of these persons in particular is a Communist," he explained that "careless" celebrity endorsements in such organizations had become a key element in the communist propaganda campaign.[100]

Matthews's testimony confirmed the suspicions Dies had of the potential dangers in Hollywood and the threat of communism that loomed more broadly in Roosevelt's New Deal. As Dies also investigated the place of communist subversion in the Department of Labor, the Federal Theater Project, the National Labor Relations Board, and the Works Progress Administration, the Roosevelt administration responded that allegations were misguided and exaggerated and a "flagrantly unfair attempt to influence an election."[101] On the other side, the Hollywood press and members of the Roosevelt administration cleverly portrayed as ridiculous the supposed threat of Shirley Temple, the eleven-year-old child star, to discredit the allegations that the Communist Party had infiltrated New Deal organizations and the Democratic Party.[102]

Though many laughed off Dies's accusations in 1938, this response, what Dies called the "Shirley Temple fabrication," made him even more convinced of the link between liberal activism in the motion picture industry and the communist propaganda efforts. While his investigation in 1938 lacked in-depth research and factual evidence, in 1940, he returned to Hollywood armed with more information about dinner parties, fund-raising efforts, and Democratic Party activities. He interviewed Humphrey Bogart, James Cagney, and Fredric March about their involvement in supposed communist-front organizations. In round two, Dies accused the motion picture industry's "high price publicity machine" of having undermined his earlier investigation.[103]

But in 1940, propelled by a surge of political activism during the election and the international crisis, entertainers fought back and defended their Americanism and political legitimacy. While Dies claimed to "expose Hollywood thoroughly," the lack of research and fact showing communist influence left the motion picture industry claiming victory—as one headline proclaimed, "Hollywood Heckles Its Hecklers."[104] Looking back at the obstacles the film industry faced in 1940, the *New York Times* noted that assertive testimonies from Humphrey Bogart, Fredric March, Robert Montgomery, and Melvyn Douglas "took the punch out" of Dies's campaign.[105] Immediately after his testimony, Melvyn Douglas went on the offensive and explained to fans in *Photoplay* that he had supported Republican Spain in the Spanish Civil War and campaigned to resolve the "problems of the underprivileged."[106] *Photoplay* featured an interview with Douglas about his political beliefs so his fans could know exactly where he stood on the political spectrum. "As a motion picture actor, he belongs to the millions who pay hard earned coins to see him," explained the magazine. "Those people have a right to know the true status of affairs." The *Photoplay* article showed both the shift from industry politics to a "patriotic politics" that began to happen in response to the outbreak of war abroad. Rather than just focusing on the interests of the industry, Douglas took part in a renewed public relations campaign that did not just assert the civic role of celebrities but also defended their rights to mobilize to defend democracy abroad.

By 1941, Hollywood spectacle was a part of politics but had not yet replaced traditional forms of party mobilization or communication. But as the Roosevelt administration redefined the role of government, making national programs and policies a more active part of individual lives, Hollywood's media outreach, knowledge, and publicity tactics proved crucial to Roosevelt to communicate with a diverse electorate, which studios had courted with great success in the 1930s. Moreover, studio executives, on both the Left and the Right, understood the economic benefits that came with the increased prestige of motion picture productions and actors. Having the cultural power to shape national conversations about events abroad gave industry leaders a seat at the negotiating table over the antitrust suits. By treating the motion picture industry respectfully as a partner in fighting infantile paralysis, bringing about economic recovery, and encouraging interventionist debates, Roosevelt developed an ad hoc system of propaganda for his international New Deal, something that would expand dramatically during the war. At the end of the day, profits trumped politics, but executives learned how profits could depend on establishing political ties to the administration and making politicians appreciate the power of entertainment—in ways that Roosevelt understood and his opponents feared.

The Hollywood Dream Machine Goes to War

During the summer of 1941, Senator Gerald Nye (R-N.Dak.) turned up the heat on the motion picture industry. Angered by the 1939 Warner Bros. production *Confessions of a Nazi Spy* and the recent release of Charlie Chaplin's *The Great Dictator*, the prominent isolationist spokesman passionately charged that Hollywood studios "had flooded" the silver screen with "picture after picture designed to rouse us to a state of war hysteria."[1] Nye dramatically accused the industry, run by "foreign born" men from "Russia, Hungary, Germany, and Balkan countries," of pushing the country to the brink of war because of their selfish desire to protect profits from their British markets threatened by the German bombing campaign. The movies, asserted this newspaper-editor-turned-politician, had inflicted "madness" for war upon unsuspecting audiences across the country. By using glamorous actors and the allure of entertainment, Jewish studio executives had "insidiously" coerced audiences into supporting military involvement in the war abroad, argued Nye, as he warned listeners how "in 20,000 theaters in the United States tonight they are holding war mass meetings."

In this emotional address, Gerald Nye attempted to arouse public support for the Senate resolutions he had just drawn up with fellow isolationists Senator Bennett "Champ" Clark (D-Mo.) and America First Founder John T. Flynn. Through this formal investigation into the propaganda efforts of the motion picture and radio industries, Nye aimed to uncover two intertwined concerns. First, he wanted to probe the political power of entertainment. The Senate resolution stated clearly that "whereas the motion picture screen and radio are the most potent instrument of ideas" and possess power to "influence public mind" by reaching the "eyes and ears of one hundred million people," the content on the screen surrounding such an important political concern as intervention in the war abroad demanded attention.[2] Throughout the investigation, Nye continued to state how motion pictures should adhere to their primary role as pure entertainment. Major studios, he contended, should not make productions that would lend weight to any one side of a political debate. He referred to the moral censorship campaign from a decade earlier, reminding listeners that the movie producers "only a few years ago filled their pictures with so much immorality and filth that the great Christian churches had to rise up in protest against it and organize the League of Decency to stop it."

Second, Nye also suspected direct collaboration between the entertainment industry and the Roosevelt administration. The senator charged that the "movie companies have been operating war propaganda almost as if they were being directed from a single central bureau."[3] Convinced that "government men" directed productions on "every studio lot," Nye argued that collaboration between government and the industry aimed to inflict on unsuspecting audiences a militaristic spirit. "What I would like to know," Nye informed radio listeners, "are the movie moguls doing this because they like to do it, or has the Government of the United States forced them to become the same kind of propaganda agencies that the German, Italian, and Russian film industries have become?" Nye concluded that he had "excellent reason to believe that this government influence had prevailed."

Many of Nye's fears rang of anti-Semitism, ultimately providing an avenue for the industry's hired counsel, Wendell Willkie, to discredit the charges. The senator's suspicion about behind-the-scenes collaborations between Hollywood and the Roosevelt administration, however, was not unfounded. The administration had praised various "warmongering" films and invited the same celebrities who voiced strong opinions about international events to birthday ball celebrations and the recent inaugural gala. Privately, Franklin Roosevelt even encouraged actors like Douglas Fairbanks Jr. to generate support for the British cause and producers like Jack and Harry Warner to continue to produce "meaningful" entertainment: movies like *Confessions of a Nazi Spy*, which Nye condemned. Nye suspected what had indeed started to happen over the course of Roosevelt's administrations: the embrace of entertainment as a tool for political communication. By calling a Senate hearing to uncover "propaganda" campaigns by the motion picture industry, Nye publicly questioned the legitimacy and legality of using entertainment to advance a political agenda. In doing so, the senator led a national debate over the definition of "entertainment" and the proper political place of "celebrities." In 1930, Hamilton Fish had declared the propaganda potential of cinema as "yet to be seen."

By 1941, Gerald Nye recognized and feared the propaganda potential of the motion picture industry. The European conflict thoroughly politicized not just individuals but also studio productions, as Hollywood activists for international intervention worked diligently to change the definition of entertainment from "pure family fun" to a tool for "enlightenment and education."

During the war, Hollywood-inspired propaganda fully came of age, as directors, studio executives, actors, writers, and producers joined together to assert the motion picture industry's patriotism. From film productions to the war bond campaigns, Hollywood Democrats and Republicans suspended partisan hostilities to serve the nation in ways that expanded the industry politics of the 1930s. Wartime collaboration with the Office of War Information (OWI) and the Department of the Treasury, in particular, gave Hollywood new ways to make its entertainment and publicity strategies not just respectable and moral but also an essential aspect of the Allied effort and expressions of American patriotism. The industry's patriotic political mobilization used the power of the Hollywood Dream Machine to improve the morale and line the pocketbooks of the Allied powers.

From 1939 through 1945, the government and the American people both placed faith in motion pictures and their stars to disseminate news, policies, and ideology. Extensive literature has explored Hollywood's World War II propaganda effort, chronicling how political beliefs, the pursuit of profit, and patriotism shaped both nontheatrical and commercial productions.[4] The motion picture emerged as a powerful weapon of war as it helped to mobilize civilians on the home front, taught proper wartime behavior, motivated troops, attacked enemies with "black propaganda," and dramatized to others around the world the intense ideological and military struggles that entangled the United States and its allies. But, scholarship focusing on the silver screen messages has neglected an exploration of how the World War II propaganda effort offered Americans a new way of seeing film and its personalities outside the "pure entertainment sphere." The war transformed celebrities from consumer icons and civic role models into patriotic leaders and government spokespersons. Beyond the short-term goals of winning the war, the inclusion of Hollywood in the war effort taught politicians lasting lessons about how to promote policies and political ideologies using Hollywood production tactics while also offering the film industry entrée into the political world it had previously seen only from the fringes. Moreover, the war bond campaigns proved that entertainment and media exploitation did not decrease civic awareness and activism. On the contrary, during World War II, integrating Hollywood personalities, production, and media spectacles into the political process increased awareness of international events and encouraged a new type of political activism grounded in entertainment structures.

Redefining the Meaning of Entertainment

In the spring of 1939, as Adolf Hitler's forces overran Czechoslovakia, domestic debates over the international responsibilities of the United States raged. President Roosevelt urged revisions to the Neutrality Act that would allow the country to provide Britain and France with military support without directly engaging in the potential conflict. Progressive Republicans, an important part of Roosevelt's domestic New Deal coalition, strongly disagreed with the president's foreign policy ideas, arguing that the war threat resulted from British propaganda and that U.S. participation would only benefit big businesses and profiteers.[5] In this volatile atmosphere, Harry and Jack Warner took steps to articulate their personal political beliefs about the evils of Nazi expansion. Fearing the dangers for European Jews under Hitler's rule, the two brothers produced the controversial film *Confessions of a Nazi Spy*. In what the *Motion Picture Daily* termed a "vigorous piece of entertainment, which is, at the same time, a powerful anti-Nazi picture," the film chronicled the recent news drama of four Nazi spies arrested, indicted, and tried in the United States.[6] Based on a true story of FBI agent Leon G. Turrou's investigation of a ring of Nazi sympathizers in New York City, the movie interspersed actual newsreels with studio-produced material to dramatize the insidious efforts of the Nazi forces to overthrow the American democratic system. While the movie carefully depicted the Nazi spy efforts as amateurish, it nevertheless warned about American naïveté and susceptibility to the Nazi threat from within the country itself.

To produce the explicitly anti-Nazi film, Jack and Harry Warner fought the Production Code Administration, withstood criticism from their fellow studio executives, and knowingly gave up lucrative international box office profits.[7] Still, the personal political agenda of the two Jewish brothers to promote an interventionist agenda abroad coincided with that of the Roosevelt administration. While the film was controversial among isolationists like Senator Nye, the Warner brothers also understood that this movie production would be a sign of good faith and gratitude for the work that Harry Hopkins, with Roosevelt's approval, had done to help defend the broader industry against antitrust legislation.[8] *Confessions*, however, did something more than serve as a tool for negotiation and favor with Roosevelt. As the *Hollywood Reporter* noted, the film "unquestionably sound[ed] out the efficacy of a new approach to purposeful entertainment."[9] Another viewer agreed and claimed that Hollywood had a "responsibility" to relay "stories of the dramatic events of modern life, of records of struggle for Democracy and the heroism of average people."[10] As a major motion picture production that aimed to enlighten its audiences about a controversial political issue, *Confessions of a Nazi Spy* showed how ideas about film content and public responsibilities articulated by the radical fringes in the mid-1930s had come to dominate a tenuous but growing Hollywood Left coalition by the spring of 1939.

Over the previous five years, as in urban intellectual areas across the country, the Left in Hollywood had grown. As exiled European Jewish filmmakers, intellectual artists from New York City, and studio workers engaged in lively intellectual political discussions about the merits of the New Deal, socialism, and communism, a Popular Front alliance spread through cocktail party conversations. Accustomed to turning out for "good causes," liberal celebrities joined radical writers at dinner parties and fund-raisers in the name of what many actors simply saw as "humanitarian gestures"— such as providing money for ambulances or medical aid for the Popular Front fighting General Francisco Franco's military forces in Spain. Spurred on by the outbreak of the Spanish Civil War in 1936, cocktail party causes soon turned into organizations like the Hollywood Anti-Nazi League, the Actors' Refugee Committee, the Motion Picture Committee for Spanish Relief, the Committee of 56, and the Hollywood Committee for Polish Relief, among many others.[11] Though frequently divided in political philosophies, party loyalties, languages, backgrounds, and intellectual outlooks, the Hollywood Left unified around a desire to use entertainment to engage the public in intellectual and political debates about the meaning of democracy in modern industrial life.[12] While studio publicity departments had sold entertainment as pure family fun through philanthropic campaigns of the 1930s, refugee artists like Fritz Lang aligned with communists, like writer John Howard Lawson, and liberals, like actor Melvyn Douglas and producer Walter Wanger, to develop strategies to use motion pictures as "an instrument of enlightenment and entertainment."[13]

Organizations like the Hollywood Anti-Nazi League brought communist writers and émigré directors to collaborate with capitalist Jewish executives like Harry and Jack Warner. By the summer of 1939, however, the ideological tensions within the Hollywood Popular Front had cracked with the August announcement of the Nazi-Soviet Nonaggression Pact. Loyal Hollywood communists who followed directives from the Communist Party in Moscow supported the party decision that maintaining the border security of the Soviet Union trumped concerns to protect European Jewry.[14] Two years later, when Germany invaded the Soviet Union, the Hollywood Left reunited in common cause against Hitler. But the political tensions that pervaded the industry in the summer of 1939 foreshadowed the tumultuous postwar divides during which conservatives would critique liberal political activism on and off the screen.

Nevertheless, the rapid Nazi conquest of Poland, and then of France less than a year later, heightened the resolve of filmmakers to dramatize on the silver screen the international and domestic threat of Hitler's expansion.[15] Since the censorship battles of the early 1930s, producers had been reluctant to develop any politically controversial movies; profits trumped politics and philanthropic rhetoric frequently disguised partisan activities. But the gravity of the international crisis propelled the Warner brothers to lead the way in using studio production tools to make a broader statement about the threat of Nazism abroad. Their political advocacy, however, went beyond the silver screen. Just as the brothers had used the contractual obligations of the studio system to encourage support of their friend in the White House, so too did they use their position as studio executives to warn employees of fascist dangers abroad. Over a year after the release of *Confessions of a Nazi Spy*, on June 5, 1940, Harry Warner delivered an impassioned speech, "United We Survive, Divided We Fall," to 6,000 Warner Bros. employees and their spouses. In this speech, Warner read excerpts from the Nazi publication *Defilement of Race*, which professed the mission of Germany to "free this world of Jews and Christians." He stressed the threat to Christianity as well as to his own Jewish beliefs, arguing that Nazism could encroach on the United States as swiftly as it had on Denmark and France. Warner stressed the importance of democracy and the evils of fascism, professing that he would "rather see my children in the earth, buried, than to live under any such system as the one I am trying to prevent them from living under." Americanism needed to be actively protected by cooperation with the FBI, aid to European Allied countries, and the purge of "all un-American organizations, especially those sponsored and paid for by enemy foreign powers." Warner introduced his employees to the local FBI agent, stressed increased production of the unprofitable patriotic shorts, and urged his employees to unify within a democratic country of equal races and religions. To ensure that all employees understood the importance of this address, Warner published it as a pamphlet. "It is my sincere wish," he reiterated, "that every employee of Warner Bros. will carefully read this booklet and profit there from."[16] Both Jack and Harry Warner took the lead in articulating anti-Nazi sentiment and warning colleagues, employees, and the broader public about the perils of Hitler's Germany.

Just as producers like the Warner brothers assumed a risk in using their studios to support their political agenda, so too did celebrities like Fredric March, Humphrey Bogart, and Douglas Fairbanks Jr. take on the costs, risks, and benefits of traveling the country and even parts of the world to promote a certain message. Douglas Fairbanks Jr. emerged as a prominent spokesman in advocating for the Allied cause and a new role for entertainment. He traveled throughout the country to generate sympathy for British defense efforts and also to address the nation's fear of propaganda. On behalf of the newly formed Committee to Defend America by Aiding the Allies, headed by William Allen White, Fairbanks articulated that he was a voting citizen, who happened to be a movie actor, pleading for the cause of freedom.[17] Emphasizing to a Chicago crowd that he was "pro-British, but *only* because I am radically pro-American," Fairbanks argued for intervention in the European war, declaring isolationism to be "impossible, impracticable, and dangerous." Fairbanks pointed to the struggles as between "two great revolutions taking place, one is called totalitarian, and the other democratic." More than arguing for an active contribution to the British war effort, Fairbanks attempted to unravel the meaning of propaganda. Declaring that "the cry 'Propaganda' rings out in the same strident voice as 'Witchcraft' did in Salem in the seventeenth century," Fairbanks attempted to distinguish between informative propaganda—the education of the public about the war principles—and subversive propaganda—that deployed by German secret organizations and "designed to foment unrest and subvert our system." Enlightened entertainment, argued Fairbanks, was necessary to combat the evils of Hitler's dark magic of persuasion.

As Fairbanks became the head of the committee's Southern California office and one of its national vice presidents, he worked with playwright and FDR speechwriter Robert Sherwood to garner popular support for the Allied cause. According to Fairbanks's autobiography, President Roosevelt urged him and members of White's committee to push the media, public opinion, and Congress toward the interventionist side, so the president could send more aid to Britain.[18] Fairbanks took this role seriously, addressing diverse audiences about Britain, the perils of Nazism, and the importance of the Lend-Lease Act. His universal appeal, cultivated in Hollywood studios, made him an attractive speaker to Rotarians, bankers, schoolteachers, youth, and farmers.[19]

Just as President Roosevelt rewarded the loyalty of studio executives, he too showed his faith in Douglas Fairbanks Jr.'s ability to influence public opinion by appointing Fairbanks to serve as a cultural ambassador to Latin America under the newly formed Office of the Coordinator of Inter-American Affairs. As he toured countries in South America, Fairbanks made speeches to his foreign fan base and their political leaders about motion pictures and American democracy.[20] Like his public role on the White Committee, his Hollywood fame attracted audiences eager to meet such a famous personality face to face. Trained by Hollywood studios to read audience reactions and desires, Fairbanks saw his ambassadorship as an important opportunity to bring back to the president a report on the popular sentiment toward the administration's policies and the ongoing European war. In his final report, "A Report on South America and a Plan for International Democratic Propaganda," Fairbanks warned of the powerful inroads that Germany had already made with a propaganda program that presented the United States as greedy and untrustworthy. Fairbanks stressed the need for an "aggressive concept of a democratic attack" to compete with the German organization, emphasizing that "no matter how many reports one reads from our Intelligence Services, it is impossible to appreciate the great advances into people's minds made by Nazi and Communist propaganda."

Douglas Fairbanks Jr.'s evolution from movie actor to diplomat paralleled the developments in the industry as a whole from 1939 through the U.S. entry into the war. Stirred by events abroad, Fairbanks spoke out against Nazism, which propelled him into further anti-isolationist statements and engagements. The success he had in talking to audiences and his involvement in FDR's reelection campaign in 1940 brought his skills to the attention of Roosevelt, who used them to promote his foreign policy in Latin America. As Fairbanks observed in his work for the Office of the Coordinator of Inter-American Affairs, the United States lacked a propaganda arm of the government and German advances in such media techniques forced the president to counter the "black magic" unleashed by Hitler's professional propaganda offices. To do this, he turned to his friends in the motion picture industry for guidance.

Eager to promote their industry as well as advance their personal political beliefs, film people, led by active Roosevelt supporters like the Warner brothers and Fairbanks himself, quickly mobilized to teach the government the power of the silver screen and the value of "exploitation"—a widely used term referring to the execution of a Hollywood-style publicity campaign. And yet, even before the administration developed an official propaganda office, both sides—President Roosevelt and Hollywood studio executives—faced intense criticism from opponents who considered the growing use of the silver screen to persuade audience members about controversial political issues immoral, manipulative, and "un-American."

The increased activism on and off the screen of Hollywood interventionists confirmed Senator Gerald Nye's suspicions, and he moved quickly to use a Senate hearing on propaganda and implicit threats of antitrust legislation to silence the industry in the fall of 1941. Nye and his fellow isolationists used all the power they could muster, and some over which they had no control, to strong-arm the industry back to producing only "pure entertainment" films that would not weigh in on the political concerns of the day. As the investigation moved forward, however, it became clear that he and other committee members had not even seen the alleged "propaganda" films. They did not want to debate the merits of the particular films but rather engage in a discussion of the ethics of unleashing the Hollywood Dream Machine upon a controversial issue that they opposed.

Nye's investigation, and the isolationist movement more broadly, played on the still-powerful negative memory of the Committee of Public Information. Nye attempted to cast the motion picture industry as the new manifestation of the infamous Creel Committee. He claimed that greedy filmmakers collaborated with the Roosevelt administration to once again force the country's involvement in another messy European conflict at the expense of American lives and resources. The hearings quickly became a circus, with Senators Nye and D. Worth Clark (D-Idaho) and their flimsy research becoming the object of derision. Hollywood producers, well organized and accustomed to defending the industry in the public eye, again went on the offensive and flooded the press with releases about the patriotism of the industry and its pride in working with the government to sell defense bonds, train troops, and raise money for the United Service Organization (USO). On behalf of the industry, Wendell Willkie asserted proudly that the industry as a whole "abhor[s] everything which Hitler represents."[21] He spoke to the prevailing public sentiment at the time and stated clearly that the motion pictures were "opposed to the Nazi dictatorship in Germany," an opinion held by the majority of Americans. If this was the central question, then "there need not be [an] investigation," declared Willkie. Throughout the investigation, Willkie and his clients all boasted about how "the motion picture screen is an instrument of entertainment, education, and information," and, moreover, "it is peculiarly American."

As the Nye investigation floundered, all of Hollywood—studio executives, the press corps, producers, and actors—declared the industry to be triumphant.[22] The editor of the trade publication *Box Office* praised the interventionist films that dramatized the evil of Hitler and gave the American public an idea of the challenges of the national defense policy.[23] "Other industries do it in terms of their specific materials," declared Maurice Kann. "Motion pictures do it in terms of celluloid—shorts and trailers for public view and army trainees." This editorial asserted the significance of Hollywood in the upcoming war efforts and also offered a strong defense of FDR and his international policy. "If oil, steel, motors, and the rest are working hand in hand with the officially declared, and pursued, administration policy," Kann concluded, "so should and must this industry. Mr. Roosevelt is still the President." Much to the chagrin of conservative Republicans, prominent voices in the motion picture industry would remain faithful to Roosevelt's personal interventionist views and also saw patriotic support as contingent on upholding a very specific New Deal liberal ideology that coalesced during war and heralded a commitment to the Four Freedoms, an international New Deal, a universal humanism, and a consumer citizenship.[24] Aspects of this liberal vision that flourished under Roosevelt, however, would fuel political fires in the postwar period and generate strength for the rising conservative anticommunism movement even before gunfire ceased.

Motion Pictures Prepare for Battle

When Japan attacked Pearl Harbor on December 7, 1941, and the United States officially entered the war, the motion picture industry had yet to attain an institutional place in the federal government. While five different government agencies had film divisions, each gave varying levels of importance to the role of motion pictures. But one person seemed to link the various agencies with President Roosevelt and the Hollywood studios: Lowell Mellett.[25] An acclaimed journalist from Indiana, Mellett started covering Democratic Party politics at the age of sixteen when the Democratic National Convention nominated William Jennings Bryan as its presidential candidate. After working with newspapers in Ohio and then New York, Mellett moved to Washington, D.C., during World War I, becoming the editor of the *Washington Daily News*. Soon after Franklin Roosevelt assumed the presidency, Mellett took a job within his New Deal administration as the head of the National Emergency Council, in 1937. A behind-the-scenes and quiet figure, Mellett accomplished the valuable task of coordinating information about various New Deal initiatives and worked with various agencies to present information to the public about the administration and its programs, a task that his years in the newspaper business had trained him to do well. Two years later, Mellett became head of the Office of Governmental Reports, where he continued to work to support the president's agenda and to work with studios to produce films for the defense effort.

Understanding the valuable role that friendly collaboration with Hollywood studios played in conveying ideas and giving access to production facilities, Mellett constantly encouraged Roosevelt to strengthen his ties with executives on the West Coast. In February 1941, as debates raged about the release of anti-Nazi films, Mellett urged Roosevelt to endorse publicly Hollywood's efforts to enlighten and educate moviegoers about the evils of Nazism on the screen. When the president of the Motion Picture Academy, Walter Wanger, invited the president to speak at the annual Academy Awards ceremony, it was Lowell Mellett who pushed Roosevelt to accept.[26] That evening, for the first time in the Academy's history, the voice of the president boomed over the radio as Roosevelt praised the motion picture industry's rise as a "national and international phenomenon of our generation," which represented "our civilization throughout the rest of the world" and the "aspirations and ideals of a free people and of freedom."[27] The evening foreshadowed how World War II would bring the industry and the Roosevelt administration closer together through patriotic political mobilization.

While Mellett focused on developing a coordinating center for gathering, producing, and dispersing media messages, through the press and the silver screen, he faced a Congress reluctant to fund agencies that could serve as a potential tool for Roosevelt's personal advancement or that of his party. Similarly to other "brain trust" advisers who held various positions in the federal bureaucracy before the Executive Reorganization Act of 1939, the motion picture industry had a variety of fragmented links to government organizations in places ranging from the Office of the Coordinator of Inter-American Affairs (where Douglas Fairbanks Jr. served as cultural ambassador) to the seemingly serious agency of the Office of Facts and Figures, which produced motion picture propaganda but clearly defined its purpose as educational and informative—just the "facts and figures."[28] As the Roosevelt administration became closer allies with Hollywood studios, Mellett became a figure central to maintaining and advancing the institutional relationship between the administration and the motion picture industry. After the bombing of Pearl Harbor, Mellett added to his responsibilities those of Coordinator of Government Film, and soon Roosevelt directed the former journalist to become an expert in Hollywood studio production, distribution, and exhibition so that he could bring this knowledge of studio operations to the Roosevelt administration as it prepared for war. Through Mellett, Roosevelt made it clear that he wanted coopera-tion, not coercion or restriction from the studios, and given the close re-lationships that had developed among the studio moguls, celebrities, and the president over the past few years, this seemed a reasonable and likely expectation.[29]

As Mellett worked to formalize institutional relationships with studios, he found a community eager to mobilize its resources for the war effort and demonstrate its patriotism. After a decade of constantly defending the place and merits of the studio community in American society, studio publicity departments quickly moved to sell the patriotic potential of en-tertainment and celebrities. The MPPDA circulated a short informational booklet, "Film Facts, 1942: 20 Years of Self Government," which reminded Mellett of the economic achievements of the industry when left uncen-sored by the federal government.[30] The slogan on the front page, "Win the War Now! Everything else is chores," stressed Hollywood's eagerness to aid the war effort while also reinforcing the idea of cooperation rather than forced wartime regulation. As factories converted to wartime pro-duction, so too did Hollywood convert its production, distribution, and exhibition branches, keen to see "this service of entertainment as a patri-otic responsibility." The MPPDA clearly articulated the scope and reach of the industry, as its theaters and employees spread from towns of less than 1,000 people to urban metropolises. Drawing in around 85 million patrons a week, paying over $410 million in taxes, and stimulating local business, motion pictures not only "furnish[ed] entertainment, relaxation, informa-tion, and inspiration" but also coordinated 276 different trades with its highly organized vertical structure. Pledging its "all out assistance to the war effort," the MPPDA made clear to Mellett and President Roosevelt that its industrial structure, experience in promotion, production capabilities, economic strength, and charitable traditions offered an unprecedented re-source for fund-raising and wartime communication and for maintaining the necessary patriotic fervor.

Immediately following Pearl Harbor, RKO studio head George J. Schae-fer mobilized the Hollywood community by establishing the Motion Pic-ture Committee Co-Operating for National Defense. Also known as the War Activities Committee, its chairman, Schaefer, sent the president a res-olution representing "12,000 theaters, and the artists, producers, distribu-tors, newsreels and trade press," which declared loyalty, dedication, and "full cooperation in achieving victory."[31] Movie stars contributed to the war effort in other ways, often before a camera or at a war bond rally. Many ac-tors, directors, and producers joined the armed forces and served time in the military campaigns abroad. However, the government often found that men like Clark Gable, Ronald Reagan, Frank Capra, Robert Montgomery, Jack Warner, and Darryl Zanuck could best serve their country by using their personalities and production talents to inspire the American public through war films, uplift the troops through performances for the USO, and finance the defense effort through war bond drives.

Studio writers also established a war mobilization branch to coordinate the skills and talents of 3,500 writers and make them available to Mellett. The Hollywood Writers' Mobilization brought together eight different writing guilds that worked with the Hollywood Victory Committee, which coordinated the use of performer talent, and the War Activities Committee, to bring experts of all types of media communication under one branch to provide an unprecedented pool of talent on call for the government. Ralph Block, the secretary of the 1940 Hollywood for Roosevelt committee, moved to Washington, D.C., to coordinate directly with government officials about war film needs. Across the industry, individuals used their positions in the well-oiled Hollywood production machine to meet Roosevelt's request for them to "inform the people of the complex problems that must be solved if peace is to become a living reality."[32]

While building on earlier philanthropic collaborations to generate support for the Allied cause, wartime mobilization also presented new challenges for Hollywood entertainers to articulate political ideologies, programs, and events on the screen. War films required cooperation between government and studios, with each needing to respond to the agenda of the other and the best interests of the country. Hollywood's critics in Washington frequently accused the industry of being unpatriotic during the war as studios continued to release feature-length films that achieved box office successes. Undoubtedly, the desire to maintain profits and prevent censorship intensified executives' eagerness to volunteer for wartime duties. Lowell Mellett faced the challenge of not only coordination with the various studios, but also cooperation, when his vision of the role of film in war conflicted with the economic goals of studio executives, the experience of storywriters, and the artistic demands of producers and directors.[33] Following the example of the "Hays Office," run for the past twenty years by the movie czar, Mellett hoped to establish a clearinghouse for all film productions. But without a central film organization, Mellett faced formidable obstacles in developing a coherent program to inform the public accurately about the war effort.

On June 13, 1942, the White House announced the creation of the OWI, with Elmer Davis, a popular radio commentator, as its chief executive.

Roosevelt gave the agency the responsibility of coordinating overseas and domestic communications, publications, and broadcasts. This agency formulated and oversaw production of international and domestic images of the U.S. war efforts, aims, and policies. Though only officially active from March 13, 1942, to August 31, 1945, the agency had roots in the controversial Committee of Public Information from World War I. But rather than relying so extensively on local speakers, or the "Four Minute Men," and the National School Service program, to promote patriotism in schools, as the Committee of Public Information had done, the OWI emphasized mass media messaging, which was now more readily available through radio and motion pictures.[34] Although filmmakers who had just created a name for themselves in Hollywood eagerly produced patriotic films to assert their American identity during World War I, film production constituted one of many "channels of communication" that the Committee of Public Information used. The OWI, however, dramatically expanded these channels of communication during World War II through Hollywood-inspired production and publicity, making theaters not just one facet of life during war (as they had been during World War I), but a central area for community engagement and information concerning the war effort.[35]

Created by executive order, the OWI coordinated radio, film, newsreels, and press releases, but did so in a way that reflected Roosevelt's interpretation of the war and its meaning. The OWI consisted of a domestic and overseas branch. The overseas facet of the OWI, headed by a former playwright and FDR speechwriter, Robert Sherwood, focused on the Voice of America program, which used its overseas branches for motion pictures, radio, and press to promote the United States and its ideals, strengthen ties with allies, and attract people of enemy nations to the side of the fight against fascism. Within the domestic branch of the propaganda agency, the Bureau of Motion Pictures jumped to the forefront of propaganda coordination and production efforts. Appointed as the head of the Bureau of Motion Pictures, Lowell Mellett worked with his Hollywood contacts to bring carefully honed professionalism and expertise to propaganda production, exhibition, and distribution. He also had the challenging job of coordinating government wartime policy with the commercial incentives of the studios. To do this, Mellett established an office in Los Angeles and appointed the editor of the *St. Petersburg Times*, Nelson Poynter, as his West Coast front man. For the first time, the government had to consider not only the capacity of film to communicate, inspire, and deceive, but also the intricacies behind production, distribution, and exhibition. During World War I, the Committee of Public Information had evaluated strategies of presenting war information via newsreels and propaganda shorts, but the organization had not attempted to direct theatrical performances.[36] By World War II, OWI officials understood the importance of entertainment films, not just newsreels or documentaries, in shaping public perceptions of political events. As a result, Hollywood figures—executives, writers, producers, directors, actors, and actresses—were thrust into politics as never before. Although Ralph Block proclaimed after the 1940 election that members of Hollywood's politically active community were "political amateurs" with good common sense, these personalities now had a responsibility to write, perform in, and edit films that communicated to the country, and even to the world, war aims, political ideology, and policies of the U.S. government.[37]

To ensure that Hollywood productions properly depicted war goals and ideology, the OWI gave each studio a very detailed and constantly expanding "Government Informational Manual for the Motion Picture Industry."[38] As a "purely advisory" manual, it articulated the OWI's desire to use motion pictures to inform and educate the country and its allies about the "truth of democracy." Seeing fascism thriving in "ignorant," "frustrated," and "poverty-stricken" countries, the OWI based its existence and involvement in motion pictures on the belief that "mass opinion is intelligent and will support an intelligent program *if informed*." The manual used the six themes of President Roosevelt's 1942 State of the Union address to shape its instructions to the film industry. The first section described the issues of the war—"Why we fight, what kind of peace will follow victory." The manual instructed motion picture directors, writers, producers, and actors to "live and breathe" Roosevelt's Four Freedoms. "Each individual must know how these Four Freedoms affect his individual life, his everyday affairs," the manual stated. "The realization must be driven home that we cannot enjoy the Four Freedoms exclusively. They must be established on a world-wide basis,—yes, even in Germany, Italy, and Japan—or they will always be in jeopardy in America." With these directions, the OWI transferred to Hollywood the responsibility of instilling in audiences a cogent and consistent New Deal political ideology. Just as Douglas Fairbanks Jr. had articulated this liberal, consumerist view of freedom and democracy in South America, now the Bureau of Motion Pictures broadened and intensified the effort by bringing this philosophy to an entire industry.

Forced to counter the ugliness of Adolf Hitler's white supremacist worldview, the guide also stressed that movies must commit themselves to presenting African Americans as equal partners in American democracy. Jewish studio heads, like Jack Warner, David Selznick, Sam Goldwyn, and Louis B. Mayer, understood the evils of prejudice, as they had confronted anti-Semitism throughout their lives. But they saw movies as an inappropriate medium to make a controversial political statement about civil rights for fear of economic repercussions at the box office. The OWI manual, however, directly asked the industry to portray the opportunities of "the underprivileged, the uneducated, the oppressed minorities" in a democracy. "The Negroes have a real, a legal, and a permanent chance for improvement of their status," emphasized the guide. "We are clearing our slums, we are establishing electric lines to out-of-the-way farmers, we are abolishing vicious tenant farming, we are improving the lot of minorities." Moreover, the guide emphasized the need for pictures to show the tolerance of a democracy and put pressure on Hollywood to teach Americans "a genuine understanding of alien and minority groups and recognize their great contribution to the building of our nation."

The manual also instructed motion pictures about the nature of the enemy, emphasizing that the roots of Nazism and Japanese militarism went beyond Adolf Hitler or the Japanese warlords. The "doctrine of force" constituted the real enemy, and thus a negotiated peace "would not be worth the ink with which it was written," and the American public could not accept anything besides unconditional surrender. Warning of the "fifth column"—enemy sabotage and spying—the OWI manual stressed the importance of constant surveillance of native sympathizers, a policy accepted by the public as Roosevelt herded Japanese Americans into internment camps to protect war plants, material, and public morale.

Along with depicting the evils of the enemy, the OWI instructed movies to emphasize the strength of the U.S. allies and, in particular, the importance of the United Nations. The manual instructed Hollywood to counter negative stereotypes of U.S. allies by emphasizing that "China is a great nation, cultured and liberal," and that despite their imperialistic past, "the British people are putting up a magnificent battle." Communist Russia proved more difficult in its treatment, and the manual insisted that "yes, we Americans reject Communism. But we do not reject our Russian ally. Where would we be today if the Russians had not withstood heroically the savage Nazi invasion of their land?" The guide emphasized the importance of showing images that would symbolize the hard work, respectability, and integrity of the allies—"Russian farmer destroying his fields before the enemy advance" or the "Chinese peasant fighting with an outdated rifle against Jap tanks and airplanes." The dramatics of the Hollywood studio provided an opportunity for the American people to see their allies "as one of us." The OWI used movies to instruct soldiers in how to train at camp or workers in how to construct tanks and bombers or housewives in how to ration and conserve. In all of these efforts, the propaganda operation forced both government and film personnel to think in terms of symbolic politics—using the mass media image, in this case the silver screen, to convey broader statements about citizenship and democracy.[39] The stringing of images had become a powerful weapon to mobilize the country for war and to imbue its audiences with a specific New Deal ideological view of the world that celebrated both consumption and the need for government intervention to promote the public good for individuals at home and countries abroad.

In 1942, the OWI Bureau of Motion Pictures faced many organizational challenges in translating its vision of motion pictures into a reality on the silver screen. Hollywood studios worked to produce three types of movies, all of which Nelson Poynter's office in Los Angeles examined for content and wartime message: feature-length films, patriotic shorts, and nontheatrical pedagogical films. The first, which extensive scholarship has explored, was the bread and butter of the motion picture industry and frequently the thorn in the side of the OWI: the box office feature. The studio desire for profits at the box office frequently conflicted with the OWI desire to present a free, democratic, tolerant, just, and victorious America on the screen.[40] Mellett had no censorship authority, and the Office of Censor could act only on overseas films. The instructional manual for the motion picture industry sought to shape the thinking of writers and producers as they prepared a feature production, but the pursuit of box office profits often involved movies with violence, misrule, and disorder, which the OWI found offensive to a country fighting totalitarianism.

The Bureau of Motion Pictures screened each studio production and evaluated whether the film offered a positive view of America and its allies, presented a neutral point of view, or characterized the country and the war effort negatively. The bureau objected to movies that portrayed Americans as "foolish and shallow" or "frivolous, superficial, with little or no understanding of the issues in the war or their part in the war effort."[41] It also found stories like the MGM production *Whistling in Dixie* objectionable because the movie featured an "unscrupulous, willing to kill" sheriff, thus making the American legal system and its agents appear "corrupt and murderous." On the other hand, the bureau praised movies that showed the integrity of Americans and the hard work of its allies. The bureau wanted filmmakers to avoid "scenes of lavish banquet, elaborate clothes, unusual use of automobiles, etc., etc., which is contrary to the restriction under which the audience has to live."[42] Although the office saw some films as solely about entertainment and as important for "relaxation purposes," these films still needed to provide a proper model for the lifestyles of their audiences during war. Leisure, contended the OWI, was not a separate pursuit from public engagement and civic responsibilities. Rather, the movies shaped public expectations of their everyday lives outside the theater.

The OWI also focused on producing theatrical "patriotic shorts," with messages on wartime behavior, ideals, and issues, rather than feature-length films, to avoid competition with the industry. Wanting to complement features rather than to replace them, these original shorts dramatized issues of the war to raise morale and enhance mobilization for the Red Cross, war production, and the armed forces. The OWI worked with various studios to produce these theatrical shorts, which accompanied feature-length movies in theaters. For example, the MGM short *Mr. Blabbermouth* warned of the dangers of gossip, rumor, and exaggeration.[43] In this nineteen-minute short, Mr. Blabbermouth, played by Ralph Peters, talked openly about his ideas of war, production, and the power of the enemy, thus giving German and Japanese secret agents inside knowledge of the war. The fear of the "fifth column" that permeated these movies emphasized to all American citizens the importance of keeping any knowledge of army locations or battles secret. Other theatrical shorts dealt with domestic conservation, such as the OWI film dedicated to food production and rationing. Orson Welles (Chester Morris replaced him due to a scheduling conflict) was slated to star with Joseph Cotten and Rita Hayworth in the one-reel short *Magic*. The OWI relied on celebrity status to create what it called "an immediate audience interest created by the star names." Furthermore, the script notes stressed the importance of using entertainment to promote the key war issues. "It is our experience that any presentation of fact is far more acceptable to audiences if there is an element of entertainment mixed with the subject matters," wrote the OWI. The dramatization of a *Welles Wonder Show* promised to engage audiences and teach them about the necessity of rationing and curbing waste in "terms understandable and acceptable to all ages (yes, kids too) and groups."[44]

Government workers for the OWI understood that no such thing as "pure entertainment" existed: each movie conveyed American values, culture, social structures, or political ideas in some capacity. The constant monitoring of the intricacies behind constructing scenes and writing scripts made OWI employees ponder and debate how to convey the right message through each on-screen image. Entertainment, in all its production stages, mattered. The OWI valued all aspects of the production process, which began with an investigation of public problems in personnel shortages, desired behavioral changes, or particular instructions for defense.[45] Relying on polls from institutions such as Ohio State University, feedback from theater owners about audience reactions, and extensive personal interviews in local communities, researchers first coordinated their findings within the Research, Reports, and Information Division of the Bureau of Motion Pictures and then entered into discussion with either government writers or studio writers about the proper imagery and appropriate dialogue.[46] Each project had a specific purpose and content and frequently a supporting government agency that had requested help in mobilization or education.[47] After Mellett and Poynter approved script lines and characters, production began in either 16mm or 35mm through the Production Division of the Bureau of Motion Pictures or through a cooperating studio in Hollywood.[48] The financing of the patriotic shorts varied, as coordination with the Hollywood War Activities Committee and industry volunteer efforts allowed for the production, distribution, and exhibition of films at far below commercial cost. According to one report, "For the Government's investment of $50,000 in the Motion Picture Bureau, they are obtaining a service that would cost the commercial returns $65,500,000 a year."[49] The cooperation of the studios, distributors, and exhibiters allowed the government to effectively and affordably communicate with the American public.

Since Congress ensured that the OWI had only a small budget, to avoid production of partisan propaganda, Mellett understood the extent to which the bureau depended on the coordination and goodwill of Hollywood resources and the studio system's vertical chain of operations. "There is nothing in the situation that warrants the assumption that a picture when made by the government can automatically reach the screen," he wrote to Elmer Davis in 1943.[50] The studio not only offered space and talent for many productions, but it also gave the OWI help in the promotion of the films, as studios' distribution companies made films available to theater owners throughout the country and helped to publicize the films through posters, newsletters, and brochures that highlighted the stars in the films.

Other theatrical releases focused on explaining actual events without the dramatics of Hollywood, and newsreels emerged as an effective way to show the American people a seemingly more "realistic" portrayal of war. Newsreels had long been an aspect of the moviegoing experience and continued throughout the war to be an important source of direct information on the war effort. Shots featured President Roosevelt meeting with Allied leaders and making speeches about the "triumph through the streets of Rome and Berlin and Tokyo" or Madame Chiang Kai-shek speaking of the

Pacific war. Audiences watched as bombs were dropped on Naples and as Polish refugees retaliated against the Nazis.[51] The newsreels also carried a more direct call to arms and instructions for home front behavior. Women performed essential factory work and government officials gave directions for consumer behavior under the rationing systems. Although movie stars less frequently served as spokespeople in newsreels, they nevertheless still appeared on the screen as the camera continued to chronicle their annual birthday ball appearances with the president and their various activities at war bond or Red Cross rallies. These newsreels used a more informational style of communication with audiences, which the OWI monitored as carefully as it did the patriotic shorts. Mellett and his assistants read weekly summaries of both newsreel content and motion picture productions to make sure that media messages encouraged the American people to sacrifice and work hard for freedom and democracy.[52]

The nontheatrical division constituted the last operational structure of the Bureau of Motion Pictures' film production, and as this branch expanded during war, its productions erased the boundaries between entertainment and daily life for Americans at war and on the home front. A comprehensive survey of the motion picture industry's involvement with various government organizations in July 1940 revealed the extent to which the War, Treasury, Justice, Interior, and Commerce departments had either government- or Hollywood-sponsored film projects under consideration.[53] The U.S. Coast Guard and the U.S. Signal Corps used government-sponsored nontheatrical films to recruit and train men about procedures, mechanization, and general life in the armed forces. The government underwrote the production of films showing the benefits of rural electrification for the Department of Agriculture, while Warner Bros. produced a two-reel pilot training program for the Department of Commerce. Initially, educational and training films provided a common ground for Hollywood and government—with studios eager to gain access to military installations and privileges and governmental organizations eager to gain the boost in public relations and recruitment that films offered. World War II, however, provided an opportunity for the expansion of nontheatrical pictures from their previously pedagogical focus to including combat footage, sales pitches, and, eventually, Hollywood celebrities.

An unexplored aspect of the World War II propaganda effort and media mobilization, the 16mm film war effort began with amateur operators who understood the potential benefits and accessibility of 16mm film structures and convinced the OWI of the ability of this overlooked medium to generate community patriotism and participation. As this film industry grew over the course of the war, it began to emulate Hollywood studio structures and used entertainment principles integral to theatrical Hollywood's success to generate community activism. The war bond campaign, in particular, provides insight into how the lessons of Hollywood entertainment and publicity strengthened civic events in local communities while helping usher in a consumer citizenship reliant on these mass media structures, which would dominate civic identity and political mobilization in the postwar period.

The OWI and Hollywood studios both produced nontheatrical films. Similarly to prewar films, these films instructed and educated specific groups on their wartime responsibilities and gave the home front motivation for sacrifice by showing war scenes and production needs.[54] These films combined documentary footage, shot with 16mm cameras and frequently in battle by combat cameramen, with government interviews of ordinary citizens, soldiers, government officials, and experts in production, conservation, and medicine, among others. The OWI commissioned these films to deal with specific wartime issues and then released them in 16mm format to war plants, colleges, and libraries. The Bureau of Motion Pictures hoped to target the specific concerns of industrial workers, farmers, or women with these films, which were to have free admission and be shown directly in places of employment to inform and instruct the public on the war effort.

The success of the 16mm nontheatrical division depended on its ability to organize a cohesive system of distribution and promotion that emulated the Hollywood studio system's vertical integration, if not its products' style and appeal. Couched in dry, factual language, the films initially faced a lack of demand from distributors and the public, and the bureau focused on increasing audience size by gaining endorsement from "leaders of public opinion," expanding the showing of these films to service clubs, unions, and churches, and tying the films into "an integrated community program so that the activities suggested in the films will be carried out in the community."[55] The nontheatrical division solicited the help of universities, leaders from a range of civic organizations, and 16mm distributors, who were quite eager to expand what had been a smaller, more amateur style of film production and exhibition, used in schools and by "roadshow" operators.[56] Reports to the OWI extolled both the success of film in raising morale among workers and families on the home front and the need for film content to provide "entertainment, recreation, and relaxation," to increase attendance and circulation.[57] C. R. Reagan, the president of the Texas

Visual Education Company, advocated expanding the role of celebrities in 16mm films. Adding the talents of Lucy Monroe, Nelson Eddy, or Bing Crosby promised to provide good material, which, in Reagan's opinion, "we need badly now [in order] to get audience participation in War and Victory meetings all over the land."[58] Reagan informed the OWI that public sentiment supported the use of movies, not only as "a magnet to move the masses" but as a means to "restore pure democracy."[59] Film, argued Reagan, had the potential to bring communities together with a fusion of entertainment and information. He and others from communities across the country wrote to the nontheatrical office with evidence supporting this belief.

Originally mandated to "carry out a mass informational and educational program designed to stimulate more effective and intelligent use of the available motion pictures," 16mm war films gradually incorporated Reagan's suggestions and moved from relating straight information to using more attractive sales techniques.[60] The entire OWI experienced this transition as well in the spring of 1943, when the new head of its domestic branch, Gardner "Mike" Cowles Jr., used his connections with the motion picture community to bring the former vice president of CBS, William Lewis, and a motion picture executive, James Allen, to the OWI.[61] When Lewis and Allen turned to Price Gilbert, former vice president of Coca-Cola, to head the writers division in the domestic branch, a "Madison Avenue" approach to propaganda overran the educational and informational efforts of writers like Archibald MacLeish and Arthur Schlesinger Jr.

Disgruntled writers publicly attacked the commercial trends of the OWI, saying that the advertising pressures made it impossible to "tell the truth" about the war. These arguments, however, reflected attitudes about the manipulative power of advertising and emotional appeals that invoked negative memories from the Committee of Public Information. But the role, use, and meaning of entertainment had changed over the course of the 1930s. In discussing the efforts of the Bureau of Motion Pictures within the OWI, Hollywood producer Walter Wanger defended the ability of entertainment to sell "truths" about the war.[62] Audiences "are not willing to be bored by clumsy pictures," declared Wanger in an article from the *Public Opinion Quarterly* read into the *Congressional Record*.[63] The producer argued that government officials from the OWI constituted film amateurs with unrealistic "fancies" of how motion pictures worked and what audiences wanted. Hollywood, on the other hand, had decades of experience in responding to audience desires and demands that came "from deep psychological *need*; no man at a desk can or should attempt to over-rule it."[64] Wanger and his influential motion picture colleagues saw the proper relationship between government and the motion picture industry in following their mantra: "Give the industry the broad lines of policy, and leave the committees within the industry the task of producing results."[65]

For different reasons, a more conservative Congress in 1943 agreed with Wanger that the OWI had overextended its authority over motion pictures. Southern senators rejected the OWI's sympathy for African American struggles through the production of films like *The Negro Soldier*. Republicans protested the pro-Roosevelt stance as Democratic electioneering. In the end, Congress drastically cut appropriations for the OWI, allocating only 27 percent of the funds from the previous year and forcing the agency to cut over 800 jobs.[66] The tightening of the purse strings threatened to strangle the effectiveness of the OWI in selling anything to the public. It appeared as if the Republican congressmen had finally achieved victory over the OWI operations.

With a budget of only $50,000 approved in the spring of 1943, the Bureau of Motion Pictures would complete films that were already in production but did not launch any new projects. The National Association of Visual Education Dealers assured Lowell Mellett of its pledge to continue distributing and exhibiting the 16mm films, and the Hollywood War Activities Committee also remained committed to disseminating war propaganda, even without the financial support of the OWI. With no money to pay government officials in the domestic branch of the Bureau of Motion Pictures, the OWI shifted its resources to the overseas branch of the bureau. This transition in the OWI allowed government-sponsored film production to continue during the final years of the war, with films focusing more on spreading the promise of American democracy to war-torn countries liberated by the Allied forces. Paving the way for postwar collaboration between Hollywood and foreign policymakers, this shift established the industry as an essential player in the postwar reconstruction efforts. In the short term, however, the collapse of the domestic branch of the Bureau of Motion Pictures allowed Hollywood producers, directors, and executives to assume control of domestic propaganda production and distribution.[67] As a result, subsequent war films increasingly followed the vision that Walter Wanger and C. R. Reagan had of using entertainment to teach "truths" and to inspire civic activism in local communities. Although the domestic branch of the Bureau of Motion Pictures continued its official role as a liaison between Hollywood studios and government industries, its filmmaking capacity depended almost entirely on the patriotic volunteer efforts of the studios.[68]

The War Bond Effort: Government, Hollywood, and the American People Unite

With such a weakened budget, the Bureau of Motion Pictures had to become more resourceful in its domestic film production, and it found one answer with 16mm film, the Department of the Treasury, Hollywood celebrities, and the war bond campaign. Since the onset of war, movie stars had emerged as key figures in the bond campaigns, as their talents and presence attracted audiences and stimulated sales. In doing this, celebrities built on the tradition of public service that stars like Charlie Chaplin, Mary Pickford, and Douglas Fairbanks Sr. had originated during World War I. During that time, local theater owners attempted to demonstrate their patriotism and cultivate local goodwill by using theaters as a central meetinghouse for war bond events. In places like Milwaukee, Fairbanks and Pickford arrived to stimulate sales and help the city exceed its sales quota.[69]

The World War II war bond campaign relied on celebrities even more in ways that both asserted the extraordinary patriotic contributions of the industry and downplayed the earlier political tensions that had plagued the use of entertainment as an educational and informational tool. The public relations committee for the motion picture industry claimed that celebrity "players"—serving without compensation and absorbing all costs of travel—visited small towns and cities to encourage war bond sales. The committee asserted that their presence in factories and plants "increased payroll deductions for bonds from 4 to 10 and 12 percent of their wages" and increased employee participation "up to 100 percent from levels of 45 percent."[70] One movie fan, Sybil Bruce Leach, attended a local Bette Davis bond rally in St. Joseph, Missouri, and claimed that she went to the event "to see a glamorous movie star" and "to bask in her scintillation." But for Leach, "seeing and hearing Bette gives people like me a grand and glorious urge to buy and buy until by and by the danger of the dictatorship passes."[71]

Photoplay Movie Mirror Magazine chronicled the journeys of stars selling war bonds alongside their relationship troubles and movie productions. While celebrities like Dorothy Lamour could not carry a gun, *Photoplay* explained, she did have a name, and "she'd make that name help Uncle Sam sell his all-important bonds."[72] The magazine detailed the war efforts of each movie star—in the service and on the home front—and sold the war as it previously had sold lipstick and hand cream. In many ways, the magazine joined with the hundreds of other industries throughout the country that used their particular resources to aid the war effort. But, for *Photoplay* readers, their favorite film stars taught them the importance of

A small community joins together to welcome Bette Davis on her war bond tour in 1942. Entertainment proved an effective way to raise money for the war effort during World War II and to encourage civic engagement on the home front. From the Bette Davis Collection, Howard Gotlieb Archival Research Center at Boston University.

buying bonds, growing victory gardens, supporting the troops through letters, and working at plants in wartime production. In the process, not only did civic responsibility, patriotism, and entertainment blur together, but also, through bond rallies and eventually with 16mm productions, movie stars became direct spokespeople for the government, drastically shifting tactics of political communication by relying on media events and dramatic spectacles to inform and persuade the public.

The 16mm war loan campaign united Hollywood production, personalities, and showmanship with the government, and, as C. R. Reagan predicted, entertainment stimulated the bond drive and introduced a new type of local democracy. Moreover, it allowed film production activities to continue as the Department of the Treasury, rather than the OWI, financed the production and distribution of films to generate sympathy, and, more important, dollars, for the war effort. Since only one-quarter of government wartime loans came from individuals, scholars have frequently overlooked the importance of the war bond campaign, emphasizing instead the role of big business in funding the effort.[73] The influence of the war bond drive, however, went beyond raising money. The drives allowed men, women, and children on the home front to engage more concretely with the war effort and achieved what Walter Wanger declared essential to sustaining morale—"participation, however vicarious."[74] Films could use images of war, whether re-created in Hollywood studios or captured during military campaigns, to connect civilians to their sons, husbands, or brothers abroad. Moreover, the war bond drives deepened Hollywood's fund-raising experience—previously dedicated solely to raising money for charitable organizations—to set an important precedent for using entertainment events to generate financial support and stimulate political involvement by invoking emotional attachments with "the cause," a strategy that astute politicians would use in the near future. As the loan drives advanced in organization, they offered inside showmanship knowledge to small-town exhibiters, who then featured films everywhere in the community: civic gatherings, libraries, gymnasiums, bus stations, war plants, and factories. The accessibility of 16mm film in particular allowed the government to use Hollywood celebrities, directors, and writers to speak directly to the people about the pressing issues of war, and in the process, it taught participants to turn to show business, not local parties, for political discussions.

In 1943, as the OWI faced drastic budget cuts, the Treasury Department also struggled with sagging bond sales, and it too turned to advertising and market-based research to increase sales. Robert K. Merton's 1946 study on famous radio personality Kate Smith's sixteen-hour marathon war bond drive revealed the extent to which these bond drives offered a unique opportunity for entertainment to initiate a two-way conversation between government programs and the people—and for Americans to see particular show business personalities as symbols of Americanism.[75] Successful bond salespeople like Smith or Bette Davis moved from entertaining the public to embodying Americanism. Merton observed that "a sense of symbolic fitness governs the choice of the person who is qualified to urge the purpose of war bonds."[76] Playing on emotions of patriotism and sacrifice rather than economic incentives, the government relied on symbolic politics to sell the bonds. Purchasing a war bond meant loving one's country and believing in the war effort and democracy, not making a responsible investment that would yield future profits.[77]

Appeals to citizens to purchase war bonds permeated every aspect of daily life. Newspapers, radio spots, theaters, and broadsides continued to remind the public daily of their responsibility to buy bonds. Every few months the Department of the Treasury would organize a national "war loan drive," to reemphasize the need to purchase war bonds. Each "drive" required novelty in order to reinvigorate the emotion of the war bond message, and celebrities found success in working with the government to create these media events. Before 1944, each community constructed its own bond drive, with theater owners frequently offering ticket deals for those who purchased bonds and movie stars traveling to bond rallies to whip up the excitement surrounding film events.[78] War films, obtained from the OWI or the Treasury Department, were often shown alongside celebrity speeches or veterans' testimonies. In some cases, smaller film operators would show 16mm films on beaches or in town halls to promote bond sales for the Treasury Department, but the showing of these films depended solely on patriotically motivated individuals.[79]

Desperate for ideas to stimulate the upcoming Fifth War Loan Drive, set to take place June 12 through July 8, 1944, the Treasury Department accepted C. R. Reagan's plea to incorporate 16mm film.[80] As in the previous war loan drives, the government hoped that increased advertising on radio, in newspapers, and in theaters would motivate citizens to help finance the new stages of war. The inclusion of 16mm films, however, offered a distinct opportunity for war films, produced by Hollywood or the OWI but funded by the Treasury, to expand their circulation. No longer would the government have to rely on theater owners to show trailers or shorts pushing war bond sales. Now it could break the monopoly of film exhibition through this smaller, more mobile format of film. With the 16mm projector, available through schools, film libraries, and independent dealers, operators could bring the message of war bonds to the people while they worked, traveled, or relaxed.[81]

During May 1944, C. R. Reagan busied himself with matters of production, distribution, and exhibition. While the OWI and Hollywood had produced many 16mm films previously, only a few states had actually incorporated these films into war bond rallies. Traditionally brought to schools, training camps, or war plants by individual 16mm operators, the 16mm industry lacked national distribution networks and resources.[82] To stage an unprecedented national distribution of the films during the upcoming bond drive, the Treasury Department sent a letter to "all 16mm projector owners in America," asking them to use their projectors "in the service of Uncle Sam for the Fifth War Loan."[83] Hoping the more-transportable 16mm film would bring the message of the war bond campaign to "every nook and corner of the land," Treasury urged projector owners to "lend it, use it to show battlefront films where ever you can: In shop, plant, shipyard, forum, library, union hall, lodge, luncheon club." The War Finance Division of the Treasury Department emphasized that "anywhere people can be assembled to see and hear this message," the film needed to be shown to communicate the government's message of war bonds.

President Roosevelt, Secretary of the Treasury Henry Morgenthau Jr., and numerous Hollywood stars officially kicked off the Fifth War Loan campaign, "The Battle of the Bonds," with a radio announcement on Monday, June 12, 1944.[84] Americans across the country listened to Hollywood stars speak about the importance of bond participation in person, on the silver screen, through the radio, or even on a projected screen outside on the beach. The Hollywood spokespeople allowed for a stronger national coordination of local war bond events as communities across the country watched or listened to these mass media–based bond appeals. The war films offered a distinct opportunity to create a more emotional atmosphere that stimulated bond purchases. As the National Association of Visual Education Dealers presented trophies to distributors for "outstanding work with 16mm films in the Fifth War Loan," Treasury Department spokesman Theodore "Ted" Gamble delivered an address that emphasized that the 16mm war films "made the difference between success and failure."[85] The key, Gamble explained, was to launch the war loan drive "at a good time and with the proper atmosphere." The war films could bring footage of the military invasion to the screens of local theaters and the walls of war plants, and letters poured into C. R. Reagan's office attesting to the power of film to increase bond sales. William Gutwein, head of industrial relations for McCall Corporation in Dayton, Ohio, claimed that showing the films *Invasion of the Marshall Islands* and *Establishing Anzio Beachhead* motivated workers to purchase 10,000 to 15,000 more bonds.[86]

Reagan urged Gutwein and 16mm exhibitors across the country to document the impact of the war bond films and also consider how more effectively to use the film showings during each war loan drive. He wanted statistics to document the number of showings, audience size, promotional tactics, and bond purchases in order to prove to the Department of the Treasury the importance of incorporating film in the drives.[87] These reports demonstrated the impact of film on audience turnout and participation in the effort.[88] One account of a film showing at a war plant noted that the audience "didn't say anything, they just sat in complete silence for nearly a minute" following the film. With clips of combat, the OWI films dramatized the struggles, aims, and ideology of the war. With Treasury footing the bill for distribution and production costs, hostile congressmen could no longer stand in the way of the production of controversial films. The winner of the National Association of Visual Education Dealers award, H. U. M. Higgins, the 16mm war film coordinator for Southern California, specifically requested a film "depicting Negro activities in the Army and abroad."[89] To achieve this, Higgins suggested splicing together *The Negro Soldier*—the film against which conservative southerners had mobilized previously—with scenes of actual combat.

Despite numerous encouraging stories, problems of distribution arose, revealing both the fragility of the 16mm industry and the inexperience of government in the filmmaking process. Films frequently arrived late or damaged, if they arrived at all, and exhibitors experimented with different publicity tactics with varying degrees of success. Before the war, Hollywood studios had dominated film production, distribution, and exhibition, and 16mm films found only a small audience in libraries for instructional purposes. But starting with the Fifth War Loan Drive and continuing through the end of the war with the Victory War Loan Drive, the OWI and the War Finance Division of the Department of the Treasury cultivated a national network of 16mm distributors to reach a larger, more diverse public. To strengthen and enhance the effectiveness of the 16mm network, Reagan and Gamble decided to teach local communities the language and strategy of Hollywood publicity.

The Sixth War Loan campaign, which took place November 20 to December 16, 1944, attempted to correct the problems in coordination, distribution, and, more significant, showmanship that plagued the previous drives.[90] To gain a more effective organization, Reagan oversaw the distribution of not only war films, but also "informational programs" to teach "media, advertisers, advertising agencies, copy writers, script writers, artists, and media specialists" how to properly inform and motivate the public during the drive.[91] The program provided clever slogans with suggested advertising approaches, and it emphasized the importance of all advertising "to follow the same general appeals." Local and state "victory volunteers" would circulate direct mailing, newspaper and magazine advertising, radio, and car cards to raise awareness and excitement for the bond drive. Showing loan trailers featuring Tyrone Power, Jennifer Jones, Eddie Bracken, and Bob Hope in the midst of actual war footage, however, gained national acclaim for its success in selling war bonds. The Hollywood War Activities Committee worked with the OWI and the War Finance Division of the Treasury Department to produce both 16mm and 35mm shorts, such as the Orson Welles–directed *Jennifer Jones Speaks for the*

"*Fighting Generation*"—in which Jones stresses the importance of victory and war bond purchases to sweethearts and wives on the home front. With the cooperation of the War Activities Committee, the OWI, and the Treasury, 12,620 prints of war bond films were distributed to local theaters and also to the growing national network of 16mm distributors, who reported a total attendance of 23.5 million.[92]

By the Seventh War Loan Drive, scheduled for May 14 through June 30, 1945, the 16mm industry, and the World War II propaganda effort as a whole, had decisively moved from educating to entertaining the American public. The featured event of the drive, the exciting *All Star Bond Rally*, provided a distinct opportunity for the implementation of Max Youngstein's new publicity style. Youngstein had served as a coordinator of advertising and publicity for Twentieth Century Fox. As the newly appointed head of the publicity department for the War Finance Division, he encouraged the use of Hollywood exploitation strategies in production and publicity to expand the reach of the war bond campaign to communities across the country. The *All Star Bond Rally* film did just that. The short film featured Bob Hope, who served as master of ceremonies, and other film and radio celebrities, including Judy Garland, Bette Davis, Dorothy Lamour, Betty Grable, Harpo Marx, Frank Sinatra, and Bing Crosby.[93] The catchy song "Buy a Bond," written by top songwriters Jimmy McHugh and Harold Adamson, became the theme song for the overall campaign.[94] The OWI noted how the film offered "fine exploitation possibilities," along with the potential to "bring home the fact that bonds can be purchased at any theatre on Saturday, Sundays, holidays, and evenings." Intentionally blurring the lines between patriotic duty and entertainment would ensure that even during traditional leisure time the American public would not miss an opportunity to contribute to the war effort.

Amid dances, songs, and comic acts, celebrities in the *All Star Bond Rally* film pointedly tell viewers that the "deadly serious purpose behind the fun of all these stars" is to buy even more war bonds.[95] "These stars have seen the other side of the war picture," Bob Hope told the audience. Emphasizing the firsthand knowledge the stars had of the war, Hope continued: "Harpo and the other stars can tell you some fantastic stores about this war we're in, stories of the horrors and the suffering, the bombings, and the magnificence of all the guys from Keokuk, Seattle, and all points east, west, north, and south." Through entertaining troops abroad with the USO, celebrities had acquired insider knowledge of the war effort, which they used to sell war bonds and articulate the government's message of sacrifice. They had become important spokespersons for the war effort, and the Department of the Treasury relied on the ability of stars to sell bonds and to extend the reach of the federal government into rural counties during the Seventh War Loan campaign.[96]

Regardless of the city or town, Ted Gamble believed in his philosophy: "You can make it entertaining; you can make it convincing; you can make a sale." And he immediately saw the potential in the *All Star Bond Rally* film to expand the reach of the bond drive.[97] Although MGM originally produced the film for theatrical release in 35mm, once Gamble previewed *All Star Bond Rally* he implored the Seventh War Loan committee to do everything possible to produce 16mm prints so that the "best selling picture the Industry has ever turned out" could reach the state and local 16mm networks.[98] Distributors received the prints of this impressive Hollywood production, along with a publicity manual, which told them that "it is up to us to give this picture the greatest possible audience and the greatest possible publicity and promotion. It is entertainment and *it will sell Bonds!*" The manual then gave a brief synopsis of the nineteen-minute short, followed by detailed templates of various press releases for distributors to release to newspapers and radio stations to generate excitement for the upcoming showings of the film. Each scripted press release offered various ways to promote the film: all the local distributor had to do was fill in the location and date of the film's premier.

As part of the broader publicity campaign of the drive that Max Youngstein organized, the *All Star Bond Rally* film, with its emphasis on celebrity performances, provided an easy opportunity to implement the Hollywood style of publicity that Youngstein stressed throughout the campaign to attract the largest possible audience to each showing. Each war bond film event should begin with an exclusive "preview," declared the Seventh War Bond Drive 16mm publicity and promotional manual.[99] "Everyone's vanity is flattered by being in on the 'know,'" shared Youngstein. "This human frailty can become the springboard for one of the most effective publicity outlets available to you." The "preview" was to be followed by a "premier," one of "the most important devices of the 35mm Motion Picture Industry," which brought local businesses in as sponsors to spur even more advertisement and participation. Along with providing ideas for previews and premiers, Youngstein organized radio spots, publicity stories, and posters for each town's premier. Distributors were instructed to hang the posters in "strategic spots" throughout their communities. He advised local chairmen in how to exhaust all advertising outlets, bringing the inside knowledge of a Hollywood public relations department to local communities throughout the country, explicitly teaching state and local leaders how to sell a story and images to the public.

Along with equipping local communities with an intimate understanding of showmanship and advertising, the war bond campaign allowed towns to unite around these film exhibitions, which occurred inside and outside of theaters. Reagan convened meetings with individuals in small towns and large metropolises to organize a national network of 16mm distribution and also to share ideas of how film and entertainment could be used to stimulate patriotic activity. As the industry expanded and began to emulate Hollywood publicity and production styles, one Chicago 16mm film manager observed that "every advance you make in this field not only benefits this campaign, and your own OWI circulation, but lays the foundation for a broader, and more effective use of the motion picture as a basis for community discussion, inspiration, and action."[100]

The war bond campaigns and 16mm war films provide a case study for how the war effort introduced the style and structures of Hollywood into the daily lives of men, women, and children on the home front and influenced democratic activity. Entertainment and advertising language and practices permeated libraries, rotary clubs, union halls, universities, and factories and brought communities together in new ways rather than simply promoting passivity. As the war bond campaign progressed, the boundaries between entertainment and civic duty increasingly blurred. Furthermore, the World War II 16mm bond campaigns proved to government officials the ability of entertainment to expand the reach of government and to communicate more effectively with the public through Hollywood tactics. The community response to 16mm films revealed the potential of film to promote civic activity on the local and national levels. The eventual incorporation of Hollywood tactics into 16mm war bond film production and exhibition spurred even more community interaction by bringing people together through previews, premiers, and celebrity rallies. Although a turn toward Madison Avenue commercialism characterized the war loan drives in the last years, the incorporation of entertainment and advertising did not bankrupt this wartime experience for individuals, but rather it deepened their emotional connection to the troops abroad and to the wartime efforts of the national government.

The war bond drives definitively blurred the lines between politics, patriotism, and entertainment, ultimately affording the motion picture industry a distinct opportunity to insert itself into the political process. Hollywood's unique talent in selling wartime ideology, policies, and actions made publicity skills, production expertise, and box office appeal a potent new asset of governance. Drawing on the philanthropic activism of the industry during the 1930s, the transformations in media strategy heralded by the Hollywood war effort in World War II would continue to permeate the partisan political process in the postwar years. In fact, even before the war's end, the Democratic Party was attempting to translate the successful wartime mobilization of the entertainment industry into concrete electoral gains.

CHAPTER THREE

The Glittering Robes of Entertainment

On February 9, 1944, *Variety*, the major motion picture industry trade newspaper, ran two articles side by side that juxtaposed liberal and conservative political mobilizations in the industry. One headline declared, with the paper's standard "catchy" abbreviations, "H'wood Alliance Formed to Combat Alien Isms in Pix; Sam Wood Prexy."[1] This article discussed the formation of a new "nonpartisan" political organization, the Motion Picture Alliance for the Preservation of American Ideals (MPA) and the election of the conservative MGM director Sam Wood as its new president. In its statement of principles, the alliance not only declared war on subversive elements of fascism and communism in Hollywood, but also made an active promise to defend "the American way of life; the liberty and freedom which generations before us have fought to create and preserve; the freedom to speak, to think, to live, to worship, to work and to govern ourselves, as individuals, as free men."[2] The other headline described the recent appearance of Vice President Henry Wallace in Los Angeles: "Vice President Wallace Points Up Need for Vital, Imaginative Pix"[3] This article chronicled the inaugural dinner of the Hollywood Free World Association (HFWA) four days earlier, at which the Democratic vice president joined 225 prominent film industry members in supporting the principles of world peace and international cooperation in the wake of World War II.

Both groups emphasized their "nonpartisanship," but they articulated political ideologies on the conservative and liberal fringes of the Republican and Democratic parties, respectively. The MPA expressed an ardent suspicion of big government and its interference in the marketplace and a deep mistrust of the manipulative nature of communist Russia. The HFWA advocated a peace that would spread New Deal ideology across the world, advance a civil rights agenda and policies for full employment at home, and pursue an amiable relationship with the Soviet Union. As their opposition to one another heated up, ideological politics waged by the Hollywood Left and Right polarized the industry but captivated the nation for its style of political engagement. Both of these organizations injected the language of entertainment into the political arena in ways that stimulated popular participation in the 1944 election and gave voices to party outsiders—notably women and religious and ethnic minorities who had the skills to draw audiences through their celebrity appeal. Hollywood's "ideological politics" linked style and substance in ways that encouraged engagement by appealing to the public as media consumers first, citizens second.

The 1944 election showed how wartime politics had expanded opportunities for entertainment to educate the American people through a particular ideological lens. The electoral context, however, generated concern over the partisan use of this communication style, which could allow radicals, "crackpots," or simply naïve or "duped" celebrities to shape political debates. Over the previous two years, liberal, progressive, and even radical Hollywood activists had worked with the Roosevelt administration and the OWI to use studio structures to sell wartime propaganda. In doing so, this patriotic mobilization created a national political recognition of the entertainment industry's communication skills and assets. President Roosevelt praised the power of scriptwriters to "present and clarify the issues of our times," and studio executives like Darryl Zanuck continued to push the industry "to make serious, worth-while pictures palatable to mass movie audiences."[4] Relishing the new responsibilities of Hollywood entertainment to inform, instruct, and enlighten the American people, Zanuck summarized the philosophy of liberal wartime celebrity activists with his speech during a 1943 Writers' Congress. He concluded that studios should "dress" pictures depicting social injustices and concerns in the "glittering robes of entertainment, and you will find a ready market." Henry Wallace reinforced these conclusions of the Writers' Congress when he spoke at the HFWA and encouraged the use of film to promote education and a "greater imagination in terms of general welfare, free world, brotherhood of man, fatherhood of God, and science."[5]

On the other end of the Hollywood political spectrum, the MPA formed to challenge the rising power and stature of progressives, liberals, and communist sympathizers in Hollywood studios over the course of the war years. The MPA argued that the turn toward "message films" constituted an economic and political threat to the future of the industry, which MPA members believed depended on "pure entertainment" and a free market. Conservative producers, actors, and writers, groomed under Louis B. Mayer in the MGM studio, saw the flourishing of liberal and progressive activism on and off the screen during war as evidence that a "subversive minority in the industry" had conspired to make films that "undermined" American democracy.[6] The MPA asserted itself on behalf of the "unorganized majority" in the film colony who "believe in, and like, the American way of life; the liberty and freedom which generations before us have fought to preserve."[7]

Scholars have frequently dismissed groups like the MPA and the HFWA as simply representing a reactionary or progressive fringe of Hollywood politics and not affecting substantial political change. And yet, a deeper analysis of both groups reveals how the war transformed the nature of political activity within the motion picture industry as activists on each side sought to control the narrative about the meaning of entertainment and the use of Hollywood forums, personalities, and publicity tools in American political life.[8] Moreover, both groups attracted the interest and frequently the participation of audiences, sometimes stirred by the excitement of the entertainment event and not necessarily by the political ideology of its stars. Both liberals and conservatives in Hollywood sought to build grassroots networks with prominent member lists to advance candidates, policies, and political ideologies and, in doing this, showed how showbiz politics provided an avenue for political empowerment for those with the ability to create the "right image" through studio productions, media publicity, and celebrity surrogates.

While this "showbiz" style generated enthusiasm among voters, it struggled to gain credibility among national party leaders and the mainstream press, both of whom its advocates frequently circumvented to advance their political agenda. Liberal organizations like the HFWA and the Hollywood Democratic Committee (HDC) did capture the interest of President Roosevelt and the DNC, which recognized the political potential of entertainment and capitalized on the appeal and volunteer efforts of liberal activists to reelect Roosevelt and bring other progressive candidates to office. But these efforts accentuated tensions over racial and economic policies within the Democratic Party. Moreover, these campaign initiatives drew constant criticisms by Roosevelt's opponents over the misuse of "glamour" in politics while also eliciting concern over the political inexperience of Hollywood activists. Celebrities had public appeal, but they were also in the process of learning how to use it politically, just as politicians were grappling with how to use entertainment to make political statements.

In 1944, Hollywood's conservative contingent fell by the wayside as the nation reelected Franklin Roosevelt. But the rhetoric of "Americanism" used by the MPA crafted a new definition of entertainment that would draw the attention of conservative anticommunists in Washington after the war. Before the war, isolationists used charges of propaganda and accusations of celebrities being "duped" by communists in an unsuccessful attempt to stop New Deal political activity among liberal entertainers. During the war, anticommunist inquisitions by the Dies Committee continued where isolationists had left off in 1941. Conservative opponents of Roosevelt within Hollywood lent weight to the wartime and postwar congressional investigations by continuing to debate the questions of "pure entertainment" versus propaganda and celebrity activism. The Hollywood propaganda machine came of age during World War II, but questions about who within the industry had control of this propaganda and its place in domestic partisan politics at home dominated the 1944 election and planted the seeds for the anticommunist "inquisition" in the postwar years. Just as accusations of "warmongering" and "interventionist propaganda" had fueled the Nye commission before the war, assertions of communist subversion became a powerful rhetorical tool for opponents of Roosevelt in the industry and in the halls of Congress to question the expansion of entertainment in American politics.

From Patriotism to Partisanship

On October 28, 1944, CBS radio listeners tuned into *Your Hit Parade*, a popular show that featured various celebrities counting down the top ten songs of the day. As the program concluded, a voice briefly introduced Humphrey Bogart to listeners on behalf of the DNC. The famous actor spoke about his wartime experiences as justification for his role as a new type of political spokesman. "I'm not going to talk politics to you, at least, not in the way the word is generally used," began Bogart. Instead, the actor recounted his experiences entertaining the troops in the USO and the touching interactions with soldiers he had met abroad. Bogart told a story about one young GI who asked the actor, "Do me a favor when you get back, will you Bogie? Vote for me." At the end of the message, Bogart concluded, "Well, I am going to do just that. I'm going to vote for him—in his place—I am going to vote for him in the sense of voting for his future. I am going to vote for the man who has demonstrated his ability to look ahead and plan ahead in war and peace. I am going to vote for Franklin Delano Roosevelt."[9]

Humphrey Bogart and his liberal Hollywood friends used their wartime experiences to involve themselves and their talents in the 1944 electoral campaign. In doing so, this liberal celebrity activism confirmed the prewar fears of Gerald Nye and other Roosevelt critics that the entertainment industry coordinated directly with the president to advance specific policies, political ideologies, and partisan agendas. Along with their work for the OWI, Orson Welles and Olivia de Havilland also crafted Democratic radio spots and toured the country in support of progressive candidates. While selling bonds, Bette Davis encouraged women to meet their civic responsibility to protect their husbands and sons fighting abroad through "the single, simple gesture that will pull the voting lever down over the name of Franklin Delano Roosevelt."[10] On the ground and over the airwaves, Hollywood liberals actively used their wartime service—whether selling bonds, writing scripts, or producing movies—as political capital to sell the incumbent and a progressive agenda to the American people.

For liberal celebrity activists, the 1944 election constituted a political awakening and a brief acceptance into the Democratic Party as they worked with national, state, and local party officials across the country to infuse Democratic campaigns with professional showmanship. The notion of the "duped actor," which Martin Dies, the conservative representative from Texas, had introduced during his prewar investigation, had continued to plague popular perceptions of actors in postwar politics, and it would later discredit Hollywood activism in support of labor union rights, full employment, and civil rights during the war. But the term itself emerged as part of the broader debate about the role of actors in American politics that had begun in 1938 and was not an accurate portrayal of celebrity activism as it took shape during the war. In fact, an exploration of the political development of Hollywood liberals during the 1940s instead reveals a committed, active, and talented group of grassroots volunteers who researched policies and endorsed candidates. Passionate about certain issues, liberal and progressive entertainers capitalized on their power to persuade to advance certain policies as well. The Hollywood for Roosevelt mobilization, in turn, created tensions about the future of the Democratic Party, with both its introduction of new campaign styles that emphasized mass media and its constant effort to eliminate isolationists and white supremacists from the party. The duped actor, in fact, proved to be an astute liberal not manipulated by Moscow agents but instead committed to the principles of Franklin Roosevelt and to the expansion of the New Deal state at home and abroad.

Bette Davis delivers a speech to an attentive crowd during her war bond tour in 1942. Two years later, these war bond speeches became a way to promote the war, the sale of bonds, and Franklin Roosevelt's reelection. From the Bette Davis Collection, Howard Gotlieb Archival Research Center at Boston University.

Consider, for example, the event that took place on April 28, 1943, at the Philharmonic Auditorium in Los Angeles, where actors and actresses participated in a dramatic presentation of the misguided and inefficient efforts of the recently elected Congress.[11] The evening defended Roosevelt and his war agenda, while pushing for policies to combat racism and support organized labor. Reenacting scenes from the *Congressional Record*, the show exposed how racism and partisan politics in particular had "killed" the anti–poll tax bill, which would enfranchise poor black and white voters in the South. The dramatization targeted the policies and rhetoric of white supremacist southern Democrats like Mississippi senator Theodore G. Bilbo and congressman John E. Rankin, who openly defended segregation and disenfranchisement through the poll tax. "We are crusading for and trying to preserve democracy in the world," declared the actor playing Florida's liberal Democratic senator Claude Pepper. "Buying it with the lives of our people, which means the break-down of the tyrannical power of a minority, shall we exhibit to the world that a tyrannical poll tax minority may dominate the course of the United States Senate?"[12] While acknowledging the idea of states' rights, the dramatization focused on the evils of racism, which had played out in Nazi Germany, to lend support to the civil rights agenda in the United States. "This gentleman from Missisippi sounds like the gentleman from Berlin!" declared the narrator of the evening, dramatically pointing to Senator Bilbo.[13]

The evening ended with a call to action and a message to Congress. The HDC urged audience members to write their congressmen in support of the war effort and reform measures for civil rights at home. "Write to 'em! Talk to 'em! Shout at 'em! Say, 'Look here, what are we paying you people for?'" Taking the lead, the committee drafted a letter which recently elected congressman Will Rogers Jr. (D-Calif.) promised to take with him to Washington, D.C., declaring support for the anti–poll tax bill, adequate child care programs, and the Tolan-Kilgore-Pepper bill—which would have granted soldiers abroad the ballot. Not only did the HDC declare its support for FDR and his liberal New Deal agenda, but the organization continued to push the Democratic Party to void its contract with white supremacist politicians, who had accumulated seniority, authority, and influence within the Democratic Party since the end of the Reconstruction era following the Civil War. Constantly emphasizing its support of small "d" candidates, the organization refused to support those it called "defeatist" politicians, who wanted to continue racial discrimination at home, whether they hailed from Los Angeles, Mississippi, or Detroit.[14]

Reaching a packed house in the Philharmonic Auditorium and several national politicians in Washington, the "Message to Washington" event foreshadowed the manner in which Hollywood political activity would draw on its OWI experience to advocate for liberal issues with the industry's unique style during the following year's election. The language of the evening reflected an important point that the OWI had articulated in its informational manual for the motion picture industry. The enemy, stressed the guide for film production, "distracts and confuses his intended victims by fostering racial, religious, economic, and political differences among them."[15] Liberal Hollywood writers, directors, producers, and actors protested the poll tax with this language, framing it as a defeatist policy that would target the unity of Americans. Beyond the specific goal of equality, the guide declared, "It is the challenge to the ingenuity of Hollywood to make equally real the democratic values which we take for granted."[16]

The "Message to Washington" evening revealed not only the internalization of this commitment to alleviating discrimination, but also the dedication many stars made to being a part of the political process at the local level. Moreover, this mobilization hinged on using dramatization to educate citizens on key issues outside the movie theater. When the DNC heard about the event, it praised the HDC's ability to simultaneously entertain and politicize. "In these critical times," wrote an assistant chairman of the DNC, "we must not be content with feeling that our organizations stand for things we believe in, but we must dramatize these questions and make our group spheres of influence in our communities."[17] The OWI had called on Hollywood writers, directors, and actors to create media spectacles to communicate war aims, ideology, and practices, and so too would the DNC see the potential for entertainment in the upcoming election to spur voter turnout and participation. The difference: the OWI told production studios what issues and ideas to convey through patriotic shorts and feature films, while during the campaign progressive Hollywood activists took control of the content they produced for the DNC to make sure it advanced their own agendas. While a heightened coordination with the DNC reinforced their place in the campaign process, their political authority rested on an ability to sell candidates, policies, and ideologies that would ultimately challenge Roosevelt's contentious New Deal coalition.

As they would over the next several years for the Democratic Party, the recently formed HDC wrote the scripts, supplied the actors, and executed successful performances. The organization's roots traced back to the formation of the Motion Picture Democratic Committee in the aftermath of Upton Sinclair's failed bid for the race for governor of California in 1934. Vowing to "never again," be defeated by the "dirty tricks" of studio executives, advertisers, and consultants, screenwriter Phillip Dunne and actor Melvyn Douglas had organized and deployed their own "tricks" for the 1938 gubernatorial race in support of California's first Democratic governor in over forty years.[18] Yet, despite this early political awakening, the group did not mobilize nationally until the 1944 election. The 1940 election revealed the fragmented and scattered nature of the Democratic Party in California, and although the Hollywood for Roosevelt organization brought together various elements of the local community in support of the president, they had yet to truly mobilize all of the industry's talents for a national political campaign.

With the conservative backlash of the 1942 congressional elections, liberals of all shades understood the importance of uniting in support of Roosevelt's reelection bid in 1944. On January 14, 1943, over 200 people assembled in the Hollywood Roosevelt Hotel and declared themselves united as "democrats with a small 'd' " in an effort to promote the progressive wing of the party. "We vote for and support the candidate who is really democratic and who whole-heartedly wants to win this greatest of all democratic wars. In short, the only kind of representative we will stand for is a patriotic

American."[19] Shortly after this initial meeting, the organization named itself the Hollywood Democratic Committee (HDC) and began mobilizing for the next election. Its research council explored the potential candidates for election and published findings in the HDC's newsletter, *Target for Today*. It was to be "a guide to action on the political scene. It suggests win-the-war candidates; it applauds win-the-war legislation; it proposes channels for your win-the-war efforts in local, state, and national affairs."[20]

Throughout the campaign, the HDC worked to translate the liberal wartime ideology of the OWI manual into concrete political change on the ground. Alleviating discrimination toward African Americans and Mexican Americans began to emerge as a principal objective. In March 1944, the HDC joined with the Los Angeles Council for Civic Unity and many other local churches, labor organizations, and educational groups at the Shrine Auditorium for a dramatization of the problems of racial discrimination. The stated purpose of the "United We Stand" rally was "to throw the spotlight on a grave situation that threatens the unity of all Americans behind the war effort, namely racial incitement against minorities."[21] James Cagney, Olivia de Havilland, and Anthony Quinn led the group of "prominent individuals" in organizing, publicizing, and carrying out the event.[22] Motivated by the recent "disgraceful episode" of the Zoot Suit Riots, in which white sailors violently clashed with young Mexican youths, the HDC and other civil rights proponents in the area urged racial equality as necessary for wartime production.[23]

The organization and execution of the rally—with the featured dramatization written by Norman Corwin, who also wrote several DNC radio spots that election year, and performed by film celebrities, who later featured in these same spots—linked local goals for civil rights explicitly to the war effort. With Hollywood "contributing its talent to give power to our message," the Los Angeles Council for Civic Unity found a way to communicate its local concerns to the national stage through patriotic rhetoric. Celebrity activists called the Zoot Suit Riots "part of a pattern of attacks against minorities all over the nation (Detroit, New Jersey, Texas) instigated by defeatists and Fifth Columnists to disrupt the war effort."[24] As a result, the rally addressed the problems of civil rights in Southern California and also caused the message "united we stand" to resonate outside the state because of its famous participants who were both war spokespersons and film stars.[25]

Patriotic entertainment emerged as a language for advancing policy changes and encouraging voter turnout and participation, and the California primary campaign illuminated how showbiz politics had transformed

California state politics. Understanding the primary elections as an important opportunity to ensure that liberal candidates appeared on the party ticket, the HDC provided 450 spot announcements, broadcasted around the clock on nine different stations, featuring several fifteen-minute radio programs and one half-hour all-star broadcast, "Hollywood for Roosevelt," during the early primary campaign.[26] During the spring, the committee also embarked on a "Let's Go Out and Ring Door Bells" entertainment drive. Cary Grant, Dinah Shore, Walter Huston, Martha Scott, William Bendix, Victor Moore, and Joan Bennett participated in broadcasts that encouraged voter registration while simultaneously endorsing a complete slate of candidates for the primary.[27] While promoted as a nonpartisan effort to encourage voter registration, these well-coordinated efforts showed a recognition of the importance of media-driven primary battles, something future presidential hopeful John F. Kennedy would realize fifteen years later. The radio event also highlighted the ability of celebrity names to encourage voter participation, turnout, and engagement during the primary process. One radio spot featured a rushed housewife who angrily answers the door: "No! *You* look. I've got a dinner to cook, two children to dress, the bathroom to clean, a full line of washing to do."[28] But then she stops, breathless, as she realizes whom she is talking to, "Cary Grant!" The actor then registers the starstruck woman to vote, invites her to join the registration committee, and graciously gives her an autograph as she promises to vote. The script probably overplayed the ability of celebrities to register individuals, but it ended with each star stating his or her voting district with a promise to be at the registrar's office the following morning, thus giving listeners a way to combine civic activity with a celebrity meeting.

Throughout the long electoral season in California, the HDC became a center for coordinating talent for mass meetings and rallies as it expanded the Democratic networks forged during Roosevelt's first three administrations. Small Democratic campaign headquarters for senatorial and congressional candidates wrote to the HDC requesting stars like Humphrey Bogart, John Garfield, Orson Welles, or Olivia de Havilland to attend rallies for their candidates. Recalling how the San Diego Democratic Committee had packed its largest meeting place when Humphrey Bogart arrived in 1940, they requested the "valuable assistance" of another "fine Democrat" to attract another record-breaking crowd to promote local Democrats in the electoral race.[29] A woman from Bakersfield pleaded for celebrities to attend her event to "really make it go over with a bang."[30] In order to generate excitement and turnout in the local community during the 1944 race, this

Democrat believed Hollywood held the solution. "The people would come out in throngs if we can get some big names to come up here."

The political activity of celebrities through the HDC soon expanded beyond California's state lines. Candidates across the country capitalized on the nationwide appeal of these West Coast activists and their eagerness to mobilize for progressive causes and candidates. The HDC began with organizing only seven congressional districts, but its national appeal brought requests from coast to coast. "Now it's the whole country," explained its secretary George Pepper in discussing the expansion of the HDC. "Salt Lake City wants Walter Huston for a big rally on the 10th—Huston will go, but we can't get him plane space. That's how I get ulcers."[31] The Committee to Elect Warren G. Magnuson as one of Washington's senators tried to stimulate his campaign through the inclusion of "an outstanding movie star such as Orson Welles, Edward G. Robinson, or Olivia de Havilland."[32] Concerned with the "tremendous influx of new people" to the political scene in Washington that year, the Democratic state chairman believed that "the names of the stars will draw these people as they have no acquaintance with any of our State officials." The one-minute spot endorsements that Magnuson received from de Havilland, Jimmy Durante, and Gene Kelly helped him run a successful campaign that would ultimately lead to nearly forty years in the Senate.

Just as the introduction of spot radio endorsements from famous Hollywood stars helped Magnuson connect with his broader-based constituency in the senatorial race, it aided other candidates throughout the nation. The collaboration between the DNC and the HDC offered Hollywood's style of political communication to politicians outside Southern California. Though only a part of broader campaigns that relied on local party networks to win, the 1944 election foreshadowed how campaigns using mass media would require collaboration with professional image makers who either came from California or looked to California for lessons in crafting and executing publicity strategies. One newspaper article understood the sales appeal that the HDC brought to the table in 1944, pointing to celebrity spot endorsements as "probably the most successful campaign technique devised by the committee."[33] The *New York Times* seemed in awe of the "entirely new publicity approach to voters" made by Hollywood and the Democratic Party working together: "It is the Democratic one-minute dramatizations, written and played by the talent of Hollywood that furnish the most striking new note in campaign publicity."[34]

These celebrity spots allowed the HDC to incorporate one of its campaign principles about the impact of entertainment in the radio speeches.

"Listeners have a discouraging tendency to tune out straight political harangues," explained the HDC campaign method guidelines. "Tie-in with local entertainment talent if possible, then ease into your speech a cause in a conversational manner. Finish with all stops out."[35] The HDC had learned lessons in organization and political salesmanship from the war effort of fusing entertainment with political messages. The committee established various divisions—radio, speakers, actors, writers, service, newspaper, pamphlet, cartoonists, publicity, and musicians—to use efficiently the depths of its talent and resources to promote not only Roosevelt but also Democratic representatives, including its own congressional nominee, the former actress Helen Gahagan Douglas.[36] This Hollywood committee sought to promote "progressive Democrats" through techniques developed to "help candidates dramatize their campaigns to the utmost through billboards, radio spots and programs, the Free Press, precinct organization, meeting telephone campaigns, and—most particularly—through hard hitting leaflets, cartoons, throwaways, and 'campaign clinchers.' " The publicity push through a variety of mediums reflected the central strategy of star promotion that defined the studio system in which all of these activists were groomed.

Promoting Roosevelt, his wartime policies, and plans for the peace formed the basic strategy in creating these radio spots and other publicity strategies, ultimately facilitating the mass circulation of spot announcements for congressional candidates that also supported the president. A standard script allowed the committee to easily insert different names into radio spots for candidates across the country. "The man to send to Congress from the ____ District is _____, who understands that in 1944 Congress must loyally support the war and peace policies of Roosevelt."[37] De Havilland, Durante, or Kelly would conclude the radio spot by saying, "Vote for Franklin D. Roosevelt and _____," ultimately filling in the blank with a list of names in key congressional races throughout the country. The HDC sent spot transcripts to Democratic candidates hoping to retain their seats, unseat a Republican, or establish a fresh presence in the halls of Congress. Its list of candidates to support, however, significantly omitted known white supremacists and isolationists, since adherence to FDR's wartime policies and a commitment to civil rights were essential components of the HDC's platform. The HDC and its sister organization in New York—with whom it would merge the following year—observed a stringent policy of "no covert endorsements." They would only use their effective and far-reaching publicity organization if the congressional candidate supported President Roosevelt and progressive policies of antidiscrimination, full employment, and an internationalist role of the United States in the postwar period. This ideological stand resulted in partisan tensions within the New Deal coalition after FDR's death and the conclusion of the war the following year.[38]

During the 1944 campaign, however, the DNC capitalized on the loyalty of the HDC to President Roosevelt and eagerly made use of the committee in some of its national initiatives. In St. Louis, Missouri, the DNC wrote an urgent telegram to George Pepper: "Women's division is extremely anxious to secure glamour actress to appear."[39] The rally, wrote the DNC member, was "extremely necessary in swinging Missouri vote so would appreciate delivery on this." The DNC considered Humphrey Bogart an important asset in attracting votes and scheduled him to be on the air following *Your Hit Parade* to ensure "a sympathetic audience" for the actor's endorsement of Roosevelt.[40] Along with salesmanship and publicity appeal, Humphrey Bogart and other celebrities helped the DNC to incorporate lessons of market segmentation and craft a more emotional appeal to voters, which made those with professional showmanship skills in the mass media more valuable in the political process.

Roosevelt's radio director, J. Leonard Reinsch, used the structure and style of what he called the "successful" California spot announcements as a template for many spot scripts that politicians and celebrities alike used to promote the Democratic Party and Roosevelt.[41] Orson Welles painted a picture for listeners across the country of the scary, uncertain future of war, depression, unemployment, and unrest that "can happen here—under a Republican administration."[42] Frank Sinatra and Joan Bennett expressed to the audience why they supported Roosevelt while also encouraging voter turnout.[43] The DNC found these radio spots, along with endorsements of Democratic candidates by well-known members of Congress and party figures, extremely effective in getting the Democratic message to all Americans. The DNC provided recordings of these radio spots for free, along with advice on broadcasting for all party leaders, to be used "at all radio stations and on all public address systems."[44] Reinsch instructed leaders to use them "for large and important rallies and to complete your present schedule of radio announcements."

The DNC recognized the appeal of California electoral strategies that emulated publicity tactics that had been honed over the past two decades in Hollywood production studios, then used in state politics, and were now deployed during the war bond and propaganda campaign of the past two years. The nationally acclaimed names helped to bring together the electoral campaigns of Democratic nominees on national, state, and local levels. "Washington sources" told the HDC that movie stars had a unique ability to appeal to the people directly about Democratic candidates.[45] Small city newspapers controlled by Republicans would "not be able to overlook the big names," thus allowing Democratic publicity to break into previously hostile territories and encourage voters to cross party lines and cast a vote for Roosevelt.

Hollywood activists were not alone in cultivating the new style of selling pro-Roosevelt Democrats, as they worked with a man whom the DNC called "advertising man extraordinary," Milton Biow.[46] The president of the Biow Company coordinated with the HDC, and the advertisers understood that the organization "has within it the mechanism to do the important thing we can hope the show world will do."[47] Milton Biow believed that his advertising vision and slogans could combine with celebrity talents to create a more active citizenship.[48] Mobilizing the Hollywood community to make radio spots promoting voter activity, the advertising company wanted "talks by stars, bands, music, entertainment; whatever is felt will serve the objective best."[49] Moreover, the company believed that the widespread appeal of key celebrities would allow Roosevelt's campaign to market key groups. In one instance, the firm emphasized the importance of Edward G. Robinson, who knew six languages and could feature in radio spots that would appeal to advertisers in foreign market stations.[50]

Coordination between the HDC and Biow's company made the advertising and entertainment industries a legitimate component of the DNC's campaign strategy and, in doing so, revealed how a mass media campaign would rely on showmanship experts rather than simply interest group leaders from the American Federation of Labor, the Congress of Industrial Organizations, or the American Farm Bureau Federation to turn out votes.[51] The HDC and Biow's campaign effort used the media to connect with and appeal directly to the people, rather than through party structures or interest group organizations. The shift toward a candidate-centered strategy rooted in entertainment culminated on the eve of the election as the Democratic celebrities joined together in a national broadcast on CBS, which explicitly linked fans to the president via Hollywood production. The DNC, the HDC, and Biow's company planned the evening to be "the structural idea on which to hang two hours of hot radio," and they made sure that top stars pledged their votes to Roosevelt on the air amid songs, jokes, and dramatizations. Judy Garland opened up the spectacular entertainment event with a catchy song, "We're on the right track, we're gonna win the war. Right behind the president, president, president for nineteen forty four."[52]

The broadcast featured Garland, Humphrey Bogart, Cliff Nazarro, and James Cagney leading more than thirty of Hollywood's most famous voices in greeting the nation and pledging their votes for Roosevelt. "Personally," declared Bogart, "I am voting for Franklin D. Roosevelt because I think he is the world's greatest humanitarian and because he leads the fight against the enemies of a free people in a free world." With a chorus of "We're voting for Roosevelt . . . Vote . . . Vote . . . Vote," various celebrity voices interrupted the catchy chorus to announce their famous names and their loyalty to Roosevelt. "Elmer Rice, playwright. Arthur Rubinstein, Pianist. Constance Bennett, Actress. We're for Roosevelt." Thus began the string of names supporting the incumbent. "This is Gertrude Berg, you know me," chimed in the well-known matriarch of the popular radio show, *The Rise of the Goldbergs*. "You know me too—I hope—Milton Berle," sang the comedian. Finally, the lineup ended with the voice of the famous crooner: "I'm Frank Sinatra. Listen to the voice. Not mine, the people's." Broadcasting from New York to Chicago to Los Angeles, this radio show brought together the rich and famous with farmers, veterans, and white- and blue-collar workers to mobilize a national electorate for Roosevelt. This star-studded program demonstrated how the war effort paved the way for Hollywood figures to enter the political sphere and then broaden it to women and ethnic and religious minorities in a celebration of the "voice" of "the people."

Leading Democrats appreciated Hollywood's unique contributions during the election. "The increasing participation of persons of stage, screen and radio in the field of political action is of great significance to our people," declared the vice presidential candidate, Harry S. Truman, to the HDC.[53] "May I express the hope that your group will continue to mobilize your unusual capacities in bringing to our people the vital issues of this election." Others—including jealous Republicans, disgruntled Democrats, and journalists—however, continued to look down on the political activities of the film colony, frequently dismissing it as superficial and lacking in solid political thought. Since 1940, the *Washington Post*, in particular, had viewed these campaign developments that linked entertainment and politics warily. During the previous presidential race, columnist Mark Sullivan had stressed the dangers of "glamour in politics," emphasizing that "to assume glamour and wisdom go hand and hand is a serious fallacy."[54] Sullivan had urged that "the country would be better off if, when it wants glamour, it would go to the 'movies' and buy a couple hours of enjoyment of that commodity for a 50-cent admission. When it wants sound thought on public problems, it would do better to seek plain men with clear minds."

The war, however, had drastically altered the ability of politicians or citizens to separate entertainment and politics as movie theaters became places of political communication about war events, behavior, and ideology. The use of advertising and the Hollywood style in the 1944 campaign showed many that the industry's participation in politics might not be only a wartime measure. It had emerged, potentially, as a continuing part of the political process, but its style and substance challenged dominant aspects of the political establishment and campaign structures. "Still," warned the *Washington Post* in 1944, "we think there are dangers in abandoning that separation of politics and entertainment which was a pillar of our traditions."[55]

The successful involvement of Hollywood liberals in the 1944 election revealed their new place in the political process and the simultaneous feelings of excitement and resentment that surrounded their contributions. Despite the willingness of the DNC to use the publicity advantages celebrities offered, a sense of political marginality still plagued the industry. The same letter from the DNC to the HDC that requested stars for various national rallies, began with the line, "We haven't forgotten our Little Hollywood Friends."[56] The letter emphasized that the celebrities used for rallies could "use prepared speeches. They won't have to be bright and argue, just make good speeches." While celebrities played a significant role in the California election—inspiring voter turnout, speaking on behalf of the president and congressional candidates, and crafting and executing dramatizations—their national contributions were still a peripheral part of the broader campaign.

Moreover, national party leaders continued to view them as inferior political minds, beginning a perceived distinction between style and substance. This view, though, ignored how, in the minds of many celebrities, their style, glamour, and entertainment made substantial statements about civil rights and labor while simultaneously achieving concrete victories for progressive Democrats and fighting white supremacy in the party. Organizations like the HDC were not driven only by partisan loyalty, but also by a liberal ideology that valued certain policies as well as accepted the place of the media and entertainment in communicating to and engaging with a mass audience. As politically active celebrities gained credibility in American society through their philanthropic work in the 1930s and their wartime service in the 1940s, they emerged as more credible in the public eye. The HDC and its liberal activists used prestige generated from local political efforts and patriotic mobilizations to justify their newfound presence in the national party. But many leading Democrats and Republicans disliked these newcomers.

President Roosevelt embraced the catchy slogans that Milton Biow passed along for his speeches and the political potential of Humphrey

Bogart's USO tours and radio speeches.[57] As a dynamic individual, a leader with a New Deal vision for the world, and a successful showman himself, Roosevelt unified a diverse Democratic structure in Hollywood, bringing studio executives like Jack Warner together with liberals like Bette Davis and Bogart (who promoted principles of the New Deal), progressives like Edward G. Robinson (who wanted to expand further the New Deal state), and communists like John Howard Lawson, all of whom found common ground on the basis of loyalty to Roosevelt, the importance of entertainment in selling political messages, and the World War II effort.[58] But, just as these activists vowed "never again" in the wake of the anti-Sinclair mobilization, so too would conservative entertainers wage war on liberalism in the movie community that year.

Partisan Divides, Hollywood-Style

At its inaugural meeting at the Beverly Wilshire Hotel, the MPA discussed the challenges that the entertainment industry faced in 1944. Sam Wood, a director at MGM, led the discussion as the organization's newly elected president. "Each of us," Wood solemnly declared, "must consider our membership in the organization a grave responsibility and must accept it as an obligation imposed upon us by our American upbringing and our common duty as citizens."[59] Wood and other members of the MPA—including Walt Disney, Clark Gable, and Gary Cooper—considered it their duty to eliminate subversive radicals from the Hollywood scene and to produce films that showed the merits of the "American way of life." During the debates on communist subversion in the postwar period, both sides claimed to defend the "free screen." For liberals, "freedom of the screen" meant creative and socially meaningful productions without outside political pressures and coercion. The MPA, however, understood that "free" meant the production of movies that would glorify "in the fullest possible measure" patriotic images of "the American scene, its standards and its freedoms, its beliefs and its ideals, as we know them and believe in them."[60]

Determined to assure the American people that Hollywood was "a reservoir of Americanism," the only requirement for membership in the MPA was an affirmative answer to the question: "Are you an American?" The application packet included a statement of principles, letter of invitation, and a blank form to sign; during the first year especially, the MPA worked to build its list of members and demonstrate the widespread appeal of the organization.[61] The statement of principles reminded potential members that the MPA had "nothing new to sell" but rather wanted to "protect what we already have."[62] Safeguarding the screen meant exposing "the methods and intent of all groups and individuals who seek to utilize the industry as a channel of propaganda for their particular aims," declared the statement of principles. "And to counteract, by exposure, any attempts by any groups whatsoever to take over and control the Motion Picture Industry for any purpose contrary to the American way of life."

With high-minded, lofty, and vague principles, the "American way of life" that the MPA endorsed contained a specific ideological agenda that sought to return to the days before the perceived New Deal radicalism overran American political life, the days when corporate studios had political and economic authority in California—the era in which Coolidge and Hoover controlled the White House and their friend Louis B. Mayer reigned in Hollywood politics. Conceived of and dominated by Mayer's political protégés at MGM, the MPA aimed to combat the growing authority of the HDC and liberal activists like Jack Warner, Humphrey Bogart, and Orson Welles in the Roosevelt administration and the OWI.[63]

Like that of the HDC, the MPA's statement of policy explicitly denied partisanship, stating, "We shall take no part in politics as an organization, leaving this field entirely to the individual, since politics—like religion—is a private business of the individual."[64] But the focus on the individual and the marketplace was powerful ideological rhetoric against the principles of the New Deal. The organization professed belief in the "freedom to speak, to think, to live, to worship, to work, and to govern ourselves as individuals, as free men; the right to succeed or fail as free men, according to the measure and ability of our own strength."[65] Blatantly challenging Roosevelt's promise to keep Americans free from want, the emphasis on personal responsibility for success and failure challenged the ideological core of the New Deal. The group found key supporters for its goals of ousting communists from Hollywood in the newspapers of William Randolph Hearst, the American Legion, and right-winged Republican clubs throughout Los Angeles—organizations that mobilized against Roosevelt in the 1944 election by attacking communist influence in the president's administration and urging the public to not be drawn in by the subversive influence of communists in the country.[66] "Leaders in the motion picture industry have awakened to action because they resent their industry's being misrepresented before the world," declared an editorial in support of the MPA in 1944.[67] "But citizens everywhere have a great responsibility to do as the citizens of the motion picture industry," continued the editorial. "If all of us are not on guard," it concluded, "we'll find a big battle on our hands in future years to preserve American ideals."[68]

Vowing to defend against America's enemies "that which is our priceless heritage," the MPA's statement of principles explicitly equated Americanism with antifascism and anticommunism while implicitly offering a radically different version of "American democracy" from that of the HDC.[69] While professing to have a broad range of forces to fight, the MPA pursued communism as its principal enemy, considering it "deplorable" that the industry had produced a "picture glorifying Communist Russia, ignoring the oppressive and tyrannical character of Bolshevism and inventing virtues for it that have never existed."[70] Conservative-leaning papers praised the MPA for taking action against the production of movies like the Warner Bros. film *Mission to Moscow* and claimed that the American public wanted "relaxation and entertainment" in its movies, not Soviet propaganda. Celebrities like Clark Gable and Gary Cooper, studio executive Walt Disney, and various writers who had formed the Screen Playwrights Guild—the conservative, studio-endorsed alternative to the liberal Screen Writers Guild—joined the MPA to fight actively the infiltration of communism in the film industry. Claiming to speak on behalf of the silent majority of the motion picture industry, the MPA sought to counter the "small but highly organized, cleverly led, and extremely articulate minority."[71]

Similarly to the HDC, the MPA used its celebrity and publicity outlets to promote its views, beginning a media battle between Hollywood liberals and conservatives that would attract national attention. A writer for the *Motion Picture Herald* responded to the publication of MPA's statement with concern for its impact on the industry. Seeing the rhetoric of communist infiltration as "highly regrettable phrases, unsupported by the introduction of a single shred of evidence, and, in fact, only supported by blanket indictment," *Herald* journalist Red Kann spoke about the dangers these "strange phrases authored by prominent men to feed the American press" could have on the reputation of the industry as a whole.[72] Another editorial pointed to the MPA's connections to Republican state senator Jack Tenney, an ardent anticommunist in California politics, and to an anti-Semitic "little clique of MGM fascists" who gave the MPA the "drive and emotional power it has."[73]

The group appeared in the *Congressional Record* when isolationist senator Robert R. Reynolds (D-N.C.) read a letter from his "friends in Hollywood" that praised the "new, decent, patriotic element" that had emerged in Hollywood to "fight the very clique against which you and other intelligent Americans made protest of years ago."[74] The letter further commended the foresight of the senator for seeing "the Trojan horse" of communist subversion within the country and previously pushing to outlaw all organizations seeking the overthrow of the government. Congressional committees had attempted to investigate communism in Hollywood before, with no real success or public support; however, the MPA welcomed and encouraged the return of the House Un-American Activities Committee (HUAC), ultimately giving internal testimonies to the influence of communists that would demand a more thorough investigation in the postwar period. Following the published letter from "A Group of Your Hollywood Friends" in the *Congressional Record*, the Hollywood Writers' Mobilization took out a two-page ad in *Variety* and the *Hollywood Reporter* to expose the pro-Nazi sympathies of Reynolds and attempt to link the anonymous letter directly to the MPA.[75] While the MPA quickly denied having authorized or even having knowledge of the writing of the letter to Reynolds, the opposing sides of the ideological debate on the role of communism in Hollywood clearly emerged in the press across the country.

The MPA publicly challenged the political recognition that the HFWA, members of the Writers' Congress, and liberal celebrity activists had gained as they began to turn wartime mobilization into partisan victories for the Democratic Party. In response, the Hollywood Writers' Mobilization and HFWA joined with other Hollywood guilds to combat what they considered to be the antilabor, anti-Semitic, red-baiting, and fascist activities of the MPA. On June 28, 1944, an Emergency Council meeting assembled approximately 1,000 delegates from seventeen guilds and unions in the Hollywood area to build a "broad program of public relations and to take action to protect the industry and its workers from anti-democratic, anti-labor attacks."[76]

Organized labor in the industry immediately interpreted the formation of the MPA as a threat to the talent guilds. With memories of the division the Screen Playwrights Guild had caused within the Screen Writers Guild in 1936, writers in particular worried about the antilabor implications of this organization. Formed in 1933 to give economic security, artistic authority, and creative credit to the writers, the Screen Writers Guild constituted the earliest, and most political and articulate, labor organization and would serve as the template for the subsequent talent guilds. As an early leader in the Screen Writers Guild, the communist John Howard Lawson attempted to link the guild with the Authors League of America, the Dramatists Guild, the Newspapers Guild, and the Radio Writers Guild to form a national confederation of writers. MGM writers and future members of the MPA James K. McGuinness, Rupert Hughes, and Howard Emmett Rogers disagreed with and protested against Lawson's policies of "collectivism," which would lower their status from artists to mere laborers. Angered by the radical element in unions that encouraged class conflict between the workers and the studios, McGuinness, Hughes, and Rogers formed a new writers' union that worked closely and more amiably with studio executives in 1936.[77] The Screen Playwrights Guild proposed a labor/management relationship that would flourish in the postwar world, according to which businesses would keep a social commitment to their workers. MGM studio executive Irving Thalberg worked with the writers to develop a contract that gave the Guild founders time off from work, meeting rooms, messengers, lawyers, and secretaries, all in exchange for assurances that they would not collectively organize with writers in other fields.[78] As an "association of writers," the Screen Playwrights Guild found many benefits in cooperating with management. "The better producers believe that the happiness and security of the writers is an asset in their business," announced the Screen Playwrights Guild in *Variety*.[79] "They have promised us complete cooperation in the solution of problems and the righting of wrongs."

In the 1930s, when labor unions primarily served the purposes of working-class Americans, an organization focused on partnership and friendly cooperation with big businesses had little chance of survival.[80] While the Screen Playwrights Guild did not last long as an organization, its ideals resurfaced in the MPA. When the talent guilds met to form a coherent opposition to the MPA, they defended not only their labor union, but claimed that the MPA's attack on "crackpots" was the most recent fabrication of efforts to silence political activity in Hollywood. They argued that despite the incredible war effort that Hollywood put forth, the accusations of communist infiltration by hardliners within the industry smeared this patriotic mobilization. During the Emergency Council meeting on that hot June night in 1944, liberal activists sought to dismantle the media narrative put forth by MPA activists. They publicized the "proud story" of Hollywood in the war and in American life and highlighted the praise and responsibility that President Roosevelt had given them when he declared, "Entertainment is always valuable in peace. It is indispensable in war."[81] With Russia as an ally, communism was not the immediate threat, argued Walter Wanger, independent film producer and head of the HFWA. "The real threat to America is disunity—disunity between America and her Allies, disunity within America between races, classes, and creeds," continued the producer passionately. While conservative critics in the *Chicago Tribune* described the Hollywood Victory Committee as "distinctly left wing and a noisy supporter of the four freedoms," Wanger emphasized how he and others within the film industry had worked diligently over the past four years to support the war effort.[82] Prominent Hollywood liberals joined

Wanger and supported the Council of Hollywood Unions and Guilds meeting, with Rita Hayworth, Orson Welles, and Dore Schary all pledging their allegiance to national unity and a free world.[83] The meeting dramatically allowed for a representative of the MPA to counter the charges brought against it, and when no member stepped forward, the meeting concluded with a presentation of research on the members of the MPA to show their connections to isolationist groups like the America First Party and to Nazi sympathizers and propaganda outlets.[84] In a strategy reminiscent of that which had proved victorious against the Nye commission several years earlier, the council meeting framed the attacks as evidence of the ugliness of anti-Semitism and isolationism.

The MPA responded to the Emergency Council meeting with an advertisement in the *Hollywood Reporter*. Acknowledging the invitation of the Emergency Council for an MPA representative to attend a "Smear Soiree," the MPA stated that they had refused to send a lone representative, "who would be required to answer a series of 'When-did-you-stop-beating-your-wife' questions," a typical tactic used by Communists.[85] James McGuinness printed a lengthy response to the Emergency Council's allegations that the MPA was anti-Semitic, fascist, antilabor, anti-administration, reactionary, and promoters of disunity.[86] Pointing to the five labor leaders and six Jewish Americans who sat on the board, McGuinness explained how its members "were bewildered" by these charges. Rather than seeing the organization as promoting disunity, McGuinness argued that "disagreement is not disunity." The article then announced the MPA's willingness to meet for an "honest intellectual discussion" with the Emergency Council. The proposed meeting, however, never happened, and instead the debate between liberals and the MPA would continue to play out in local trade papers and national newspapers and magazines.

Walter Wanger saw the MPA's broad allegations and reliance on the press as evidence of the inaccuracy in the organization's wild accusations. If the MPA had proof of communist subversion in film production, it could easily appeal to the Production Association, the "responsible groups charged with directing industry policy and picture content," insisted Wanger. Instead, it went to the press, which eagerly published the "slanderous statements" against the industry in the hope of selling papers. The MPA and liberal groups like the HFWA all capitalized on their publicity appeal as celebrities promoted their causes on each end of the political spectrum. But, although liberals had the organizational and research support of the OWI and the HDC for their causes, the MPA relied on arousing the emotions of the public through colorful language and bold indictments. The president of the Screen Writers Guild, Emmet Lavery, sued MPA member Lela Rogers, the mother of actress Ginger Rogers, for libel and slander after she spoke on the radio about the communist implications of Lavery's new play. Calling the play a "plot to foist foreign ideology on the public," Lela Rogers later admitted, to her and the MPA's embarrassment, that she had not read the play but had made the accusation based on a studio reader's assessment she had overheard at a dinner party.[87]

After the first year, the MPA dedicated time and energy to more specific investigations of labor disputes and it carefully monitored the editorial content of *People's World*—the "west coast organ of the Communist Political Association."[88] The following year, the MPA began to publish pamphlets discussing Communist Party tactics, circulated monthly reports in its newsletter *The Vigil*, and sent members to "speak for freedom" at organizations throughout Los Angeles.[89] Until the FBI and HUAC investigations into communist influence in Hollywood, however, the MPA lacked the institutional support for extensive research to back up its frequent and bold assertions of communist infiltration.

The dominance of the Hollywood Left during the war ultimately hurt the effectiveness and the reputation of the MPA and initially made membership controversial. Critics pointed to the organization's "friends," the Americanism Defense League and former America First members—both organizations that had supported isolationism before the war.[90] Facing accusations of fascism and Nazism from the talent guilds, the organization also received national criticism from the director of the OWI, Elmer Rice. The MPA, argued Rice, was "deeply tinged with isolationism and anti-unionism."[91] Moreover, Rice saw a connection between the MPA and "Bundists," and the "defendants in the Washington sedition-conspiracy trial." Studio executives ridiculed the organization by nicknaming it "the Motion Picture Bund," "the Brain Storm Troopers," or the "Fighting SB's," and Lela Rogers reported on the intense animosity the MPA faced in its early years.[92] When the organization invited staunch Republican David O. Selznick to join a meeting, the studio executive blasted the group during one meeting for being "anti-everything."[93] In response, Rogers told Selznick that he and other studio heads were "politically blind" and could not see that "their pictures are being infiltrated with Communist propaganda or unrest and anti-American feeling."

The debate about the role of entertainment that permeated the Nye investigation and had been quelled by the war effort resurfaced in industry trade papers and social circles in response to liberal and progressive mobilization during the 1944 election. Columnist Hedda Hopper agreed with Lela Rogers that communists represented a definite threat to the community, and she saw a cunning minority manipulating the "stooge writers, directors, and stars, who fell for the 'progressive' line that they were serving humanity by turning out pictures dealing with 'real life.' "[94] To Hopper, the MPA sought not only to expose the communist attempts at propaganda, but also to wage a fight against "messages in movies."[95] Most of Hollywood dismissed the organization as a reactionary element seeking media attention, but, despite its right-wing conservative ideology, the MPA did influence national discussions about communist subversion in Hollywood and the role of entertainment in American politics more broadly.[96] Over the next three years, the MPA dedicated itself to exposing communists and restructuring labor relationships as it also continued to condemn propaganda in movies. Like Hopper, conservatives across California and the country began to listen and to speak out against "message movies," reasserting the belief that "entertainment is the sole purpose of the movies."[97]

From "Swimming Pool Parties" to "Ideological Battleground"

The MPA fueled the debate about the place of Hollywood in American politics that had captured the attention of Martin Dies and Gerald Nye before the war and would garner even more national attention at the HUAC hearings three years later. By professing a commitment to upholding the American way of life, however, the MPA pushed the industry even deeper into American politics. An editorial written in support of the MPA claimed that "they will encourage the making of pictures that create a better knowledge of America, and high understanding of American principles and ideals, and a deeper appreciation of American privileges and rights and blessings."[98] Despite its commitment to separating entertainment and politics, defining America through the silver screen forced a marriage between the two realms, while also foreshadowing how anticommunist rhetoric would allow Hollywood to connect its products with national interests during the Cold War in a way that emulated, and ultimately expanded, what liberal activists had done during World War II.

Moreover, while the growing anticommunist crusade allowed prominent industry spokespersons to assert Hollywood's role as the safeguard of democracy, in 1944 this was a media battle between the two sides for control of the narrative about the shape and meaning of Hollywood's "ideological politics." While this publicity-driven style of politics, which depended on colorful statements and dramatic stories of "impending doom," drew attention, it also incited frequent derision outside of Hollywood as negative assumptions about the naïveté and superficiality of such celebrity political activity permeated media coverage of these battles. *Time* magazine reported in a light, easy manner on the ideological polarization that divided the MPA from Hollywood liberals in 1944. "Over the room temperature burgundy and chopped chicken liver, politics came to Hollywood."[99] Listing the players on each side of battle, the article concluded that "from now on, no Hollywood hostess was safe. Try as she might to keep her Max Factor powder dry, her very next swimming-pool party might become tomorrow's ideological battleground." The focus on the luxuries of Hollywood and its social atmosphere—swimming pools, wine, and makeup—reflected the dominant press coverage of film personalities and their activities, which dismissed its political activities as shallow and inauthentic pursuits even while readers consumed these stories. In protest, Orson Welles responded that "the politics of movie makers is exactly what isn't funny about Hollywood."[100] Welles argued that luxury did not "invalidate" political opinion and that Hollywood filmmakers and actors should be commended for the "recognition of the fact that every movie expresses, or at least reflects, political opinion." Precisely because entertainment reaches "the biggest section of human beings ever addressed by any medium of communication," Welles asserted that Hollywood's political ideology and activities should be taken seriously.

The 1940 election and prewar debates about Hollywood's interventionist activities and film productions introduced key political lessons about the potential Hollywood held for influencing voter decisions. The World War II war effort further paved the road for industry mobilization in shaping electoral appeals in the 1944 election and constructions of Americanism in the postwar years. Different definitions, however, battled one another in Hollywood and the national media during the last years of World War II. Both the Left and the Right sought to control media narratives about the political meaning and uses of entertainment. The Hollywood Writers' Mobilization, the HDC, and the HFWA wanted to transmit images of racial equality, promote international cooperation, and expand New Deal liberalism to encourage further government protection abroad and equal rights for struggling citizens at home. Aligned against this, the MPA wanted an Americanism that emphasized the individual and free enterprise and made no compromises with any system that would threaten capitalism and the market. After its first year, the MPA looked back at the "unprecedented attack on us" and surmised that "had we set ourselves up as the Society to Encourage Opium Smoking by Infants or the Association to Provide for the Widespread Dissemination of the Black Plague, we could not have been subjected to more obloquy than was pitch-forked on us for stating: We believe in and like, the American way of life."[101] And yet, despite the drama that ensued, or what *Variety* called "venom and bitterness with their claims and counter claims," the core concern of the polarization centered around the fact that "these organizations are either anti- or pro-Roosevelt. All the name calling stems from that."[102] But the Hollywood version of the 1944 election emphasized drama: heroes, villains, and promises of a world renewed or the end of democracy.

In 1944, the drama that polarized the industry faded away with the electoral success of a slew of progressive Democratic candidates during the landslide election results. Proud of its prestigious role in the 1944 election, the HDC also continued its work to mobilize popular support for arms control and international cooperation and a push toward civil rights, full employment, and labor support at home. While many members wrote, directed, and starred in movies with powerful social statements, the HDC itself went beyond film production to develop a stronger and more cohesive organization of progressive citizens by joining a national association that united artists with scientists and other progressive professionals across the country. The Independent Citizens Committee of the Arts, Sciences, and Professions, Inc. (ICCASP) worked with the HDC and the DNC during the 1944 election. Although the ICCASP pushed for a formal merger with the HDC during the election, the HDC declined because it had committed not only to aid President Roosevelt's reelection, but also to "work for a Congress that will support the president's policies."[103] Nevertheless, because many Hollywood personalities overlapped in membership, the HDC remained very close with the ICCASP, and following the election the ICCASP again formally invited the HDC to join the national organization. The membership merger would allow the HDC to exert its influence across the country in a more organized manner. In considering the future challenges of maintaining a concentrated focus on "an intensive legislative and educational program during the post-election period," the HDC understood the benefits of a more formal relationship with the ICCASP.

With this merger, in the early months of 1945, the HDC changed its name to the Hollywood Independent Citizens Committee of the Arts, Sciences, and Professions (HICCASP), and ICCASP gained a valuable resource with the production capabilities and talent of the HDC.[104] The Hollywood committee agreed that its branch would specialize in producing film and radio dramatizations and organizing caravans of stars to travel the country to garner popular support for policies of postwar peace and international cooperation. HICCASP allowed Hollywood liberals to join a national network committed to pushing for policy changes between election years and a closer connection to Washington, D.C., with the establishment of an office near Capitol Hill.

As the war drew to a close, Hollywood liberals continued to exert their influence in Democratic politics through institutional collaborations, but they also wanted to bring a newfound political awareness to filmmaking that would keep entertainment a source of "education and enlightenment." Writers, producers, and even some studio heads followed Darryl Zanuck's advice from the 1943 Writers Congress to use entertainment to discuss serious issues. Films like *Crossfire, Gentleman's Agreement,* and *The Best Years of Our Lives* highlighted the ugly nature of racism and the class struggles of the postwar period. Along with the introduction of documentary filmmaking—made possible by the 16mm film advances during the war—liberal writers, directors, and studio executives aspired to reintroduce a social conscience into American films with a firm belief that winning the peace abroad and at home required meaningful entertainment.[105]

More broadly, the wartime collaboration between DNC and OWI personnel—from the Roosevelt administration and from the movie industry—helped legitimize the expertise and skills of entertainers in the national election. But it also reignited concerns over the manipulative power of entertainment, which also appeared in the aftermath of the anti-Sinclair campaign and the 1941 Senate hearings on motion picture propaganda. Liberal mobilization in the 1944 election, and the conservative response to it, especially within the Hollywood community itself, provides insight into the spread of anticommunist hysteria in Hollywood and the infamous 1947 HUAC hearings. When the MPA lost the publicity battle in 1944, the organization urged HUAC committee members to come to Hollywood and investigate the communist threat that they felt had triumphed during the election, and during the war effort more broadly. Moreover, the postwar concern over communist infiltration in motion pictures stemmed more from a concern over who would control and influence the newly important political productions constructed in Hollywood studios (or replicas arising in Washington, D.C., and New York City). Franklin Roosevelt's death in April 1945 devastated individuals in the industry, who had come to know the president on a personal and professional basis. Without an ally in the White House, the political and financial future of Hollywood, whose leaders faced an uncertain international market and battles over antitrust legislation at home, was uncertain. The war had changed the meaning of entertainment while strengthening the economic position of the industry. But what would come with peace and a new president?

CHAPTER FOUR

Defending the American Way of Life

In the fall of 1945, OWI film reviewer Dorothy Jones evaluated the transformation that Hollywood had undergone throughout the war. "Traditionally, the motion picture industry has maintained that the primary function of the Hollywood film is to entertain," wrote Jones.[1] However, the war had opened up new responsibilities and opportunities, and thus "traditional notions about film making which have so long governed the industry are slowly yielding to more progressive ideas about the function of film in the world today." Jones, along with government officials and Americans across the country, eagerly waited for Hollywood to unleash its power in uniting the world in peace and shining a light on domestic strife at home.

President Harry Truman also appreciated what he termed the "outstanding wartime record" of the industry and understood its potential for influence in the postwar world. Soon after the war ended, Truman welcomed industry leaders to the White House, praising their trade as "one of the most effective and forceful media for spreading knowledge and truth" and also expressing the hope that the industry would "perform a public service of increasing importance."[2] Truman appointed John R. Steelman, head of the Office of War Mobilization and Reconversion, to "establish a single point of contact" between government and Hollywood, which would link "the functions of production, distribution, and exhibition" to allow films to "make major contributions to public understanding of many serious postwar problems."[3]

As Truman and Steelman attempted to develop a working peacetime relationship with the motion picture industry, building on the work Roosevelt had begun, Republicans increased their criticism of the "New Deal propaganda" they said had permeated film during the war.[4] Republican

Senate leader Robert A. Taft of Ohio declared that propaganda could be justified in wartime but had no place in a peacetime government. "Production should be left up to commercial companies in order to preserve our economic system," argued Taft.[5] In rhetoric strikingly similar to that of his Senate colleague Gerald Nye on the eve of war, Taft urged the film industry not to get "mixed up" in a "New Deal plot" to continue selling liberal propaganda in pictures. New Deal critic and Speaker of the House Joseph Martin (R-Mass.) targeted the postwar collaborations between the movie industry and the Office of War Mobilization and Reconversion. Martin expressed confidence that the Republican majority in Congress would use the power of the purse strings to derail these efforts.[6] As the Republican-dominated Eightieth Congress convened, *Variety* looked uneasily at its potential to launch another investigation. "There are Republicans convinced that the motion picture industry has been so strongly pro–New Deal that it makes good sense to put the fear of God and the U.S. Congress into it," warned the trade paper.[7] Having found favor with Roosevelt's long and influential administration over the past twelve years, the paper feared that in 1947 it made "good sense for Hollywood to expect the worst."

Although Dorothy Jones and Harry Truman eagerly anticipated how the motion picture industry could translate wartime achievements into peacetime political prestige and opportunity, Franklin Roosevelt's death and the rising tide of anti–New Deal conservatism reinvigorated national concerns about the political place of the West Coast communications industry, which had proven its power to shape public opinion and advance a liberal agenda during wartime. The 1947 HUAC investigation into the communist activities of the motion picture industry occurred within this broader debate about New Deal film propaganda and the role of Hollywood in American politics more generally. While observing the preparations and spectacle that surrounded the postwar HUAC hearings, Leo Rosten surmised that because of the international appeal of Hollywood, the investigation would become a global debate about the connection between entertainment and propaganda during the intensifying Cold War. Rosten argued that a principal problem at the heart of political discussions of the industry and questions of communist subversion emerged from a belief that movies were either "pure entertainment" or something vaguely called "propaganda." According to Rosten, "This muddy distinction implied that what is entertaining cannot be significant and what is significant (dealing with group rather than individual problems) cannot be entertaining."[8]

The HUAC hearings broadcast for the world to see the debate in which Nye and Roosevelt and the MPA and the HDC had engaged over the past decade. While driven by the rhetoric of communist subversion, the hearings became a way to express lingering suspicions about celebrity political activism that had begun under Martin Dies's investigation in 1938 and continued in Gerald Nye's hearings in 1941. And yet, while HUAC members claimed they wanted to separate entertainment from American politics, they purposely staged the hearings to use entertainment for political ends, just as New Dealers had done during the war. The HUAC drama and the Cold War propaganda campaigns illuminated how Republicans, too, saw the opportunity to use the political language of entertainment in the same ways that they had attacked their political opponents for using. By making Hollywood productions and personalities integral to the defense of democracy abroad, Cold War collaborations between the government and the motion picture industry legitimized the political use of entertainment in ways that made advertisers, consultants, and presidential contenders see its partisan potential to win elections in the television age.

Scholars frequently view HUAC specifically, and anticommunism in the industry more generally, as having stifled creativity with the Hollywood Blacklist and the subsequent political pressures to conform to the national Cold War agenda.[9] But a look at individual and institutional responses to the hearings demonstrates how top Hollywood figures took advantage of the "Red Scare" to create a demand and respect for their professional skills in American politics, first in the ideological struggle against communism and then during the 1950s electoral campaigns that played out on television.[10] Strident anticommunism anaesthetized silver screen productions, but it also opened new doors for partisan advancement, power, and authority for Hollywood activists like Jack Warner, Walter Wanger, Ronald Reagan, and George Murphy to assert their credibility as public figures in promoting democracy at home and abroad. Hollywood as an industry engaged in the "politics of Americanism," which built on and extended previous types of activism as individuals promoted the industry's interests, proved their patriotism, and advanced particular political ideologies.

Convened by congressmen angry over liberal celebrity activism and "message films" during the war years, the HUAC hearings profoundly damaged the Democratic political networks in Hollywood. But the dramatically staged event showed how Republicans simultaneously attacked and emulated, and then surpassed, the success of the Hollywood Left in advancing the political language of entertainment, ultimately making the industry a player in the Cold War campaign and the Republican Party during the 1950s. In the 1930s, studios publicized the "pure family fun" of Hollywood entertainment and the role of celebrities as philanthropic leaders to ward off moral censorship campaigns. During the Cold War, executives responded to the anticommunism investigations and concerns about political censorship with an active promotion of Hollywood celebrities' role as faithful spokespersons for democracy throughout the world. Driven by pragmatic concerns to boost the box office and assert the patriotism of the industry, many Roosevelt supporters abandoned their New Deal loyalties and embraced the conservative political landscape. They did so, however, in ways that continued to help them advance professionally and politically and that would ultimately make studio productions a valued part of the political process.

Splintering on the Left

Celebrity activists who had enjoyed so much recognition and success in the battles within the industry during the 1944 campaign had already started to "expect the worst" as the war came to an end. Saddened by the death of their friend in the White House in the last months of the war, liberal celebrity activists initially sought to work with his successor's administration and responded eagerly to Truman's call for entertainers to continue their public service during the postwar period. One such person was Olivia de Havilland. Though she played sweet, demure characters on screen, de Havilland demanded recognition for her artistic work and for the liberal causes in which she believed. In 1944, she campaigned tirelessly for Franklin D. Roosevelt and also won a landmark legal suit against Warner Bros. Studio. That year the California Supreme Court ruled in favor of de Havilland, who challenged the rights of the studio to extend her contract while also suspending her without pay for refusing roles—a common studio tactic to ensure that stars remained legally bound to a studio without the power to negotiate their own films through independent contracts.[11] Advised by the up-and-coming talent agent Lew Wasserman to assert her power as a major film star, de Havilland joined a growing cadre of independent celebrities uninhibited by studio rules to control so stringently their professional and political actions.[12] De Havilland's legal victory opened up the negotiating power of individual celebrities (and of talent agents like Wasserman) in production contracts. This freedom undermined the power of studios to control their employees' public and private actions and it emboldened celebrity activists to speak out politically, as they did in the election. But actors soon realized what studio executives had long understood—that their political activity could undermine their silver screen popularity (and thus future film options), which depended on public faith and support at the box office.

Invigorated by legal victories and driven by a liberal ideological political passion, de Havilland joined other industry New Dealers, including studio executive Dore Schary and the newly elected president of the SAG, Ronald Reagan, to promote the use of "message movies" in educating and informing Americans of postwar social problems. But in the postwar period, the Hollywood Left felt the void of Roosevelt's death. "When Franklin Roosevelt died," declared de Havilland on April 14, 1946, "something died in all of us."[13] Feeling "confused and bewildered," de Havilland confronted an equally confusing liberal landscape in Hollywood as the radical/progressive/liberal coalition of the war years began to fray. Franklin Roosevelt had been a bridge for philosophical differences within organizations like the HDC, and the war had also unified liberals with communists as they worked with the OWI to defeat Germany and Japan through the power of film.[14] But without the wartime context and Roosevelt's leadership and amid growing tensions with the Soviet Union, this coalition quickly fell apart. Traveling to Seattle during the 1946 congressional elections, Olivia de Havilland looked over her speech, written by former communist Dalton Trumbo, and stopped in her tracks when she read the communist-oriented passages that linked racism to capitalism and condemned nationalism as reactionary and Hitler-like. Recalling the story in his autobiography, Ronald Reagan declared that de Havilland refused to deliver the speech because of its communist propaganda.[15] Other accounts suggest that she did deliver the speech but added a strong indictment of fascism and communism that sent Trumbo into a rage.[16]

After Winston Churchill delivered his "Iron Curtain" address in the spring of 1946, indicting the Soviet Union's attempts to divide Europe into "free" versus "communist" states, and with Joseph Stalin soon thereafter delivering an election speech declaring the inability of communism and capitalism to coexist, a hardening line between communism and capitalism and democracy emerged in international politics.[17] Several months later, concerned about the rising power of communists in organizations like HICCASP, liberal activists joined forces to "smoke" out the communists during a July meeting. In his political autobiography, Reagan dramatically remembered how this line between communists and liberals came to be clearly drawn. Reagan recalled how he sat beside MGM studio executive Dore Schary and watched Jimmy Roosevelt address the members about his concern that HICCASP had been accused of being a communist-front organization.[18] To protect its reputation, Roosevelt asked the executive board to issue a policy statement that would repudiate communism. Reagan described the pandemonium that broke out: a "well known musician sprang to his feet" and offered to recite the Soviet constitution, which was "a hell of a lot more democratic than that of the United States." Another member, a well-known writer, passionately declared to the crowd that "if there was ever a war between the United States and Russia, he would volunteer for Russia." In the midst of the "hubhub of dismay," Reagan stood up in support of Jimmy Roosevelt, only to find himself "waist high in epithets such as 'Fascist' and 'capitalist scum' and 'enemy of the proletariat' and 'witch-hunter' and 'Red-baiter' before I could say boo." The hysterical response of radicals to the suggested policy created an "emotional atmosphere" so high that one woman fell to the floor with a heart attack. A dozen liberals walked out of the volatile meeting with smiles and secretly reconvened at Olivia de Havilland's apartment. In the hope of "smoking out the 'others,'" de Havilland, Roosevelt, and Schary had set up this "preconceived plot" in order to see exactly how many communists had infiltrated the council and the true intentions of these communists. Since Reagan had proved his anticommunist beliefs by standing up for Roosevelt, Schary invited him to the meeting. As de Havilland and Roosevelt "concocted the disinfected resolution," Reagan recalled grinning at de Havilland because, until that evening, Reagan had thought she "was one." De Havilland smiled right back at Reagan and told him, "I thought you were one, until tonight that is."

Written in 1964, Reagan's account carefully reconstructs the event to assert his conservative anticommunist credentials. Nevertheless, anticommunism had started to tear apart the Popular Front political coalition, which did rupture during this July meeting. The next day, the HICCASP executive board refused to introduce de Havilland's proposed resolution: "We affirm our belief in free enterprise and the democratic system and repudiate Communism as desirable for the United States." Jimmy Roosevelt, Olivia de Havilland, her sister Joan Fontaine, Ronald Reagan, and others present in de Havilland's apartment the previous evening offered their resignations.[19]

The conflict between communists like John Howard Lawson and liberals like Olivia de Havilland and Ronald Reagan illuminated how the politicization of the industry had previously depended on the personal connection to Franklin Roosevelt and the wartime context. During the 1944 election, these political networks had generated conflict from within the industry itself over the direction and use of celebrity authority to shape political outcomes. But in the postwar period, the place and shape of Hollywood's ideological politics generated conflict from outside the industry, as national politicians struggled to harness the power of propaganda and control it for their political advantage. The HUAC investigations began within this broader debate about "message films" and celebrity activism in American politics. *Variety* predicted that the investigation would unleash a press battle, and Leo Rosten anticipated that it would become an international event. Both were right.[20]

The investigation of "Communist Infiltration of Hollywood Motion Picture Industry" began on May 12, 1947, in Los Angeles. Congressman J. Parnell Thomas (R-N.J.) joined fellow congressmen John McDowell (R-Pa.) and John Wood (D-Ga.) and investigators Robert Stripling and Louis Russell. The committee met with several strident anticommunists in Hollywood, including many members of the MPA, who eagerly told of the attempts of radicals to insert propaganda into motion pictures, to incite labor union violence, to manipulate voting behavior, and to raise money for the Communist Party through front organizations. These initial hearings took place behind closed doors to avoid publicity, as the committee hoped to uncover specific evidence of communist subversion that it could then use to build a more public case against particular individuals and films. Throughout the hearings, Stripling served as head investigator. He asked witnesses to name individuals they suspected of communist leanings, and he also inquired about the broader political activity of well-known personalities. The purpose of the investigation of the industry, claimed Congressman McDowell, was not to "dig into the private affairs of the industry." The committee professed a concern about "everyone in the movie industry who might be used as agents of a foreign power in an effort to destroy our country."[21]

The committee believed that enough evidence existed, though these were only broad accusations based on rumors, for it to hold a public hearing that would enlighten the American people about the attempt of communists to overthrow the country through entertainment. J. Parnell Thomas announced the recommendation of the committee to make a "full dress hearing" for the public that would feature "very important witnesses, very prominent persons."[22] The fame of its witnesses would provide the "great element" of "public exposure" so that the hearings could serve as a morality play to teach the American people about the evils of communism, at the expense of Hollywood's reputation.

As subpoenas filled the mailboxes of writers, directors, actors, and executives, resentment and criticism toward HUAC and fear of censorship reunited liberals and radicals in protest. Publicly vowing to protest government regulation of the silver screens and to uphold the rights of individual political beliefs, William Wyler, John Huston, George Stevens, Norman Corwin, Billy Wilder, and Philip Dunne—a group of anticommunist liberals—formed the Committee for the First Amendment. Various liberal actors and actresses quickly joined the group and worked to develop a strong protest against HUAC and its investigation tactics. Through radio programs and newspaper ads, the Committee for the First Amendment declared that it was "disgusted and outraged by the continuing attempt of the House Un-American Activities Committee to smear the Motion Picture Industry."[23] The group stood on the principles of the Bill of Rights and argued that "any investigation into the political beliefs of the individual is contrary to the basic principles of our democracy." The director of *The Best Years of Our Lives*, William Wyler, told television audiences of the ramifications of censorship and an atmosphere of fear. "You will be deprived of entertainment that will stimulate you," stressed Wyler.[24] "You will be given a diet of pictures which conform to some people's arbitrary standards of entertainment and Americanism."

The Committee for the First Amendment saw the upcoming HUAC hearings as undermining the prestigious position Hollywood had achieved in American society through its wartime service. It defended the industry's patriotic political mobilization and pointed out how the U.S. government had "called upon the American motion picture industry to extend itself further in presenting the democratic way of life to people in other lands."[25] In October 1947, twenty-five Hollywood figures traveled to Washington, D.C., to protest the hearings. Humphrey Bogart, Lauren Bacall, and Gene Kelly headlined the Committee for the First Amendment's direct confrontation with HUAC, while Frank Sinatra, Katharine Hepburn, Spencer Tracy, and many others lent their support to the committee by participating in a nationwide radio broadcast, "Hollywood Fights Back." The attention the committee generated provided a national criticism of HUAC, a defense of Hollywood's political rights, and a forum for promotion of the industry during what the committee called smear attacks that were strikingly reminiscent of those launched during the 1944 battle. In the radio ad, the Committee for the First Amendment urged the American public to "listen to the real Hollywood," the "proud" Americans who speak for "decency, tolerance, and democracy," and begged listeners to "help us to keep the screen free. We will help you to keep free the America we love."[26]

Upon leaving Washington, D.C., John Huston remarked that the "little contingent of writers, directors, and actors felt that they had performed some slight service."[27] Despite the positive media coverage of the Committee for the First Amendment in Washington, when its members returned to Hollywood, Huston felt they faced "a decidedly hostile atmosphere." Huston's impression quickly proved to be accurate. Louis B. Mayer and Jack Warner defended the product of the industry as 100 percent American under oath in Washington and were visibly upset with the hearings. And yet within two months, on November 25, 1947, these executives assembled in New York's Waldorf Astoria and issued a public statement condemning the actions of the "Hollywood Ten," whom Congress had cited for contempt. Stating that these men "have been a disservice to their employers" and have impaired their usefulness in the industry, the declaration dismissed all ten from their employment contracts and vowed that no studio would knowingly employ a communist.[28] The statement ended by reminding the American public of Hollywood's "invaluable aid in war and peace." While pointing again to the wartime role of the industry, the statement reflected the political savviness of industry leaders, who anticipated which way the wind was blowing and jumped on the anticommunist bandwagon to, once again, protect their businesses in the emerging Cold War environment. With memories of the Catholic Legion of Decency boycott from a decade earlier, and perhaps fearful of the potentially negative ramifications at the box office now that entertainment itself had faced an inquisition, the producers quickly took matters into their own hands and imposed a new type of self-censorship that resulted in support for anticommunism and a promotion of consensus.

Though weakened, liberalism survived in Hollywood, but only by making a vocal and strident commitment to anticommunism and renouncing the actions of the ten men who were cited for contempt of Congress. Seven months after Humphrey Bogart prominently stood alongside his friends in the Committee for the First Amendment, adamantly protesting the HUAC hearings, he penned an article in *Photoplay* titled, "I'm No Communist."[29] In the article, Bogart reaffirmed his faith in American democracy and capitalism and reminded readers that he did not support the "Hollywood Ten," but rather "we were there solely in the interests of freedom of speech, freedom of the screen, and protection of the Bill of Rights."[30] Bogart's article made light of how "actors and actresses always go overboard about things" but emphasized the sincerity of Hollywood's commitment to the public good and how the industry's deep-seated Americanism motivated actors and actresses to donate money to causes, play at benefits, and "volunteer our time and services to help sell bonds or just sell America to the rest of the world." He wrote that he might be a "dope" but that he was an "American dope."

In less than four years, Bogart went from active Roosevelt campaigner, wartime entertainer with the OWI and the USO, and national Democratic

Party advocate to an "American dope" who felt pressured to apologize publicly for his political activities. While not a communist, nor even a "fellow traveler," Bogart—along with other prominent liberal celebrities like Olivia de Havilland and Edward G. Robinson—experienced professional and personal consequences for his prominent activism during the postwar years. Edward G. Robinson would also face this humiliation when he bowed to political and professional pressure and admitted that the "Reds made a sucker out of me."[31] To survive professionally in Hollywood during the early Cold War years, entertainers had to repent publicly for their liberal ideological political activism during the war. Moreover, the anticommunist inquisition scarred the Democratic Party, which turned away from celebrity associations and its effective campaign style for over a decade. But the Republican Party welcomed conservative Cold Warriors in Hollywood with the expertise and skills to help wage an international war against communism and soon after a battle for the White House.

Bogart, Robinson, de Havilland, and other members of the OWI and the HDC wanted to use entertainment to educate the American public on what they saw as the pressing domestic and international problems of the postwar period, promote New Deal liberalism, and elect progressive candidates to office. While these policy goals and electoral efforts faced a nightmarish reality with the rise of the Cold War, the wartime and postwar efforts of liberal celebrity activists showcased the political potential of entertainment, which conservatives first feared and then tried to emulate. The substance of Hollywood's liberal ideological politics was stunted by HUAC, but the style prevailed. These hearings silenced liberal activism, but the investigations opened doors for anticommunist entertainers to use the rhetoric of the Cold War to open new political and professional opportunities on the Right.

Navigating the "Seamy Side of Liberalism"

At the same time that Franklin Roosevelt's death shifted presidential leadership responsibilities to Harry Truman, Will Hays announced plans to retire, leaving studio executives to seek a new leader in Hollywood. In 1921, Hays had come to the industry in the midst of murder and sex scandals and the moral panics that had ensued as police found dead starlets aboard luxury yachts at parties hosted by prominent celebrities like Fatty Arbuckle. As studio executives discussed Hays's replacement in the spring of 1945, they found a promising candidate in Eric Johnston. With experience in foreign affairs, expertise in business, and strong government connections,

Johnston had a résumé that impressed motion picture industry leaders. A Republican and former president of the Chamber of Commerce, Eric Johnston had gained a national reputation among New Dealers and corporations alike for his labor management skills and his promotion of a "people's capitalism" and a "middle way" for labor and management to compromise with one another. That summer, Louis B. Mayer and the Warner brothers led a group of moguls on a recruitment trip to Washington and convinced Johnston to accept the lucrative post.[32]

During Johnston's time as president of the MPPDA, he brought a strong business sense to Hollywood producers that turned the divisive ideology of anticommunism into concrete gains in the marketplace and the political arena as the entertainment industry became the "ambassador of democracy" in the postwar period. Domestic and international challenges abounded for the native of Spokane, Washington. He faced growing concerns about communist infiltration, labor divides within the industry, antitrust suits from Washington, and international tariffs on Hollywood films that threatened box office receipts. To pursue remedies for these problems, Johnston used his labor management skills and implemented his economic philosophies of cooperation and production to push the government to accept, celebrate, and capitalize on the potential for movies to enhance American prestige and credibility abroad. In the process, Eric Johnston used the rhetoric of anticommunism, which up until 1947 had torn the industry apart, to reassert the essential cultural, economic, and political role of motion pictures in selling the "American way of life" across the globe. This "politics of Americanism" promoted the interests of a struggling industry, advanced a more conservative political philosophy, and rebuilt the political credibility of actors (arguing that their glamour advanced democracy abroad). The end result made Republicans like Eric Johnston and George Murphy happy, as these Cold War campaigns paved the way for the Republican Party's resurgence in the television age.

Johnston accepted the offer from Hollywood executives because he believed in the power of motion pictures to voice American principles of democracy and sell American goods in an international marketplace. Calling it the "most powerful medium for the influencing of people that man has ever built," Johnston believed that "it is no exaggeration to say that the motion picture industry sets the styles for half the world." In his address to Hollywood workers in the summer of 1946, Johnston urged Hollywood to popularize the "doctrine of production" by setting a new style of living and thinking.[33] Moreover, from his own experience, he knew that Hollywood celebrities could sell capitalism and democracy. During World War II,

Johnston had served as an emissary to South America and then Russia on behalf of the U.S. Commission of Inter-American Development. Through these travels, Johnston learned of the power to communicate that motion pictures held throughout the world. He later recounted that in 1944 the only thing the Soviet Union really knew about America came from Hollywood movies. "They knew who Douglas Fairbanks was, and Mary Pickford and Charlie Chaplin," recalled Johnston in 1959. "But, they had no idea really of American leaders."[34] During this trip, Johnston found that Hollywood imagery and personalities formed a common ground between the Soviet Union and the United States and that the "motion picture was a wonderful means of communication," with a potential to play a "leading part" in postwar political understanding between nations.

Johnston's belief in a corporate liberalism intricately connected to Hollywood productions found favor with Republicans in the postwar period, who also sought to find ways to promote the party of big business and reshape the trajectory of a New Deal ideology that had transformed communities across the country.[35] In Hollywood, Eric Johnston faced a volatile community polarized about the New Deal, the role of communism, and labor strikes. On the right, Johnston found an ideological supporter in the MPA. Johnston's view of labor/management cooperation that eliminated labor radicalism and promoted free enterprise aligned with many of the MPA's principles. As the Hollywood Left splintered over issues of labor rights and international relations, the growing Right, though divided over competing definitions of conservatism, began to find commonalities with one another through a shared commitment to anticommunism, individualism, and freedom in the marketplace and on screen.

Moreover, the growing postwar labor disputes strengthened conservatism in Hollywood by highlighting the contradictions and tensions within the industry's New Deal coalition. Studio lots experienced massive strikes and labor unrest in the immediate postwar years as two different unions, the Conference of Studio Unions (CSU) and the International Alliance of Theatrical Stage Employees (IATSE), competed for recognition. The CSU worked to establish a more democratic labor union not corrupted by greedy gangsters and power-hungry industry leaders (the IATSE had historic links to organized crime in Chicago run by Al Capone and Frank Nitti).[36] By 1945, the leader of the CSU, Herb Sorrell, successfully recruited nearly 10,000 members by bringing unorganized laborers into his union and, in doing so, threatened to force studios to raise wages and improve working conditions in ways that the IATSE had failed to do. As the two unions battled for recognition by studio executives, the CSU launched an eight-month strike in early 1945, and studios, in particular Warner Bros., used violence to end the strike.

While the National Labor Relations Board supported the CSU, the labor violence divided the liberal coalition that had unified moderates like Jack Warner with progressives during the war. For Warner, profits trumped his New Deal sympathies, especially in the wake of Roosevelt's death. Warner believed the CSU strike picketed his studio first because the union hoped his past support of labor and the New Deal would ensure a sympathetic ear. But since the strike was about jurisdiction and representation, Warner went against the CSU and refused to recognize the legitimacy of the strike. In response, Warner claimed that radicals like Ring Lardner Jr. sent him threatening telegrams accusing him of bringing in "goons to destroy the union labor."[37] The radicalism and violent tactics further alienated Warner from a New Deal coalition that he had led politically over the past twelve years.

Ronald Reagan also pointed to these strikes as the beginning of his disillusionment with liberalism as he worked within the SAG to develop a compromise between Roy Brewer and Sorrell. At the end of the war, Reagan classified himself as a "hemophilic [sic] liberal" who "bled for causes."[38] Completing his service in the offices of the Army Air Corps, Reagan held high expectations for postwar progress. "If men could cooperate in war," Reagan wrote, "how much better could they work together in peace."[39] The brutal labor conflicts that permeated the motion picture industry in the immediate postwar years shattered Reagan's "make believe" world by introducing him to the reality of communism and its role in creating class conflict. All of this had begun to expose, in Reagan's words, the "seamy side of liberalism."[40]

Unlike Warner and Reagan, both of whom became disillusioned with their New Deal liberalism through the union strikes, Eric Johnston came to his new job determined to curb radical ideas that had been introduced by those he called "quacks and cure-alls." A moderate Republican, Johnston wanted to purge the class-conflict rhetoric, which he saw as destroying the common ground between workers and studio executives.[41] "Nothing gives such unholy joy to the Communists," Johnston declared fervently, "as industrial disorder in the U.S.A."[42] Any type of radical politics on the left threatened his vision of "America Unlimited" because it curbed the power of capitalism by urging government regulation of market relationships. Striking should be a last resort and only rarely used as a tool for negotiation by labor unions, asserted Johnston. While management had the "right to the lockout, they [should] rarely use it," wrote Johnston. Labor should act the same way toward striking because "these are the times when rights can mean ruin."[43] The labor strikes between the IATSE and the CSU, in Johnston's eyes, were both "ridiculous" and "outrageous" because they simply involved a jurisdictional dispute between the two unions, which disagreed over "who should do what work and who should collect dues from whom." Such a disagreement, Johnston argued, made labor strikes seem immoral to the American public, and, more important, they impeded the drive of American success, that is, production. Ridding labor unions of this divisive rhetoric would help maintain a cooperative working relationship in Hollywood studios, which in turn would increase production and profits for all. "If we fortify our democracy to lick want, we'll lick communism—here and abroad," asserted the new movie czar.[44] "Communists can hang all the iron curtains they like," continued Johnston, "but they'll never be able to shut out the story of a land where free men walk without fear and live in abundance."

While the labor strikes splintered liberal networks and strengthened the growing anticommunist sentiments in the industry, Johnston, Ronald Reagan, George Murphy, Robert Montgomery, and Jack Warner all believed that only a small number of communists lived in Hollywood. They testified privately and publicly that communists had not achieved any success in infiltrating the silver screen, and thus they tolerated the 1947 HUAC investigations, even as they were not pleased by what Johnston called the "script-burning, head-hunting and publicity-seeking" investigative tactics used by HUAC.[45] Before, during, and after the hearings, Johnston remained a staunch defender of freedom of the screen. His view of freedom, however, coincided with that of the conservative MPA rather than with the one professed by the more liberal Committee for the First Amendment. He wanted a screen that told the story of American abundance, and he discouraged the production of films like *Grapes of Wrath*, which "deal with the seamy side of American life."[46] Just as he believed that regulations, taxes, and tariffs harmed efficiency in production and slowed down the American economy, he viewed government censorship of the movie screen as both hurting the box office and striking at the core of American democracy by denying freedom of expression and choice for private industries. An "instrument of entertainment," Johnston emphasized that the motion picture now had a role that went beyond sheer entertainment. "Like the press and radio," he argued, "it is a potent purveyor of ideas and information."[47] As Johnston traveled to Washington, D.C., in the fall of 1947, he remained suspicious of the ulterior motives of the HUAC committee. Convinced it wanted publicity and to instill an unrealistic fear of communism in the

American people, Johnston defended his belief in "freedom of speech" even as he took the stand in the old House Office Building.[48]

As Johnston, Warner, and Reagan prepared for their congressional testimonies, the media spectacle they encountered upon their arrival in Washington confirmed their fears that the investigation stemmed from "publicity hunting politicians." Each day of the investigation, spectators competed furiously to claim one of the 300 seats available. Inside the room, stations for three major radio networks, a press table for 120 reporters, Klieg lights, and six newsreel cameras were ready to capture the show. Outside the caucus room, another performance took place. Holding informal press conferences, Humphrey Bogart, Gene Kelly, and Lauren Bacall articulated the opposition they and the Committee for the First Amendment felt toward HUAC and its trampling of the rights of artists in Hollywood. While they mounted a successful critique of the impending hearings, the "friendly" witnesses, who pushed through the crowd with a police escort, went to the center stage of the room to answer questions posed by members of the congressional committee. A freshman Republican congressman from Southern California, Richard Nixon, joined the committee members who had traveled to Los Angeles earlier that spring and Congressman J. Parnell Thomas began the hearings, which he carefully designed for "maximum impact on the public consciousness."[49] With lights and cameras set, it was time for action.

Because they fueled the anticommunist fire that HUAC stoked, MPA members headlined the inquiry and provided dramatic stories that targeted not only suspected communist sympathizers but also liberal celebrities' political activities and social messages in film. The FBI criticized the HUAC investigation for its "shoddy" research because it relied on stories, not facts. Even leading Republicans, like former and future presidential nominee Thomas Dewey and Speaker of the House Joseph Martin, urged Congressman Thomas to stop the hearings. While they too did not like the spread of New Deal propaganda during war, they feared the hearings would appear as a "Republican witch hunt," which could hurt their chances for election the following year.[50] But having already undergone unsuccessful attempts to attack Hollywood liberalism and openness to New Deal propaganda during his efforts as part of the Dies Committee, Thomas refused to back down, especially now that he had eager and vocal hardliners from the MPA ready to testify.

Like the Dies and Nye committees before it had done, the HUAC investigators did not take the time to watch the alleged communist-inspired movies and discuss their merits. Rather, the committee focused attention on discussing the power of celebrity and entertainment to blind and manipulate audiences. James McGuinness told the committee that the Communist Party had already capitalized on the draw of celebrity by using big name stars to sell its ideology. "Glamour is appealing," explained McGuinness. "The communists have made very shrewd and excellent use of that for their purpose."[51] McGuinness further discussed how organizations like the Hollywood Anti-Nazi League and the Joint Anti-Fascist Refugee League and fund-raisers for ambulances and orphans during the Spanish Civil War took advantage of Hollywood's philanthropic tendency to use star names and money to fund the Communist Party. Celebrities could also use their glamour and status to obtain secrets for Moscow and hurt the national interests of the country, claimed writer, film critic, and witness John C. Moffitt. He noted how various left-wing stars would "bedazzle" military officials and young scientists. By taking them to expensive restaurants and surrounding them with the glitz of Hollywood, communist actors could "induce" government officials to "a state of mind where they might disclose information entrusted to them, and that such disclosures would be detrimental to the national defense."[52] This generalized accusation revealed a suspicion and even a fear of the potential power that celebrity and glamour held to manipulate ordinary citizens.

The hearings also discussed the various ways that film could promote or subvert democracy and capitalism with even brief moments of propaganda. To show the attempt of communists to promote the party line, Moffitt named several movies that contained one moment of the "ya-ya editorial," a "technique by which you in the strongest and most specific terms possible level accusations against the existing form of government and the existing way of life."[53] Quickly following the moment, Moffitt claimed, the writer would insert a patriotic speech that "convinces nobody" to protect them from suspicion. As an example, Moffitt discussed Warner Bros. wartime production *Pride of the Marines*, written by Albert Maltz (the soon-to-be blacklisted writer)—whom Moffitt described as an expert at inserting the "ya-ya editorial." The witness pointed to a hospital scene when injured soldiers discussed the racial discrimination that permeated the United States but did not provide any conclusive answer about how to combat American prejudices. "The inference of the scene," explained Moffitt, "was that there was absolutely no answer to this except flag waving." Ultimately, Moffitt and other witnesses over the course of the hearings argued that communist subversion in film was subtle but powerful because of the use of imagery and symbols. Actor Adolphe Menjou saw the class struggles in the Academy Award–winning film *The Best Years of Our Lives*—an exploration of the challenges veterans faced as they returned home from war—as another example of a dangerous film that combined "superb entertainment" with a criticism of American class structures. Menjou argued that "if it is good entertainment, it is dangerous, because then the people will go see it, many people are not conscious of it."[54] Slowly, these Hollywood anticommunists believed, communist writers would force Americans to question and lose faith in the structures of government.

Wartime records emerged as another hot topic during the hearings. Jack Warner defended the war effort of the industry overall and his studio in particular. As he faced the congressmen, he made "no apologies" for any of the movies produced for the war effort, including the controversial film *Mission to Moscow*, which cast Russian war efforts in a favorable light.[55] Arguing that the film helped promote goodwill at a time when the government felt Stalin suspected the depth of American commitment to the European theater of war, Warner described the coordination that occurred between his studio and the Roosevelt administration. Robert Taylor also recounted the wartime pressures on studios from the government in his experience with playing the male lead in *Song of Russia*. Lowell Mellett had urged Taylor to accept the role, which romanticized Russian society and softened the differences between the United States and Russia.[56] *Song of Russia*, *North Star*, and *Mission to Moscow* all came under investigation, and not only for their positive portrayals of the country's wartime ally. It was further charged that the production of these movies stemmed from a deliberate collaboration between government officials and studios to infuse theatrical productions with a higher political purpose. After focusing on the process by which the entertainment industry and government collaborated during the war, Congressman McDowell emphasized his belief that "pictures ought to stay in the pure field of entertainment" and not mix with politics.[57]

The question of entertainment's role in politics was hotly debated inside and outside the old House Office Building. Inside, men like Eric Johnston, Jack Warner, Louis B. Mayer, and Ronald Reagan focused on Hollywood's political integrity and rights for freedom on the screen. As the president of the SAG, Ronald Reagan occupied the stand in a conservative double-breasted brown suit, quoted Thomas Jefferson, and encouraged motion pictures to fulfill their role of keeping the American people informed with "all the facts." Reagan ended his testimony by urging his country to never "compromise with any of our democratic principles through fear or resentment."[58] Louis B. Mayer insisted that he had always "sought to maintain the use of the screen for public good" and that studios alone should be responsible for silver screen content.[59] Johnston also warned the committee against any attempt to censor the screen. Calling the sensationalism of the investigation "grossly unfair to a great American industry," Johnston further criticized the committee for using laws, intimidation, or coercion to "choke off free speech or seriously curtail it."[60] With his quick wit, Eric Johnston also offered a subtle indictment of the HUAC investigators by frequently responding to committee members with what *Variety* called "snappy comebacks" that handed investigators "five yard losses."[61] At one moment, after Robert Stripling had "ridden Johnston raw" when the movie czar explained how the decency clause guided self-censorship in the industry, Johnston quipped dryly to the head investigator, "That's about sex. You've heard of that I presume."

More than anything, industry executives feared that the HUAC hearings would stir up public criticism of the industry's self-censorship policy and reinvigorate past debates about the need for federal censorship. After the movie stars left Washington, Johnston, Warner, Mayer, and other industry leaders had to confront four issues: what to do about the "Hollywood Ten," whom Congress had cited for contempt for refusing to answer questions about their political affiliation; how Hollywood, as an industry, should deal with the question of communist employees; how to restore public faith in the industry; and, most important, how to improve lagging box office profits. As the industry leaders gathered in New York in November, they first decided to dismiss the "Hollywood Ten" from studio employment, not because of accusations of communist leanings, but rather, executives argued, because they violated the morality clauses of their contracts. As Johnston later recalled, "Their contracts were severed because we thought they had brought disrepute upon the industry by going to jail," not because of their political beliefs.[62] To deal with the broader issues of communism, studio executives promised to "not knowingly employ a Communist," a practice that newspapers, television networks, universities, and numerous other employers would adopt over the next few years.[63]

The issue of motion picture content and celebrity political activity remained a more difficult question. Over the course of the investigations, Stripling asked each witness why studios had not produced anticommunist films. To remedy this, he and J. Parnell Thomas attempted to outline possible ways that cooperation between Hollywood and government could exist. After questioning "friendly" witnesses about the attempts of communists to secretly insert images of class struggle into movies, Chairman Thomas frequently concluded by asking the witness for personal thoughts on the future production of anticommunist films. "Don't you think," Thomas asked Gary Cooper, among others, "that it would be a good idea now if the moving picture industry produced anti-Communist films showing the dangers of Communism in the United States?"[64] Despite the constant claim among HUAC investigators that politics and entertainment "don't mix," they continued to propose ways to transform the motion picture industry into a vehicle to advance anticommunist messages, with which they agreed ideologically

MPA witnesses reiterated the conservative message that had floundered during the 1944 election but had won the national publicity campaign with the HUAC hearings and the broader Cold War. Gary Cooper responded that more pictures should be made about "what really is Americanism." The American people, according to Cooper, needed to be "resold" on the "idea of what we have got in this country, which is the finest thing in the world." Another member of the MPA, Robert Taylor, agreed with Cooper. Taylor urged actors to combat communism by articulating Americanism on the screen. Evaluating script potential from the standpoint of entertainment rather than propaganda would not only eliminate communist propaganda but also "promote a lot of good Americana because the stories that have entertainment 99 times out of 100 are good American stories."[65] The opinions of Cooper and Taylor on the stand would resonate in the post-HUAC Hollywood world, where liberal-message films lost their place in the studio production room to a conservative style of entertainment that took on the political responsibility of defining and promoting "Americanism."

Becoming Ambassadors of Democracy

In February 1948, Lillian Ross penned an article for the *New Yorker* magazine that discussed the repercussions of HUAC in Hollywood. "Hollywood," she began, "is baffled by the question of what the Committee on Un-American Activities wants from it."[66] A nervousness pervaded "business as usual" in the industry, and a political self-consciousness imbued social functions, where guests splintered into "sub-groups, each eyeing the others with rather friendly suspicion and discussion of who was or was not a guest at the White House when Roosevelt was President—one of the few criteria people in the film industry have set up for judging whether a person is or is not a communist." Studios forbade partisan discussions on the lot and shut doors of employment to well-known leftist writers. The liberal political networks had crumbled, and Democratic politicians distanced themselves from those supporters who had brought dramatic publicity innovations just four years earlier.

Historians have retold this story of fear, insecurity, and division when explaining how the studio system collapsed.[67] The HUAC hearings placed the entertainment industry on trial and forced Americans across the country to wonder if their box office dollars had funded the Communist Party. After a successful box office year in 1946, which broke records for audience attendance at movies, 1947 ushered in a decline in audience numbers, showing a loss in patronage for the first time since the Great Depression.[68] In the hope of reviving its domestic film industry, Great Britain imposed a tax on American imported films that gave 75 percent of profits to the British exchequer. By effectively closing the profitable British market to American films, the tax threatened to lower the revenue of the entire industry by 20 percent, which would, in the view of Samuel Goldwyn, bring "the complete end of independent motion picture production."[69] By the end of the year, it became clear that the pending Justice Department antitrust decision would render a crushing verdict to the industry. The following May, the Supreme Court ruled, in *United States v. Paramount Pictures*, that the vertical integration that had linked production, distribution, and exhibition violated the country's antitrust laws.

The advent of television and the rise of suburban neighborhoods also stood as a threat to the industry, as the new technology offered other entertainment opportunities outside the movie theater. And yet, while the dominant narrative of Hollywood portrays an industry on the verge of collapse in the postwar period, in this new business environment opportunities abounded for politically ambitious actors to craft a new role for their profession, and themselves, in American society. In fact, the instability Hollywood faced in the midst of these changes motivated industry leaders to explore new areas for professional advancement. The broader crusade against communism made the industry central in crafting foreign policy and articulating a conservative social and economic philosophy that would open new markets abroad while also reinvigorating the Republican Party with the structures and lessons cultivated in the studio system at home.[70]

Soon after the hearings, MPA member Ayn Rand penned a new *Screen Guide for Americans* that the MPA widely distributed to Hollywood producers, directors, writers, and actors. This screen guide helped to unite the MPA with Eric Johnston's economic philosophies of a people's capitalism while also providing an ideological link for Hollywood conservatives to join with free-market conservatives across the country. As a right-wing response to the control that the Left had gained over Hollywood productions through World War II and the OWI motion picture manual, Rand developed thirteen principles for producers and executives to be aware of as they evaluated scripts. The first, "don't take politics lightly," reinforced Rand's belief that "politics is not a separate field in itself." Rand saw every picture as supporting one side or the other of the ideological Cold War of capitalism versus communism. Freedom and democracy, proclaimed the guide, would follow the success of the free enterprise system because Americanism was "inseparable" from it, "like body and soul." Seeing the pillars of society as "individual rights, individual freedom, private action, private initiative, and private property," the guide urged producers to not smear "the free enterprise system," "industrialists," "wealth," "the profit motive," "success," or the "independent man."

Glorifying the "collective" or the "common man" also threatened important social ideals of individual initiative and private business, and the guide drew an important distinction between cooperation and collectivism. Cooperation was the cornerstone of American society—"the free association of men who work together by voluntary agreement, each deriving from it his own personal benefit." However, naive producers could confuse this important aspect of capitalism with collectivism—"the forced herding together of men into a group, with the individual having no choice about it, no personal motive, no personal reward, and subordinating himself blindly to the will of others." Rand's personal philosophy, and one of the underlying tenets of the guide, urged Hollywood to correct the negative view of money, self-interest, and profit that the Great Depression and Franklin Roosevelt had popularized during the previous two decades. "Put an end to that pernicious modern hypocrisy," begged the guide. "Everybody wants to get rich and almost everybody feels that he must apologize for it."[71]

MPA members eagerly mailed and handed out the pamphlet, which one critic called the "raw iron from which a new curtain around Hollywood would be fashioned."[72] While the guide remained only a voluntary code for studio productions, producers reading scripts found themselves adhering to it as a new form of self-censorship. "It's automatic, like shifting gears," one studio executive told Lillian Ross. "I now read scripts through the eyes of the DAR [Daughters of the American Revolution]."[73] Though framed in the language of Americanism, the guide, as well as the organization that produced it, actively used fear of communism to undo the political developments of the New Deal period and also to encourage a new type of political activism of defining America through images in Hollywood.[74] Through seemingly nonpartisan words of Americanism, Hollywood became a powerful force in reinserting business and the rhetoric of capitalism and individualism back into American politics and culture.

Eric Johnston, the HUAC hearings, the MPA, and its *Screen Guide for Americans* all gave Hollywood the responsibility not only to produce entertainment but also to actively preserve American freedom by spreading the principles of the free market. Ideologies and motives varied. The HUAC committee members sought publicity to enhance their popularity in the next election year. Eric Johnston strove to protect his new industry from censorship and in the process found an opportunity to preach his ideology of individualism and his belief in cooperation, not coercion. A range of concerns regarding labor unions, film content, and the wartime expansion of Hollywood's liberal/radical activism inspired MPA members to join the anticommunist crusade and construct new political networks for the Republican Party.[75] Lela Rogers traveled through Southern California stumping for the party while preaching the MPA's message of Americanism. The overwhelming financial response she received at fund-raising dinners following the HUAC hearings gave Rogers hope for Republican victories in the upcoming 1948 elections.[76] Passionate about the principles of private enterprise, Ayn Rand worked to make Hollywood's post-HUAC makeover coincide with the views of anti–New Deal businessmen like Leonard Read and W. C. Mullendore, the ideological inspiration behind the Foundation for Economic Education, a conservative think tank dedicated to spreading the gospel of free enterprise.[77]

While the motivations of conservative activists ranged from ideological to partisan to pragmatic, the growth of a conservatism grounded in the rhetoric of anticommunism and driven by concerns over the changing economic structures of the industry and fears of its decline in public opinion shaped new opportunities for collaboration with anticommunist politicians. Nonpartisan organizations like the Motion Picture Industry Council (MPIC) aimed to overcome the political polarization that had plagued the industry since 1944 in a common effort to salvage Hollywood's reputation. In an active effort to rebrand the meaning of entertainment and the public role of celebrities following the HUAC hearings, MPIC built on the many government connections the industry had forged through the OWI during World War II and worked to ward off criticisms by congressional Republicans that links between the industry and government necessarily produced "New Deal propaganda." MPIC organizers worked with Truman's head of the Office of War Mobilization and Reconversion, John Steelman, to develop a long-term link between the industry and government, which in the postwar period was to depend only on voluntary collaboration to give the industry political and economic benefits.

Through the MPIC, Eric Johnston worked with industry leaders to rees-
tablish Hollywood's prestige in the postwar world in a way that would join
his economic philosophies with the MPA's principles while also forcing the
Truman administration to make a permanent place for the industry in the
ideological Cold War battle against communism.[78] Firmly committed to
anticommunism and the economic interests of the industry, Roy Brewer,
Walter Wanger, and Dore Schary put former ideological differences aside
to reunite a divided Hollywood. Aware that the industry's economic prosperity, social prestige, and political power depended upon respect for
celebrities in American civic life, the MPIC focused on a public relations
campaign to enhance the image and credibility of Hollywood. Exhibitors
and distributors joined producers in a public campaign to promote the
"good" side of Hollywood, ward off local and state censorship efforts, and
expand the appeal of films at home and abroad. To do this, MPIC leaders
focused on ways to integrate entertainment in public life at the grassroots
level as well as in the international struggle for democracy. Walter Wanger
urged celebrities to "take more interest in civic affairs." If individuals asso-
ciated with Hollywood could gain the respect of their local communities,
"the rest of the people would not be so hard to conquer."[79]

Wanger saw the motion picture industry as "not only . . . a major economic enterprise, but also . . . an important social institution."[80] As in his
battles with isolationists before the war, he realized that only through an
active media campaign would politicians and the public appreciate the social, cultural, and political legitimacy of the industry. By planting articles,
such as one in *Kiplinger Magazine*, the MPIC went on a public relations
campaign to "fight back" against negative reports and popular criticism
of celebrities. "The film people," announced the article, "are fed up with
criticism of their morals, politics, and pictures." For those who assert that
Hollywood "is immoral, dominated by the Reds, subservient to Wall Street,
trembling before the onslaught of television, and lacking the guts to turn
out good pictures, their answer is simple: Look to the facts."[81] The article
then released statistics compiled by the MPIC research wing about its di-
vorce rates, educational achievements, charity contributions, and political
affiliations. Comparing the statistical averages in Hollywood, declared the
article, showed Tinseltown to be just like any other town. The difference,
proposed the magazine, was the "Stromboli complex": the great number
of press correspondents looking for scandals and publicity at the expense
of telling the truth about Hollywood.

In a massive public relations surge, studios joined together through
organizations like the MPIC to flood media outlets in an effort to expand

During the Cold War, many opportunities arose for Hollywood entertainers to perform for the armed forces and sell the "American Way" abroad, in the process celebrating their role in spreading democracy. Here performers stage a live performance recording for the Armed Forces Radio Service in 1950. Standing in the front row, from left to right: actor Frank Morgan, actress and singer Judy Garland, three unidentified actresses, actor and comedian Bob Hope, actor and comedian Jerry Colonna, actor and comedian Jimmy Durante, and actor and singer Frank Sinatra. Live Performancy by the Armed Forces Radio Service, courtesy of the Harry S. Truman Library.

audience interest in Hollywood personalities and clear up misconceptions about the influence of communists or other unfit role models on the screen. Driven by a concern for lagging box office returns, the MPIC decided to work with studios to embark on a "Movietime U.S.A." tour to revive the industry by emphasizing its political, economic, and cultural role in American civic life. Eric Johnston, Ronald Reagan, George Murphy, and Walter Wanger led the Movietime U.S.A. offensive, which encouraged organizations such as "Rotary, Lions, Kiwanis, Veterans' organizations, PTA clubs, Knights of Columbus, women's clubs and even churches of every denomination through personal contact" to raise their awareness about the importance of the motion picture industry in their local towns.[82] As they joked about the ridiculous Hollywood stories made popular by "rabble-rousers," "rumor mongers," and "self-seekers" about "legends of leopard-skin couches and incense," speakers refuted these stories and disseminated the basic message of the good moral nature of Hollywood.[83] Through the MPIC public relations campaigns, celebrity surrogates promoted the importance of religion, volunteerism, the free market, consumption, and, of course, anticommunism in American life.

More than any other element, however, anticommunism helped the industry forge a link with national politics in a way that further institutionalized entertainment in the political process. The anticommunism campaign began as a way to defend the industry from the negative reputation incurred during the HUAC hearings before it developed into a way to promote its economic interests through the rhetoric of preserving democracy and freedom abroad. Introduced as "screen actor by profession, Red-fighter by choice," Ronald Reagan spoke to a Kiwanis International Club in St. Louis about how he "assumed command," "struck back at the Commies," and "led some 35,000 film employees to a notable victory." Reagan and his friend and colleague Eric Johnston emphasized the important role of Hollywood as democracy's guardians at home and its "ambassadors abroad." Prominent entertainers went on speaking tours to extol the diplomatic virtues of the industry, which successfully highlighted values of individualism and consumption to its viewers across the world.[84] Reports came in from countries on both sides of the Iron Curtain about the power of Hollywood productions in selling the high quality of life possible under democratic leadership.[85] In 1953, Representative Joseph F. Holt (R-Calif.) told Congress that if it had not been for the "unheralded services of Hollywood" in spreading American goodwill, and the luxuries and benefits of the American way of life, through entertainment and not "obvious indoctrination," the diplomatic war against communism would already have been lost.[86]

While Holt exaggerated the role of Hollywood in singlehandedly winning the Cold War in 1953, he was correct in the key role that entertainment played in the ideological battle for people's minds. The new type of warfare—which used sales, advertising, and emotion rather than traditional military battles—depended on Hollywood's unique talent to sell ideas and values through motion pictures. Ralph Block, a former screenwriter and member of Hollywood for Roosevelt, explained the importance of "propaganda" from his post–World War II position as a member of the Department of State's Office of Information. Propaganda, he explained, "has increasingly overshadowed diplomacy as an instrument for influencing the course of international events."[87] As an Iron Curtain divided European countries, a new act opened in Hollywood politics that brought show business strategies to the rising conservative movement and linked free-market philosophies with morality concerns under the guise of anticommunism. Not surprisingly, the financial roots and ideological growth of this movement took place first in Southern California through an embrace of these communication and "cultural engagement" strategies rooted in Hollywood studios.[88]

Not everyone supported the connection between the entertainment industry and the Cold War state. Many liberal opponents of HUAC and the MPA, from HICCASP members to those who formed the Committee for the First Amendment, refused to cooperate with industry leaders in fighting the Cold War. Ralph Block noted how "uneasy" the American public remained about the political reliance on information and the media to wage battles abroad. He surmised that "it is possible that more Americans approve of the use of the atom bomb in defensive warfare than approve the use of propaganda to forestall war."[89] But within this controversial and anxiety-filled atmosphere, entertainers who joined the Cold War propaganda battle found new opportunities within the Truman and Eisenhower administrations to shape national policies and promote the interests of the industry.

Consider, for example, Walter Wanger's political journey, which provides insight into both the shifting political opportunities afforded celebrities and the broader transformation of the meaning of entertainment in American politics and culture. Starting in 1938, Walter Wanger defied the usual assumption that Hollywood films were merely "simple, clean entertainment," lacking in educational and enlightenment value. His films dealt with international issues of the Spanish Civil War and showcased the horrors of fascism abroad. Two years later, as president of the Academy of Motion Pictures, he became close to Lowell Mellett and advocated for President Roosevelt to support the idea that entertainment could play an essential role in informing and educating people across the world of the international dangers of totalitarian rule. During the war, Wanger brought his message about the power of entertainment to sell wartime messages to Congress, and he urged its members to allow producers to accept Hollywood professionals as legitimate partners in the war effort. When the MPA attacked the liberalism of the OWI, the Writers' Congress, and the HFWA, Wanger again led a defense of the industry, its political activism, and the shift toward "message films" to win the war and pave the way for the peace. As a member of the HDC and the president of the HFWA, Wanger embodied the diligence with which individuals within Hollywood worked to actively change the interpretation of "entertainment" that reigned in the

1930s and also develop political networks that could influence local, state, and national policies.

Six years after Wanger had harangued the MPA for its anti-Semitism, irresponsibility, and unpatriotic assertions of communist subversion in the industry, the producer accepted the local leadership of the Southern California Crusade for Freedom and wrote a letter to the MPA that apologized for these earlier criticisms. He explained that communists had manipulated his wartime comments in a way he "never expected" and that he "was guilty of wishful thinking as was many another who hoped that Russia, then our ally, could be made into a friendly neighbor."[90] Now that the MPA's warnings of attempts at communist manipulation had proven to be true, Wanger hoped to "shovel the earth over the dead issue."

Walter Wanger's transition from vocal interventionist to liberal wartime activist to strident anticommunist parallels the broader transformations of the industry since the 1930s and illuminates how the pressures of the Cold War transformed political rhetoric and limited the types of activism available to entertainers, who were dependent on public goodwill and audience loyalty for their economic success. Embracing anticommunism opened up new opportunities for political collaborations, which had personal, professional, and economic benefits for pragmatic entertainers. Cold War institutional collaborations through organizations like the MPIC brought benefits to those who embraced the anticommunist rhetoric and, in the process, laid the groundwork for reestablishing the Republican Party in Hollywood as a political force with the patriotic rhetoric of Americanism. Throughout the 1950s, men like Ronald Reagan, Jack Warner, and Sam Goldwyn would move toward the Republican Party for several reasons. Roosevelt's death and the labor strikes disillusioned their New Deal loyalties, and anticommunism became a practical rhetorical embrace for an industry that had to cater to public opinion during the Cold War. Dwight Eisenhower, like Roosevelt before him, made personal appeals to these entertainers while also supporting international and domestic policies that helped the struggling studios during the 1950s. However, unlike the DNC, which feared that collaboration with entertainers would bring on accusations of communist propaganda as it had in the 1940s, the Republican Party saw how collaboration with the industry during the Cold War could benefit partisan campaigns, especially as the party struggled to adjust to the possibilities of television. During the Cold War, entertainment became a staple of American foreign policy, resulting in the legitimization of the practices, styles, and expertise of Hollywood personalities in ways that made advertisers and consultants look to California politics as they struggled to adapt to the "television age."

CHAPTER FIVE

Building a Star System in Politics

On Wednesday, June 4, 1952, the town of Abilene, Kansas, prepared for what the *New York Times* called its "biggest event since the Union Pacific arrived just after the Civil War."[1] Over 100,000 visitors crammed the streets, which Abilene had decorated with colorful red, white, and blue banners, balloons, and huge posters welcoming home the guest of honor. Tens of thousands cheered, and the school band played jubilantly when beloved military general Dwight D. Eisenhower walked off the train toward a long dusty dirt road that led to his childhood home. Having just relinquished his post at NATO and offered a resignation of his position as president of Columbia University, Eisenhower formally left the military establishment that he had famously led during and after World War II.[2] Amid signs that proclaimed "Ike for President," the "most favorite son Kansas ever had" returned home to deliver his first political speech as a contender for the Republican Party's presidential nomination.[3]

On that summer day, journalists and photographers joined news reporters and camera crews to report on Eisenhower's much anticipated speech. Citizens for Eisenhower, a volunteer organization run by some of Eisenhower's wealthy friends in the advertising and television industry from New York City, saw the political potential in broadcasting the Republican's first speech as a contender for the presidency and organized a costly maze of telegraph, telephone, radio, and television cables.[4] In living rooms across the country, Americans shared in the excitement of the frenzied event as they sat around televisions to hear where the popular general actually stood politically on the pressing issues of this election year. In the newly dedicated Eisenhower Park in Abilene, over 15,000 people gathered in the sport and picnic arena to witness the speech.

As the evening approached, so too did the rain. The television cameras had a safe haven in a nearby barn, but the crowd withstood the wetness and the mud. Touched by such perseverance, Eisenhower refused suggestions that he deliver his speech to cameras in the barns. He wanted to talk with his loyal supporters gathered in Abilene. Cameras rolled as Eisenhower walked to the podium with each page of his speech carefully protected from the rain. Thunder rumbled in the background, rain came down in sheets, and a vicious wind blew the few strands of hair Eisenhower had. Television viewers watched a soaking-wet presidential hopeful in a clear plastic raincoat discuss his stance on foreign policy, taxes, and civil rights while water dripped from his glasses.[5]

Two viewers in particular were appalled by what they saw on their television screens: Bruce Barton, a senior partner in the advertising firm Batten, Barton, Durstine & Osborn (BBD&O), and Robert Montgomery, a Hollywood actor and former president of the SAG. In the message and in the medium, both men saw Eisenhower as succumbing to the traditional style of Republican campaigning—electoral appeals to party operatives and interest group leaders rather than to the broader public.[6] As political scientist Samuel Lubell had observed several months earlier in his book, *The Future of American Politics*, the Republican Party in 1952 remained "fundamentally unchanged, trapped by its own inner contradictions."[7] To win the election, Lubell wrote that the party needed to "transform itself." Both Barton and Montgomery saw television as an opportunity for Eisenhower to do just that. Through television, Eisenhower could build a new Republican coalition by persuading a growing and unorganized middle class to cross party lines and vote for the popular general. Each man frantically urged Eisenhower to throw the standard Republican electoral strategy to the wind and embrace the age of the mass media, an approach that would require the expertise of both of them.[8]

Several weeks later, Eisenhower defeated Robert Taft in the Republican race for the nomination. As he prepared for the national campaign against the party that had held the White House for the last twenty years, he had a decision to make. Would Eisenhower follow Thomas Dewey's strategy and respond to demands from and negotiations with factions within the party? Or would he listen to Barton and Montgomery and embrace the political possibilities of television? Would he appeal to voters as "blocs" defined by region or economic interests, or would he engage them as "media consumers"?[9] The popular and memorable 1950s campaign slogan, "I like Ike," has continued to evoke ideas of a one-dimensional campaign in which a famous World War II general captured the political support of the nation during a time of domestic consensus. But the simplicity of the slogan, its lasting charm, and its appeal across voter lines all show the path Eisenhower chose.[10] Following what Robert Montgomery would later term the "Abilene debacle," the general worked closely with Hollywood figures and advertisers to navigate the new mass medium of television to transform political communication and the Republican Party during the 1950s. In the process, Eisenhower's administration moved away from the divisive party politics that had plagued previous Republican presidential campaigns and, instead, thrust the party into the new era of mass media, which depended on the knowledge and expertise of professional image makers, from both Madison Avenue and Hollywood.[11]

During the 1950s, Hollywood Republicans engaged in electoral politics that not only helped Ike win the presidency but also started to remake the executive branch and the Republican Party in the image of Hollywood studios by finding opportunities to cast the president as the nation's "leading man."[12] Hollywood's "electoral politics" began with Louis B. Mayer and his efforts to urge Herbert Hoover to incorporate glitz, glamour, and the media into his election campaigns.[13] But while Hoover saw Mayer's suggestions as a sideshow to winning elections, twenty-four years later Eisenhower gave central importance to using the mass media to attract a wider range of voters in order to create a Republican majority.[14] The introduction of television in 1952 dramatically escalated a working relationship between Eisenhower and professionals on both coasts to make presidential politics a prime-time television event.[15]

Advertising executives from BBD&O and the Young & Rubicam advertising agency (Y&R) transformed Cold War propaganda efforts and personal friendships with Eisenhower into institutional partisan collaborations among Hollywood studios, Madison Avenue, and the Republican Party. Historians, political scientists, and media scholars have examined how the growth of television facilitated the flourishing of political advertising in the 1950s. Scholars have examined how the commodification of candidates on television dramatically escalated campaign costs, "homogenized American politics," and exploited emotional, and increasingly negative, themes at the expense of democratic and rational discussion.[16] Moreover, political advertising in the 1950s aided the rise of political consultants and pollsters. Overwhelmed by advances in campaign technology, candidates felt they needed to hire professionals to craft "artful" and effective media in order to have any chance at electoral success. By turning to advertisers for support, Eisenhower strengthened a growing link between publicity experts and politicians, which would soon dominate

With the guidance of Hollywood entertainers, a prime-time television studio began to take shape at 1600 Pennsylvania Avenue, with Robert Montgomery and President Eisenhower at center stage. Here Eisenhower prepares with Montgomery for his address to the nation on the situation regarding the integration of schools in Little Rock, Arkansas, September 24, 1957. Courtesy of Dwight D. Eisenhower Presidential Library.

the political process, as the age of the political machine gave way to the age of the consultant.[17]

And yet this narrative overlooks the role of Hollywood in paving the way for and shaping this process. Newly empowered consultants turned to California and the Hollywood studio system for lessons on how to navigate the mass media terrain. Moreover, actors like George Murphy and Robert Montgomery generally appear only in passing, but these two men led the Hollywood Republican mobilization in 1952 that motivated key figures, including Samuel Goldwyn, Ronald Reagan, and Jack Warner, to abandon their New Deal loyalties and embrace the potential economic and partisan rewards offered by the party of big business.[18] By the 1956 campaign, the Citizens for Eisenhower Committee had developed a national coordination between celebrity talent and advertising firms that used Hollywood style and technical skills to encourage voter turnout and influence ballot box decisions. During the Cold War, Hollywood had sold American ideals abroad, but under the Eisenhower administration, celebrities sold Hollywood tactics to politicians, who eagerly consumed the lessons to attract a media-hungry public. The visions that Louis B. Mayer had for the use of entertainment and the mass media to reinvigorate the GOP in the 1920s finally took shape.

Hollywood and Madison Avenue Like Ike, and Each Other

Television drastically altered the political landscape during the early 1950s. Only 2.9 percent of families had owned television sets in 1948, but television sales had resulted in an astonishing 52 million sets by 1953. By 1956, over 80 percent of families had one as a centerpiece in their living rooms.[19] This dramatic growth forced politicians to grapple with the anxiety-ridden implications of the new medium—how to present themselves and their policies through celluloid images rather than newspaper articles or radio broadcasts.[20] During the 1956 campaign, both Democrats and Republicans turned to television as a political tool to sell policies and personalities, but in very different ways. The Democratic presidential nominee in 1952 and 1956, Adlai Stevenson, looked with disdain on the new medium, which sold presidential candidates as commodities. "The idea that you can merchandise candidates for high office like breakfast cereal," Stevenson remarked bitterly, "is, I think, the ultimate indignity to the democratic process."[21] Wanting to discuss issues and deliver eloquent speeches rather than make television spot commercials, Stevenson refused to listen to his media advisers.[22] On the other hand, Ike listened, however grudgingly, to men like Montgomery and Barton.

The actor and the advertising executive, like their respective industries, had long been involved in American politics. Barton and his advertising firm had offered publicity advice to Republican presidential contenders beginning with Calvin Coolidge in 1924. Donating money and talent, the firm urged Republicans to make use of the mass media, from radio to television, to attract new voters into the party. Yet much of their advice went unheeded, and the Republican Party struggled to compete with a media-savvy Franklin Roosevelt, an economic depression in which big businesses lost respect, and a powerful New Deal coalition backed by labor interests and with a southern dominance. Like Hollywood, advertising as an industry worked to overcome a social stigma, and advertisers also asserted their civic role and patriotism during World War II.[23] Just as the war proved to be a boon for big business and the motion picture industry, so too did it propel advertising, as powerful firms grew along New York City's famous Madison Avenue in the postwar period. But, as with Hollywood, economic success did not guarantee political authority. During the 1948 election, the Republican presidential candidate, Thomas Dewey, listened to advisers who saw BBD&O as a direct threat to their political power. As a result, Republican Party operatives frequently tried to shield the candidate from Bruce Barton.[24]

Actor Robert Montgomery had likewise been a disciple of the Hollywood Republican tradition begun by Louis B. Mayer. A new convert to the party in 1940, Montgomery joined George Murphy in Willkie's and Dewey's campaigns. Anticommunism also attracted him to the party as Montgomery joined Reagan and Johnston in their travels to the "friendly" HUAC hearings. In 1948, Montgomery became vice president of the Hollywood Republican Party under George Murphy. The two men worked to deliver California votes and stage publicity opportunities across the state for Dewey. These stars attempted to make Dewey more palatable as a public figure to voters. Murphy encouraged the nominee to "spill gravy on your vest" and "fluff" while answering questions, in order to make him appear more human. But Dewey dismissed many of these suggestions or, like Hoover before him, saw them as unimportant. Hollywood insiders in the California Republican Party still remained political outsiders on a national level.[25]

Amid the dramatic growth of television, Eisenhower changed this dynamic as he made admen, television executives, and prominent Hollywood figures a part of his inner circle, which ultimately brought economic, partisan, and professional advantage for those involved. Robert Montgomery soon signed on as Eisenhower's television adviser, and George Murphy served as his liaison to studio executives and California Republican networks (and money).[26] Bruce Barton and his company, BBD&O, happily accepted the Republican Party account for the 1952 election, ultimately giving the firm official control in crafting the television and radio portions of the campaign. The various partners developed a strong relationship with the candidate, and Eisenhower listened to the information, which, he acknowledged, were "things that I should have been told at the start and that nobody told me."[27] Barton and his partner Ben Duffy explained to Eisenhower the different television strategies that he should employ over the course of the campaign. They encouraged the candidate to use notes rather than reading from a script in order to show the candidate as "talking to people as one frank, unassuming American to his fellow Americans."[28]

Perhaps nothing conveyed this desire for a carefully crafted honesty and openness with television as well as the spot program that Rosser Reeves designed, "Eisenhower Answers America." Duffy and Barton were not the only advertising men eager to jump on the Eisenhower bandwagon and usher the Republican Party into the media age. Advertising histories frequently retell the story of the wealthy Republican oilmen who decided on the golf course during the summer of 1952 to hire the advertising hotshot from the Ted Bates Company, Rosser Reeves, to combat the Democratic slogan that had given Truman an edge in 1948: "You Never Had It So Good!"[29] Reeves developed a concept that would integrate Barton's advice and assert the importance of advertisers in the campaign process. Selling the plan to the RNC and the candidate himself, Reeves explained the democratic potential of short-spot television advertisements to "stimulate voters to go to the polls and vote for the candidate."[30] Emphasizing how television could represent the "essence of democracy" by informing the electorate through twenty- or thirty-second "spots," Reeves ultimately convinced Eisenhower to accept the political spot advertisement campaign, "Eisenhower Answers America," over lunch.

The Republican Party did not simply come to embrace the television age with just one lunch, however. Hollywood entertainers had already begun the process that admen further engrained in American politics during the 1950s. In Hollywood, advertisers, consultants, and studio executives dominated the 1934 gubernatorial election. A decade later, during electoral contests across the state, liberal celebrities collaborated with advertisers to make entertaining short radio spots that spurred voters to action, an important lesson remembered by not only bitter Hollywood Republicans like George Murphy and Robert Montgomery but also New Deal Democrats like Jack Warner, who became disgruntled and unhappy with the party in 1952. Madison Avenue and Hollywood had a mutually dependent relationship that, with the political demands begot by television, took shape more formally in 1952 and would result in intimate collaboration four years later. While advertisers focused on selling a message—drafting storyboards, constructing catchy slogans, and researching voter tastes—Hollywood Republican activists helped to design professional spectacles to form emotional bonds between "Ike" the personality and potential Republican voters in the same way they had turned moviegoers into starstruck fans of individual celebrities.

As prominent entertainers worked with national party and government institutions to translate their showmanship skills into philanthropic efforts, propaganda campaigns, and Cold War initiatives, contemporary political scholars started to notice the ways in which the entertainment industry had influenced local and state politics over the past twenty years. Political scientists saw how the California political environment, shaped by its combination of progressive reforms, suburban landscape, diverse demographics, and the powerful economic interests of the motion picture industry, held answers for understanding how national politicians and political parties could adjust to technological, cultural, and spatial changes of the post–World War II period. In 1958, as one political scientist sought to understand the "new look" in American campaigns in which professionals "raise money, determine issues, write speeches, handle press releases, prepare advertising copy, program radio and television shows, and develop whatever publicity techniques are necessary for a given campaign," he argued that scholars needed to look to California, where this professionalized image making had "flourished in the past two decades."[31]

California, it seemed, had the answers to political success in the television age, and the California "showbiz politics" style started to appeal to national Republicans as more than simply a sideshow. With liberal activists receding from the public arena, through frustration and fear from the HUAC investigations, George Murphy led the Republican charge in Hollywood to gain the support of Democrats unhappy with the Truman administration. Before the 1952 Republican National Convention, former Franklin Roosevelt supporters Jack Warner, Samuel Goldwyn, and Darryl Zanuck looked to Dwight Eisenhower as the hope for the nation to conquer communism and alleviate the economic struggles of their industry. Having so effectively organized Roosevelt's reelection campaign in 1944, these men built on their previous political experience to develop publicity strategies and fund-raising efforts to support Eisenhower's candidacy. As Southern California representatives of Citizens for Eisenhower, Goldwyn, Warner, and Zanuck stressed Eisenhower's nonpartisan appeal and emphasized how he, as a person, embodied principles of patriotism and Americanism in which they could trust. As they sent letters to Hollywood Democrats and Independents, Zanuck and Warner constantly stressed that "you must judge the *character* of the man." Yes, they too had voted for Roosevelt because of their faith in his leadership abilities, but in 1952, "from the standpoint of character, integrity, and experience, no one runs even a close second to Dwight D. Eisenhower."[32] The industry and patriotic politics that had previously driven and shaped Hollywood activism served as a basis for a deeper political involvement that would beget partisan benefits for the Republican Party and nurture a Hollywood conservatism that stressed anticommunism, patriotic rhetoric, and a pro-business attitude.

Goldwyn, Warner, and Zanuck struggled economically under the Truman administration as the antitrust suits broke up the vertical integration of the industry, television legal battles threatened the ability of the studios to reap the financial benefits of the new medium, and high tariffs hurt the international box office. The British tax crisis in 1947 began the mobilization of studio executives against the Truman administration, based on the economic arguments in favor of the free market and deregulation. Republicans like Eric Johnston and Walt Disney led the charge against Truman, and soon former Roosevelt supporter Samuel Goldwyn joined the cause. Goldwyn linked his appeal to Cold War rhetoric when he penned a letter to President Truman that called the tax a threat to the economic survival of such an important industry and a "definite deterioration in the quality of picture which will represent the American way of life not only at home but abroad."[33] While Truman worked to lower the trade barriers, his failure to produce results provided another reason for studio executives to find a new presidential candidate to support.

When Eisenhower won the Republican nomination in 1952, the formerly Democratic studio executives put their time, money, and experience into electing their favorite general. But first, a conflict within the party demanded resolution concerning the organization and structure of the presidential campaign.[34] In Southern California, volunteer political activists Warner, Goldwyn, and Zanuck campaigned vigorously for Eisenhower to get the nomination through the Citizens for Eisenhower organization, which stressed cross-party organization and supported the use of entertainment to expand the reach of the Eisenhower message.[35] Conservative party regulars, however, resented this "invasion" of the Republican Party, which took the nomination away from Robert Taft. Darryl Zanuck learned firsthand of the "deep bitterness on the part of the Taft backers" when he attempted to organize a post-convention fund-raiser for Eisenhower and found that every member of the MPA had declined an invitation and that other long-term "die hard" Republicans remained "on the fence."[36]

To curb the tensions within the party that permeated local Republican chapters, candidate Eisenhower insisted on what Zanuck called a "combined unified effort" between volunteers and party officials, to be worked out on the state level.[37] Following Eisenhower's instructions, George Murphy helped to negotiate a middle ground between the moderate and conservative Republicans as he set up the Hollywood Republican Club, which literally stood side by side with Warner, Zanuck, and Goldwyn's newly refocused Entertainment Industry Joint Committee for Eisenhower-Nixon organization. Officially, Murphy's Hollywood Republican Club and Zanuck's entertainment committee remained separate entities, but they maintained adjacent offices, frequently shared stationery, and consistently worked together to deliver Southern California to the Republican Party.[38]

Murphy, Warner, Zanuck, and Goldwyn immediately went to work to persuade their friends in the Hollywood studios to donate their time, talents, and money to the Eisenhower campaign. They reminded them that "our industry has been kicked around by the present Administration," building on anger about the pending television suit that the Democrats supported, which would "give them our films on television for free."[39] Pure political calculations motivated this Democratic policy proposal, Zanuck wrote to Warner. By sabotaging the economic interests of the motion picture industry, Democrats wanted to use the case to "demonstrate that the Democrats are looking after the 'people'—even if they wreck another industry in doing so." These former Democrats flooded the mailboxes of other liberals with letters emphasizing the inability of Stevenson to deal with national security and his lack of commitment to the economic interests of the struggling motion picture industry. Many liberals remained committed to the Democratic ticket, in particular, Humphrey Bogart, Frank Sinatra, and Dore Schary, but the Hollywood Republicans found that their message resonated with the growing conservative movement in Hollywood built around the "politics of Americanism," in which activists could assert their anticommunism while defending the industry's economic interests.

Developing an elaborate public relations campaign, Murphy's and Warner's committees planted newspaper advertisements in "strategic areas" and developed radio and television spot announcements written and delivered by professionals from their studios.[40] The committee organized campaign appearances for vice presidential nominee Richard Nixon to return to his home state in style, and George Murphy led groups of Hollywood personalities to fund-raising and publicity events up and down the state. Upon Darryl Zanuck's recommendation, Nixon made a "whistle stop"–style tour tailored for television, in which he stopped briefly with a celebrity entourage in critical areas, withheld from the press the text of his speeches to "augment curiosity," and concluded with a "big appearance on television."[41]

The joint committee drummed up publicity, dollars, and Independent and Democratic votes for the Republican ticket in California. Committee members informally shared their expertise with advertisers and politicians involved with the national campaign. After watching several Eisenhower television spots, Warner advised the New York campaign office on how to appeal effectively to viewers through commercials. Warner warned that the public did not enjoy excessive and boring commercials.[42] "If you see a spot announcement once or twice, it is interesting but if you see the same one repeatedly, it begins to annoy you and look like an obvious 'sales campaign.'" Incorporating catchy Eisenhower songs or images from a political entertainment rally could be used as thirty-second spot announcements, which Warner assured would sell. The Republican Campaign Plan emphasized that all television productions should be made "with the best directional technical facilities employed," and BBD&O eagerly ate up the valuable advice (offered for free) of entertainment professionals like Warner.[43]

The campaign efforts of the joint entertainment committee paid off as Eisenhower swept California and the majority of the country. He became the first Republican president since Herbert Hoover, and Murphy organized celebrity supporters for the upcoming inaugural celebration. Determined to show the country that the "motion picture industry will support the Republican inaugural as strongly as it has supported the Democratic ones," the inaugural committee invited the joint entertainment committee members to travel to Washington and "bring whatever stars you can."[44] As director of entertainment, George Murphy promised to produce "one hell of a show."[45] Juggling the National Symphony, the New York City Ballet, and West Coast actors and actresses, Murphy made sure that the Hollywood glitter complemented but did not overwhelm the more traditional forms of inaugural entertainment. As Eisenhower took his presidential oath, the turnout of entertainers at the inaugural pleased the entertainment director and helped to solidify his place as the liaison between Hollywood talent and the social, political, and economic needs of the Republican administration.

From Cold Warriors to Political Insiders: Hollywood Goes to the White House

Murphy was not the only Republican pleased by the prominent place of Hollywood in the campaign and inauguration. Eric Johnston looked with great excitement on the potential for the industry to capitalize on its potential Cold War contributions to gain much-needed economic opportunities. The 1952 campaign clearly signaled to Madison Avenue and Hollywood alike that the image and mass communications businesses would, at last, have a respected and valued place in Washington, D.C. Throughout the next four years, Hollywood figures would become valuable political insiders, who would use their roles as cultural diplomats and media consultants to advance the economic and political interests of the struggling industry. Partisan collaboration had its rewards.

A long-time Republican, Eric Johnston welcomed Dwight D. Eisenhower to the national political scene and found new opportunities to continue his crusade for cooperation and free enterprise in Hollywood and across the world. Constantly referring to the industry he represented as "America's Traveling Salesman," Johnston heralded the ability of film to stimulate production and consumption to enhance the quality of life across the globe. To him, the motion picture industry stood as the epitome of American business potential to stimulate the marketplace through the "power of suggestion—the suggestion of new styles, new devices, new methods."[46] Celebrities could protect the capitalist system and promote a democracy of goods throughout the world. Eisenhower appreciated Eric Johnston's insight on economic matters and his charismatic salesmanship, which the new "movie czar" had developed during the past five years of selling Hollywood. As Eisenhower moved into 1600 Pennsylvania Avenue, Eric Johnston accepted a new government position as chair of the International Development Advisory Board.[47]

Over the next eight years, Eric Johnston traveled internationally with a dual role of promoting the interests of the motion picture industry and of the Eisenhower administration. With one eye on expanding potential markets abroad and another on containing the spread of communism, Johnston found Hollywood films an effective tool for U.S. economic and ideological expansion. Johnston worked with Eisenhower to develop film programs in Africa, ascertain public opinion in Middle Eastern conflicts, and explore possibilities of film exchange with the Soviet Union. Hoping to foster goodwill toward America through "accurate" film portrayals, Johnston developed international trade agreements that opened new markets for the industry and also allowed Hollywood films to promote democracy, capitalism, and the United States beyond the Iron Curtain.[48]

Johnston also traveled domestically across the United States to advocate the social responsibility of the motion picture industry, its important Cold War role, and Eisenhower's foreign policy to Republican forums months before the 1958 congressional elections.[49] At Eisenhower's request, Johnston organized a "giant rally" to generate popular support among Republicans for the president's new foreign aid program. Proposing to "muster support for the project and sell it to a hostile Congress," the rally stimulated a "healthy discussion" of the proposed $3.9 billion program.[50] The *Washington Post-Herald* called the rally a "smash hit" and proclaimed that "no show business entrepreneur ever assembled a more star-studded cast for a one-day stand than Eric Johnston."[51] At the end of the rally, Johnston took the lead in forming a permanent group dedicated to "educating Americans to the urgency of foreign aid" and reaffirmed his commitment to Eisenhower's leadership in the Cold War crusade.[52]

By intertwining his professional, political, and personal interests, Johnston taught the administration the importance of salesmanship and "education" through spectacle—whether it be a Disney film or a foreign policy rally—abroad or at home. Robert Montgomery also believed that the Republican Party had to actively "re-educate" American citizens about the meaning of "genuine Americanism." In a motivational speech to rev up the Republican Party before the 1952 election, Montgomery emphasized the need to protect voters "from the beguiling propaganda of the advocates of something-for-nothing they are spreading across the land."[53] Because New Deal liberals had so effectively sold their messages or "propaganda" of collectivism, socialism, and the welfare state, the Republican Party, argued Montgomery, needed to embark on a massive public relations campaign to teach voters about the importance of private enterprise, the free market, and the dangers of communism. Montgomery urged Republicans to translate Hollywood's Cold War efforts to sell "Americanism" into electoral benefits for the party at home.

As both Eric Johnston and Robert Montgomery understood with their Hollywood backgrounds, fighting the Cold War and returning the Republican Party to political power demanded effective salesmanship through the mass media, a skill that Eisenhower initially lacked. While Johnston focused on using Hollywood films to sell democracy abroad, Robert Montgomery joined Eisenhower's executive staff at the White House as his television adviser. Montgomery remembered watching the Abilene broadcast before he made a "frantic long distance call" to Eisenhower's campaign manager with basic suggestions to salvage the potential president's image on television. The poor lighting and lack of stage direction "ruined political communication," claimed Montgomery.[54] Following Eisenhower's election, Montgomery volunteered his services and knowledge to help the president conquer the medium of television and avoid a disastrous repeat of the Abilene incident.

Frequently referred to as Eisenhower's "coach," Montgomery moved into his own White House office in 1954. The official presence of a Hollywood actor and television producer as an Eisenhower adviser quickly made newspaper headlines across the country, which demanded to know Montgomery's precise role. Montgomery assured the public that he had assumed the role as a technical adviser in order to help the president with

President Dwight Eisenhower depended on the media advice of actor Robert Montgomery to navigate the challenges of television. Montgomery, here advising Eisenhower before he declared his intention to seek a second term as president on February 29, 1956, served as the first television adviser on Eisenhower's White House staff. Courtesy of Dwight D. Eisenhower Presidential Library.

lighting, camera angles, and microphones to transmit the president's personality to viewers without distractions. Montgomery strongly argued that he never attempted to influence the content of Eisenhower's televised speeches or manipulate his celluloid character. "For me or anyone else to try to direct him or give him a different personality would be downright silly," explained the actor. "And most of all, the president wouldn't stand for it."[55] Constantly stressing the technical nature of his job, Montgomery advocated for the political benefits television could bring through its ability to connect politicians and constituents. Voters could better evaluate the ideas and stances of candidates, claimed Montgomery, because "it is impossible for a candidate on television to get up before a vast audience and tell a series of untruths to 100 million people in this country and get away with it."[56] To Eisenhower's advisers, the embrace of television would "pick up where FDR left off in the establishment of contact with the public through mass communications media."[57]

As Eisenhower worked closely with Robert Montgomery to develop new strategies for political communication, the president, his administration, and the American people all learned the basics of the Hollywood production process and got a "television education" as the actor shared his technical expertise with newspapers eager for stories about how the new medium worked.[58] News reports chronicled the details of the White House television studio—the thirty by fifty-five foot old kitchen in the basement, where cameras and hanging lights had replaced racks of pots and pans.[59] Stories circulated about how cameramen, technicians, secret service agents, photographers, and makeup girls rushed around the studio testing lights and camera angles while Robert Montgomery rehearsed the upcoming speech carefully with the president. The television productions improved in quality and effectiveness, but the real fun, declared one article from the *Washington News*, was the great show "behind the scenes."[60]

Montgomery taught basic Hollywood technical strategy and, in the process, helped the country adjust to the new role of television and showmanship in American life. Eisenhower's endearing smile and likable nature allowed Montgomery to remind people of the positive contribution television could make in clarifying issues and presenting candidates to the American people. He constantly emphasized how television "could be a force for good, capable not only of improving politics as a calling, but of raising the quality of the public servant."[61] Some critics looked negatively on the "Hollywood invasion" of Washington, but Montgomery and Eric Johnston constantly explained to the American people the benefits motion pictures and television offered in the promotion and expansion of democracy.[62] Only the skills and knowledge of Hollywood, they explained, could communicate the famous general's true personality or show foreign countries the real meaning of the American way of life.

In preparation for the 1956 election, Montgomery moved from Republican spokesman and television adviser to active campaigner. Working extensively with George Murphy, Montgomery developed production ideas and strategies for the Republican National Convention. Having also televised the convention four years earlier, the RNC was determined in 1956 to "improve our show" by cutting back long speeches and adding staged "pageants or other spectacle to enliven dull stretches."[63] Actor Wendell Corey hosted the "songs, ceremonies, and fanfare," which also included the unveiling of a new Irving Berlin song written just for the president, "Four More Years."[64] Montgomery put aside criticisms in the press that "conventions are being converted into TV spectaculars," just as he had done with negative comments about his advisory role to the president. He understood the potential for more vibrant political communication that television held, and he wanted to focus all his efforts on harnessing this new tool.[65]

A Prime-Time Presidency

Montgomery and Eisenhower both stressed the actor's role as a technical adviser, but he also used his Hollywood fame to promote the Republican Party and create favorable publicity for its electoral candidates. Hollywood Republicans offered their expertise to a party that worked diligently to embrace the mass media to remake its public image, build a majority coalition, and more broadly transform the party, as Samuel Lubell had suggested in 1952. Eric Johnston and Robert Montgomery worked for Eisenhower and also traveled the country giving speeches on behalf of the national Republican Party, stressing the importance of free-market ideals, privatization, and the dangers of collectivism, which Republicans felt Roosevelt and Truman had made so palatable to many Americans.[66] Back in California, George Murphy continued his work on behalf of Republican candidates during the 1954 congressional race. He produced an elaborate show featuring the president with Hollywood performers to attract national coverage for California's Republican ticket.[67] Warner, Goldwyn, and Zanuck diligently campaigned for candidates "who are pledged to the support of the magnificent program which the President has proposed."[68]

President Eisenhower also understood and appreciated the importance of these party-building strategies. During his administration, he worked to bridge the divide between the extrapartisan Citizens for Eisenhower Committee and the formal Republican Party structures following his election. Rather than "preying" on the party, the president hoped to expand its reach and popularity by using his own personality.[69] To do this, Eisenhower set up party-building workshops in Washington, D.C., that not only focused on teaching how to set up local precincts and raise money but also instructed Republicans in how to use the "press, radio, and TV" effectively, as Eisenhower, and the committee that had helped get him elected, had done in 1952.[70]

By the 1956 election, Warner, Zanuck, and Goldwyn had become a formal part of the broader effort to rebrand the Republican Party in the image of "Ike." During the campaign, the entertainment committee worked with Republicans across the country to provide parades of stars to generate turnout, excitement, and dollars. George Murphy wrote Hedda Hopper requesting her appearance at a Kansas City rally to fulfill the local Republican committee's request for "outstanding personalities to assist Missouri, and through the test method set up, the rest of the nation."[71] Television cameras promised to make the Missouri rally an event worthy of national coverage if a celebrity could join the program to sell it to networks across the country. When the president traveled to Los Angeles in October, a parade of stars greeted him and television cameras broadcasted their hour and a half entertainment feature that preceded his talk.[72]

The success of such events showed how the partnership between Hollywood and the Republican Party far exceeded the Democratic Party's earlier collaborative efforts. Moreover, the HUAC probes into the political activism of liberal celebrities put the Democratic Party on the defensive against charges of propaganda that had emerged from these earlier associations. The RNC, however, quickly moved to institutionalize these innovative media strategies into their party-building efforts and give Republican showmen authority within the national party. In his influential 1956 book, *Professional Public Relations and Political Power*, prominent political scientist Stanley Kelley Jr. observed how the merchandising of Eisenhower's personality became integral to the Republican Party's victories in the presidential and congressional races in 1952 and ultimately taught party leaders an important "lesson for future party recruitment of candidates."[73] The presidential candidate needed to capture the public imagination to propel the entire party to a victory, and this role of the "leading man" required a "systematic, large-scale, privately sponsored publicity build-up." The Citizens for Eisenhower Committee served as the central extrapartisan organization that helped advance the former general's political interests. The challenge for the broader Republican Party in the 1956 election lay in unifying all factions of the "publicity build up" into one organization with a coordinated electoral purpose.

During the 1956 election, wanting to "appeal to all kinds of people" through a "variety of forms," the Citizens for Eisenhower Committee brought Hollywood salesmanship to the national Eisenhower campaign and demonstrated how entertainment could relate important messages about Eisenhower as a person and a politician to help rebrand the Republican image. The Citizens for Eisenhower Committee developed various styles and formats for its television programs to sell the idea of four more years under Eisenhower. Armed with the resources of their Hollywood friends, the committee emphasized the need to "make the principles and the President's promise the meat of most our efforts." The RNC and BBD&O maintained the responsibility to "handle the past and the GOP record." Working with Y&R and Hollywood Republican activists, the Citizens for Eisenhower Committee, therefore, concentrated its attention on appealing to the emotions of its viewers through variety shows, five-minute and one-minute spots, and savvy commercials, all stressing the theme of four more years in various ways to "appeal to all segments of the population."[74]

The committee focused on the content, style, and placement of its television productions. First, it needed to develop shows that would attract the interest of television viewers while also plugging the Eisenhower line. As a basic production premise, Y&R wanted to avoid boring or controversial political debates and instead "give our programs an atmosphere of action and entertainment."[75] The content frequently varied with the length of the show. The one-hour program proposed for the eve of the election would rely extensively on entertainment acts and celebrity drawing power to "attract and hold their interest." Hoping to draw in viewers from the previous show, the committee understood that unless top names starred in the Eisenhower production, viewers would turn off the television at 11 o'clock that night. Moreover, a "star studded thematic show" would relate the "many reasons why all kinds of people are voting for Eisenhower-Nixon" and the variety format would offer new "opportunities for our message."[76]

One "national town meeting" intermixed Eisenhower's celebrity supporters with "little people from all walks of life and from all over America" and included carefully rehearsed vibrant dialogue that highlighted the achievements of the Eisenhower administration.[77] The goal of the broadcast was to convince "lukewarm Democrats" and Independent or "disinterested" voters to turn out on Election Day and cast ballots for President Eisenhower. The strategy: "To leaven the loaf of political content with as much entertainment as possible." To persuade the uncertain or apathetic voter, wrote a Y&R advertising executive, these television shows needed prominent movie stars to endorse Eisenhower and relate the campaign issues intelligently and quickly. Rather than a traditional partisan appeal, these entertainment events needed to promote Eisenhower in an informal manner that was "the very opposite of the set political speech." Since disinterested citizens might tune out explicitly political speeches, a show that featured a "celebrity and his home" would allow prominent stars to give movie fans personal home tours on camera while implicitly promoting Eisenhower's candidacy.

For an election eve show, in particular, when the committee could make its final impact on voter decisions, Y&R emphasized how "the stars are a *magnet* to draw viewer interest and to build up as large an audience as we can."[78] The proposed performance, "Salute to Ike," would capture the excitement of a political rally and feature dance routines of famous performers, like MGM stars Marge and Gower Champion, "rousing music," and brief endorsement speeches from celebrities, "to the point and rehearsed." The performances and remarks "would all tend to achieve for us a point of view that reflects the enthusiasm of America for Eisenhower the man, Eisenhower the leader, Eisenhower the next President." To make its "final and effective political contribution," the all-star show needed to combine politics and entertainment to "contain enough sell of the Eisenhower principles and Eisenhower's program for the future of America."

Political entertainment like "Salute to Ike" relied on extensive coordination with Eisenhower's Hollywood supporters. The president of Twentieth Century Fox, Spyros Skouras, worked with the Citizens for Eisenhower Committee to develop a feature-length film, *Four Full Years*, which would "pin point the contribution that Eisenhower and his great team have made in bringing about this new era of security and good times for all of the American people."[79] Having discussed the film with Eisenhower himself, Skouras developed script ideas with the Citizens for Eisenhower Committee, pledging "the full support of his company to collaborate with us in the production of this film and has assigned top people to work with us." Volunteer appearances of television and film stars helped the committee execute its plans to use entertainment to transmit the message to reelect Eisenhower. Skouras's film used Gary Cooper to narrate the various pictures of the "flavor, the excitement, and the atmosphere" of the Eisenhower years.[80] One Y&R advertising man who had also worked with Eisenhower as a radio consultant during World War II, David Levy, wrote the committee asking for the names of Hollywood stars who supported Eisenhower and would be willing to participate in his campaign programs.[81] After stressing the extreme urgency and importance of getting a list of "any and all pro Eisenhower personalities," Levy found that the extensive list of celebrity supporters eager to host programs for the incumbent proved to be an invaluable asset. Other professionals experienced with "show demands," like Robert Montgomery, Ed Sullivan, Bob Hope, and George Murphy, were instrumental in Y&R's efforts to convey effectively an exciting message about Eisenhower that "induces action."[82]

The Citizens for Eisenhower Committee also worked diligently to bring in top studio writers, film editors, and television directors.[83] In the *Four Full Years* film, for example, a professional studio editor spliced scenes of events over the past four years with Eisenhower's speeches, Cooper's narration, and optimistic scenes of future prosperity under Ike. Other Eisenhower productions also relied on Hollywood formats to hold the audience's attention and relate the best possible images of the president using studio production tactics. Y&R urged the president to move from his makeshift studio in the small former kitchen in the White House to a professional studio in the Washington area, which could effectively "duplicate the Presidential setting."[84] Requesting a "top lighting expert," the committee planned rehearsals and makeup trials to improve the president's appearance. Despite Robert Montgomery's help with camera angles and lighting, Y&R believed that the president's televised appearance "has never reflected his own healthy and vigorous look," and the firm requested a "stand in"—"a man whose skin texture is like the President's and test him under various conditions as Hollywood does for its stars."[85] With Eisenhower's recent heart attack concerning voters, the television advertisements needed to make sure that the president had "the best possible personal appearance." Moreover, because the Citizens for Eisenhower Committee focused its efforts on selling Eisenhower "the man," the physical appearance of the president promised to be of "as great interest to viewers as the very subject he will present in his address."[86]

Along with constructing longer filmed programs, from the "Salute to Ike" to the colorful, New England–style "Town Meeting," the Citizens for Eisenhower Committee employed its advertising and show business expertise to produce short one-to-five-minute commercial advertisements. An effective commercial would "get our story across in a fast moving, entertaining fashion" by incorporating star personalities and animation devices.[87] Commercials juxtaposed ordinary citizens—a "down to earth farmer from the Dairy State of Wisconsin" or "a Negro Doctor"—with prominent figures to show the wide range of people who supported Eisenhower's leadership.

Y&R worked with the Citizens for Eisenhower Committee to prepare potential "vignettes" that the committee felt confident would combine "the elements of imagination and persuasion that will drive home as an 'emotional hit on the jaw.' "[88]

Along with influencing content and style, the motion picture industry also contributed important market segmentation strategies to help advertisements transition from commercial to paid political programming. A Citizens for Eisenhower Committee report stressed the importance of a five-minute "integration" of the advertisement with the preceding show to help the political spot "hold the circulation these shows deliver so that we can get our shot in."[89] With personal and professional connections in the television world—from Robert Montgomery, who filmed a weekly show on NBC, to William Paley, who built CBS into a leading television and radio network—the Citizens for Eisenhower Committee convinced network shows to end five minutes early and then bought these prime slots following top entertainment shows that featured some of the same actors that they recruited to perform in their advertisements. The committee also brought local stations into its market strategy by instructing state subsets of the Citizens for Eisenhower Committee to purchase the break spots following these national programs. "Local station break spots are very effective," wrote the committee's director of public relations, Richard Tobin, "particularly when they follow or precede a nationwide TV program of the same advocacy."[90] Advertisements followed such programs as the *Robert Montgomery Presents Television Show*, during which the Eisenhower adviser served as host and presented "a number of other actors and artists who are pro-Ike."[91]

The most important program for local and state committees to buy up local advertisement time was the election eve "Salute to Ike." The hour-long presentation, which aired on the three major networks, stood as the "climax" of the National Citizens for Eisenhower campaign.[92] Having obtained high Nielsen ratings from the election eve program in 1952, the committee worked even harder to wage the campaign "with top strength to the very end."[93] Despite the plans to use maximum entertainment to "induce" viewers to vote, the committee decided to replace "all elements of commercial entertainment previously considered" and instead maximize the "emotional use of President Eisenhower himself." NBC news anchor John Cameron Swayze hosted President Eisenhower, his wife, Mamie, and Vice President Richard Nixon and his wife, Pat, in Washington for an evening of reflection on the achievements of the Eisenhower administration and the course of the campaign events. The election eve program combined live camera shots and prefilmed coverage of political rallies and carefully rehearsed interviews with Eisenhower supporters from across the country. Swayze told viewers that "tonight, there are hundreds of V-I, 'Vote for Ike,' rallies now in progress," which the show would visit before hearing the final appeal for votes from Eisenhower himself.[94] The show emphasized Eisenhower's leadership and his fulfillment of the promises that he had made in 1952, from achieving peace in Korea, to bringing economic prosperity and a high quality of life to Americans, to ending inflation, to protecting social security, to ending discrimination in businesses that work with the federal government. Featuring supporters from across the country, the program highlighted the principles for which Eisenhower stood and depicted the wide range of supporters who reaffirmed "that the promise of 1952 has been fulfilled plus their personal reasons for voting for Ike."[95] The program concluded with Eisenhower addressing the audience about his promises for the next four years and a reminder that "tomorrow is election day—it is your duty to vote."[96]

The election eve program, which traded commercial entertainment for a more direct Eisenhower appeal, embodied the overall approach of the Citizens for Eisenhower Committee and its more subtle use of Hollywood style to rebrand the Republican Party in the image of Ike. Because the committee saw the American public as consumers of the mass media, it used basic philosophies of Hollywood studios to elicit television viewers' emotions and then gain their electoral support. The committee relied on studio production and editing tactics, but the personal appeal from Eisenhower himself was the highlight of the program. Communicating Eisenhower's principles and programs to the American people stood as the committee's number one priority, and it was willing to use all assets to achieve this goal, whether the president himself or his celebrity supporters.

Eisenhower first accepted the importance of the mass media, both television and radio, and then turned to show business professionals to learn how to use it to win two presidential elections and advance his vision for the country and his party. Experts from the advertising, television, and motion picture industries finally gained access to and influence within the national party, which sought innovative strategies to challenge the electoral dominance of the Democratic Party. The vision for electoral strategy that Louis B. Mayer had articulated to Herbert Hoover almost thirty years earlier found acceptance in Eisenhower's administration. Eisenhower saw the value in a political style rooted in California and dependent on popular appeals to voters through the media. Working with the Citizens for Eisenhower Committee, he had a professional production studio and staff dedicated to convincing voters to abandon traditional voting habits and cross party lines through a concerted effort to showcase Eisenhower as a leading man of the people, not necessarily a representative of the traditional Republican Party.[97] Campaign films replayed World War II footage to "show Ike as a hero to Democrats" and remind them of his valiant service under presidents Roosevelt and Truman.[98] Entertainment could show why "all kinds of people are voting for Eisenhower [and] Nixon"—not just Republicans but voters across the political spectrum.[99] As a result, the Citizens for Eisenhower Committee used mass media images—from pictures of an African American doctor to those of a small-town farmer, all showing people who were supporting Eisenhower—to advance their ideological vision of a moderate Republican Party. Their success, during the 1950s at least, transformed the party structures in place across the country by making media messages, and those who constructed them, central to political communication and party mobilization and identification. A decade later, conservatives would attempt to change the ideological outlook of the party but would continue to rely on the place of the media to connect presidents and party leaders to local constituencies.

Stevenson, the DNC, and the "Deadliness of Straight Political Speechifying"

The Democratic presidential challenger, Adlai Stevenson, lacked Ike's World War II fame and professional sales staff. The Illinois governor had little patience for the changing technology that emphasized the importance of image, and he openly criticized the Republican use of political advertising. During his acceptance speech at the Democratic National Convention in 1956, Stevenson attacked the administration's use of men who "evidently believe that the minds of Americans can be manipulated by shows, slogans, and the arts of advertising."[100] Despite his critique, Stevenson remembered how Eisenhower even as a media novice had outshone him on television four years earlier, and by 1956, he acquiesced to his advisers and various Democratic Party leaders who insisted that he incorporate Madison Avenue techniques into his campaign. Nevertheless, despite the DNC's efforts to develop imaginative campaign spots in collaboration with advertising experts, electoral success for Stevenson and the Democratic Party hinged on reasserting the New Deal coalition and using party operatives to turn out the vote. As the Democratic Party had traditionally done, Stevenson merchandised policies for interest groups, not his personality for television viewers, and he faced defeat.

When looking ahead to the 1956 election season, the DNC chairman, Paul Butler, recognized the need to help Democratic candidates compete with Republicans during the television age, and he crafted a new wing of the party dedicated specifically to developing television and radio resources and strategies.[101] Senate Majority Leader Lyndon Johnson encouraged and praised Butler for "moving rapidly in the Television-Radio field as it is one of the most important to all of us."[102] Other congressmen, who were inexperienced or underfunded for this expensive communications field, also expressed their gratitude that the national party would assume responsibility for coordinating television efforts for the Democratic Party in the next year.[103]

Hoping to develop a more aggressive advertising strategy for the 1956 election, the DNC also hired a new advertising firm, Norman, Craig & Kummel (NC&K). Top companies on Madison Avenue shied away from the Democratic Party for fear of offending their friends and colleagues in the big business party; but NC&K worked diligently with the DNC to develop campaign strategies that sold the party and Stevenson as a candidate without offending the governor with excessive commodification.[104] The firm's publicity plan began by acknowledging the Democratic Party's aversion to the term "propaganda," which, though an accurate description for their plans, "has acquired vaguely sinister connotations."[105] The firm offered clever slogans for newspapers, radio announcements, and television to remind the voters of the Republicans' broken promises, the laziness of the incumbent, and, most important, the need to vote for the "party for you, not the party of the few."[106]

Through clever slogans and anti-administration rhetoric, the DNC pursued a more traditional political campaign at the expense of expanding its voter base through effective media mobilization. During the 1950s, while Republicans sought to rebrand their party in the image of "Ike" and generate voter turnout by appealing to media consumers, Democrats relied on the power of labor unions to spread the party message and get voters to the polls. With efficient party machinery in urban areas and labor unions firmly committed to the party, the Democratic Party did not have a strong enough motivation to embrace publicity men and electoral strategies in 1952, especially in the wake of the ongoing HUAC investigations, which frequently targeted former liberal celebrity activists.

Extensive DNC research into the media ineffectiveness of the Stevenson campaign in 1952, however, forced the party to reconsider this strategy and explore how television could expand campaign efforts. The DNC worked with advertisers to fix the mistakes of the first televised election.

To initially save money and allow Stevenson the forum to address constituents through longer speeches, the DNC had bought half-hour television spots in the previous campaign during off-peak hours, which had bored the small viewing audience during the 1952 race.[107] In a University of Miami study of the influence of television on the 1952 election, the researchers concluded that "Republican programs and speeches were timed to coincide with the periods of larger viewing audiences." Democrats, on the other hand, saved money but lost audiences by scheduling programs "in periods when political viewing was at a low ebb."[108]

Four years later, the DNC worked with NC&K to emulate successful aspects of Eisenhower's earlier campaign. Dividing the television spots into ten seconds, thirty seconds, one minute, and five minutes, NC&K relied on short spots, which followed shows like the *Jackie Gleason Show* and *Kraft Theater*.[109] However, rather than linking the entertainment programming with the political commercial, as the Republicans had done to sustain viewers' interest, NC&K advocated a different philosophy, as it told the DNC that audiences found "5 or 10 minute news programs were more welcome than almost any other type of program after their star studded shows." Therefore, a political announcement structured as a "news report would insure a continuation of the audience attracted by the big star shows."[110]

The spots followed Stevenson's instructions to avoid excessive commerciality and Hollywood-style entertainment and instead emphasize the issues and the candidate. While Eisenhower as a person had become a beloved figure, the public perceived Stevenson as an "egghead" out of touch with the daily lives of Americans.[111] NC&K understood that electoral success depended on selling "the man as well as the issues" and worked to build a stronger media personality for Stevenson.[112] Political broadcasts featured the candidate mingling with crowds of people—to emphasize his "connection" to the everyday person—at his home in Libertyville, Illinois, or beside familiar landmarks in Washington where the candidate casually spoke with other people, mostly Democratic Party figures, about the problems with the Soviet Union, on farms, or in schools. The short commercials wanted to connect the candidate to the television audience by giving Stevenson an opportunity to "state in a direct, positive way, his views of specific issues."[113] Stevenson's open dislike of the manipulative power of television fueled NC&K's reluctance to stage a more attractive sales campaign that used Hollywood salesmanship to reach voters. The governor rarely conversed or cooperated with the hired agency, ultimately forcing the advertisers to rely on newsreel footage and clips of speeches rather than staged, dramatic, or even rehearsed productions.

Despite Stevenson's resistance to commercial advertising strategies, the candidate did attract the support of various celebrity figures eager to mobilize for the liberal candidate in both of his presidential campaigns. The anticommunism crusade in Hollywood had severely damaged the liberal political networks in California that had sprung up during the Roosevelt years, but Stevenson's candidacy in 1952 reinvigorated liberal activity. When Stevenson captured the Democratic nomination, grassroots California Democratic clubs, including the Hollywood for Stevenson organization in Los Angeles, welcomed the visiting candidate to the state with the Hollywood Dream Machine, which had become a staple in California politics. Volunteer groups worked with liberal celebrities, like Humphrey Bogart and Lauren Bacall, to use Stevenson's California visit to get national publicity in campaign events orchestrated to show the grassroots excitement surrounding the candidate.[114]

And yet Stevenson and the national Democratic Party maintained distance from a "showbiz politics" style in the national campaign. One Hollywood for Stevenson-Sparkman member wrote to the DNC with ideas on how brief radio and television spots that featured entertainers like Frank Sinatra, Eddie Cantor, Ava Gardner, and Tony Martin could promote Stevenson's candidacy through song and dance.[115] After a month of production efforts, the Hollywood for Stevenson Committee presented the DNC a "gift" of free film and radio advertisement spots. "The price tag on this kind of package they are delivering would run about a million dollars," noted Thomas Durrance, the DNC liaison with the group.[116] Despite its efforts, however, the Hollywood for Stevenson Committee saw the DNC fail to properly distribute this effort to Democratic campaigns outside of California. Labor unions and "sundry organizations" were trying to find pro-Democratic material to fill their local television and radio time, but they remained "unaware of the material produced by Hollywood for Stevenson."[117]

Frustrated by the lack of "education" about the availability of its production material, the Hollywood for Stevenson Committee urged the DNC to teach party organizers about "the effectiveness of entertainment coupled with politics, which is keynote of all Hollywood for Stevenson material, as compared with the deadliness of straight political speechifying."[118] The committee hoped to counter the "tune-offs by radio and TV listeners," which, they argued, ultimately proved fatal to the Stevenson campaign. But in the end, when it came to communicating to voters and understanding their desires and needs, the DNC relied on labor leaders like George Meany, not on celebrities like Frank Sinatra or Humphrey Bogart.[119] Dore Schary did ultimately develop a personal relationship with the candidate—frequently offering Montgomery-like advice to improve Stevenson's television appearances—but the Hollywood for Stevenson Committee found openings to collaboration with the Democratic Party only in fund-raising.[120] With a candidate clearly lukewarm about its potential contributions to the national campaign, the Hollywood for Stevenson Committee's push to replace traditional forms of party communication with entertainment in the 1952 election failed, ultimately lacking the political organization and drive that the Republican Party had developed with the Citizens for Eisenhower Committee.

To Adlai Stevenson, and many other party leaders and public intellectuals, however, television and advertising were negative and dangerous tools that threatened to replace the democratic system with a public relations game, which could have perilous consequences, as Adolf Hitler's propaganda regime had demonstrated less than a decade earlier.[121] Many others agreed with the Democratic candidate. In 1956, John Schneider's *Golden Kazoo* hit bookshelves with what the *New York Times* called a "somber and frightening" forecast of how Madison Avenue would soon control the electoral process.[122] With candidates sold to "the lowest common denominator," only playing "a bit part in a spectacular that will demonstrate a vote-winning point," Schneider's story presented a dismal view of the democratic system under the advertisers' control.[123]

The Golden Kazoo reflected the broader fear of the encroachment of mass media in American life and politics. Since the 1920s, motion pictures, radio, and now television had slowly transformed almost all aspects of the traditional political landscape in ways that made show business knowledge increasingly valuable and essential. While men like Adlai Stevenson resisted what they considered the debasement of democracy by television, Stanley Kelley Jr. argued that the "adman" did not undermine traditional political structures but rather took over "from the big city boss with new campaign techniques to mold the mind of the voter."[124] Rather than building a block of voters committed to one party through the ties of patronage, the public relations man "fights his battles in the mind of the voter." The new politics used campaign funds to mold public sentiment, not dispense political favors. Constituents, in return, gained more individual choice in selecting their candidates, and they developed a more emotional, personal relationship with their leaders at the expense of receiving concrete "kickbacks" from their party.

The shift toward consultants and advertisers, moreover, reflected a changing attitude about voters' desires and interests.[125] Politicians began looking at voters as media consumers—as television audiences first and citizens second. Political consultants stressed to candidates that "propaganda as a political weapon" could engage those Americans whom interest groups and "precinct workers" had "been unable to bring into previous political battles."[126] Rather than focusing on attracting blocs of voters based on economic interests or geographical location, consultants encouraged politicians to gain votes in the same way that celebrities had generated box office sales: "stimulating" voters through exciting media spot announcements. Publicity men, whether from Hollywood studios, television networks, or advertising firms, successfully convinced politicians of the merits of a "showbiz" political style, because they too had studied California politics to learn about the political application of the "star system."[127] Stanley Kelley Jr. observed that the "attitude" of the new type of political boss "parallels that of the early movie magnates toward their players." Moreover, in his research, which commanded attention from political hopefuls seeking to understand the television age, Kelley argued that "there is evidence that the star system in politics, as in Hollywood, pays dividends."

Mass media politics made "star quality" an essential component of politics, ultimately deepening the niche for Hollywood personalities and salesmanship. The studio system sold personalities, stories, and products unlike any other industry could, and it set the sales standard that Madison Avenue and television companies, and eventually political parties, consistently emulated. And yet the introduction of professional salesmanship and commercialism did more than change the "style" of electoral campaigns; it also reintroduced the assets of the marketplace to American politics, particularly to those on the right who understood the business benefits of "persuasion" and willingly adopted the new modes of communication to reorganize Republican Party structures.

Hollywood, as an industry, attained a distinct place in this new political hierarchy. Eisenhower's personal and professional relationships with Eric Johnston, Robert Montgomery, and George Murphy and his political appeal among patriotic, business-minded studio leaders like Jack Warner, Samuel Goldwyn, and Darryl Zanuck invigorated the Republican resurgence in Hollywood as the president gave these Hollywood leaders a more prominent place in his administration. Through his personal appeal and policy incentives, Eisenhower tapped into the frustrations with big government and regulations that were hurting box office profits. In the end, Eisenhower's ability to transcend traditional party loyalties rebuilt the

Republican Party in Hollywood and made the motion picture industry a key player in Republican politics in a way that Richard Nixon struggled to understand in 1960 but would be forced to depend on later to achieve his political success. During the 1950s, Hollywood political activity in the Republican Party gave consultants advice and tools for the party to use to "wage political war." This new electoral strategy resulted in more than changed perceptions of voters and new types of "bosses. It also changed political perceptions of the skills required for presidential leadership. As Kelley concluded, "Currency of name, the outline of the public personality, adaptability to the various media of communication, the power to command the skill and resources necessary for the build-up and the presales campaign" became the factors that would determine a candidate's success.[128] In short, presidential contenders in the age of the consultant needed to themselves become celebrities to gain political legitimacy.

Asserting the Sixth Estate

Though only six years apart in age, Hubert Humphrey and John Kennedy appeared to be a generation apart in their efforts to secure the Democratic presidential nomination in the early months of 1960. During the Wisconsin primary, Humphrey followed Adlai Stevenson's campaign approach as he traveled the state with the educational director of the United Rubber Workers, who strummed his guitar and sang folk music to appeal to the midwestern state's farmers and workers. After his campaign speeches, Humphrey engaged in intense debates with voters over particular issues, attempting to win over the crowd with his mastery of the details of farm prices and labor union politics.[1] According to journalist Theodore White, Humphrey "stuck to the issues, always a mistake in a primary campaign."[2]

John F. Kennedy avoided this "error" as he pursued a media campaign carefully crafted to generate enough votes and excitement to force the Democratic Party to nominate him during the summer convention. Incorporating lessons learned from the Hollywood studios his father ran and he had visited as a young adult, the senator's campaign strategy centered on creating "Jack Kennedy fans" across Wisconsin.[3] Kicking off his campaign with a personalized version of Frank Sinatra's recent hit, "High Hopes," Kennedy stirred the excitement of screaming teenage girls, who trampled one another for the senator's autograph. A station wagon with two large speakers on its roof broadcast the catchy lyrics for all of Wisconsin to hear: "Everyone is voting for Jack, 'cause he's got what all the rest lack. / Everyone wants to back Jack, Jack is on the right track; / Cause he's got high hopes, he's got high hopes, 1960's the year for his high hopes. / So come on and vote for Kennedy, vote for Kennedy, and we'll come out on top."[4]

According to one newspaper account, "Senator Kennedy, supported by a slick high-octane machine, is a celebrity to folks here. His supporters compared him to a movie star. He spent as much time signing autographs

With the backing of a "slick high-octane machine," John F. Kennedy's campaign created "Jack Kennedy fans" on the campaign trail in 1960. Cornell Capa, photographer, Magnum Photos.

as he did shaking hands. Often he was almost mobbed by autograph seekers."[5] Referred to as a "Battle of Contrasts," the Wisconsin primary—which pitted a traditional, issue-oriented campaign against the politics of image and showmanship—showed the effectiveness of Hollywood publicity at work in an electoral race. Unlike Stevenson and Humphrey, John Kennedy embraced television, advertising, and the role of entertainment in politics. A political unknown before the 1956 Democratic Convention—at which he nearly got the vice presidential nomination—John Kennedy used his intimate knowledge of the mass media, his Hollywood connections, and his family's wealth to generate excitement, publicity, and political legitimacy.

While Franklin Roosevelt emerged as the first media-savvy president and Dwight Eisenhower the first "prime-time" television president, John F. Kennedy, or simply "Jack," became the first celebrity president. Kennedy did not rely just on Hollywood personalities to produce positive television or radio spot advertisements, sell a particular political ideology, and teach him the "tricks of the trade," as Roosevelt and Eisenhower had done. Kennedy used his personal fascination with Hollywood stars and his father's professional connections in the studios to make him a celebrity in his own right. The Hollywood Dream Machine at work during his campaign not only expanded the reach of his political message, as it had with his predecessors, but it also allowed Kennedy to make himself a viable political candidate from the beginning. Kennedy's 1960 electoral success—from the primary to the national campaign—ultimately made media image, the primary campaign trail, television, and strong financial backing necessary to winning national political attention.

Television during the 1960 election, contend many political scientists and historians, transformed the electoral process and ushered in the modern celebrity presidency.[6] Historians frequently focus on the role of the television debates and how John Kennedy's attractive, charming television image helped him defeat the nervous and sweaty Republican nominee, Vice President Richard Nixon.[7] And yet, even before Kennedy's presidential campaign, both the Republican Party and the Democratic Party had accepted the importance of crafting appealing television images for their candidates. Republicans, in particular, worked with network executives to absorb publicity lessons from the Hollywood star system that had shaped California politics over the past two decades. Many of the aspects of the "celebrity presidency"—specifically the use of entertainment to stimulate voter interest, behind-the-scenes collaboration with Hollywood figures, and a coherent advertising strategy that focused on selling political personalities—had been developed during the Roosevelt and Eisenhower administrations.

Kennedy, however, became a media celebrity to gain political legitimacy. This did not happen just because of his "natural" good looks or talent, but rather this was a consciously designed strategy to take advantage of new avenues to gain political power. Hollywood's electoral politics during the 1950s paved the way for the success of a showbiz politics in the 1960 election. Much more than merely including endorsements or advice from entertainers to generate political attention, showbiz politics required a candidate to use the tools of the star system—from creating advertising spots to responding to public opinion polls to making live television appearances— to appeal to voters as not just media consumers but as fans. Scholars frequently allude to Kennedy's "celebrity appeal" by simply pointing to the flashy Sinatra theme song, the swarms of excited young girls who screamed when he arrived, and the confident way he spoke to audiences through the television camera at the debates. But this narrative overlooks the fact that John Kennedy, with the help of his brother Robert and father, Joseph, decided to pursue a mass-mediated campaign specifically designed to use advances in advertising and communications technology to prove to party bosses the electability of an Irish Catholic.

John Kennedy's media campaign, from the primary battle to the general election, mirrored the style and organization of campaigns that had been successful over the past twenty years in California state politics. Kennedy's 1960 campaign used strategies of the Republican offensive during the 1934 California gubernatorial campaign and the liberal mobilization on the California congressional primary trail in 1944. Though controversial at the time, his victory later created a bipartisan political belief in the power of showbiz politics, which opened the doors for actors like George Murphy and Ronald Reagan to gain acceptance not just as advisers but as candidates in their own right. Kennedy's 1960 campaign ultimately forced the Democratic Party to recognize that constructing a celebrity image and building a well-oiled media exploitation campaign could be more than a controversial sideshow or a distraction to American politics. This strategy would help the Democratic Party win the White House, as it also made extrapartisan, private resources crucial to success and diminished the authority of party leaders and interest group endorsements. For the Democratic Party, this showbiz politics would promote a system of popular governance that, in turn, demanded innovations in fund-raising that would bring Hollywood and the president closer while separating the White House party leader from his base.[8]

"Jack Is on the Right Track"

In 1959, both Senator Kennedy and the Democratic Party had visions for how to take back the White House that the Republican Party had occupied for the past seven years. Having only tenuously entered the world of television, party leaders decided to use the new medium to link Democratic chapters across the country, honor their rich history, and raise money through a closed-circuit Truman Diamond Jubilee production that featured "the great political and entertainment leaders of today" in a "spectacular" television program to honor the former president.[9] Featuring Democratic leaders Adlai Stevenson, Lyndon Johnson, Sam Rayburn, and, of course, Harry Truman, the program presented a "one hour kinescope" of brief political speeches, historic newsreel clips, music numbers, and performances by top entertainers, including Jack Benny, Jimmy Durante, Melvyn Douglas, and Mort Sahl. The television event also included a film dramatization of Truman's life from his World War I service to his presidential challenges, which Dore Schary conceived, produced, and narrated.[10] The organization memo acknowledged the motivation for including Hollywood celebrities in the event: the hope that spectacular entertainment would "induce attendance in a political off-year" and generate excitement and dollars for the upcoming campaign.[11]

Deemed a success because it "help[ed] your treasury" and "advance[d] the cause of the Democratic Party in your area," the event provides a window into the Democratic Party's transition into the age of the mass media during the 1950s.[12] As the event attempted to unify the Democratic Party, television literally replaced traditional structures of party mobilization and communication. State and national party officials collaborated extensively on publicity strategies and efforts to ensure that the closed-circuit television system functioned properly. To stimulate interest in the affair, the DNC promised local organizers that Hollywood celebrities would be available to talk via phone to "build enthusiasm for the event."[13] The turn toward using celebrities as political assets and even partisan spokespeople marked a significant shift for the Democratic Party in the late 1950s. Eisenhower and the Republican Party had recognized the potential electoral appeal of actors like George Murphy and Robert Montgomery and welcomed them as political assets, but Democrats had remained wary of the close connections, which had brought so much controversy at the time of the HUAC investigations—a historic event that the Truman Jubilee, of course, left out. In this atmosphere, a candidate with media savvy and wealth could simultaneously push the party forward into the television age and make a name for himself in the Democratic Party. The son of a former studio executive, John F. Kennedy felt he was up to the task.

With the help of his brother-in-law, actor Peter Lawford, Kennedy used the talent and fame of his Hollywood friends to generate voter turnout and popular support for his candidacy throughout the primary elections. Having married Kennedy's sister, Patricia, in 1954, Lawford played a prominent role in linking the candidate to Hollywood performers throughout the campaign. Many newspaper reporters wondered if Lawford would become "Kennedy's Bob Montgomery" and serve as an adviser on camera angles and lighting.[14] The Kennedy family, however, had a long background of Hollywood experience, which made John Kennedy already aware and experienced in staging effective performances and exploiting media opportunities.

The Kennedy family patriarch, Joseph, had been involved in the motion picture industry since the 1920s. As a stockbroker on the rise in 1923, he had made his first millions by buying local movie theaters in Massachusetts and then a production company in the thriving motion picture industry on the West Coast.[15] Running three studios by the end of the 1920s, Joseph Kennedy oversaw film productions, built careers for young stars, and learned the importance of crafting a successful public persona.[16] Y&R, Robert Montgomery, Jack Warner, Eric Johnston, and George Murphy had taught Eisenhower how to construct effective advertisements and promote his personality to win political points. John F. Kennedy, on the other hand, had learned the tricks of the Hollywood Dream Machine from his father, a former studio executive.

As executive of FBO and then Pathe studio, Joseph Kennedy had worked with the power elite of the rising industry to develop a business-style approach to the creative medium.[17] His commercial savvy and media instinct flourished in Hollywood's rapidly changing environment in the late 1920s. He constantly wooed the press with colorful stories that simultaneously sold papers and heightened his professional status in Hollywood and his reputation back on the East Coast. His Hollywood story paralleled the industry's rise in Democratic politics. He too engaged in "industry politics" to advance his economic and professional interests. His active support of Roosevelt's administration helped him secure a subsequent political role as ambassador to Great Britain in 1938.[18] Just as Hollywood celebrities stood outside national politics as amateurs at this time, controversies that surrounded his diplomatic services in Britain during the outbreak of war showed that he had skills in publicity but not necessarily in diplomacy.

"Demanding" that his eldest son enter politics, Joseph Kennedy turned his attention to grooming Jack into the future president of the United States after Joe Jr. died during a risky bombing mission in World War II.[19] Jack Kennedy not only had a father with unique knowledge of the mass media world, but he also had personal experience with Hollywood studio productions and relationships with actors and actresses, which had taught him lessons in communication that would prove increasingly valuable as television and advertising took hold of American politics in the 1950s. Joseph Kennedy sold his Hollywood studios at an enormous profit before the stock market crash, but he kept one eye on the motion picture industry and stayed in touch with prominent actors and executives, frequently bringing his son with him to Southern California. Recuperating from his World War II injuries, Jack spent time with prominent figures like Gary Cooper, Olivia de Havilland, and Marion Davies.[20] Growing up as a privileged youth with a fascination for Hollywood films, Jack Kennedy basked in the glamour and beauty of the young starlets while also learning how cameras, lighting, and staging worked in Hollywood studios.

With his father's financial backing, Kennedy advanced politically in the House of Representatives and then won a Senate seat against Henry Cabot Lodge in 1952. Joseph Kennedy remained a constant presence looming over his shoulder. Scholars continue to debate the policy influence of the former ambassador in Kennedy's congressional career, and clearly the Kennedy patriarch remained committed above all else to using his connections, from William Randolph Hearst (until he died in 1951) and his son, William Randolph Jr., to J. Edgar Hoover, to create publicity opportunities and filter out any potentially damaging reports of his son's womanizing.[21] His financial support of Jack, however, remained a source of contention in the Democratic Party as New Deal liberals looked with suspicion on the integrity, sincerity, and loyalty of the Massachusetts senator, whose political success had been so strongly tied to his father's finances.[22]

Following the 1958 congressional elections and Kennedy's successful re-election to the Senate, his campaign to win the 1960 Democratic presidential nomination began to take shape. Prominent Democrats looked with disdain on this new style of politics that relied on ever-escalating mass media expenses, which John F. Kennedy represented. On December 7, 1958, ABC aired an episode of *College News Conference*, which featured an interview with Eleanor Roosevelt. The former first lady and matriarch of New Deal liberalism harshly criticized the campaign tactics and questioned the political legitimacy of John F. Kennedy.[23] Undoubtedly, Kennedy was a "young man with an enormous amount of charm," Roosevelt conceded. The senator, however, lacked political independence because "his father has been spending oodles of money all over the country and probably has a paid representative in every state by now."[24] Aware of the potential ramifications of such a strong indictment from a well-respected figure in the Democratic Party establishment, Kennedy immediately wrote Roosevelt a personal letter explaining that she had been the "victim of misinformation," and he requested concrete evidence of these "paid representatives."[25] Roosevelt refused to back down, replying that it "seems commonly accepted as fact" that Kennedy's father openly said he would spend "any money to make his son the first Catholic President of this country," and she reprimanded the practice of "giving too lavishly" because it "indicates a desire to influence through money."[26]

Roosevelt's critique of John Kennedy's primary campaign exposed the central conflict between shifting strategies to gain the party nomination. The Kennedy family wealth was indeed essential for John Kennedy to achieve victory in the primary campaign because Kennedy's media strategy focused on generating popular support through television appeals. It made possible the "systematic, large-scale, privately sponsored publicity build up" that Stanley Kelley Jr. had noted as essential for capturing the "public imagination" as a party outsider or political unknown.[27] Kennedy hired Lou Harris to conduct public opinion polls that he used to shape his image and his policy stances to appeal to voter preferences.[28] He commissioned Jack Denove Productions to film his speeches and interactions with voters and to then edit the footage to create effective television spot advertisements. This tactic enhanced the celebrity status of the presidential hopeful when voters watched him on television for several days before he arrived in small towns and crowded cities. In the Wisconsin primary, fifty-two twenty-second television spots played across the electoral battlefield, with paid newspaper and radio announcements to publicize what new Kennedy spots were coming.[29] As Kennedy arrived at local city halls with "High Hopes" playing from the loudspeakers, fans screamed with excitement and besieged him with requests for autographs.

Primary, Robert Drew's documentary of the Wisconsin race, highlighted the different responses of Wisconsin voters to the two candidates. As Hubert Humphrey spoke to small, scattered crowds with an introductory joke about his Polish roots and coffee habits, John Kennedy entered an overcrowded, loud, and excited hall where every participant joyously sang about the senator's "high in the sky, apple pie hopes."[30] The atmosphere of energy and celebrity surrounding Kennedy's campaign, which Drew so effectively captured, was a strategic political move to use Hollywood publicity strategies to force the Democratic Party to accept the legitimacy of John Kennedy as a presidential contender. Having met Kennedy in 1959 while filming *Oceans 11* in Las Vegas with Peter Lawford, Frank Sinatra decided to help his new friend on the campaign trail by producing the personalized version of "High Hopes." This song became a tool to raise funds, increase publicity, and engage voters across the country. During these primary campaign events, miners in West Virginia and Polish Americans in Milwaukee received copies of the lyrics before Kennedy's arrival. Those who wanted memorabilia from the event or who wanted to support the senator from afar could send a dollar to the Kennedy campaign and, in return, receive a vinyl record of Sinatra's song.[31] The song emerged as more than a "soundtrack" to the campaign; rather it served to energize voters and foster an emotional connection between the candidate and his supporters, in ways that Louis B. Mayer had envisioned three decades earlier.

As had Eleanor Roosevelt, Hubert Humphrey looked with disdain on his opponent's high-cost media strategy, which demanded immense personal wealth, frequently referring to Kennedy as "Jack who has jack."[32] After outspending the Minnesota senator by more than four to one in primary races, John Kennedy traveled to the Democratic National Convention armed with victories that he hoped would convince party bosses to support his candidacy. To do this, he had to compete for the nomination with the most powerful Democrat in the country, Senate Majority Leader Lyndon Johnson. While he had not run in any primaries, Johnson had climbed the party ladder over the past two decades and possessed negotiating skills that were already legendary.[33] With only sixteen primaries open to presidential hopefuls, Kennedy had to show his electability in key demographic areas, like Wisconsin and West Virginia, and to use this perceived popularity to convince powerful party figures like Chicago mayor Richard Daley that he, not Johnson, should headline the ticket to defeat Richard Nixon in the national race. In 1960, winning the Democratic nomination required backroom negotiations with party officials and labor union leaders and the ability to trade dollars for political support.[34] The Kennedy wealth bought not just media time but also delegates from state and local bosses. Ironically, the media campaign that Kennedy pursued so effectively would, over time, be the key factor in diminishing the political authority of these same local and state party bosses less than a decade later.

Taking place in Los Angeles, the Democratic National Convention reflected the shift toward mass media and entertainment that figures like Stevenson, Roosevelt, and Humphrey regarded with suspicion. In fact, the DNC used the glamour and appeal of the local entertainment industry to engage television viewers across the country. The convention opened on July 11, with over two dozen celebrities, including Sinatra, Lawford, and Sammy Davis Jr., appearing on stage in a "Parade of Stars." After being ushered into the elaborately decorated, ultramodern arena by 200 "Golden Girls" from Southern California, these celebrities joined together to sing the National Anthem and to recite the Pledge of Allegiance. The *Chicago Daily Tribune* noted that while entertainment provided the high point to many viewers, it angered "party professionals," who criticized "the glamour brigade's distracting attention from the serious business of the convention."[35] Political drama clashed with Hollywood spectacle as a last-minute Draft Stevenson movement by disenchanted liberals fueled an intense battle between the two-time unsuccessful Democratic nominee and Kennedy. Pro-Stevenson delegates made emotional and loud appeals for his nomination, but the primary victories and promises to party leaders combined to propel Kennedy to victory.[36]

Kennedy's success showed that primary elections mattered and that a media-centered strategy could win the presidential nomination. At the same time, the Radio and Television Division of the DNC continued to investigate how to use television and image to generate more political participation among voters outside the convention halls, making the political

John F. Kennedy addresses both delegates at the Democratic National Convention in Los Angeles and television viewers as he accepts the Democratic presidential nomination on July 15, 1960. Kennedy won the nomination after pursuing a mass-mediated campaign on the primary trail carefully designed to make him a celebrity to gain political legitimacy. As this picture shows, the behind-the-scenes production strategy proved successful. © The Estate of Garry Winogrant, courtesy of Fraenkel Gallery, San Francisco.

process more open to average citizens and less dependent on backroom negotiations. J. Leonard Reinsch, head of Franklin Roosevelt's successful 1944 publicity campaign, coordinated the 1960 Democratic convention and stressed the importance of using television to educate voters on the party's platform and candidates both during the convention and on the campaign trail.[37] After John Kennedy secured the Democratic nomination, his personal political production team joined with the DNC in an effort to convince the nation that the Massachusetts senator could "get the country moving again" as president. While the DNC hired advertising agency Guild, Bascom & Bonfigli, Kennedy continued to work with Jack Denove, who had so effectively crafted his primary campaigns. Relying on Denove as Kennedy's personal "advertising manager," the Kennedy team frequently disregarded ideas from the DNC advertisers. Without a clear coordination plan between Denove Productions and Guild, Bascom & Bonfigli, the campaign ineffectively produced television spot productions that drained campaign finances.[38]

Kennedy and the DNC did agree on the importance of the senator's television image in the campaign. Believing that Republicans held editorial power in newspapers across the country, Democrats saw film spots on television as an effective way to communicate with certain voting blocs. Even before he gained the presidential nomination, John Kennedy had worked to gain the support of key entertainers to help him with the market segmentation strategies that Eisenhower had so effectively used. In the hope of keeping African Americans in a party that also relied on conservative white southerners for support, the DNC produced television spots featuring Harry Belafonte, Ella Fitzgerald, and Nat King Cole.[39] However, it was Kennedy, not the DNC, that got the support of civil rights entertainers, especially Belafonte, by forging a relationship with the movement's leader, Martin Luther King Jr.[40] The paid political advertisements focused on short televisions spots of under a minute, rather than the five-minute spots that Eisenhower had incorporated into the ends of popular entertainment shows. Warning Democrats about angering viewers by cutting their favorite programs short, CBS president Sig Mickelson reminded them that a person who had tuned in to watch a Western might be "irritated by intrusion" of politics into the program.[41] Jack Denove agreed that shorter, snappier advertisements that focused on the Democratic "theme line" would better help get the Kennedy message out, and, as Herbert Alexander would later observe when researching campaign costs of political broadcasting, these emerged as the "most economical way for some candidates to reach the electorate."[42]

Due to these innovations, the Democratic Party amassed the largest campaign deficit in its history. As funds ran low, Kennedy's campaign focused less on constructing pricey advertisements and more on creating media events during which Kennedy would appear as a guest—on news shows or with his opponent in the television debates. Extensive scholarship has researched the Kennedy-Nixon debates, and the contrasting images of a healthy, vibrant Kennedy versus a sweaty, nervous Nixon dominate the discussion of these debates and the 1960 election.[43] These media events, however, emerged as only part of the shifting use of television executed by Kennedy's campaign team, which sought to propel the candidate to the center of the television stage rather than rely on advertisements alone to sell his candidacy. Mickelson explained to the DNC that focusing too much on "paid political performances" was a "great error by political professionals in their use of television," because they "fail to recognize the day-to-day news coverage." While viewers had become savvy in recognizing, and were even annoyed by, paid political advertisements, they continued to watch news programs like *Douglas Edwards with the News* in audiences ranging from 12 million to 20 million.[44] As guests on network shows, candidates got effective and free exposure, but they had less control of the production and structure of the show, which meant that charisma and ease before a camera became an important asset.

Denove urged Kennedy to appear on a variety of news shows to take advantage of popular interest in his personality and to use these appearances as a way to reinforce his basic campaign message. The debates emerged as part of the effort to saturate news shows like *Meet the Press*, *Face the Nation*, *Person to Person*, and *Presidential Countdown*, and even the more entertainment-based *Jack Paar Show*. During these shows, Kennedy consistently had higher audience ratings than his Republican challenger, and J. Leonard Reinsch happily reported the statistics showing that "more people are interested in Senator Kennedy."[45] The director of the presidential debates program, Don Hewitt, remembered how Nixon and Kennedy approached the television program very differently. Considering it "just another campaign appearance," Nixon showed up looking "like death warmed over," while Kennedy arrived at the studio savvy to the importance of news events in the broader media strategy of the campaign.[46] More than 70 million viewers tuned into the debates, and the event, Hewitt claimed, changed the American political process by making it "hostage to money." While advertisers and Hollywood advisers had previously stressed the powerful potential of television to shape elections, the memory of the television debates after the election transformed this opinion into an accepted fact of American politics by the end of the decade. The perception that Kennedy won with his media image, however, cemented the place of publicity experts and machinery as essential to future political success. "From that day on," Hewitt lamented, "nobody has ever run for office in the United States without amassing a war chest to buy television time." But it was not just television time that cost money. These coffers also needed to finance a team of professionals to develop advertisements, edit footage, plant stories, monitor public opinion, and advise the candidate. In the 1960s, political parties came to believe that they too needed professional studio resources to win elections, and, as a result, parties had to find financial backers to expand their production and publicity capacities.

More broadly, Kennedy's campaign, which hinged on using new forms of television production and pushed the candidate to the center of these productions, made show business knowledge an even more essential component of waging an electoral campaign. Because of the "enormous complexities of the television performance as well as the intricacies of purchasing time," Mickelson saw hiring a professional advertising agency for campaigns as an "indispensable requirement."[47] Networks and political parties would continue to debate questions of purchasing time "discounts" and the "public good" over the course of the twentieth century. But the perception of advertisers and pollsters as necessary to help candidates navigate the "complexities of television performance" made collaboration with Hollywood insiders vital. In the aftermath of the election, the *New York Times* observed, "Hollywood—even the Republican part of it—was congratulating itself today on having won a presidential election. . . . From a bipartisan standpoint, opinion was unanimous that it was the dramatics of television toward which Hollywood has a justly proprietary attitude that had yielded Senator Kennedy's decisive margin."[48]

Liberal Activism in the Anticommunism Era

Despite the prominent role of Frank Sinatra, Peter Lawford, and other celebrity supporters during the campaign, the legacy of the HUAC investigations and earlier controversies surrounding celebrity activism shaped public debate about the impact of their contributions. Just as the memory of the HUAC investigations just over a decade earlier had made the DNC concerned over accusations of "propaganda," so too did it make Sinatra and other liberals in Hollywood cautious during electoral campaigns throughout the 1950s. As one newspaper writer observed in 1958, after years of "promiscuous blacklisting" when "most of show business gave up its rights of democratic free speech," Hollywood was "tentatively, timidly, and very cautiously beginning to regain its political consciousness."[49]

The Cold War and the legacy of HUAC quickly resurfaced during the 1960 election when Sinatra hired blacklisted writer Albert Maltz for his upcoming production, *The Execution of Private Slovik*. A flurry of intense public and private criticism quickly ensued, targeting not only Sinatra's choice of writer but also John Kennedy. In a rebuttal, Sinatra took out an advertisement in *Variety* that declared, "I and I alone will be responsible" for the filmmaking decisions. Connecting John Kennedy to his choice of screenwriter was "hitting below the belt," declared Sinatra. "I make movies. I do not ask the advice of Senator Kennedy on whom I should hire. Senator Kennedy does not ask me advice on how he should vote in the Senate."[50] Ultimately, Sinatra bowed to the intense public pressure and dismissed Maltz as the film's writer, announcing, "The American public has indicated it feels the morality of hiring Albert Maltz is the more crucial matter, and I will accept this opinion." In assessing the events, the *Los Angeles Times* concluded that "Frank's done himself a great deal of harm, not to mention the harm he'll do for Sen. Jack Kennedy if he goes out campaigning for him as he declares he will do."[51]

The Albert Maltz incident exposed how the legacy of the HUAC investigations continued to restrict liberal political mobilization in Hollywood. As Sinatra jumped aboard the Kennedy bandwagon and used his connections and talent to promote the candidate, his political activities quickly became linked to the memory of HUAC and its investigation into communist subversion in the industry. By 1960, many of the "Hollywood Ten" had avoided the blacklist with pseudonyms, but HUAC continued its investigations into the following year, and anticommunist sentiment still dominated American politics and culture. Liberals like Frank Sinatra, Humphrey Bogart, Bette Davis, and Fredric March, all of whom had been monitored by the FBI for their leftist sympathies, remained committed Democrats, but disparate grassroots clubs across the state had only started to revive networks to promote the liberal issues for which they had campaigned in 1944.[52] The HUAC hearings themselves had explicitly targeted the potential for manipulation inherent in celebrity politics, and organizations like HICCASP had faded away with Henry Wallace's national prominence after 1948.[53] While Republicans commanded the national support of anticommunist entertainers during the 1950s, liberal Democrats found that after the HUAC smoke lifted, the struggling civil rights movement offered a new opportunity to advocate for racial equality, but not through grassroots mobilization, as the HDC had a decade earlier. Rather celebrity activists could use their performance skills at benefit concerts.

Since the 1930s, the entertainment industry had been a profitable source of funds for charitable organizations and civic "causes." In fact, the ability of the motion picture industry to raise donations for the National Infantile Paralysis Foundation, among other philanthropic groups, helped to advance the "industry politics" during the Roosevelt administration. Following the HUAC investigation, the MPIC led the campaign to reinvigorate Hollywood's reputation as a civic-minded and generous community. New organizations developed not only to coordinate the demands for Hollywood talent from benefit organizers across the country, but also to protect the entertainers who had just faced an inquisition about their donations to seemingly worthwhile causes, like supporting orphans during the Spanish Civil War, which HUAC later targeted as communist front fund-raising efforts.

In 1953, theatrical organizations across the country developed the idea for the Theatre Authority, which joined performers from the SAG, the American Federation of Television and Radio Artists, the Actors Equity Association, the American Guild of Variety Artists, the American Guild of Musical Artists, the Authors League Fund, the Negro Actors Guild, and the League of New York Theaters, among others, into a national organization to "cooperate with legitimate benefits and charity events to the reciprocal advantage of the charity, the public, and the performers who participate."[54] Racketeers, promoters, and illegitimate charity organizations had taken advantage of the willingness of performers to donate their talents for a worthy cause, with only a fraction of the money raised actually going to the said destination, claimed the Theatre Authority. The organization set out to provide a clearinghouse for entertainment requests to "protect individual performers against excessive or unfair demands upon their time and talents" and to ensure that a "benefit is not being given for improper purposes or unworthy causes." The Theatre Authority required a written request outlining "the date, time, the place, type of event, the beneficiary or purposes, how the proceeds are contributed and distributed and by whom, the price of admission, anticipated gross, terms for any promoter, producer or impresario, names of performers you contemplate requesting to donate services or to appear for payment" no less than sixty days prior to the event. It then helped to negotiate contractual terms between potential stars and benefit organizers. The Theatre Authority did not "provide performers," but rather permitted "the performers to appear—if they are willing—in a properly cleared benefit." The Theatre Authority wanted to weed out manipulative promoters, whether driven by greed or a communist doctrine, from taking advantage of Hollywood's "heart."

In establishing coordinating centers in New York and Hollywood, the Theatre Authority helped to pave the way for Hollywood liberals to reenter the national political scene on a fund-raising basis. While the McCarthy-era communist purges had opened avenues for anticommunism collaboration between government and Hollywood, it had also silenced overt liberal activism during the 1950s. The conservative political pressure, combined with the Democratic Party's reluctance to collaborate with entertainers, especially concerning the contentious issue of civil rights previously broached by organizations like the HDC, limited opportunities for Hollywood activists. With fewer outlets for political participation within the Democratic Party, liberal celebrities redirected their focus to new types of political activities with outside organizations, such as Martin Luther King Jr.'s Southern Christian Leadership Conference (SCLC), and with the protection of organizations like the Theatre Authority.

In 1957, following the successful boycott protest against the discriminatory policies on public buses in Montgomery, Alabama, Martin Luther King Jr. joined civil rights advocates and black preachers to pursue a nonviolent campaign to challenge the system of racial violence and segregation in the South. As one of the wealthiest groups of African Americans in the country, black entertainers proved instrumental in donating money and raising awareness of the importance of the civil rights campaign, and they used their talents to generate ticket sales for benefit events.[55] Harry Belafonte worked closely with the NAACP, SCLC, and Martin Luther King Jr. to mobilize as many prominent members of the entertainment industry as possible for the burgeoning movement. Even brief performances by these top-billing entertainers could generate much-needed funds for civil rights organizations, which faced severe financial pressure as they challenged white supremacy in the American South.

Unlike many activists on the Left who feared the political and economic ramifications of speaking out, Harry Belafonte sought to use film performances, fund-raising, and political pressure to change government policy and cultural attitudes about race.[56] As a musician and actor, Belafonte used his talents and social contacts to motivate other entertainers to support the movement. In 1957, Sammy Davis Jr. followed his example by publicly joining the NAACP as a Life Member, an act that generated a positive buzz about the organization, which the NAACP gleefully reported, "spread like wildfire."[57] Immediately, the NAACP and SCLC inundated him with requests for performances, from Columbus, Ohio, to Atlanta, Georgia.

Working with the Theatre Authority, the NAACP identified three upcoming opportunities for Davis to generate publicity and money for the movement.[58] First, Davis took advantage of his social networks to sell his friends tickets to a November fund-raising dinner featuring Duke Ellington. Davis then worked with the NAACP to record songs with fellow celebrities boosting the cause of equal rights with an independent recording company, which allowed the NAACP to sell the records for the upcoming holiday season and generate publicity in the process.

Benefit concerts, however, emerged as the most effective way for the NAACP to stimulate interest in the civil rights agenda and raise money. Through the Theatre Authority, the NAACP requested Sammy Davis as the headline entertainer at an upcoming benefit at the Apollo Theater in New York City. Other comedians and dancers also gave performances, but for seven straight days, Davis performed two shows a day to audiences that paid between one and two dollars per show.[59] The Theatre Authority negotiated the travel and lodging arrangements for Davis and the Will Mastin Trio and also established pay of $300 per day for the stars, which Davis ultimately donated back to the NAACP. Other members of the Will Mastin Trio did not donate the money back, and the cost of the show turned out to be quite high, at $15,586. In the end, the Apollo Theater owner and Sammy Davis Jr. received the disappointing news that their efforts netted the NAACP a profit of only $3,859.14.[60]

But the Apollo Theater concert gave Davis valuable experience in organizing benefit events, and he soon began recruiting his celebrity friends to the NAACP cause, sending letters urging them to take out life memberships in the organization, give benefit performances, donate money, and speak out on civil rights issues. "We artists have set an inspiring example of tearing down race barriers in our own field," wrote Davis to his friends. "Now we must put our time, our money, our whole-hearted efforts on the line with our conscience."[61] In February 1960, Davis joined other prominent black entertainers, Sidney Poitier, Nat King Cole, and Belafonte, in forming a new subset of the SCLC dedicated to raising money to fight impending tax evasion charges against Martin Luther King Jr. by the state of Alabama. "The Committee to Defend Martin Luther King, Jr. and the Struggle for Freedom in the South" used the name power of top stars to garner media attention for the protest, of which civil rights leader A. Philip Randolph declared: "The plot to jail Dr. King through a trumped up tax charge is the shabby means by which Alabama's prosecutors hope to put out of action one of the nation's foremost inspirational leaders and thereby weaken the Negro movement in the South."[62]

Sammy Davis Jr. also brought his famous white friends into the cause, and before members of the "Rat Pack" backed Kennedy in the 1960 presidential race, they advocated for equal rights. Throughout the 1950s, the Rat Pack gained fame and notoriety as a tight-knit group of top Hollywood actors, musicians, directors, and producers that held secretive parties and controlled Hollywood society. The *Los Angeles Times* reported that Rat Packers "live close to each other, often go to the same tailor, drive the same kind of car, own homes in the same area in Palm Springs. They travel as a group and even have their own language, a cross between bop talk and high-school slang." Gossip columnists frequently debated who was in or out of the Pack, but conceded that Frank Sinatra stood as the "reigning monarch," with Davis, Peter Lawford, and Dean Martin as core members.[63]

Media accounts focused on the group's womanizing, excessive drinking, potential Mafia connections, and frequent violent outbursts by its leader, Sinatra. The Rat Pack, however, also supported Sammy Davis's work in financing and publicizing the civil rights cause. Frank Sinatra had long been a proponent of equal rights. Having featured in a World War II short film educating young children on the importance of racial and religious tolerance, Sinatra also released the hit song "The House We Live In," which brought that silver screen message to radio listeners across the country. Previously investigated by J. Edgar Hoover for his civil rights sympathies, Sinatra remained an outspoken proponent of integration. "Prejudice and good citizenship just don't go together," Sinatra told *Ebony* readers in 1958.[64] Optimistic about the future of racial equality, Sinatra bluntly stated that "integration is inevitable and bigoted dimwits cannot prevent it."

Along with Dean Martin and Joey Bishop, Sinatra showed how the Rat Pack's support for Davis and the NAACP could produce massive financial returns. In a January 1961 "Tribute to Martin Luther King Jr.," the four Rat Packers joined together in a "spectacular" performance at Carnegie Hall in honor of King and in support of SCLC.[65] Front-row seats sold for $100, and box seats drew $200 each for the event.[66] The willingness of "stars of such a magnitude" to lend their "enormous prestige and influence" to the movement constituted an "amazing development," wrote fellow actor Sidney Poitier in promoting the event. "It is also a sign of the times, and further proof that a new wind of freedom is blowing across the land."[67] Billed as a "once-in-a-lifetime" event, the benefit attracted church groups, civil rights supporters, and Rat Pack fans and raised a net profit of $26,326.51 for the SCLC in one night.[68] According to one columnist, the Rat Pack performance and efforts by other African American stars—Belafonte, Poitier, Ella Fitzgerald, Duke Ellington, Count Basie, and Dinah Washington—should earn the entertainers a special recognition from the NAACP. In 1959, southern ministers stood out for their efforts, and Freedom Riders were vitally important in 1960, but "the entertainers have come onto the battlefield with a bang and the NAACP honor for the year 1961 belongs to them."[69]

And yet the political influence of entertainment fund-raisers in 1961 went beyond the civil rights movement. Seven days before the "once-in-a-lifetime event" at Carnegie Hall, the same performers honored president-elect Kennedy with an inaugural gala, which reporters considered "the most stunning assembly of theatrical talent ever brought together for a single show."[70] Its organizers, Frank Sinatra and Peter Lawford, cancelled Broadway shows for the evening and flew performers in from all over the world to make sure that the best talent in the entertainment industry came together in Washington to welcome Kennedy to the White House. The entertainment event that night in the Washington Armory assembled talented singers, including Ella Fitzgerald and Harry Belafonte; eminent composers, such as Leonard Bernstein; and silver screen stars, including Janet Leigh, Sidney Poitier, Tony Curtis, Bette Davis, Fredric March, and Gene Kelly. The list of gala participants shared many names with those who had headlined civil rights benefits over the past three years. Perhaps even more revealing, the list shared many similarities with that frequently scanned by J. Edgar Hoover and HUAC investigators over the past fifteen years. Sinatra, Davis, March, and Kelly were all frequently monitored by the FBI for their support of potentially subversive "communist fronts." Benefit concerts emerged as a way for liberal activists to reengage in the political scene, and both the civil rights movement and the Democratic Party eagerly capitalized on their newfound avenues of activism.

The "Tribute to Martin Luther King Jr." and the Inaugural Gala had more in common than shared participants: the two "unprecedented" and "spectacular events" had identical underlying functions—to raise money and publicity with professional political performances. Despite the hype of the huge Hollywood celebrity presence at Kennedy's inauguration, the need to pay off the unprecedented $3.2 million Democratic campaign deficit was the primary motivation, not the desire to stir audience emotions, create positive publicity for the president-elect, or bask in the glamour of celebrity—although Democrats appreciated these results as well. The *Hartford Courant* observed that the "greatest take in show business history" to bail out the winning political party from its campaign deficit indicated "how closely the entertainment industry is now being embraced by the politicians" and that this revolutionary fund-raising event "might well be a milestone that social historians may some day find interesting in the developmental history of these United States."[71] The fund-raising efforts by liberal entertainers indeed emerged as an important political change in media mobilization and campaign finance. The civil rights fund-raising campaign reinvigorated Hollywood liberal activity and taught figures like Sinatra, Davis, Fitzgerald, Poitier, and Belafonte important lessons in fund-raising to help politicians looking for sources of financing outside the party structure. Having developed a media strategy that transformed him into a celebrity, Kennedy, and the DNC, needed the box office returns to pay off the production costs of the 1960 campaign.

Financing the "War Chest"

Advances in mass media and the emergence of primary elections as a po-litically significant battlefield contributed to rising campaign costs in 1959 and 1960. John Kennedy's primary campaign expenses totaled nearly $1 million, and he outspent his main opponent, Hubert Humphrey, in every primary election in which they competed.[72] While Kennedy's celebrity strategy won him "free" media attention as his travels attracted newspa-pers and television cameras, the initial expense of this approach meant that Kennedy began his national campaign with a deficit of $217,000. The DNC assumed the debt, as it began the party's most expensive presidential campaign to date.

The introduction of advertising companies into political campaigns during the 1950s made each vote more expensive to capture. Herbert Alex-ander's research for the Citizens' Research Foundation provides a statisti-cal breakdown of the changes that came to campaigns during the 1950s and 1960s. His work demonstrates that from 1912 through 1952 the cost of elections per vote cast remained relatively stable, at nineteen to twenty cents per vote. By 1960, each vote cost twenty-nine cents, and this figure doubled by the 1968 election.[73] During the 1960s, the turn toward television accounted for the increase in campaign expenditures as Democrats and Republicans alike bought airtime for costly political spots.

The Democratic Party struggled to keep up with the rising costs of po-litical elections in the television age—a problem that the new Hollywood-based strategy would exacerbate. Having traditionally lagged behind the Republican Party in support from large corporations, Democrats under-stood the financial difficulties they faced with rising campaign costs dur-ing the 1950s. Fund-raising depended mainly on two efforts, "Dollars for Democrats" and $100-a-plate Jefferson-Jackson Day Dinners. The Dollars for Democrats campaign started as a national party effort in 1956.[74] In the hope of "strengthening party organization" and generating income from small donors, state and local party leaders implemented a "door to door canvass" program to encourage Democratic families to donate. During "D-days," local volunteers would ask Democrats to contribute money to the national committee and also engage in voter registration activities and recruit precinct workers for the upcoming campaign, thus bringing in money for the party and strengthening the partisan connections at the grassroots level. But by the 1960 election it became clear that no more than 10 percent of the escalating DNC budget could be covered by such drives, thus to augment these efforts, the DNC also pursued a "political dinner formula" with its Jefferson-Jackson Day Dinners.[75] In honor of two historic presidents, Democratic supporters gathered regionally in the spring of each year for an evening of affordable chicken dinners and political speeches by state party figures.[76] Considered a "mainstay" of the DNC during the 1950s, these dinners were profitable, but the financial pressures on the DNC following the 1960 election pushed the committee to consider ways to increase the per-plate donations by turning fund-raising dinners into more elaborate entertainment events.

The 1961 Inaugural Gala provided an important lesson for Democrats in how to raise money with star power, just as the growing civil rights movement had so effectively done over the past few years. Eager to contribute to the excitement of Kennedy's upcoming administration, Sinatra and Lawford spent December developing plans for an inaugural event that would go above and beyond what George Murphy had planned for Dwight Eisenhower. It seemed a difficult task to overshadow the 1957 inauguration—Murphy, as the chair of the entertainment division, had brought in what seemed like "half of Hollywood and three-quarters of Broadway" to perform at four inaugural ball events. Observers declared in 1957 that "no previous inauguration came close to matching . . . for variety, splendor, and—once again—spectacle."[77] Frank Sinatra, however, would show that while Hollywood and politicians had "rubbed shoulders" in previous inaugural celebration, the 1961 gala would prove Hollywood's worth in terms of dollars.

Of the five inaugural balls held in honor of President Kennedy, the Inaugural Gala stood as a separate inauguration event planned by Sinatra and Lawford for the DNC. Other inauguration festivities—including a Governors' Reception, Inaugural Concert, Parade, Young Democrats Reception and Dance, a Reception for "Distinguished Ladies," and the Inauguration Ceremony itself—were planned by the Inaugural Committee.[78] By invitation only, the inauguration itself, the ball, and various receptions honored

Democratic administrators, cabinet officials, presidential appointees, Supreme Court justices, ambassadors, loyal contributors, and campaign workers. Events like the Young Democrats Reception and the Inaugural Concert opened up ticket sales to the public, with tickets ranging from five to fifteen dollars. Also selling tickets, souvenir programs, commemorative medallions, and concessions, the Inaugural Committee reported that it made more money than any other inauguration in history.[79] All profits went to either the Guaranty Fund, which provided financial support as a "backstop against a financially unsuccessful inaugural" in the future, or the designated charity, United Givers Fund.

Unlike the other inaugural events, the Inaugural Gala directly benefited the DNC. General admission tickets required a $100 donation to the Democratic Party, and the boxes, which sat ten people in comfort and afforded a better view, cost $10,000. Also different from the inaugural balls, which required invitations, anybody willing to pay $100 could attend the gala extravaganza with the president-elect. A week before the inauguration, ticket receipts and the successful sale of seventy-two boxes for the event promised a gross revenue of $1.9 million. Despite the steep entrance fee, performances by Sinatra, Lawford, Belafonte, Nat King Cole, Ella Fitzgerald, Sidney Poitier, Gene Kelly, Shirley MacLaine, Henry Fonda, Fredric March, Red Skelton, and others promised audience members an evening of entertainment, which, the *Washington Post* observed, "the average couple couldn't hope to see in a lifetime, unless they splurge this year's entertainment budget and buy $100 tickets to the gala."[80]

The star-studded event heightened the excitement surrounding Kennedy's inauguration and showed the importance of the entertainment industry to the Democratic Party's fund-raising efforts. "I don't know what we would do without people like Frank Sinatra," declared the DNC treasurer, Matthew McCloskey.[81] "If it weren't for this the Democrats would be out passing the hat." Relying on Hollywood performers to "bail" the Democratic Party out of its spending—resulting from the turn toward advertising and television to which Hollywood had introduced politicians in the first place, and from which it benefited economically and professionally—showed how closely entertainment had become linked to the political process. With the first fund-raising Inaugural Gala just days away, only Mother Nature seemed able to curb "one of the largest gatherings of enthusiastic Democrats since Andrew Jackson's mountain boys came here 128 years ago."[82] A winter blizzard barreled through the city, bringing travel to a halt and canceling or delaying many of the inaugural events. The snowstorm delayed the "Kennedy Gala" and left the armory only half full; yet the performances of the night astonished audience members who fought the snow.[83]

At the end of the gala, Kennedy told the crowd that "the happy relationship between the arts and politics, which has characterized our long history, I think, reached a culmination here tonight."[84] Indeed, the three-hour celebration presented many of the most famous stars in film, music, and theater, while also relying on the behind-the-scenes talent of famous directors, producers, and technicians. Frank Sinatra opened the evening by articulating the dual role as politician and actor that Kennedy had "played" throughout the campaign. "Our performance will be over in a couple of hours, but the president-elect will be going on stage for at least four years before an audience that has been known to bang on the desk with a shoe. We hope he is a smash, we wish him good luck and may God be with him." While the performances honored Kennedy's political achievements, the evening also stressed the importance of Hollywood in supporting a political process that had drastically changed—financially and stylistically. As she came to center stage and asserted that "show biz" had become the "sixth estate," Bette Davis hammered home the evening's message about the importance of entertainment in American politics.[85]

The evening blended the seriousness of the occasion with comedy, song, and dance. Joey Bishop brought a lighthearted sense of fun to the event by blaming the weather on the poor sportsmanship of the Republican Party, which had yet to give up control of the Weather Bureau. Yet, even in the midst of his jokes, Bishop stressed the overlap between politics and stardom. He introduced dancer and actress Juliet Prowse as "a young lady who is also being elected, only to stardom." Sinatra served as the unofficial host and also dedicated two songs to the president-elect: "You Make Me Feel So Young" and "What America Means to Me," both of which spoke to Kennedy's youthful presence and the importance of politics in Sinatra's life. Composer, conductor, and Kennedy supporter Leonard Bernstein led the orchestra in the Hallelujah Chorus from Handel's *Messiah* and dedicated the song directly to Kennedy because of the "hallelujah" feeling Bernstein had experienced when Kennedy won. In another comic moment, Hollywood couple Janet Leigh and Tony Curtis staged a skit exploring the obscure nature of the Electoral College, with Leigh saying, "I thought Kennedy went to Harvard."

The evening ended in the same manner that Kennedy's campaign had begun a year earlier. In an up-tempo version of the campaign theme song, "High Hopes," all the participants joined in to transform Kennedy's political ascendancy into musical entertainment. Each performer rose to sing about the various challenges that Kennedy had faced, from the Democratic Convention and the addition of Johnson to the ticket, to defeating Nixon in such a close election. Frank Sinatra crooned about Kennedy's celebrity aura by comparing it to his own. "That old Jack magic had them in his spell. / That old Jack magic that he weaved so well. / The women swooned, and it seems a lot of men did too. / He worked a little like I used to do." Sinatra's lyrics celebrated the success of Kennedy's media strategy, which had cast a "spell" over voters by appealing to them as "fans."

The final act offered a historic tribute to Abraham Lincoln. A sober reenactment by Fredric March of Lincoln's 1861 speech emphasized the importance of Inauguration Day. By invoking history, Sinatra attempted to show the serious side of Hollywood as understanding the meaning of political activism. Following the "Moment with Lincoln," Kennedy made a concluding speech. He expressed his delight in the performances of the evening, and in particular with the efforts of his brother-in-law and of Frank Sinatra. Kennedy remarked, "I'm proud to be a Democrat because since the time of Thomas Jefferson, the Democratic Party has been identified with the pursuit of excellence and we saw excellence here tonight." This particular moment highlights Hollywood's role as the "sixth estate" in politics. Musicians, actors, writers, comedians, and producers paid tribute to Kennedy as the supreme celebrity, and the Democratic Party experienced the financial perks of Hollywood entertainment. In return, Kennedy placed these talented people within the historic tradition of political excellence in the Democratic Party and acknowledged the importance and legitimacy of their contribution to politics. The smile on Sinatra's face while Kennedy lauded his efforts told the entire armory that his hard work over the past two months had been time well spent.

Cutting the Democratic campaign deficit in half, the gala represented what one newspaper called "a new frontier in the art of political fund-raising."[86] Soon after the Inaugural Gala, the DNC developed the concept of the "President's Club," which could create the notion of elite political events with extravagant entertainment and new access to the president for wealthy Democrats who contributed $1,000 per year to the party. Rather than focus on the Dollars for Democrats program, the DNC shifted its attention to expanding the political dinner formula by creating an elite group of annual large contributors who would receive special invitations for cocktail events, dinners, and exclusive movie premieres.[87] By 1964, the President's Club had over 4,000 members, who each paid the annual fee and in return could attend exclusive social events, including opportunities to meet the president. Under Kennedy, the President's Club raised $1.9 million from events the president attended. These fund-raising events spared no expense to ensure that attendees had a good time, and the voluntary appearance of Hollywood celebrities elevated the "fun level" of the functions by replacing political speeches with entertainment.

Before the 1960 election, the idea of "fund-raising" meant the Dollars for Democrats Drive or the $100-a-plate dinners that featured local and state politicians. Primarily organized by state and local party members, these events would give portions of earnings to the DNC but would dedicate the remainder to maintaining local party operations. Winning the nomination as a "party outsider," Kennedy did not make it his priority to raise money for the party once in office; instead he focused on raising money to pay off debts incurred by his campaign, which had functioned as a private publicity machine dedicated to his election.[88] With a group of loyal Democratic performers experienced in benefit performances and eager to use their talents to raise money for Kennedy, the DNC turned toward a fund-raising strategy that relied on larger donors and big returns from extravagant affairs. These fund-raising affairs—which served the dual role of raising money and generating publicity—made the entertainment industry an important political partner. The reliance on "big affairs" and extrapartisan connections, however, expanded the celebrity status of the president as it also weakened the Democratic Party by encouraging the president to "prey" upon party resources rather than initiate programs that would strengthen them and maintain a more consistent support base.[89]

The President's Club also received criticism for possible special treatment for members. When Anheuser-Busch Inc. officials donated $10,000 through the President's Club a week before the Justice Department dropped an antitrust case against the company, suspicions of corruption arose.[90] During the 1960s, questions surrounding campaign finance lacked political saliency and the interest of the public, but these questions became more pressing with the struggle for campaign finance reform during the 1970s. But despite the changes of the post-Watergate campaign finance laws, the Democratic Party would remain committed to the fund-raising model developed during the Inaugural Gala, which relied on star-studded entertainment to attract supporters to political events.[91]

The Republican Party responded very differently to the changing economic demands of this shifting political environment. According to Democrats at the time, the Republicans had the support of "big business" and thus had a constant flow of large corporate donations.[92] But, along with support from big businesses, Republicans also pursued a mass-solicitation, direct-mail strategy, which never took hold for the Democrats. By shifting attention to the idea of many small donations, the Republican financial strategy created a stronger base of Republican constituents who gave annually to the Republican Party. The Republican Sustaining Fund focused on many $10 contributions per year per contributor. During its first year, 1962, the mailing campaign brought in $700,000. By the end of the decade, the Republican Sustaining Fund surpassed returns of $2 million a year.[93] Moreover, this turn toward grassroots financial support reflected the broader goal of the Republican Party to restructure American political coalitions and create a Republican constituency that expanded beyond "big business" and attracted white- and blue-collar workers in the suburbs and the booming Southwest.[94]

Moreover, unlike the Democratic Party, Republicans sought to integrate "extrapartisan" organizations, like the Citizens for Eisenhower Committee, into the national party structure; through this tactic of party building, the Republican Party embedded Hollywood resources and activists deeper into the party itself.[95] The Republican resurgence in Hollywood contributed to this broader restructuring of the national party, as George Murphy, Ronald Reagan, and Jack Warner worked to infuse their local Republican Party with Hollywood business sense in a manner very different from that of Hollywood liberals. In the fall of 1955, George Murphy sent Warner material about the Republican Associates (RA). As Warner read the free-enterprise Republican philosophy behind the organization of Republican business leaders in Los Angeles, he soon decided to join, and over the next four years he became an active board member. A nonprofit organization dedicated to working with professional politicians in the Republican party, the RA wanted to bring a "business sense" to the Republican Party as it emphasized a constant, year-round reeducation of local citizens about the merits of small government and the free-enterprise system and the dangers of "quasi socialist concepts."[96] Through educational outreach courses, a research facility of current political material, radio and television programs, and annual "publicity clinics," the RA taught young Republicans not only political philosophy but also "practical techniques of campaigning" to prepare them to run for office in the near future.

Jack Warner and George Murphy brought the important Hollywood connection to Republican Associates, helping solidify the place of Hollywood corporate studios in the restructuring of the Republican Party in California. In the spring of 1959, Jack Warner worked with RA leaders on the "100 Days Campaign" to restructure the Southern California Republican Party to follow the example of the RA and its "businesslike approach" to political organization. The 100 Days Campaign sought to transform the

Republican Party into a corporation with the purpose of increasing money, publicity, and loyalty for the conservative movement that had been growing in California politics over the past decade.[97] The RA urged the larger Republican Party to become more professional, with full-time, paid directors of finance, publicity, and precinct organization, in order to ensure a year-round "merchandizing" of the party. Noticing its achievements, Vice President Richard Nixon expressed praise for the "widespread impact of the program" because of its ability to raise money and morale.[98] The RA would continue to be an important source of expanding the base of Republican support in Southern California and taught important lessons on the need for constant voter education and publicity, on which Richard Nixon and the New Right would draw over the next two decades.

Opportunities and Limitations of Celebrity Political Activism

On both the Left and the Right, Hollywood emerged as an important financial asset to subsidize the increasingly expensive effort to communicate with voters through the media. Based on contrasting experiences from two decades, both parties turned to the entertainment industry, but with different requests. With a history of urging conservative actors to get involved in reshaping the party, the Republicans continued to welcome prominent personalities into the full range of political activities: from policy discussions about the Cold War to collaboration over advertising strategies to evaluations of campaign finance efforts. Democrats, on the other hand, maintained a relationship with supporters that centered on political fund-raising with the goal of building a war chest dedicated to presidential electoral successes. More so than their counterparts, many Democrats remained wary of close connections with entertainers outside fund-raising campaigns. Although Robert Kennedy had advocated a Hollywood media strategy during his brother's primary campaigns, he consistently pushed for John, once in office, to distance himself personally from Sinatra because of the singer's alleged connections to the Mafia.[99] In addition, the marriage of Sammy Davis Jr. to Swedish actress May Britt had stirred controversy in the Democratic Party, which was divided over the question of civil rights. Having received "boos" from conservative southerners after performing at the national convention, Davis found his interracial marriage a political liability. The performer, who had been so instrumental in connecting the civil rights benefit organizations to the Democratic Party, was noticeably excluded from the gala in an effort to prevent a repeat of the convention experience—a slight Richard Nixon would use to bring Sammy Davis Jr. into the Republican camp nine years later.[100]

Sinatra's presence at the Kennedy family compound in Hyannis Port later that year provoked still more criticism. *U.S. News and World Report* ran an article in October 1961 that pointed out this growing concern. "Now it seems to be President Kennedy's turn to come under fire for his associations—sometimes through members of his family—with what is called the 'Hollywood set.' "[101] This article quoted a Cape Cod resident, who complained, "It's about time that President Kennedy does something about these people. Although they are not strictly his guests, he could lay down the law to his relatives if he really wanted to." The president also received a telegraph from a citizen urging "more confidence" for the president than "will come from your playing with Sinatra and Rubirosa."[102] Like Sinatra, Porfirio Rubirosa, the former ambassador from the Dominican Republic, had frequently appeared in the gossip columns for his womanizing lifestyle and had also visited the Kennedy compound in Hyannis Port during Sinatra's stay. At the end of the year, *Private Affairs Magazine* put out a press release that told of its upcoming edition, which would contain "an unknown fact about Sinatra that should raise quite a few eyebrows including the President's!" The magazine claimed to hold no antagonism toward Sinatra: "We just think that the high office of the Presidency calls for a little more circumspectness in its private relationships with people who can only detract from the dignity it represents."[103]

Republicans tried to exploit this divide and fuel opposition to the president by asking, "Do you recall—any of you—Sinatra types infesting 1600 Pennsylvania Avenue in the Eisenhower days? Or twisting in the historic East Ball room? Or wild swimming pool antics shocking to all the country? Or all-night parties in foreign lands?"[104] Republicans claimed to be appalled at the celebrity nature of this presidency. And yet, even as they played into this popular distrust of the use of the celebrity culture for political gain, they were rebuilding their own party even more thoroughly with star power behind the scenes. Nevertheless, this criticism once again attests to the novelty of and controversy provoked by Kennedy's electoral innovations. Eisenhower had certainly taken advantage of Hollywood's electoral politics to help him communicate to voters, but Kennedy had used his celebrity status to establish his political credentials. It had gotten him elected, but it had proven to be a contentious issue, during and after his election.

Kennedy ultimately distanced himself from Sinatra as the singer's mob connections increasingly plagued the administration, showing how, in 1960, "showbiz politics" was a campaign strategy, but most definitely not an accepted style of governance. During a March 1962 visit to the West Coast, the president had planned to stay at Sinatra's home, and the star had enthusiastically renovated his house, constructing a presidential wing for his visitor. However, right before the trip, Kennedy changed his plans and stayed with a prominent Republican, Bing Crosby, instead. While accounts vary as to what motivated this change, the press coverage that emerged the following year linking Frank Sinatra directly to the mob provides possible evidence for Kennedy's decision. The *Chicago Daily Tribune* reported on Sinatra's friendship with Sam Giancana, whom it called a "Chicago hoodlum, regarded as the leading light in Cosa Nostra, the national-wide crime syndicate." This article concluded that Sinatra's "social range encompasses both J.F.K. and Giancana," a public statement that would concern any presidential adviser.[105] Alienated by the president and then later by Bobby Kennedy's formal investigation into his Mafia connections when Bobby served as attorney general, Sinatra, like Sammy Davis Jr. before him, felt betrayed by the Kennedy family, and an astute Richard Nixon would capitalize on these resentments to bring the effective campaigner to his camp years later when he attempted to emulate Kennedy's path to the presidency.

In the summer of 1964, a panel of journalists, local politicians, and movie stars joined together on a Hollywood Press Club panel to address the question: "Should Hollywood and Politics Mix?" Debating the moral right of a performer to "influence followers toward his own personal political, or other belief," the panel concluded that celebrities "could, and should" become active participants in American politics.[106] "Politics is and should be everyone's business and Hollywood is and should be everybody's business," declared one panelist. "I can't think of a more perfectly mixed cocktail." This mixture, however, signaled a decisive shift in party politics that angered many within the Democratic Party, as the controversy over Frank Sinatra illuminated. By accepting the friendship and political support of the Rat Packers during the primary and national campaigns, Kennedy transformed himself into a celebrity and became further dependent on the fund-raising potential of Hollywood, which turned the inaugural proceedings into ones of commercial gain and made the party dependent on extravagant social events to finance party functions.

This fund-raising focus of the Democratic Party and the rising importance of the political primary would drastically weaken party structures on the Left, making media spectacle a necessary strategy for candidates or protestors to gain national attention. During the 1960s, demonstrators—from those promoting civil rights to the New Left—also relied on television cameras and media spectacle to promote their political causes. Harry Belafonte, Sidney Poitier, Sammy Davis Jr., Frank Sinatra, Dean Martin, and Count Basie continued to headline events for the NAACP and SCLC.

Forming the "Stars for Freedom," this celebrity activism frequently went beyond fund-raising, as these stars emerged as an important component of the 1963 March on Washington and the subsequent Selma voting rights campaign.[107] As reporters and photographers meticulously documented the actions of the movement's celebrity supporters, these Hollywood civil rights activists hoped to use their celebrity to "make our weight felt," declared Paul Newman. "We're desperately trying to raise ourselves above the gray mass of people who refuse to be committed."[108] The efforts on the part of Martin Luther King Jr. and other civil rights leaders to use Hollywood celebrities to raise money and attract attention to the cause reflected the movement's broader goals to attain political success through dramatic images broadcasted over television.[109]

The New Left and anti-Vietnam protesters emulated the media strategy that King and the civil rights movement had so effectively used to pressure Congress to pass the Civil Rights Act in 1964 and the Voting Rights Act in 1965. Staging dramatic media spectacles emerged as a powerful way for college students and left-wing radicals to critique the military-industrial complex that they felt had brought an imperialistic war to Vietnam.[110] Hollywood celebrities, emboldened by their civil rights contributions, joined antiwar protests, again giving more publicity and dollars to the opposition to President Lyndon B. Johnson and his foreign policy. When Johnson traveled to Los Angeles in 1967, over 200 Hollywood personalities joined protests over his conduct of the Vietnam War and used their talents and resources to "sponsor books, records, pix, and TV to disseminate their protest."[111] As the studio system crumbled under economic stress, actors gained more authority and independence as they negotiated contracts for only one picture at a time, which released them from the contractual obligations that figures like Warner, Mayer, and Goldwyn had so effectively used to regulate star behavior.

On the Left, fears of communist accusations faded as actors found a voice in movement politics in which they believed. From Jane Fonda's Hanoi travels to John Lennon's political rallies for peace and the legalization of marijuana, movement politics relied on celebrities to use their talent and name recognition to raise money for causes, bring attention to political ideas, and engage youth through entertainment, from risqué film productions to music festivals to living theater performances in the street.[112] In this environment, then, a presidential candidate needed to do more than become a celebrity to gain attention on the campaign trail and votes on Election Day—he needed a permanent staff to engage new voter attitudes and keep him a star in the public eye all year long.

CHAPTER SEVEN

The Razzle Dazzle Strategy

On November 7, 1962, a bitter and tired Richard Nixon held what he called his "last press conference."[1] Discussing his recent defeat by Democrat Pat Brown for the California governorship to a group of a hundred reporters at the Beverly Hilton Hotel, the former vice president made what the *New York Times* called a "valedictory of his national political career." With a quavering voice, Nixon delivered a fifteen-minute monologue, which ended with his famous last words to reporters: "Just think what you're going to be missing—you don't have Nixon to kick around anymore." The California native showed his anger over losing the electoral battle in his own state, a state he had carried two years earlier in the presidential contest with Kennedy. But at the heart of the resentment was a feeling that the press had continually favored his opponents over the course of his political career. Nixon understood that the media culture had started to shift and that communicating to voters through the mass media was essential to political success. The problem: he felt that media coverage with a liberal bias had prevented him from doing this. Over the next six years, the California native found a solution rooted in publicity strategy that had developed around him since his youth.

On September 16, 1968, Richard Nixon made explicit the extent to which he had changed his political strategy when he appeared on a television show that had captivated the nation with its fast-paced, slapstick comedy. After making its debut the previous January, *Rowan & Martin's Laugh-In* had quickly soared to a number one rating with humor that targeted everyone—black, white, male, female, conservative, liberal, young, and old. Now opening for its second season, the show extended its influence beyond the television screen as it expanded the hip lexicon with popular phrases like "sock it to me," "you bet your sweet bippy," and "here comes da judge." T-shirts, napkins, sweatshirts, bags, joke books, bubblegum cards, cartoon strips, and greeting cards quickly flooded the marketplace, making *Laugh-In* the cultural phenomenon of 1968. Celebrities—from John Wayne to Sammy Davis Jr. to Kirk Douglas—appeared, often for just a minute, to utter the show's signature phrase, "Sock it to me!" In response, the show "socks it to 'em" by belting them with marshmallows, a hammer, or some other type of prank, to the delight of the viewing audience. The *New York Times* suggested that the show's influence "may exceed that of any previous TV offering."[2]

The highly anticipated second season of the show began with the mayor of "beautiful downtown Burbank"—where the show was famously filmed—introducing co-hosts Dan Rowan and Dick Martin and welcoming the audience back for the second season of *Laugh-In*. The show quickly "socks it" to them with a shower of golf balls. The regular performers follow suit, declaring "sock it to me," and in return they lose their clothes, are doused in water, or are hit on the head with a hammer or clock. Then the studio phone rings, and the recent victim of a prank bucket of water falling from the door, a shivering English secretary, Judy Carne, answers a phone call, supposedly from New York governor Nelson Rockefeller. "Oh no, I don't think we could get Mr. Nixon to stand still for a sock it to me." But, to the surprise of the national viewing audience, the next shot is of Richard Nixon, the Republican presidential nominee, turning to the camera with a feigned look of surprise. "Sock it to me?" he awkwardly asks.

The "sock it to me" heard around the nation made explicit the historic juncture between presidential politics and popular entertainment. Scandalous and shocking to many older viewers, including Nixon's opponent, Vice President Hubert H. Humphrey, who refused the show's invitation, many Americans thought it undignified for a presidential candidate to appear on such a foolish program. But the appearance on *Laugh-In* fit perfectly into Nixon's new media objectives for 1968: connecting with the under-thirty generation, making the candidate a constant part of popular consciousness, relying on a "hit and run" sales strategy, and, most important, using entertainment television to bypass the press and actively construct a public image of a likable, popular personality to assert his political legitimacy.

Nixon resurrected his political career through an embrace of showbiz politics—a conscious and purposeful turn toward studio publicity, production, and salesmanship structures and philosophies to win the presidency. John F. Kennedy successfully transformed himself into a celebrity candidate during the 1960 electoral campaign, but Richard Nixon's constant effort to control his media image and then his embrace of this as a permanent campaign strategy once in office made Hollywood a permanent part of American politics. Less than a month after winning the 1968 election, the television producer–turned–political adviser Roger Ailes began to make plans for Nixon's next presidential campaign. Formalized with the creation of the Committee to Re-elect the President (CREEP) two years later, a full-time Hollywood production center took shape and recruited entertainers to work for Richard Nixon throughout the year to promote his policies at home and abroad. Nixon worked to develop personal relationships with both celebrity supporters and powerful Hollywood executives in an effort to ensure constant collaboration on camera, in social circles, on the campaign trail, and behind the scenes. By 1972, Nixon had professionalized conservative entertainers in a way that rebuilt the Republican Party into an effective corporate media organization and made the president the number-one media attraction.[3]

At the same time, as the Democratic Party fractured, celebrities also expanded their role in party politics, and by 1972 George McGovern also relied on showbiz politics in his campaign, although a lack of organization and oversight made the electoral achievements of liberal celebrities pale in comparison to their conservative counterparts. The Republican Party functioned like a corporate studio, the "Old Hollywood," and Nixon collaborated with studio executives, who had organizational skills, money, and connections. The Democratic Party, on the other hand, lacked the top-down media structure and ultimately resembled the "New Hollywood," which celebrated liberal cultural trends on the screen and propelled to fame new and unlikely stars, from Barbra Streisand to Dustin Hoffman. On both sides of the electoral battle in 1972, however, the campaigns placed faith in showbiz politics to raise money, generate awareness, communicate to voters, and gain political power. The 1970s saw the triumph of the consultant, the pollster, and the entertainer in American politics, all of whom reinforced the other's political authority when advising candidates on how to navigate political structures that had been dramatically changed by the open primary, the Twenty-sixth Amendment, and the expansion of mass media.

In Kennedy's Footsteps

On the eve of the 1968 presidential election, two candidates made their last-minute appeals to the American public for their votes. Determined to learn from his mistakes against Kennedy during the 1960 primary campaign, the Democratic presidential nominee, Hubert Humphrey, emulated the "Coffee with Kennedy" call-in events that he believed had carried his opponent to victory eight years earlier. As questioners surrounded the vice president and viewers phoned in their concerns, the presidential hopeful engaged in a discussion of campaign issues on camera. Humphrey's DNC media team then cut down the two hours of taped footage to a thirty-minute televised event that showed Humphrey competently handling panelists' and callers' questions with confidence and ease. Aiming to place Humphrey in a "natural setting," the producers even left out empty coffee cups and television wires for the viewing audience to see. Humphrey's election night "telethon" sought to use particular media advances, such as cutting and editing film footage, and to limit the candidate's long-winded answers with orchestrated phone calls to tap into the vice president's campaign message of his honesty versus Nixon's constantly morphing identity.[4]

Nixon also followed the media strategy that he felt Kennedy had used so successfully against him during the 1960 national campaign. Convinced that his opponent's celebrity media style had accounted for his small margin of victory, Nixon carefully controlled his image throughout the campaign. The election eve "telethon" began with actor Jackie Gleason introducing the program and stressing his belief that "this country needs Dick Nixon, and we need him now."[5] The camera then turned to Nixon, who sat in a carefully lit studio crafted by Jack Rourke, the set designer for a popular NBC program, the *Merv Griffin Show*. Working with four different cameras to ensure a flattering angle for the candidate, a media team carefully rehearsed questions from viewers. Paul Keyes, the head writer and producer for *Rowan & Martin's Laugh-In*, fielded caller questions and then "rephrased" them to match what he had written in advance to make sure that no caller could "trip up" the president with an unrehearsed question. No wires or empty cups or chairs appeared on screen. With the top television producers and writers carefully overseeing the event, the evening tolethon went off without a glitch

Looking healthy and confident, Nixon answered a caller's question about the role of image in the campaign by assuring him, "I'm not a showman, I'm not a television personality."[6] Although both candidates were trying to emulate John F. Kennedy's successful media campaign in 1960, Humphrey and Nixon wanted their viewers to believe that they were politicians and not performers. And yet both relied on new media strategies to communicate their candidacies and stances on issues to voters through a conscious use of the techniques from television and film production studios. As Nixon's media strategist, Roger Ailes, watched the Republican nominee's successful election eve appeal, he understood what Nixon and Humphrey frequently did not want to admit. Politicians forever more "would have to be performers."[7] Ailes proclaimed the incorporation of Hollywood studio strategy into presidential politics to be "the beginning of a whole new concept," but, in fact, the 1968 election shows the attempt by both parties to incorporate very specific lessons from the 1960 election.

Eight years earlier, both Humphrey and Nixon had looked publicly with disdain (and privately perhaps with a bit of jealousy) at the celebrity style of Kennedy. While Humphrey's emphasis on discussing farm issues and strumming labor union songs on a guitar pointed to his inexperience in media exploitation, the fact that Nixon failed to defeat Kennedy in the realm of the mass media came as a surprise, considering the well-established media organization that the Republican Party had developed under Eisenhower. Boasting connections with advertising firms and Hollywood personnel, the Citizens for Eisenhower Committee proved extremely effective in raising money and developing talent and ideas for television spots during the 1956 campaign. Eisenhower understood the important role the committee had played for him in the previous campaign, and he worked to help Nixon establish a similar committee, "Volunteers for Nixon." Despite Eisenhower's effort to get the organization moving in 1960, Nixon overlooked the importance of this committee, lagged in naming a director, and faced a $3 million shortage of operational funds just two months before Election Day.[8]

In many ways, this "lag" showed the problems of party building initiatives that centered around the personality and ideas of President Eisenhower himself as much as it showcased the growing ideological cleavages emerging within the Republican Party. Advocating for the expansion of a "Modern Republicanism," the president worked with moderate party leaders and independents in the Citizens for Eisenhower Committee to emphasize cooperation with the New Deal state and keep control out of the hands of what he called a "ludicrous partnership of the Old Guarders and the McCarthyites."[9] And yet Eisenhower was only partially successful, and as the standard-bearer for the party in 1960, Richard Nixon faced this party divide nationally and in Hollywood as well. Right-wingers in Hollywood strongly criticized the moderate foreign policy stances of the Eisenhower-Nixon administration—from the censoring of Joe McCarthy to pursuing negotiations with the Soviet Union over nuclear testing.[10] In both his 1960 campaign and his subsequent gubernatorial campaign two years later, Nixon spent time, energy, and resources to negotiate these intraparty divides rather than pursuing a mass media appeal to independent, and perhaps even Democratic, voters.[11]

Nixon's lack of enthusiasm for the Volunteers for Nixon Committee, however, also reflected his broader effort to preempt reproaches for using advertising to construct or manipulate his image. During the 1952 election, Nixon took to television to ward off criticisms that he had hoarded a secret campaign fund. In an effort to salvage his candidacy for the vice presidency, Nixon took advantage of television in a brilliantly effective appeal. He appeared on television with his wife, outlined all of their financial holdings, and celebrated the "respectable Republican cloth coat" that his wife Pat wore. As he ended the address with his famous promise to keep the family dog, Checkers, who had come from a supporter in Texas, an outpouring of support came in from viewers across the country, solidifying his place on the ticket. This very address, which helped him win the vice presidential nomination, also brought on accusations from liberals that he was indeed "Tricky Dick" and would do anything to get elected. In the eyes of journalists like Walter Lippmann, who had criticized the ability of the mass media to manipulate the American people since the 1920s, Richard Nixon posed a threat to rational, intellectual public conversations about pressing social problems.[12]

With little participation in Eisenhower's prime-time presidential operation and aware of the criticisms that circulated among liberal intellectuals at the time, Nixon approached television like Humphrey, Eleanor Roosevelt, and Adlai Stevenson had. Throughout his vice presidential career, Nixon attempted to present himself as a mature politician who was qualified and knowledgeable, not manipulative and self-serving. In the 1960 election, the vice president campaigned on the idea of a "New Nixon" who was a respectable and deserving public leader capable of succeeding President Eisenhower.[13] In his television advertisements, he appeared in an office setting and spoke directly to the cameras, in direct contrast to Kennedy's use of catchy jingles. Moreover, while he did hire an advertising agency to help him construct a media strategy, the organization, Campaign Associates (a small subset of the RNC's hired agency, BBD&O), set up an office on Vanderbilt Avenue, a side street in Manhattan a block away from Madison Avenue, in an effort to disguise its activities as advertisers.[14] Nixon also refused Eisenhower's offer to have Robert Montgomery advise him on his television appearances.[15] Nixon understood the prominent role television would play in the campaign. And yet he did not acknowledge the changes in campaign tactics required to master the medium. Montgomery and Eisenhower watched the vice president in the debate and were "flabbergasted" by the potential negative ramifications of Nixon's television handicap. Eisenhower had listened to Montgomery's suggestions about makeup, dress, and lighting over the past eight years, but Nixon had not been a part of these conversations.

Moreover, as a native of Southern California, Richard Nixon did have connections to and support from the entertainment industry, but he used these resources differently than both his predecessor and his current opponent had.[16] Throughout the campaign, Nixon accepted the support of the Celebrities for Nixon-Lodge organization, but he neglected to incorporate its efforts into the broader Volunteers for Nixon Committee—as Eisenhower had done with his Citizens for Eisenhower Committee—or use its knowledge and talent to support his candidacy in any organized capacity. John Kennedy generated massive amounts of publicity and dollars from his public supporters in Hollywood and also from his deployment of showbiz politics to gain political legitimacy. Nixon, on the other hand, viewed Hollywood political activity as a subsidiary of his campaign, not a strategy in and of itself. Nixon relished the personal relationships he had formed with stars like George Murphy and eagerly wrote to the actor he nicknamed "Murph" about the latest Hollywood gossip.[17] "Murph" did support his friend on the campaign trail. But, when he found that the Republican Party could not compete with the glamour of the reinvigorated liberal celebrities turning out for Kennedy, the Celebrities for Nixon committee Murphy organized stressed that although its members might "not be the most popular at the moment, they have dignity and the right image."[18] Celebrity supporters—including John Wayne, Ginger Rogers, Helen Hayes, and Irene Dunne—attempted to show American voters that the Democratic Party did not monopolize Hollywood loyalties, an idea the televised Democratic National Convention in Los Angeles seemed to convey.[19] John Wayne even used his release of the movie *The Alamo* and his purchase of a three-page advertisement in *Life* magazine to link the heroism of Texans in their independence struggle a century earlier to that of Nixon.[20]

Similarly to Adlai Stevenson, Nixon welcomed the support of celebrity political activists in state and local politics throughout California but neglected to use effectively the tools of Hollywood studio structures in his national campaign. While Kennedy proved innovative in his use of the media and entertainment strategies to stimulate interest in his candidacy, Nixon, the man previously deemed "savvy" on television, had become "flatfooted."[21] The vice president worked to present himself as "fair-minded, clean-cut, and clean-intentioned" and criticized his opponent for reliance on media.[22] Publicly warning of the "cheap publicity" Kennedy was receiving from "the element that is supporting him," Nixon's campaign attempted to turn lack of overt advertising and media strategy into an asset for the vice president.[23] In doing this, Nixon followed the same strategy of those liberals who had publicly reviled him throughout his career, again revealing the novelty of Kennedy's campaign strategy and the broader suspicion of media manipulation that remained in American society during the 1960 election. In fact, the triumph of Kennedy's showbiz politics style emerged not because his glitz and glamour necessarily won him votes. Rather, it emerged because a bitter Richard Nixon firmly believed that it did and used this interpretation of the 1960 election to shape his "comeback narrative" eight years later.

Emulating Reagan: The Image as the Reality

Watching Kennedy squeak out enough votes in Illinois and Texas for victory, Nixon concluded that his opponent's success lay in his mastery of television, not of the issues. Two years later, having suffered defeat in the race for governor of California, Nixon bitterly linked his exit from the political world to the media in his famous "last press conference." The *New York Times* reported Nixon's defeat in 1960 and 1962 as a "tragic story" of a man who rose and fell in politics too quickly. The biggest problem Nixon faced, *Times* columnist James Reston argued, was his "preoccupation with the machinery of politics." While Nixon "attacked planning," he also planned everything, and despite his best efforts to appear honest, "everything seemed to be contrived, even the appearance of naturalness."[24] Nixon always believed that the press was "kicking him around." In fact, he emerged at a time when the relationships between the media and politicians had drastically changed.[25] His efforts to control his image only motivated journalists to dig deeper to uncover what tools he, and other politicians, used to craft their media personas.

While Nixon suffered defeat in a political atmosphere that increasingly relied on image, George Murphy and Ronald Reagan rose to national political prominence because both men understood that television was not just another tool for political communication. It needed to be the central component of a political campaign. George Murphy's work with Eisenhower and the California Republican Party made him an increasingly valuable asset in a state political system that had long valued and practiced "media-driven performative politics."[26] In 1964, Murphy constructed a media-savvy campaign that united Independents, Democrats, and conservatives across the state to defeat Kennedy's former press secretary, Pierre Salinger, in a remarkable senatorial upset.[27] Murphy's win signaled that electoral victories increasingly demanded an attractive, likable persona that could appeal across party lines the way that Hollywood films had so successfully done during the studio years. Moreover, Murphy's political success demonstrated a clear shift in public views of celebrity. After depending on entertainers to fight for democracy abroad and advise politicians on how to campaign and even govern with television, voters accepted that these individuals also had the qualifications for political office. The public relations campaigns of the 1950s, which stressed the public service of Hollywood stars and their rising political authority within diplomatic, party, and civic organizations, had changed popular perceptions of "celebrity."

Reagan followed Murphy's lead. As he gained political contacts through his work with General Electric and the MPIC during the 1950s, Reagan began to make friends in conservative Republican circles across the country. As a frequent speaker at Republican events, Reagan capitalized on the broad public interest in the behind-the-scenes activities of Hollywood studios and frequently began speeches attacking big government regulation and taxation with anecdotes about his Hollywood film career and studio production practices.[28] Just as Murphy had, Reagan gained prestige in the California Republican Party, and in 1964 he led enthusiastic Hollywood conservatives in Barry Goldwater's Southern California grassroots campaign for the presidential nomination.[29] As Reagan used his conservative credentials, Hollywood fame, and television skills to win national attention with his compelling endorsement of Goldwater's presidential candidacy, he also laid the groundwork for his 1966 race for California governor against Pat Brown.

Brown had defeated Nixon four years earlier, but Reagan brought the governorship back to the Republican Party by speaking the language of the silver screen and appealing to the emotions of voters. As two contemporary political scientists observed in the aftermath of the election, Ronald Reagan followed the Eisenhower playbook from 1952. The California Republican Party recruited an "attractive, conservative candidate with virtually no political experience and placed him under the skilled management of one of the most successful political public relations firms in the nation, which created an image of a political moderate acceptable to all."[30] One significant difference existed between the two men. Eisenhower was a popular personality because of his fame leading Allied forces during World War II. Reagan's popularity hinged on his experience as an actor. Brown used this acting experience to attack Reagan, but in the end this did not stop voters from casting their votes for the former star. In fact, observers noted that Reagan's claim that he was a "citizen politician" rather than a "professional" stirred a "Jacksonian chord in the public mind."[31]

Ronald Reagan based first his acting career and then his political career on public opinion generated through media messaging. Capturing the "imagination of the people wherever he goes," Governor Reagan quickly emerged as a potential candidate for the Republican presidential nomination in 1968.[32] Also having an eye on a future presidential nomination, Richard Nixon collected extensive research on Reagan and studied his political strategy and media style. Combing through speech after speech, he realized the root of Reagan's political effectiveness. "We may think this is demagoguery, but it is very effective," Nixon wrote to his top advisers in 1968. Reagan, observed Nixon, "reaches the heart. We reach the mind. . . . Do we not miss an opportunity in failing to reach the hearts and not just the heads?"[33]

During the mid-1960s, Nixon remained out of the public eye but very aware of the possibilities of reasserting his candidacy in the 1968 election and determined to develop a new media strategy that would appeal to the hearts of the American voters. While Reagan studied Murphy's political success in 1964 to help him rise in the ranks of the Republican Party, Nixon studied Reagan's. Through his extensive research on the former actor, Nixon learned how, for the California governor, "image is the reality."[34] One report on Reagan's political success noted that the governor was not a "political fraud," but rather a "suburban politician who communicates the message his audience, largely in the South, largely immigrant in origin and parentage, wants to hear."[35] Along with revealing to Nixon the "right ingredients for a mass lower class appeal" that could restructure the Republican Party, Reagan's political success in California showed a "political style that is well suited to an age of mass media" because the governor had a "way of stating the issues that is unfailingly newsworthy, if not new."[36] Trained in the Hollywood studio system, Reagan knew how to appeal to a diverse crowd and root common values in a diligently constructed "politics of Americanism."

Studying how Reagan won the race he had lost, Nixon believed that to achieve his political goals he had to construct a media strategy that emphasized Hollywood personalities and publicity styles in ways that he had previously ignored. Celebrity endorsements, like the ones he had received throughout his career and during the 1960 election, were not enough to win an election, but implementing a studio production system to promote himself as a star potentially could. Even before he reentered politics in 1967, his friend and television producer Paul Keyes had urged him to remain in the public imagination by associating himself with entertainers at home and abroad. When Nixon went on a European tour in 1963, Keyes urged him to visit "American movie stars on location making films."

By mingling with Hollywood celebrities in Europe, Keyes explained, columnists like Hedda Hopper would mention Nixon, and "papers and magazines where people who don't read editorial pages, etc., can see him."[37] Keyes constantly reminded Nixon of the importance of using entertainment forums—from columnist discussions of his celebrity encounters to developing an appearance for Nixon in 1963 on the *Jack Paar Show*—to enhance his popularity with the American public.

As a lawyer working in New York City in 1966, his colleague Leonard (Len) Garment reinforced Keyes's message and urged Nixon to consider returning to public life during the upcoming campaign. As Nixon slowly moved into the public eye again through a 1966 appearance on *Meet the Press*, Garment urged him "to poke fun at the questioners and at yourself, and at the general scene."[38] Rather than putting emphasis on specific issues—which Nixon had done in the 1960 election—Garment stressed emphasizing his personality as "reflective, humorous, complex." After all, argued Garment, "I don't know anyone in public life who looks better on the screen while actually laughing." Humor could develop charisma and an emotional connection between Nixon and the television viewer. "Today's candidate," Garment told Nixon, "must learn to grapple, to cope, and to conquer television—refine and project a 'saleable' television image—in order to become attractive to the electorate."[39] Crafting this image, however, demanded time, practice, resources, and experience.

Garment was not alone in his belief in Nixon's potential to win the 1968 election through a more determined, focused, and elaborate media strategy. A schoolteacher from Pennsylvania, Bill Gavin, urged Nixon to pursue the Republican nomination, assuring him that with the proper television strategy, he could win. After all, Gavin wrote Nixon, "nothing can happen to you, politically speaking, that is worse than what has happened to you."[40] Gavin urged Nixon to go on the offensive with television, and he saw possibilities of Nixon "revolutionizing" the medium. Gavin's ideas and encouragement caught Nixon's attention, and he sent Garment to Pennsylvania to find out more about the teacher and evaluate his interest in working on a campaign to win the Republican nomination the following year. Well versed in mass communication theory, including Joseph Klapper's *The Effects of Mass Media*, Gavin brought new ideas on how to wage a television campaign and connect to the "soul" of Americans.[41]

Harry Treleaven, an advertising man who had recently crafted George H. W. Bush's successful congressional campaign in Texas, joined Garment and Gavin in the fall of 1967 with ideas on how to interest voters in Nixon's candidacy by using images that simplified complex issues. Treleaven saw political candidates as "celebrities" similar to Johnny Carson and Batman, and therefore the political campaign had to capitalize and expand this popular perception to interest voters, who were frequently bored by detailed policy analyses.[42] Former *New York Herald Tribune* editorial writer Ray Price soon joined the growing campaign staff, bringing talent and expertise in crafting speeches and television scripts. A television executive at CBS, Frank Shakespeare, also saw potential in Nixon and joined the media team that was forming in 1967. The successful producer of *The Mike Douglas Show*, Roger Ailes, met Nixon in 1967 as the presidential hopeful prepared to go on the show as a guest. As Nixon chatted with the producer, he sighed with frustration over the "gimmicks like this" that were needed to be elected. Understanding the potential of television to reach voters and communicate through images, Ailes shook his head and told Nixon that "television is not a gimmick." Determined to have a new approach toward the medium that still haunted his memories of the 1960 election, Nixon told Garment to hire Ailes to round out the media strategy team.[43]

With the Republican primaries on the horizon, Nixon had gathered a talented group of advertising and television men all united around a common belief that his media strategy had cost him the election in 1960 and a determination to not make the same mistakes again. Like Kennedy in 1960, Nixon needed to show his electability through primary contests; therefore, he gathered consultants dedicated to him, not to the GOP. But, unlike Kennedy, who had used his carefully constructed popularity to establish himself as a party leader, Nixon now used a carefully crafted image to reassure party leaders that the public image of Nixon was not that of a "loser." Nixon had credibility and authority within the party, and now he needed to show that he had popularity with voters. By 1968, the Republican Party lacked a dominant leader to unite rival factions, which ranged from Goldwater conservatives on the Far Right, to moderate Republicans, like New York governor Nelson Rockefeller, who were willing to work within the New Deal structures as Eisenhower had done. In 1964, Goldwater captured the Republican nomination through an effective grassroots campaign that gained strength in the Sunbelt by espousing vigilance against communism, the importance of self-reliance, and a strident, uncompromising patriotism.[44] The Arizona senator's resounding defeat in the national electoral contest, however, reminded Republicans of the need to reach voters across the country, including many who regularly voted for Democrats.

Nixon kept this important lesson from 1964 in mind as he began his primary campaign. The team of television producers incorporated lessons from Hollywood studios about lighting and camera angles and also about how to appeal to a diverse audience. To Nixon's team, the 1968 campaign had "become a national campaign in a more complete sense than ever before."[45] These advisers discussed how regional and geographic political divisions had "given way to the new politics of media campaigning." Rather than focusing on policy details, which Nixon had prided himself on mastering in 1960, Nixon's team found it more important to emphasize "the issue of the spirit" and to use television as the central means to establishing an emotional connection between Nixon and voters.[46]

Appealing to "New Voter Attitudes"

In January 1968, *Time* magazine predicted that the upcoming electoral contest would cater to "the human factor rather than the statistical and fiscal in defending domestic programs" through "heavy use of sophisticated television advertising." As Bill Gavin read the article, which focused primarily on Lyndon Johnson's potential electoral strategy, he wondered, "Has the old boy been reading our mail?"[47] By 1968, politicians and the American public had accepted the place of television in campaigns. Four years earlier, both Johnson and his opponent, Barry Goldwater, had hired advertisers and deployed Hollywood celebrities to raise money and create publicity for their campaigns. Johnson's production of the powerful "Daisy" advertisement helped him win control of the media narrative when it cast Goldwater as the extremist candidate.[48] In the aftermath of the election, President Johnson even began initiatives to use committed entertainers to help sell his legislative agenda, the "Great Society." Bess Abell, social secretary to Lady Bird Johnson, urged the president to take advantage of the eagerness of celebrities who "believe in your program, in your hopes for a great society and are eager to participate."[49] Abell urged Johnson to form a "steering committee" of celebrity supporters, which could coordinate the schedules of entertainers to develop star-studded recruitment and fund-raising events for programs like the Peace Corps or National Service Corps.

While the Johnson administration took steps toward developing a more concrete organization dedicated to celebrity coordination, the conflict with liberal Hollywood supporters caused by the Vietnam War tore apart any potential electoral network by 1968. Moreover, Johnson never saw Hollywood supporters as more than a sales tool or fund-raising machine. He had yet to understand that a Hollywood sensibility was not just fluff in the political process but a central and legitimate style of political communication. Johnson saw political clout in terms of backroom negotiations, during which he could use his commanding personality, towering figure, and knowledge of private lives to force through legislative change.[50] Media image was a secondary, albeit a frequently frustrating, concern to Johnson—simply a tool to sell a message, not a central source of political power in and of itself.

Murphy and Reagan, on the other hand, understood that the expansion of the mass media had fundamentally changed the nature of American politics and the avenues to gaining power and establishing authority. To win office, each had ignored criticism that he was "just an actor," without political qualifications. Their celebrity appeal and media expertise gave them political authority by the mid-1960s. The success of these two California Republican political pioneers helped to convince Nixon to turn to "showbiz" professionals and allow them to work their sales magic and make television central to his campaign. His media team coordinated with professionals in advertising and also with seasoned producers, directors, and screenwriters, giving Nixon successful and innovative opportunities to use entertainment to attract new types of voters to the Nixon camp.

With the talent of experienced behind-the-scenes staff, Nixon crafted a campaign that relied on image, showmanship, and the media but at the same time cleverly mocked the superficiality of celebrity influence in American life. To attract the increasingly skeptical younger generation, Bill Gavin suggested producing an interview with "an imaginary college student," who would ask Nixon "hard questions." The candidate would reply with answers that revealed his belief that "the younger generation hates hypocrisy, cant, 'image,' and distrusts the smooth operator." Most important, Gavin wanted the "mass-distributed" production to show that "Dick Nixon does not try to gain admirers among the under thirty generation by insulting their intelligence. . . . Dick Nixon doesn't 'sell' his face, his image. . . . He just tells it like it is."[51] The idea of constructing an "imaginary" question-and-answer session that would be carefully written, directed, edited, and distributed to show that Nixon does not "sell" messages or craft images for electoral gain seems to be a contradiction. It certainly reflects, however, the broader attempt to use elaborate studio production to promote a trustworthy image of Nixon to win loyalty and votes from television viewers by turning them into fans of Nixon. Len Garment and Bill Gavin believed that the ineffective media campaign from 1960 could be blamed on the "tinker-toy set," which had lacked coordination of campaign messages.[52] Nixon had lost many opportunities to present his candidacy and policies in a "dramatic" way on television that "would catch the public eye."[53] After all, wrote another member of the media team, Ray Price, "it takes art to convey the truth from us to the viewer."[54]

According to these campaign advisers, a poorly constructed image and market strategy had failed in 1960 and 1962, not the candidate.[55] Convinced by this interpretation, Nixon dedicated himself completely to pursuing a showbiz politics strategy devised by his media team. Roger Ailes, Paul Keyes, Bill Gavin, Len Garment, Ray Price, Harry Treleaven, and Frank Shakespeare planned to change Nixon's image as "a loser" by "attacking the problem in public" with "wry good humor."[56] The media team believed that "personal" reasons for voters to dislike Nixon emerged from a "gut reaction, unarticulated, nonanalytical, a product of the particular chemistry between the voter and the image of the candidate." The media strategy in 1968 had to take advantage of new opportunities presented with the "television generation."[57] Treleaven identified three essential questions that they would have to answer throughout the campaign. Number one: What to communicate. Two: How to communicate, with what audiovisual techniques, style, and tone of voice. Three: Where to put the message so it will "reach the most voters in the most effective way possible at the lowest cost." In considering these questions, Treleaven concluded that media strategy should not be so concerned about discussing ideas of the "New Nixon," emphasizing that "it's the new voter attitudes that's important."[58] Treleaven articulated what Stanley Kelley Jr. had argued in his groundbreaking book on political consulting in 1956 and what Kennedy had put into action in 1960. In the television age, Kelley had argued, most citizens are media consumers first and voters second, and thus entertainment was a necessary tool to delivering political information to voters and encouraging them to vote on Election Day.[59]

Nixon and his media strategists attempted to play into this "new voter attitude" and appeal to voters by projecting an image of the candidate as a hip, friendly, and popular personality. Harry Treleaven recognized the negative characteristics of Nixon in the public mind as someone who lacked "newness," "glamour," "humor," and "warmth," and he committed his advertising campaign to changing these public perceptions. Nixon and his media associates recognized that they had to appeal to the television generation: the under-thirty voters, whom John Kennedy and Bobby Kennedy had inspired during their presidential campaigns. Bill Gavin believed this appeal needed to be about emotion rather than logic, a "total experience" that "doesn't arrange itself in compartmented, linear, logical patterns[;] it's a collection, an assemblage, of random impressions, not necessarily connected except by the coincidence of their coexistence."[60] Gavin continued to declare that the successful way to court the votes of this younger generation was to make them simply "like" the candidate.

"They're emotional, unstructured, uncompartmented, direct; there's got to be a straight communication that doesn't get wound through the linear translations of logic."

Nixon's campaign team worked tirelessly to integrate the candidate into the contemporary political environment, which simultaneously relied on and distrusted the television image. His behind-the-cameras team evaluated angles, expressions, statements, and gestures on screen to ensure that the most attractive image of the presidential hopeful was telecasted into American homes. Catchy music, memorable phrases—like "Nixon Now!"—and montages of images sought to attract the "voter eye."[61] Understanding that television was a "hit and run medium," Roger Ailes stressed the importance of quick, memorable spots that promoted Nixon's personality.[62] Moreover, the campaign also had to make Nixon a constant part of everyday life. He must always be before the public eye in a variety of forums, stressed Gavin. "When he is not part of the daily consciousness of the average citizen as that consciousness is formed by the media (esp. t.v.), he seems to actually not exist."[63]

Concerned more about the "quantity" than the "quality" of media exposure, the team pushed Nixon to pursue a variety of television appearances: from staged question-and-answer sessions on local stations as he traveled the country during the primary season, to nationally broadcast shows like *Meet the Press* and his cameo appearance on *Rowan & Martin's Laugh-In*. While scholars have frequently dismissed the twenty-second *Laugh-In* spot as a publicity stunt, Nixon's decision to appear on the show, more so than other television appearances, exposed the crux of the candidate's media strategy and the profound shift in American culture and politics that had occurred since the vice president's previous political attempt in 1960.[64]

Laugh-In illustrates Bill Gavin's description of the post-television generation, who responded to "a collection, an assemblage, of random impressions, not necessarily connected except by the coincidence of their coexistence." The show dedicated one minute or less to scenes showing its regular actors and actresses spitting out one-liners—such as "If Shirley Temple Black had married Tyrone Power, she'd be Shirley Black Power"—and being the victims of gags such as falling through hidden trapdoors, being doused with pails of water, or taking a hammer to the head. Although the hosts dressed in tasteful suits, the performers on the show wore the latest fashions, short skirts, bright colors, long hair—all visual representations of the mainstream success of the countercultural and sexual revolutions. Printed phrases appeared across the bottom of the screen: "GEORGE WALLACE YOUR SHEETS ARE READY," and the stars of the show took their punches at national political figures: "Texas produced some great men: Sam Houston, Stephen F. Austin, and Lyndon Johnson. Two out of three isn't bad." Or: "Spiro Agnew: Your new name is ready."[65]

Dan Rowan described the show as not new in substance but new in style. "The pace is the most important thing," declared Rowan. "No one is really interested anymore in sitting for a long time listening to or watching one thing. The old days are over."[66] The *New York Times* similarly attributed the show's success to its fast-paced style. "*Laugh-In* is hilarious, brash, flat, peppery, irreverent, satirical, repetitious, risqué, topical, and in borderline taste—it is primarily and always fast, fast, fast! It's attuned to the times, It's hectic, electric." The show's structure demonstrated the elaborate television techniques that had evolved in the studios over the decades. Each episode required over 400 separate pieces of tape, four full-time editors, and a script of more than 250 pages. Furthermore, the background for the show was a studio production center, and the inefficiencies of the camera and cue cards were often victims of the show's jokes. Thus, not only its pace but also the open acknowledgment of the process of filming, editing, and advertising made *Laugh-In* appeal to the post-television audience, which understood and responded to one-liners, striking images, and quick actions. Executive producer George Schlatter understood his principal audience to be twelve to twenty-five years old, the generation raised on television, which had "seen more show business than the professional of 10 or 15 years ago."[67]

The Nixon media campaign incorporated a variety of lessons of *Laugh-In*. Moreover, Paul Keyes provided Nixon with an opportunity to promote his "likable," humorous persona on prime-time television with a guest appearance on the show. Nixon delivering his famous (or infamous) "sock it to me" was an effort to keep the candidate constantly in the media consciousness and to use entertainment formats to appeal to a broader range of voters. The appearance fit into Gavin's belief that just showing Nixon "with famous people doing things" evoked an important statement that the country needs "not just someone better, someone excellent: Nixon, Now!"[68] Nixon's campaign managers also used the show for more indirect political benefits as well by frequently airing his campaign advertisements during the commercial breaks. The controversial Nixon advertisement that split images of war, rioting, and starving children with the picture of a grinning Hubert Humphrey aired during a *Laugh-In* episode. The commercial ended with the bold letters: "VOTE LIKE YOUR WHOLE WORLD DEPENDED ON IT."[69] Although protests from the Democratic Party forced the Republicans to remove the grinning Humphrey from the commercial, the advertisement used editing and visual techniques that were similar to those of *Laugh-In*. Even the concluding statement came across the screen in headline fashion, reminiscent of the one-line news flashes from the show.

By assembling men familiar with Hollywood-rooted production strategies—whether through academic study, television experience, or advertising expertise—the Nixon media team talked about campaign challenges in terms of celebrity appeal. Comparing Bobby Kennedy to a Rock Hudson movie in color and Hubert Humphrey's campaign to "an old Alice Faye musical in which everything turns out o.k.," these experienced men stressed the importance of the "right" Hollywood theme for Nixon to use. Gavin believed that using the style of *On the Waterfront* would be helpful to Nixon, which used "realism" to "get over a statement to the audience."[70] To his consultants, celebrity meant more than simply name recognition. It meant an artfully constructed emotional and personal appeal focused on Nixon as a star himself, appealing to fans through his media persona. This celebrity construction, they believed, would win the presidency.

A Hollywood sensibility pervaded the 1968 campaign. Despite Nixon's continuing claim that he was "not a showman," he had hired showmen to create a "saleable television image." While Humphrey had the support and expertise of advertisers—an essential part of the campaign process by 1968—he lacked the talent of a media team armed with intimate knowledge of the production process and new strategies to make the candidate a constant media personality. Nixon centered his presidential aspirations in 1968 on the ability of his production team to emulate Kennedy's showbiz media strategy from 1960. Nixon won the election and delivered a decisive victory for the consulting, advertising, and polling professionals, who would find permanent employment in the mass media age ushered in with the expertise, insights, and skills of Hollywood entertainers.

Richard Nixon's stunning comeback during the 1968 campaign, which reporter Joe McGinniss turned into a best-selling exposé, *The Selling of the President*, told a story of how artfully crafted media messages and entertainment philosophies honed in Hollywood studios could turn the loser of the 1960 presidential election into the winner in 1968. Consultants, pollsters, advertisers, and media professionals carefully chronicled Nixon's political career as one that faltered in front of the cameras in 1960 but was resurrected by show business professionals in 1968. This narrative, in turn, helped transform the political landscape and pad their wallets as politicians across the country flocked to this burgeoning industry to perform the same "Nixon miracles" for their own careers. In 1957, forty-one public relations firms offered campaign services, among other services. By 1972, over sixty firms dedicated their entire businesses to political advertising, and over 200 others focused at least some of their services on electoral campaigns.[71] Political hopefuls throughout the 1970s looked to image professionals as a sort of "Wizard of Oz," the highly paid and incredibly powerful men who could control the electoral process through smoke and mirrors. Rather than understanding how this new world of the politics of mass media worked, candidates paid the high consulting fees and let these "wizards" work their magic.

While the story of the "Nixon miracle" has validated the political consultant profession, a deeper analysis of Richard Nixon and his journey from Southern California to the White House shows how his political development occurred within, and reflected shifting attitudes about, entertainment, celebrity, and media mobilization. The age of the consultant depended on the transformations begot in the political process by the entertainment industry, first in California, then in national politics. Just as these Jewish immigrant filmmakers struggled for cultural and political acceptance into an American society dominated by the East Coast businesses, universities, and Protestant churches, so too did Richard Nixon, who grew up as a Quaker and attended local Whittier College rather than an Ivy League school. Just as the entertainment industry rose in national esteem and gained new political opportunities through World War II propaganda collaboration and its reluctant embrace of anticommunism, so too did Nixon, who won a congressional campaign in 1946 and made a national name for himself through the Alger Hiss hearings before HUAC two years later. In 1952, Dwight Eisenhower gave Hollywood stars Robert Montgomery and George Murphy an opportunity to shape his national campaign because of their media expertise, and he also offered to give Nixon this same opportunity as his vice president.

As a fan of Hollywood and a native of Southern California, Nixon loved the movies, and he understood the importance of projecting an image on the television screen; but in his own presidential campaign in 1960, Nixon crafted a public image as a statesman, honed through his years as vice president, emulating the traditions of the "eastern establishment" more than the institution that had shaped his youth. While he had celebrity endorsements from stars like Ginger Rogers and John Wayne, he did not tap into the studio structures of publicity, fund-raising, and image making to gain legitimacy the way his Democratic challenger, John F. Kennedy, did, perhaps seeing entertainment as a personal leisure choice, the constructed definition of the "Golden Age of Hollywood" in the 1930s. To

Richard Nixon, in 1960, Hollywood meant entertainment and perhaps a useful sideshow that could help him win in California, not a central strategy for a national presidential contest that demanded party delegates and an appeal to interest groups.

Unlike Nixon, John Kennedy understood that becoming a celebrity himself was a means for gaining national political authority, and whether this actually had made the difference in the national election, Richard Nixon believed that it did. Eight years later, Nixon hired a team of show business professionals, who reinforced this belief that he lost in 1960 because he neglected to include mass media and show business strategies in his campaign. Rather than focus on serious presentations on the "issues," this media team focused on selling Nixon the way that Hollywood studios had constructed and sold personalities over the past forty years. As a result, Nixon's comeback narrative solidified the belief that central components of Hollywood from the studio system era—crafting entertaining stories, producing the stories with talented actors and directors, marketing the product with advertising strategies, monitoring public opinion concerning the product, and raising funds for subsequent productions—determined political success. The perceived difference between Nixon the loser and Nixon the president hinged on media innovation. As a result, the 1972 election became a battle of showbiz politics. While the Nixon and McGovern camps pursued different uses, attitudes, and approaches toward Hollywood style, both equally valued entertainment as necessary, forging a belief shared by both parties in its power and necessity in the political process.

1972: Professionalizing Hollywood

On the evening of August 22, 1972, President Richard Nixon flew into the Miami International Airport to help kick off the Republican National Convention with a rally carefully designed to create excitement around the nomination process. Over 8,000 young supporters jammed into the Miami Marine Stadium to see performances by top entertainers, including Pamela Powell, a television actress with a famous family name, and Sammy Davis Jr. In what one newspaper called the "razzle dazzle plan to woo the young, first-time voters and slice into that exclusive Democratic base of support, the blacks," the event brought an aura of unrestrained excitement to Richard Nixon's reelection campaign.[72] As Nixon approached backstage, news of his arrival prompted the audience to interrupt Davis's performance, chanting, "Four more years! Four more years!" When Nixon

On August 22, 1972, in front of a youth rally of more than 8,000 supporters, Sammy Davis Jr. spontaneously hugs Richard Nixon on the stage. After accepting the Republican presidential nomination, Nixon attended the rally as part of his "razzle dazzle" strategy to appeal to youth and African American voters. Though the unplanned hug caught the president by surprise, Nixon claimed he was thrilled by the "wide coverage" it received in the press. AP Photo/Jim Palmer.

walked onto the stage, cheers erupted and he literally stole the spotlight as he walked toward Davis, who stood in the center of the stage. The former Democrat, whom Nixon had personally courted to join the Republican Party and participate in the campaign, reached out to welcome the president and then spontaneously embraced the incumbent. The hug caught the president, who had planned every detail of the national convention over the past two years, by surprise. Unsure of what to do with his hands, President Nixon just laughed awkwardly and accepted the gesture from the entertainer.

A cameraman captured the moment, and newspapers across the country featured the picture. Richard Nixon rejoiced when he saw the "wide coverage in the press" that followed the "hug."[73] Shortly after the convention, he sent Davis a signed copy of the photograph and thanked the singer/actor for his work in making the rally a "personal highlight of the convention" that he would always treasure. For many observers, the clear awkwardness of the embrace was reminiscent of the "sock it to me" moment, when Nixon attempted to embrace popular entertainment only to emerge as a clearly uncomfortable figure in the new political milieu. The 1972 election, however, served as a triumph of Nixon's ability to project an effective and powerful media message through a full-scale studio production that showcased him as the premier star of American politics. He read from a perfectly crafted script that highlighted his achievements over the course of the past four years, and he had a cast of supporting stars in Powell and Davis, audience members who shouted for the candidate on cue, and an elaborate stage setting with lights and cameras to capture the action. The hug exposed the difficulty the president had with impromptu changes to the script, ultimately highlighting how much his media-savvy campaign relied on planned, staged productions for political consumption.

The production strategy for Nixon's reelection campaign started immediately after the 1968 election ended. By the end of November, Roger Ailes had compiled a confidential report on the need for immediate implementation of a long-term media plan to control Nixon's presidential image during his administration and to develop new strategies for 1972. "Television was used well in this campaign," wrote Ailes. "But in four years it will have to be better."[74] Ailes understood that just as Hollywood studios had to push the envelope in publicity and production strategies to attract audiences, so too would campaigns have to stay on the cutting edge of innovative communication strategies; staying stagnant, as Nixon had done in 1960, was detrimental to political success. While Nixon had used various entertainment forums to navigate the airwaves in 1968, Ailes advocated the immediate reorganization of a "celebrities for Nixon" network, which he saw as crucial to the 1972 reelection campaign.

During the 1968 campaign, John Wayne and Jackie Gleason emerged as two prominent celebrity supporters. Wayne delivered spot announcements on radio and television that reiterated Nixon's "Silent Majority" message by reminding voters "that there's a heckuva lot right with America too."[75] Jackie Gleason proved instrumental in the election eve telecast, as he grabbed viewers' attention at the start of the show and reminded them of the importance of voting for Nixon the following day.[76] Despite these various shows of celebrity support, the campaign had focused more on behind-the-scenes strategies on how to turn Nixon into a likable media personality with entertainment messages and forums, like *Laugh-In*, to promote the candidate. In the wake of his victory, the president's closest advisers, and those in charge of reelection strategy, sought to expand the role of entertainment in the next election by recruiting celebrities to serve as surrogate speakers for the president. His celebrity operation in 1972 demonstrated that the successful approach to the "new politics" in 1972 demanded a rigorous coordination with professional image makers, both behind the scenes and on screen. The goal: to make Nixon the ultimate movie star with an all-star supporting cast that would dominate media narratives of the election.

Once in office, Nixon never stopped campaigning, and thus the media production team had year-round, full-time jobs. The permanent campaign, in turn, demanded a permanent place for Hollywood publicity structures. To oversee this collaboration, Nixon eventually set up CREEP, which put campaign strategists in close communication with top White House advisers.[77] As the organization responsible for various illegal activities—most famously the oversight of the White House Plumbers' break-in at the DNC's Watergate offices—CREEP has received considerable attention from historians.[78] But the focus on the scandal in Nixon's administration overlooks the significant developments in media exploitation, campaign strategy, and party mobilization that CREEP used to cultivate and expand Republican loyalty. Alongside its darker functions, CREEP functioned as Nixon's primary public relations organization. When the heat of Watergate began to make Nixon and CREEP members sweat, they initially viewed the scandal as a "PR problem" that this talented group of image makers could solve with the right "script."[79] CREEP marked the culmination of the Republican move toward campaign operations dependent on the use of mass media and advertising that had begun under Eisenhower. Moreover, its overwhelming success in the 1972 campaign illuminates how Hollywood style had become an instrumental tool to establishing alternative partisan networks to penetrate suburban living rooms across the country.

In the fall of 1971, CREEP staff noticed that Nixon had failed to cultivate celebrity support over the previous three years. White House aide Charles Colson noted the inefficiency of the celebrity operation and the "lack of White House functions." Responding to H. R. Haldeman's request that Colson or "someone else with his head screwed on" develop an organizational plan, Colson urged the chief of staff to invite key entertainers to the White House during the upcoming social season to establish personal relationships between Hollywood figures and the president.[80] While various older celebrities—from Kirk Douglas and Lucille Ball to Rat Packers Sammy Davis Jr. and Frank Sinatra, who had been snubbed by the Kennedy family—had expressed loyalty to Nixon, the noticeable lack of younger entertainers disturbed his staff.

In many ways, the inclusion of older celebrities revealed the success of the strategy, begun under Eisenhower, to revitalize the party with studio stars. Although the acting days of men like Ronald Reagan and George Murphy lay in the past, late-night television featured older movies that promised free publicity and continued name recognition. As Hollywood movies from the 1930s, 1940s, and 1950s played on television during the 1960s, many viewers became acquainted with Murphy and Reagan for the first time as strong, heroic, masculine, and protective characters. The "good guy" image helped both Murphy and Reagan win votes at the polls on Election Day. As Murphy explained to a reporter, when his constituency watched his late-night films in bed, it gave him "a more intimate association with my constituents than any other candidate."[81] Moreover, the free television time and nature of the image reinforced Republican messages of traditional values at a time when movement politics challenged these same values.[82] Although Nixon and CREEP wanted younger celebrities in ordor to appoal to youth, they remained more successful in attracting those celebrities cultivated under the Hollywood studio system who upheld values the MPIC had promoted so vigorously years before. Nixon's campaign functioned like a corporate studio of Hollywood's "Golden Age" and it featured stars of that era, who reinforced the message of stability and nostalgia that permeated the broader campaign and its appeal to the Silent Majority.

To add to the short list of "popular" celebrity supporters, CREEP's assistant director, Jeb Stuart Magruder, used the "tremendous selling tool" the administration had: positive policy developments for the industry from the past three years.[83] Industry politics, in which executives had engaged since the 1920s to cultivate political favor, now became a way for the president to cultivate political support, ultimately showing how Hollywood as an industry had risen in public and political stature over the past forty years. Nixon needed the industry as much as it needed him. Working with Attorney General John Mitchell, Magruder recruited studio executives who had benefited economically under the Nixon administration's tax initiatives, financing opportunities, and antipiracy legislation.[84] With the help of Taft Schreiber, longtime Republican and influential head of Music Corporation of America (MCA), Mitchell invited the power brokers of the motion picture industry to the White House in November of 1971. During the meeting, Mitchell emphasized the administration's support for the financial interests of the industry before delivering a "plea for advice and assistance in recruiting celebrities."[85] The roomful of wealthy, sympathetic Republicans discussed with Mitchell how to "maximize celebrity participation in the 1972 campaign" while also identifying potential celebrity supporters for the upcoming campaign, "most importantly those with appeal to the more youthful voters."

With more organizational experience, influence, and money, the studio executives would work with the business-friendly political party to implement a vertical media campaign that would highlight President Nixon and his agenda through a variety of forums in the public eye. Taft Schreiber worked with CREEP to mobilize "prime movers" within the industry, to develop a central coordinating committee for celebrity organization, and to hire a prominent lawyer for the entertainment industry, Joe Horacek, as a full-time staff member to fulfill the responsibilities of "Executive Director of the Celebrities Committee."[86] By allocating budget resources and a professional position to coordinate celebrity political activities, CREEP altered the established policy within the Republican Party. Rather than relying solely on volunteer organizations like the citizens' committees, White House aides acquired celebrity endorsements through a professional, top-down plan. Celebrity recruitment efforts became part of the national Republican budget paid by CREEP because "the celebrities' function was national in scope, and not a part of the California State Committee."

Over the next months, the Celebrities Committee compiled lists of names for prominent officials—from Henry Kissinger, to Spiro Agnew, to Nixon himself—to contact in order to persuade celebrities to join the Republican Party and also to travel the country giving speeches and recruiting voters as surrogates for the president. Initially, CREEP focused celebrity political activity on two demographic groups: youth and African Americans. CREEP seriously considered "having our approach to Blacks be that of going via black celebrities who are for us," and Sammy Davis Jr.'s recent White House visit became a positive public relations opportunity for Nixon to stress his commitment to equal opportunity and black capitalism.[87] Davis promoted the philosophy that Nixon and the Republican Party also embraced as he emphasized "buying the bus, not fighting for a position on it," and "working within the System because the System won't let you fight it."[88] Nixon's aides believed that Davis's personal success and move to the Republican Party had become an important symbolic image for Nixon to use to appeal to a mistrustful African American constituency. Moreover, having Davis entertain at the White House during the campaign would help to reconnect the entertainer to the president in the public eye, honor "a man who has risen from poverty to the top of his profession," and "spotlight" the president's "commitment to equal opportunity."[89]

The famous (or infamous) hug that Sammy Davis Jr. gave the president at the Miami Republican Convention, though awkward, arose from the personal and political relationship Nixon had developed with Davis over the course of the campaign. A former supporter of John Kennedy and Robert Kennedy and a civil rights activist, Davis underwent a personal transformation following a physical collapse only a year earlier from excessive drinking, partying, and drug use. The Nixon administration capitalized on Davis's subsequent sobriety and used the president's drug abuse program to bring Davis into Nixon's campaign and also to motivate him to promote the president's antidrug initiatives by traveling to drug centers across the country and in Vietnam.[90] Moreover, while meeting with President Nixon in the fall of 1971, Davis learned that Nixon had appointed him to the National Advisory Board for the Office of Economic Opportunity.[91] Having developed a more intimate bond with Nixon, Davis felt he could trust the president, and he told his fans, "There's an honesty about the man I love."[92]

While Davis enjoyed the closeness he had established with the president, civil rights activists across the country felt he had betrayed the movement when he so vigorously endorsed and campaigned for the incumbent. One "embarrassed black man" wrote a letter to the *Washington Post* declaring his outrage that Davis would "demean himself by virtually selling his soul for the opportunity to be one of Richard Nixon's entertainment supporters."[93] Other African Americans also felt betrayed by Davis's participation in the Republican Party's "black blitz" to attract votes, but Davis defended Nixon's record on welfare, education, and affirmative action initiatives.[94] Moreover, like Sinatra, Davis felt that John Kennedy and the Democratic Party had cast him aside after the 1960 election, but now Nixon actively courted the prominent entertainer. The personal relationship between the

The support Nixon received from Hollywood during the 1972 campaign came after diligent efforts by the president to gain favor with entertainers behind the scenes and through policy initiatives. Here Sammy Davis Jr. and President Nixon meet in the Oval Office on March 4, 1973. White House Photo Office Collection, courtesy of the Richard Nixon Presidential Library.

two men motivated Davis to return to the political process, but on a different side. For Davis, his ideological belief in black capitalism coincided with his desire for personal prestige to motivate his controversial support of the Republican president.

Sammy Davis's situation demonstrated the complexity of celebrity participation that CREEP carefully orchestrated during the campaign. Firmly believing in the power of celebrity activism to swing potential voters and create meaningful media spectacles about the president's commitment to a cause or a demographic group, Nixon aides researched potential supporters and the issues dear to their hearts before approaching them about joining the campaign. Deeming the "traditional method of approach to these celebrities ineffective," the coordinating committee urged research on policy preferences of celebrities, particularly to sway younger performers to support Nixon.[95] Moreover, CREEP wanted to discuss policy decisions, encourage political activism, and teach details of the Republican platform that would keep these stars committed, not just to Nixon as a person but also to a Republican Party rooted in the mass media.

Ideas that had been informally discussed in earlier administrations, like Bess Abell's proposal for a steering committee of celebrities to promote Johnson's Great Society, became formalized within Nixon's reelection campaign. CREEP held celebrity recruiting parties at which committed and uncommitted stars would join administration spokesmen to discuss topics such as "Russia and China," "the Economy," and "Domestic Policy."[96] During May 1972, Kissinger traveled with Attorney General Mitchell to the California home of Richard Zanuck, son of Darryl Zanuck, to meet and greet and discuss foreign policy with stars. Kissinger's trip aimed "to make an effort to have the celebrities feel 'a part' of the campaign; let them hear about foreign policy (a subject most of them are interested in) from one of their favorites in the Administration; and give them an opportunity to hear a little about campaign strategy."[97] Understanding the unique ability of celebrities to convey key messages from the president to voters during the campaign, Kissinger, John Ehrlichman, Dwight Chapin, Donald Rumsfeld, and John Mitchell fully complied with the requests from the celebrity coordinating committee for appearances and policy discussions, ultimately deepening the personal relationships between the White House and Hollywood Republicans, while also teaching celebrities strategic electoral and policy initiatives and expanding the base of informed, interested, and active Republicans in Tinseltown.

Despite the early organization of the Celebrities Committee and the successful recruitment of influential entertainers like Sammy Davis Jr., Frank

Sinatra, Elvis Presley, and actor Charlton Heston, who, before Nixon, had supported Democratic candidates, the committee still lacked the younger Hollywood celebrities that it had hoped to gain to attract the eighteen- to twenty-five-year-old vote. Moreover, in the cases of Davis and Presley, their embrace of Nixon and the antidrug campaign further distanced these Nixon surrogates from a younger constituency, which no longer saw either artist as "hip" in 1972. The Celebrities Committee collaborated extensively with CREEP officials and Hollywood studio producers on how to rectify the fact that in the spring of 1972 the campaign remained "still soft in the young performers area."[98] To step up its recruitment effort, the Celebrities Committee took the advice of Sammy Davis and planned a West Coast party that would bring President Nixon into direct contact with current and potential supporters. According to Davis, a Hollywood party with the president would help "make the difference among the 'now' generation of younger celebrities."[99]

The San Clemente party planned for the summer of 1972 became a key focus point for gaining younger Hollywood support. Scheduled to follow the Democratic National Convention in order to sway disappointed Hubert Humphrey or Edmund Muskie supporters, the party hoped to bring Democrats and uncommitted Hollywood figures to the Nixon campaign while also inspiring and motivating confirmed supporters to campaign more actively for the president. As Haldeman previously noted, "The list of committed entertainers is of little use until they are locked in to a carefully planned series of speaking engagements, rallies, appearances, etc."[100] Rather than relying on supportive celebrities to simply place their names on advertisements in support of the president, Haldeman wanted informed celebrities to travel to campaign events "where they will have the biggest impact." The San Clemente party aimed to recruit, inform, and inspire stars whom Nixon personally asked to join his reelection team and represent him and his policies during the campaign.

The Hollywood party took place on July 14, 1972. Specifically excluding the press, the event was not designed to promote short-term publicity but rather aimed to develop a lasting collaboration upon which the entire party would depend. The reception focused on motivating political participation, not placing "the President prominently in the midst of celebrities."[101] With a purpose to "woo" potential supporters with personal contact from the president, the committee carefully planned an atmosphere of informality, with Taft Schreiber standing alongside the president to offer more intimate introductions. Deemed a "huge success" because of its "fantastic motivation aspects achieved with our committed celebrities," the party did convince various entertainers to support Nixon. However, the event, which boasted what the *New York Times* called "a guest list dominated by vintage Hollywood," did not achieve its goals of attracting younger Hollywood role models.[102]

Refocusing its efforts to employ the celebrity support it did have in the most efficient way possible, CREEP commissioned a Republican supporter familiar with the motion picture industry to assess the celebrity operations in place and make recommendations for future activities. In response, Ray Caldiero submitted a plan for using the media, publicity, and electoral potential of Hollywood. In what Caldiero called a "public relations/sales function," the plan outlined specific programs that went beyond personal recruitment of new celebrities at San Clemente to ensure that the existing celebrity structure achieved its full potential and to "take advantage of this media opportunity."[103] The "Caldiero Plan" sought not only to assure stars' presence for already scheduled campaign events, but also to create "new visual opportunities" for these personalities as a vehicle for President Nixon's message. Caldiero prepared a "briefing book" for each entertainer, which contained specific information on the president's accomplishments and stances on issues to ensure their familiarity with the Republican platform. A detailed "celebrity media plan" would exploit all opportunities for stars to appear on talk shows, prime-time specials, and interviews, during which they could put in a plug for the Nixon line. "This will give us a 'mass media' approach rather than a rifle shot here and there," explained Caldiero, to ensure the constant "party line flow of information" from an all-star ensemble. While he also discussed the importance of using entertainers to raise money, Caldiero emphasized their ability to navigate the mass media and bring Nixon's message to diverse groups of voters.

The Caldiero Plan achieved what CREEP "had been after for months"— it offered coordination among entertainers, athletes, musicians, and politicians.[104] Through planned media events, the Caldiero Plan and the Celebrities Committee gave Nixon increased opportunities to get out his policy messages and electoral promises through entertainment forums and personalities. Researching the particular demographic appeal of each committed celebrity allowed CREEP to incorporate key lessons of market segmentation into campaign strategy. While structuring an institutional network of celebrities appeared as a top-down strategy designed to make actors and actresses into puppets mouthing the Nixon line, in reality, the Celebrities Committee depended deeply on Hollywood's business sense, publicity knowledge, and past political experience to execute effective strategies in these new media games.

Since 1928, Hollywood entertainers had stressed the importance of their knowledge, talent, and expertise. Driven by personal ambition, ideological conviction, patriotism, and personal relationships, these men and women eagerly shared their ideas with political parties and had pushed their way into a political sphere that regarded their glamour and fame with a curious suspicion. Over the next forty years, ambitious politicians slowly saw the potential political reach of snappy advertisements, catchy songs, glamorous appeals, and entertaining skits. Not until Richard Nixon's successful presidential campaigns, however, did journalists, politicians, and advisers celebrate the ability of showbiz politics to help win elections and even govern a nation.[105] CREEP deepened the ties of Hollywood Republicans to the national party and, in the process, fully institutionalized and professionalized celebrity activists and entertainment philosophies during the 1972 campaign. The postelection plans reiterated the importance of an organized system of celebrities to sell policies and candidates beyond President Nixon. A "Celebrity Advisory Service" promised to keep these entertainers invested in the future of the Republican Party, which would help local and state Republicans win in 1974 and 1976 and also allow the party to add "flair and glamour to the White House" with "constant contact with our many celebrities."[106] Moreover, as Caldiero pointed out with excitement, "by setting up this small office we can get our celebrities to work for the Republican Party all year long!"

The "Sparklies" Wage War

Having worked so diligently to prepare a permanent place in the Republican Party and Nixon's campaign for Hollywood, Ray Caldiero saw the constant media attention on the glamorous McGovern celebrities as a personal slight with potentially negative electoral ramifications. After reading a *Newsweek* article discussing the role of "show biz in politics," Caldiero began an angry letter to the magazine. Upset by the cover shot of actress Shirley MacLaine and the article's focus on the glitz and glamour of McGovern's celebrity activists, Caldiero told *Newsweek* editors that their article "gave a most unfair impression to your readers" about the political activities of Hollywood. Caldiero reprimanded *Newsweek* for overlooking the dedicated group of entertainers working just as diligently for President Nixon's reelection. Why focus on MacLaine, asked Caldiero. "She is less credible than James Stewart, less charismatic than John Wayne, older than Pam Powell, and less entertaining than Bob Hope." Moreover, he continued, MacLaine and her famous friends, like Warren Beatty, supported the

Democratic presidential candidate not because of the "courage of their convictions" but rather because of the "publicity potential of supporting extreme candidates like George McGovern." As Caldiero saw it, despite the success of Nixon's campaign in attracting distinguished and committed celebrities who provided "entertainment suitable for rallies for young people," he seethed at *Newsweek*'s unfair media coverage, which ignored these events and instead perpetuated a "so-called division of families by generation, a division in which the young people always support Senator McGovern." The magazine, Caldiero wrote, continued to show its "well-known bias" by ignoring the Nixon campaign's achievements while simultaneously attempting "to revive the faltering McGovern candidacy with this puff piece on another radical millionaire backing the Prairie Populist."[107]

The huge media attention that Hollywood liberals generated angered Nixon aides, who worked hard to use famous Republican supporters to drum up symbolic images for the incumbent. But the prominent place of celebrity supporters in McGovern's campaign reflected the broader differences between the two candidates' contrasting interpretations of "Hollywood" and of the meaning and pursuit of "showbiz politics" in the Democratic and Republican parties. If the Nixon administration functioned like the corporate studio of the past, the McGovern camp resembled the New Hollywood built around the cultural revolution of the 1960s. Director Steven Spielberg later remembered the New Hollywood of the 1970s as a time when "a kind of age restriction was lifted, and young people were allowed to come rushing in with all of their naiveté and their wisdom and all of the privileges of youth."[108] As cheap and revolutionary films like *Easy Rider* and *Bonnie and Clyde* cut down the barriers of entrance for new writers, actors, and directors in Hollywood, the Twenty-sixth Amendment to the Constitution, which gave the vote to eighteen-year-olds, and changes in the nominations process of the Democratic Party created new opportunities for youth, women, and minorities to reshape and influence the party's future.

While Nixon emerged as the incumbent with campaign structures dedicated first and foremost to his reelection and then to other state and local candidates, McGovern bitterly battled other Democratic contenders within a deeply divided Democratic Party. During the tumultuous 1968 Democratic convention in Chicago, young antiwar activists, who wanted a say in selecting the presidential nominee and writing the party's platform, had violently clashed with traditional Democratic Party authorities—as epitomized in Mayor Richard Daley, who refused to let youthful protestors bring chaos into his city.[109] As police beat protestors outside the convention hall, delegates on the convention floor selected Vice President Hubert

Humphrey as the presidential nominee despite his not having competed in any primary campaigns. Minnesota senator Eugene McCarthy galvanized many on the Left with his antiwar stance and had gained support in primaries throughout the country; yet party leaders ignored his candidacy in favor of the vice president. The uproar inside and outside the Democratic National Convention led many figures within the party to push for a formal nomination procedure that would rely on primary election results, not the whims of party regulars.

Following Nixon's victory in 1968, Senator George McGovern headed a Commission on Party Structure and Delegate Selection. Hoping to "invigorate our party with a massive injection of democracy," McGovern declared that the commission had put an end to the "day of the bosses."[110] The McGovern-Fraser Commission changed the rules of the Democratic Party, which had been wavering since Kennedy's successful primary campaigns in 1960 had introduced new ways to capture the nomination. Rather than being fodder for political bosses to gain favor and privilege in the party, delegates were won in primary elections and distributed proportionately, depending on percentages of the vote candidates attained in each state. In this new atmosphere, a slew of candidates emerged as potential contenders for the Democratic nomination, and they traveled across the country to collect as many delegates as possible in state primaries. As Kennedy's 1960 campaign foreshadowed, however, primary elections incurred high costs, which candidates who lacked personal wealth struggled to meet. In this atmosphere, as George McGovern's campaign illuminated in 1972, celebrities filled an essential funding and publicity void, making them an integral and unchallenged part of the political process.

To wage a successful primary campaign, McGovern did what Nixon had done so effectively in 1968.[111] Neither candidate could count on support of party regulars and instead reacted to strands of "disenchantment" and aroused the emotions of the American people across the country to show their electability. One "less obvious similarity" between Nixon's and McGovern's campaigns, noted an article in the *Chicago Tribune*, was their use of "celebrities-by-the-bushel to add a wisp of charisma-by-association to their own rather glamorless facades."[112] Nixon understood Hollywood's image-making power, and he worked extensively with CREEP to expand the celebrity arm of the Republican Party. So too did George McGovern. In fact, for McGovern, as he traveled the primary circuit with limited funds as the "dark horse" contender for the nomination, celebrities of the entertainment world—from film to television to sports—emerged as essential tools to attract free media coverage and to invigorate his candidacy. The 1972 campaign quickly emerged as a battle over celebrity political organization, with the parties relying on drastically different strategies.

For McGovern, celebrities did not just help sell his policy messages—as Nixon surrogates did—they actually allowed his campaign to gain speed, attention, and respectability. With the California primary an essential race for McGovern's political success, his campaign workers found that all "huge media buys were booked and the money to pay for them was in hand."[113] What to do?—use celebrities as "secondary speakers" to attract a news camera when they spoke for McGovern at country saloons, college campuses, or supermarkets. The McGovern campaign carefully cultivated a list of celebrity endorsements and compiled an elite collection of unlisted telephone numbers. Politicized by the civil rights movement and the Vietnam War, Hollywood liberals eagerly responded to calls from the McGovern campaign to become active participants in organizing, funding, and publicizing campaign events. Using their advertising power and communication abilities, celebrities "reinforce morale, and boost attendance and gate receipts," reported a campaign worker. Most important, celebrities "play media games."[114] As these stars traveled the country as representatives of the youth and vigor of the Democratic campaign, they sometimes played music in concert halls and other times mingled on college campuses, but they always performed these political activities in the media eye.

Like Nixon's, McGovern's campaign attempted to keep the senator's name constantly on the lips of the American public. Campaign manager Gary Hart appreciated the media attention these celebrities, whom he called "sparklies," created. Hart went beyond the tradition of Democratic fund-raising with Hollywood and welcomed figures like Warren Beatty, Goldie Hawn, Jack Nicholson, Shirley MacLaine and Barbra Streisand into the campaign.[115] In return, McGovern entertainers celebrated their place in the political arena as part of the transition to a more open political process. "Actors have for a long time been used as shills in politics," declared Burt Lancaster. But their position had changed by 1972. "Instead of being paper-mache characters, they have come out as interested citizens."[116] Dependent not just on their fund-raising abilities but also on their willingness to speak for his candidacy, McGovern treated his celebrity supporters, in particular Beatty and MacLaine, as trusted campaigners and advisers. MacLaine later remembered how she traveled to small towns, union rallies, ladies' lunches, and college campuses to talk about military spending, the tax system, and urban decay, seven days a week. Eager to learn more about the issues, she frequently called policy experts "so that I could answer questions with more facts and deeper knowledge."[117] Warren Beatty occupied an even more intimate place in McGovern's inner circle. Similarly to Montgomery and Murphy before him, the actor worked behind the scenes of McGovern's campaign to direct its communications strategies and present the candidate in the best light possible for television cameras.[118]

Drawing on the party's embrace of entertainment fund-raisers since the 1961 Inaugural Gala, Beatty also organized political rock concerts, which brought stars from the music, theater, film, and television worlds to perform at rallies for the senator across the country.[119] Ticket prices ranged from $8 to $100 apiece for a Madison Square Garden performance, and the rally attracted thousands with promises that Goldie Hawn, Raquel Welch, Candice Bergen, Dustin Hoffman, and Paul Newman would serve as ushers. Peter, Paul and Mary performed, followed by Bob Dylan and Simon and Garfunkel. After the performances, McGovern ended the rally with a brief speech. Not only did these "Rock'n'Rhetoric Rallies" raise money; they also encouraged voter participation and engagement in the campaign, which for the first time sought votes from youth under the age of twenty-one. The promise of celebrity encounters brought voters to Madison Square Garden but also led to disappointment for many fans when Warren Beatty, Raquel Welch, and Bette Davis failed to appear.[120]

McGovern's campaign acknowledged that in 1972 "politics has replaced both art and charity as an acceptable social pastime," and celebrities from the film and theater worlds organized events for McGovern and other liberal causes.[121] Tom Wolfe famously dubbed the fashionable turn of celebrities toward politics the "Radical Chic" with an exposé that revealed how wealthy white artists and socialites had embraced political organizations like the Black Panthers as a statement in status rather than a show in true political conviction.[122] Just as Republicans had done to derail the HDC in 1944, Nixon's campaign derided liberal political activism as superficial when Ray Caldiero labeled McGovern supporters as "radicals" engaged in "puff" politics.[123] As Hollywood moved into the political arena over the last forty years, political figures had accepted their talents but also maintained that glamour and politics should not mix. Some actors had undoubtedly embraced politics with an eye toward trendiness, but committed celebrity activists drove the convergence of entertainment and politics through a firm embrace of "ideological politics." Like the liberal mobilization in 1944, this activism has depended on policy analysis and a desire to promote cherished issues and candidates.

In 1972, McGovern's and Nixon's campaigns understood the political potential of a mutually beneficial relationship with Hollywood, something entertainers had pursued since the 1920s. Both parties actively reached out to committed activists in Hollywood, taught them about policy initiatives, promoted their professional and economic interests, and relied on them to go out on the campaign trail. While Nixon developed a top-down organization of celebrities, McGovern relied on liberal entertainers to organize rallies and tour the country in support of his candidacy on their own accord.[124] Moreover, as the campaign continued to rely on the fame of its performers to attract attention, the spectacle of Beatty, MacLaine, or Lancaster frequently outshone the candidate's message. The "sparklies" brought a "politics of ecstasy" to the McGovern candidacy, which enlivened the political rallies with "rock'n'rhetoric" and attracted new people to the political arena. But in the end, the reliance on sell-out entertainment events was not enough to win the election.[125]

On the surface, Nixon's landslide victory over McGovern in 1972 showed that even as corporate studios had failed to find a popular audience for their expensive movies, they had effectively mobilized a popular electorate for Richard Nixon. Nixon's campaign did not receive the publicity that McGovern's celebrity supporters generated, much to the irritation of Ray Caldiero, but it did mobilize an organized network of entertainers who traveled across the country to urge the electorate to vote for Nixon on Election Day. McGovern may have attracted young and "hip" celebrity activists, but his campaign lacked the structure, focus, and constant media exploitation with which CREEP achieved such success. Rather than focusing on big fund-raising events, like rock concerts held in New York City, Los Angeles, Cleveland, and Lincoln, Nebraska, CREEP consistently incorporated musicians, actors, and athletes into all its campaign events as frequently as possible. In the process, CREEP developed more concrete connections between operations in Washington and pro-Nixon celebrities who traveled across the country with CREEP.

It is difficult to gauge how entertainment events influenced actual voter decisions at the polls, but the 1972 campaign revealed that both Democrats and Republicans turned to entertainment to communicate with voters and to make a name for themselves. As one McGovern aide wrote, campaign managers previously stood on the sidelines and "chewed cigars and handed out turkeys," but now they had to generate excitement, turn out crowds, and attract media cameras for news coverage.[126] This atmosphere saw Hollywood experience as necessary, and, as the 1970s progressed, celebrities found that not only could they help politicians succeed, but they too could emerge as powerful political contenders themselves. The two parties incorporated showbiz politics in different ways, but they both relied on "media driven performative politics" rooted in California politics. As political scientists have observed, during the 1970s, changes in nomination rules and voting requirements combined with technological advances in mass media to transform political institutions, from electoral campaigns to political parties.[127] In this environment, innovative politicians worked to create new political traditions, which though they seemed "no more ancient than television and shopping centers," in fact relied on lessons, assumptions, and values that had originated in Hollywood studios forty years earlier. On and off camera, celebrity activists had worked to establish alternative networks for political communication and engagement and, in doing so, created new political practices that relied on consumption, entertainment, and the mass media. The style and appeal that originated in the studio system would continue to spread these traditions across the country over the twentieth century. The democratization of American politics resulted in the Hollywoodization of the process.

The Washington Dream Machine

In 1960, Robert Drew launched his new company, Drew Associates, which planned to employ mobile video technology to chronicle events as they happened, much the way *Life* magazine had so successfully done. Drew hired an up-and-coming filmmaker, a pioneer of a film genre that would soon be known as "cinema verité," to record on video the primary campaign in Wisconsin between Hubert Humphrey and John F. Kennedy. Working with Drew, D. A. Pennebaker captured the celebrity presence of the Massachusetts senator and the effects of a well-oiled publicity machine, which created Jack Kennedy fans wherever he went. The crowds, the autographs, and the Frank Sinatra song "High Hopes" showed a new campaign style in progress, the impact of it yet to be determined. The final product, *Primary*, showed Kennedy launching his political career, and it also launched the career of D. A. Pennebaker. Three years later, the filmmaker documented a president in action. The film *Crisis* chronicled how the Kennedy administration navigated the tumultuous waters of desegregating the University of Alabama. Four years after that, Pennebaker filmed different experiences of the music industry and its potential for growth in *Don't Look Back*, a documentary of folksinger Bob Dylan's tour of England, and another film, *Monterey Pop*, that featured the organization and execution of the Monterey Pop Festival.[1]

Three decades later, Pennebaker again saw an opportunity to capture American politics in action, from the campaign trail to the national election, and he took a gamble on baby boomer and presidential hopeful William J. Clinton. Pennebaker saw an opportunity to capture Clinton the political celebrity and turn him into the star of his new documentary. Though disappointed not to have direct access to the candidate,

Pennebaker found the real story chronicling not the celebrity candidate but rather the celebrity-making machine behind the scenes. *The War Room* dramatized the political prowess of consultants, especially James Carville, and media advisers, like Clinton's director of communications, George Stephanopoulos. This dynamic duo led the campaign staff in a media battle as they monitored and then shaped potential news stories around the clock. As Pennebaker filmed the campaign team, it became clear that if the Clinton campaign won the "spin" competition—slogans, advertisements, and, most important, interpretation of events—it would win the election. As the film documents, the team accomplished both feats.

The war room became a star of the 1992 election, and as James Carville emotionally stated in an election eve speech to the staff, "We changed the ways campaigns were run."[2] Looking back on the campaign from almost two decades later, Carville, Stephanopoulos, and other members of the war room talked about how, in 2012, their efforts at spin seem commonplace, but in 1992, the idea of having a war room to develop media strategy, anticipate news events, and shape media strategies around these events was a dramatic electoral innovation—one designed to meet the challenges of a campaign that ran not just on three networks, but also on twenty-four-hour cable news stations.[3]

In many ways, *Primary* and *The War Room* highlighted dramatic changes in the size, responsibilities, functions, and daily tasks of campaign staffs from 1960 to 1992. Candidate Kennedy sat in a station wagon with the lyrics of Frank Sinatra blasting out of a loudspeaker on top of the car. Candidate Clinton traveled with Secret Service protection and aides who followed and debriefed him at all points. Kennedy assembled a well-oiled media team consisting of his brother, his father, and Jack Denove Productions. Clinton headed a war room filled with professional pollsters, consultants, and "spin doctors"—media professionals who shaped story lines and interpretations of events.

Despite these differences in scale, the legacy of Kennedy and the 1960 election was present in the principles of Clinton's war room. Throughout the 1992 campaign, Clinton constantly told the story of meeting President Kennedy as a high school representative from Arkansas at Boys State, an educational program sponsored by the American Legion to learn about government and citizenship. Clinton frequently invoked the memory of Kennedy and his call for service as a motivating factor for his presidential campaign. And yet the Arkansas governor did more than use Kennedy's rhetoric. Just as Kennedy saw the potential for a party outsider to win the presidency by embracing innovative media strategies that seemed potentially dangerous and unconventional, so too did Clinton approach the path to the presidency with an eye on media, innovation, the Kennedy celebrity legacy, and lessons from the Nixon comeback narrative (the original "comeback kid").

In the age of cable television, sound bites, and twenty-four-hour news, a candidate's political production team works around the clock to monitor his or her public image, and on the surface, many changes had taken place in the years between *Primary* and *The War Room*. But the principles and lessons that Hollywood entertainers had taught Roosevelt, Eisenhower, Kennedy, and Nixon remained firmly in place for candidates like Clinton who wanted to serve in the Oval Office. Like Roosevelt, Clinton cultivated personal relationships with entertainers and encouraged celebrities to participate in generating awareness and money for causes like AIDS research and the environment. Eisenhower had Robert Montgomery to shield him from ineffective media presentations like the Abilene debacle. Bill Clinton had a team of publicity experts to shape the presentation of not only his public image but also the news and policies of the administration. Clinton did not simply follow Kennedy's celebrity-driven media strategy to win electoral points. He expanded the place of Hollywood entertainers in financing the Democratic Party war chest. Through the President's Club, which Kennedy had started, Clinton asked celebrity friends like Barbra Streisand and George Clooney to perform at fund-raising dinners so that wealthy supporters could bask in the celebrity of the president and movie stars. Like Nixon, Clinton attempted to appeal to youth and new voter attitudes of the MTV generation by participating in the "Rock the Vote Campaign" and famously playing the saxophone on Arsenio Hall's late-night talk show.

By the time of Bill Clinton's election, the line between politics and entertainment—which was hotly debated during the 1920s and 1930s, feared during the 1940s and 1950s, and slowly accepted by the 1960s and 1970s—had fully disappeared.[4] Despite popular belief that the election of Ronald Reagan in 1980 initiated the modern "celebrity presidency," the former actor capitalized on inroads made by entertainers before him and a dramatic shift in the conception of entertainment and political structures of authority. Ronald Reagan used his Hollywood experience and financial connections to win the governorship of California, establish himself as a national political contender, and rise to victory.[5] As president, Reagan launched his administration with an inaugural celebration shaped by a glamour and glitz reminiscent of the "Golden Age of Hollywood."[6] When in office, the former actor used the language of the silver screen to communicate to the American people.[7] He talked of *Rambo* and

Star Wars in ways that used Hollywood movies to explain his domestic and foreign policies, and he employed a full-time media team to control, monitor, and protect his public image and to stage the news to benefit his political agenda.[8] But, more significant, like Kennedy and Nixon before him, Ronald Reagan's rise to the presidency reinforced the political belief that entertainment and media savviness won voters and public support. In fact, research has shown that Reagan's approval numbers were significantly lower among voters, and that it was journalists, congressional leaders, and political "insiders" who were more "wooed" by him. They believed he was the "Great Communicator," and they reported stories about his administration that reflected this belief and gave the president the political power to push his legislative agenda through Congress.[9] The 1980s, writes sociologist and media scholar Michael Schudson, saw the triumph of "the belief in Washington, by now an article of faith, that politics today is in the television age and that a man with Reagan's evident personal charm on the television screen has practically irresistible power to shape public opinion."[10]

Bill Clinton—a baby boomer and an embodiment of this new voter whom Nixon was attempting to reach in 1968—won office with the help of a political staff that did not necessarily hail from Hollywood but that came of age politically in the era of showbiz politics and also accepted these principles as a fundamental political truth. Entertainment was a weapon as powerful as television advertisements and public opinion polls, and Clinton and his advisers did not hesitate to employ, or even question the use of, Hollywood styles, structures, and forums to communicate with voters and shape public perceptions of who he was as a person and a politician. As Clinton experienced over the course of his political career, however, by discarding the line between politics and entertainment, he also removed the line between public and private. Over the course of his administration, the public treated him like a celebrity, held him accountable for public and private actions, and demanded to know intimate details of his sex life, just as they demanded to know such details of movie stars George Clooney and Leonardo DiCaprio at the time. Clinton instinctually looked to voters as fans, and by the 1990s, voters instinctually looked to leaders as celebrities. No longer did presidential hopefuls have to create a celebrity image to win elections—they had to be a star with a professional production team in place to even try out for a position on the political stage.

As D. A. Pennebaker's film showed, Bill Clinton won the 1992 election through a "Washington Dream Machine." In an effort to start shaping the legacy of his presidency, Clinton made the White House itself a production studio and became the first president to star in a motion picture as president. Philip Rosenthal, the executive producer of the hit television show *Everyone Loves Raymond*, produced the short film *Final Days* for premier at the Washington Correspondents' Dinner in the spring of 2000. In *Final Days*, Bill Clinton rides a bicycle in the halls of the White House, answers phones on the switchboard, poses with a cardboard cutout of himself for a tourist, makes lunch for his wife, who was campaigning for her own seat in the New York Senate race, and mows the lawn.[11] Through scenes of him playing "Battleship" with his chief of staff, setting up an email account, and ordering a ham on eBay, the movie generates laughs that build on the expansion of political satire in the showbiz politics era. Since Richard Nixon, presidential hopefuls have recognized the usefulness of engaging with popular entertainment and satire, a legacy that plagued his successor, Gerald Ford, who endured Chevy Chase's many lampoons of him on *Saturday Night Live* as a dense, absentminded klutz over the course of his presidency.[12]

During a compelling scene in the short production, Bill Clinton holds an Academy Award trophy and says to the mirror, "I always wanted to be an actor." Kevin Spacey sneaks up behind him to give him an almost pitying look as he asks the president to give back his award. Spacey provided this cameo appearance in the film and was at the Correspondents' Dinner when the film aired. The mingling of entertainment and political celebrities during the actual dinner itself seemed to confirm the observation made by Jack Valenti, president of the Motion Picture Academy and former aide to President Lyndon B. Johnson, that "politicians and movie stars spring from the same DNA."[13] In the age of showbiz politics, Valenti's observations most certainly were accurate. On April 29, 2000, the White House Correspondents' Dinner celebrated the connections, both real and fabricated, among the television program *The West Wing*, motion pictures like *Wag the Dog* and *Primary Colors*, which chronicled aspects of the Clinton administration on the silver screen, and the actual executive branch in Washington.[14] But, though accepted as fact in the 1990s, the similarities between actors and politicians were not preordained or inherently ingrained. Rather, this connection emerged from a longer, more controversial development in political institutions, strategies, cultural beliefs about sources of political authority, and assumptions about the electorate.

The Final Days showed how naturally showbiz politics came for Bill Clinton. But this accepted truth about the political power and place of entertainment came as a result of specific interpretations by politicians and advisers about how John Kennedy and then Richard Nixon won the presidency. Moreover, as Nixon's resignation following the Watergate scandal solidified distrust in established political leaders and traditional institutions, the opening of the primary system through the McGovern-Fraser Commission and expansion of the electorate with the Twenty-sixth Amendment allowed more people opportunities for political participation. In this atmosphere, the message that Ronald Reagan used on the campaign trail in California, that of a citizen-politician, paved the way for celebrities to voice their political beliefs and for entertainment forums, especially television shows like *Saturday Night Live* (which launched in 1975), to become places for political engagement. While voter turnout rates from 1972 to 2000 showed a constant decline, the place of entertainment emerged as more and more powerful in public conversations and in shaping political awareness, suggesting that, especially among youth, new types of engagement continued to develop outside traditional party politics. Criticisms abounded in the 1980s about what media scholar Neil Postman feared, that Americans were "amusing themselves to death" and that entertainment had trivialized American politics.[15] During the Clinton era, as voter turnout reached a low in 1996, intellectual criticism reached a high, with studies revealing how Americans lacked community and a civic identity because of the torrent of entertainment from mass media—from television to video games to movies.[16] According to one political scientist, "If citizens are home watching television or its future counterpart, they cannot be out participating in politics."[17]

But during the 1950s, Stanley Kelley Jr. recognized that television could serve as a new tool for political engagement for people who did not necessarily engage with traditional precinct organizers. Despite popular concern about the disappearance of the divide between politics and entertainment, political scientists who have taken popular culture and entertainment seriously have concluded that entertainment can engage as much as it can trivialize in an era in which politics is packaged.[18] This is something that Louis B. Mayer told Herbert Hoover in 1928, that Douglas Fairbanks Jr. explained to Franklin Roosevelt on the eve of World War II, and that the HDC showed the DNC in 1944. During World War II and the Cold War, Roosevelt and Truman celebrated the positive place of entertainment in American society. Motion pictures served as a vehicle to inform, educate, and unite the American people, and the war bond campaign proved to many government officials that entertainment could enhance civic activism. Dwight Eisenhower accepted these principles as he crafted his appeals in 1950, and John F. Kennedy opened up the political process to youth in ways that valued their perspectives, even if these attitudes were first crafted by televisions in postwar suburbs. Even if voters were media consumers first, they were still voters, and their support on the campaign trail, their support as fans, made Kennedy president.

Many contemporary scholars and pundits have continued to bemoan the prominence of a showbiz politics. Journalists, political scientists, and media scholars have focused on the undemocratic implications of modern media politics. Sex scandals command substantially more attention than policy debates, news shows emphasize conflict over consensus, polling data skews public debates, and sound bites make leaders more concerned over the appearance of what they do rather than the content of the bills they craft.[19] Presidential scholars have noted that the celebrity demands of the president have ultimately undermined his effectiveness in policy-making as administrations focus on crafting a popular media image over governing.[20] Life has become a movie, critics argue, and democracy and community are threatened by the manipulation of the uneducated and emotional voter through the powerful culture of celebrity.[21]

And yet implicit within these contemporary critiques is an idealization a great nineteenth-century "golden age of American democracy," during which almost 80 percent of voters turned out on Election Day and listened to three-hour debates between candidates on the issues. This "golden age," however, is a romantic memory, not a historical reality. Nineteenth-century party politics, though boasting high voter turnout rates, limited participation to only white men and often relied on voter intimidation, fraud, violence, and corruption. Moreover, scholars have found that voters were no more informed during this nineteenth-century "golden age" than they are today.[22] Parades and picnics commanded the attention of voters at partisan events, not necessarily the long speeches or debates. Moreover, while contemporary journalists and scholars frequently deplore the importance of image in American politics, the construction (and potential for manipulation) of the presidential image has been a central concern since the presidency of George Washington. During the nineteenth century, parties, not candidates, controlled and created political images to help inspire voter turnout at elections, especially among poor, working, and nonlandholding men.[23] As progressive reformers challenged the urban machine during the early twentieth century, the merits of presidential leadership and political authority were debated by party men and intellectual reformers, many of whom believed that the media could be a way to combat the power of the political machine.[24]

But the makeup of the entertainment industry complicated the efforts of intellectual reformers to regain control of the political process through new media outlets because motion pictures were controlled by political newcomers: Jewish immigrants who lacked a traditional American education and political pedigree but had image-making skills that worked with the new technology of motion pictures. Through decades of negotiation over the meaning, role, and use of entertainment and celebrity in the political system, men, women, minorities, and immigrants brought their talents into a political system that valued and depended on appealing to a diverse audience. By the 1970s, professional entertainment had become a central means to communicate with the electorate and stimulate civic activism. In this atmosphere, professional entertainers—those people who have succeeded at selling stories and personas to the masses—held expertise and knowledge that had become valuable politically. The twentieth-century expansion of consumer culture and mass media technology changed the nature of American citizenship. *Showbiz Politics* shows how Hollywood studios embarked on campaigns to make the motion picture industry and its stars a part of this changing body politic. As a result of institutional collaboration between the entertainment industry and the government, celebrities emerged as public figures and political figures became celebrities. Politics has always been theatrical, but theatrical performance has become necessary to, and at the forefront of, modern politics to communicate to and engage with voters.

As the people of California experienced during the 1934 campaign, this open political process relies on the expertise of showmen, values emotional connections, and encourages popular participation through entertainment events. For better or worse, Bill Clinton's presidency demonstrated that showbiz politics is here to stay, and those who embrace the potential to engage, communicate, and inspire through entertainment have reaped the rewards. With the expansion of the internet, technological changes now offer opportunities for innovative politicians to expand the use of entertainment to communicate to audiences and bring renewed civic interest, through Twitter feeds, Facebook pages, and YouTube channels. As a two-term president, Barack Obama has appeared on entertainment shows like Jon Stewart's *The Daily Show* and *The View* to appeal to viewers as media consumers first and voters second. He worked with musicians Beyoncé and Jay-Z to raise money and advance his political agenda during his presidential campaigns. Moreover, while in office, he has used these same tactics to govern by "rapping" the news with Jimmy Fallon on late-night television to promote his student loan policies and appearing on the internet show, "Between Two Ferns" with Zach Galifianakis to encourage younger viewers to sign up for the Affordable Health Care Act. Barack Obama's presidency reminds us how the age of showbiz politics has both set the stage and provided essential lessons for political success in an age of social media.

Notes

ABBREVIATIONS

AMPTPF	American Motion Picture and Television Production Files
COREC	Congress of Racial Equality Collection
CRCC	Community Relations Committee Collection, Jewish Federation Council of Greater Los Angeles, Oviatt Library, California State University, Northridge, California
CRPC	Committee for the Re-election of the President Collection
DDEL	Dwight D. Eisenhower Presidential Library, Abilene, Kansas
DNCP	Democratic National Committee Papers
DNCR	Democratic National Committee Records
EAJP	Eric A. Johnston Papers, Joel E. Ferris Research Library, Spokane, Washington
FDRL	Franklin D. Roosevelt Presidential Library, Hyde Park, New York
HDCR	Hollywood Democratic Committee Records, Wisconsin Center for Film and Theater Research, Madison, Wisconsin
HRHC	Harold Robbins (H.R.) Haldeman Collection,
HSTL	Harry S. Truman Presidential Library, Independence, Missouri
HUAC Records	House Committee on Un-American Activities, Records of the U.S. House of Representatives, House Committee on Internal Security, RG233, National Archives and Records Administration, Center for Legislative Archives, Washington D.C.
JFKL	John F. Kennedy Presidential Library, Boston, Massachusetts
JLWP	Jack L. Warner Papers, School of Cinematic Arts, University of Southern California, Los Angeles
LOC	Library of Congress, Washington, D.C.
MHL	Margaret Herrick Library, Academy of Motion Picture Arts and Sciences, Beverly Hills, California
MPICR	Motion Picture Industry Council Records
NAACPR	National Association for the Advancement of Colored People Records
OWI	Office of War Information, RG6, Archives II, College Park, Maryland
POF	President's Official File
PPF	President's Personal Files
PPP	Pre-Presidential Papers
RFKP	Robert F. Kennedy Papers
RMNL	Richard M. Nixon Presidential Library, Yorba Linda, California
RNCF	Republican National Committee Files

VPP   Vice Presidential Papers
WCFTR   Wisconsin Center for Film and Theater Research, Madison
WHCF   White House Central Files
WHCNF   White House Central Name File
WHSF   White House Special Files

INTRODUCTION

1. For a discussion of Arnold Schwarzenegger's gubernatorial campaign in 2003 and his use of celebrity politics to engage voters, see Ross, *Hollywood Left and Right*, 363–407.

2. Douglas Churchill, "Return of Terror," *New York Times*, November 18, 1934, X5.

3. "Film and Politics: Hollywood Masses the Full Power of Her Resources to Fight Sinclair," *New York Times*, November 4, 1934, 5.

4. Sinclair, *I, Governor of California*.

5. A description of these radio and stage performances can be found in Sinclair's account of the 1934 campaign, *I, Candidate for Governor*. The battle between Sinclair and the movie industry and the tensions that this battle caused with Roosevelt are outlined in Mitchell, *Campaign of the Century*.

6. See Cruikshank and Schultz, *The Man Who Sold America*, 295–305, which chronicles the role of the Lord & Thomas advertising agency and the ways in which it worked with Whitaker & Baxter. Mitchell, *Campaign of the Century*, focuses attention on the role of Whitaker & Baxter.

7. For more details on the role of Mayer in the anti-Sinclair campaign, see Ross, *Hollywood Left and Right*, 51–88.

8. Mitchell, *Campaign of the Century*, 370.

9. Cruikshank and Schultz, *The Man Who Sold America*, 305. Other scholars have pointed to the 1934 campaign as the beginning of modern media politics. See Kelley, *Professional Public Relations and Political Power*; Nimmo, *Political Persuaders*; and Mitchell, *Campaign of the Century*.

10. McLuhan, *Understanding Media*.

11. Volumes have been written debating McLuhan and his theories. For a recent overview of ways to discuss technological determinism and the debate that has ensued, see Kovarik, *Revolution in Communications*. More recently, Susan Douglas presented a paper examining ways to move beyond "technological determinism" in reassessing presidential history. See Douglas, "The Presidency, Media Affordances, and Media Aptitudes."

12. Balogh, "'Mirrors of Desire.'"

13. The literature on modern conservatism is too extensive to cite here, but for a thorough overview of this recent historiography, see "Conservatism: A Round Table." Southern California has been highlighted as central to the development of modern conservatism and the rise of the Sunbelt in American political and economic life in the post–World War II period. For a look at the role of federal policy in the growth of Southern California and the Sunbelt more broadly, see Schulman, *From Cotton Belt to Sunbelt*. On how anticommunism flourished in Southern California suburban neighborhoods and its place in the rise of the modern conservative movement, see McGirr, *Suburban Warriors*. For

a discussion of the impact of evangelical religion that shaped Southern California communities and then influenced the broader conservative movement, see Dochuck, *From Bible Belt to Sunbelt*.

14. Bell, *California Crucible*. For a discussion of the role of race in California politics, see Self, *American Babylon*. The place of sexuality in California is discussed in Clayton Howard, "The Closet and the Cul de Sac: Sex, Politics, and Suburbanization in Postwar California," a manuscript-in-progress.

15. The term "media-driven performative politics" is from Bell, *California Crucible*, 2. The term "cultural engagement" is from Dochuck, *From Bible Belt to Sunbelt*, xv.

16. This idea of the new mode of success being dependent on media image is further expanded on in Barbas, *Movie Crazy*, 96–108.

17. "Studio Plan Awaits Vote," *Los Angeles Times*, October 14, 1934, 18.

18. Sinclair, *I, Candidate for Governor*, 167; Mitchell, *Campaign of the Century*, 227–28.

19. Quoted in Kelley, *Professional Public Relations and Political Power*, 50.

20. Cruikshank and Schultz, *The Man Who Sold America*, 300–301.

21. Details on the formation of the Production Code Administration can be found in Sklar, *Movie Made America*, 161–74.

22. Reactions in the aftermath of the election can be found in Mitchell, *Campaign of the Century*, 551–82.

23. Sinclair, *I, Candidate for Governor*, 223–29, discusses his allegation of election fraud.

24. Ibid., 3.

25. Ibid., 166.

26. A terrific overview of the business structures of Hollywood and how they developed in the broader context of the broadcasting industry is in Hilmes, *Hollywood and Broadcasting*, 26–36.

27. The dominant twentieth-century political scholarship looks to the arrival of mass media, television, and advertising as evidence of the growing commodification of American politics, which has simultaneously generated political apathy and contributed to the declining voter turnout trend of the twentieth century. For a look at the impact of the mass media and the rise of extremist advocacy groups on civil identity and activism, see Skocpol and Fiorina, *Civic Engagement in American Democracy*; and Putnam, *Bowling Alone*. For a look at the commodification of politics because of television, see Ansolabehere, Behr, and Iyengar, *The Media Game*; Didion, *Political Fictions*; and Jamieson, *Packaging the Presidency*.

28. Nimmo, *Political Persuaders*; Sabato, *Rise of Political Consultants*.

29. Kelley, *Professional Public Relations and Political Power*, 10–91. In the first section of his groundbreaking study of the rise and impact of public relations in politics, Kelley studies the rise of Whitaker & Baxter through the 1934 campaign and also direct referendum voting on legislative and regulatory policies during the 1930s and 1940s. For more on the lessons of California politics, see Pitchell, "Influence of Professional Campaign Management Firms in Partisan Elections in California," 278–300.

30. Cannon, *President Reagan*, 20–21.

31. Baker, *Affairs of Party*.

32. The phrase "media-driven performative politics" is used to describe California's unique political style, in Bell, *California Crucible*, 2.

33. "John F. Kennedy Inaugural Gala," January 19, 1961, Washington Armory, Washington, D.C. (Michael Hirsch Productions), Audio Visual Archive, JFKL.

34. The longer, more detailed connections between Nixon and the movie industry specifically can be found in Feeney, *Nixon at the Movies*. The standard account of Richard Nixon and his media struggles and successes is Greenberg, *Nixon's Shadow*.

CHAPTER 1

1. Ross, *Hollywood Left and Right*, 61–64.

2. For an extensive discussion of the ways in which Mayer engaged in local and national Republican Party politics during the 1920s and with the Hoover administration, see ibid., 51–88.

3. Critchlow, *When Hollywood Was Right*, 18–21.

4. Quoted in ibid., 18; and Ross, *Hollywood Left and Right*, 64.

5. David Greenberg graciously shared his manuscript-in-progress on presidential spin with me. This upcoming monograph discusses William Irwin's career and his relationship with Hoover.

6. Irwin, *The House That Shadows Built*.

7. Letter, Will Irwin to Herbert Hoover, September 13, 1928, Folder, Correspondence— Irwin, Will, box 38, Campaign and Transition Files, Herbert Hoover Presidential Library, West Branch, Iowa.

8. David Greenberg, manuscript-in-progress on presidential spin.

9. Robert Sklar examines this popular perception of movies as immoral and problematic for the social and cultural elite, in *Movie Made America*. Starr, *Creation of the Media*, 233–346, also examines the moral censorship campaigns and the economic pressures and policies developed from these campaigns. For a focus on the silent film censorship campaigns and the moral concerns behind them, see Grieveson, *Policing Cinema*, which examines progressive concerns about the moral behavior of working-class laborers as they increasingly turned toward the dark nickelodeon theaters, which offered no segregation based on ticket price. As part of the broader campaign to regulate immigrant behavior and actions, reformers and police officers developed state censorship boards, which focused on regulating the content of the silver screen. For a look at the role of women in particular in these campaigns, see Parker, *Purifying America*, which focuses on the Woman's Christian Temperance Union's role in censoring the early motion pictures and the use of maternal activism to target the production and consumption of popular entertainment on the silver screen.

10. A terrific discussion of Hays and his work in the Motion Picture Producers and Distributors of America in the 1920s and 1930s and lobbying efforts more broadly can be found in Welky, *The Moguls and the Dictators*, 55–65. Will Hays also discusses his activities and his priorities as the new "movie czar," in *Memoirs of Will H. Hays*.

11. Muscio, *Hollywood's New Deal*, examines this shifting political culture of the New Deal and the collaborations that turned citizens into audiences.

12. U.S. Congress, *Investigation of Communist Propaganda, Report 2290*, January 17, 1931, 80–81. Critchlow discusses the Fish investigation more broadly, in *When Hollywood Was Right*, 18–22.

13. David Greenberg, in his manuscript-in-progress on presidential spin, examines the inroads made with advertisers and journalists during the Harding, Coolidge, and Hoover administrations. Balogh, "'Mirrors of Desire,'" looks at how Herbert Hoover initiated a process of merchandising policies to interest group leaders to gain electoral support. During the 1928 campaign, as Hoover worked with prominent advertisers like Albert Lasker and Edward Bernays, he emphasized "merchandising" his policies not for the "masses" but for interest group leaders.

14. Balogh, "From Corn to Caviar," examines shifting perceptions of voter attitudes and desires. He argues that the political authority of political parties, then interests groups, then pollsters rested on their ability to translate voter desires for political leaders.

15. Beginning in 1907, radical labor unions used the new celluloid medium to recruit laborers. The American Federation of Labor, the Industrial Workers of the World, and the Western Federation of Miners used moving pictures to battle for the loyalty of unorganized workers in the workplace and at the ballot box. The use of films in labor battles in the early twentieth century is discussed in further detail in Ross, "The Revolt of the Audience." A deeper examination of this working-class activism in early film can be found in Ross, *Working Class Hollywood*.

16. Eyman, *Lion of Hollywood*, 31.

17. Ibid., 30–79; Ross, *Hollywood Left and Right*, 54.

18. This debate between new ideas of sexuality and freedom and the Victorian standard that had reigned in middle-class circles since the nineteenth century is further explored in the context of New York City nightclubs, in Erenberg, *Steppin' Out*. The broader role of Hollywood in navigating the discussion of sexuality through silent films can be found in Lary May, *Screening Out the Past*. The class dynamics between Jewish immigrant entrepreneurs and the Protestant middle and upper classes is explored in Sklar, *Movie Made America*.

19. Eyman, *Lion of Hollywood*, 49.

20. Ibid., 66.

21. Rosten, *Hollywood*, 15. The argument about how in the twentieth century the cult of personality replaced the nineteenth-century culture of character appears in Susman, *Culture as History*.

22. Sklar, *Movie Made America*, 132; Zukor, *The Public Is Never Wrong*, 3–5.

23. Robert Sklar discusses the construction of the studio system, which he calls "the house that Adolph Zukor built," in *Movie Made America*, 141–57.

24. Ceplair and Englund, *The Inquisition in Hollywood*, 1.

25. Discussions of the Southern Pacific Railroad machine and the impact of progressive reforms in California politics can be found in Owens, Costantini, and Weschler, *California Politics and Parties*; and Hichborn and Jones, "The Party, the Machine, and the Vote," 349–57. For a more recent assessment of the rise of Los Angeles and its local politics, see Deverell, *Whitewashed Adobe*.

26. The system of cross-filing and its impact on the broader political structures in California is discussed in Bell, *California Crucible*, 11–30. See also Owens, Costantini, and Weschler, *California Politics and Parties*, 77–96; and Pitchell, "The Electoral System and Voting Behavior," 459–84.

27. For literature on the "long campaign" as a modern part of twentieth-century politics, see Gould, *Modern American Presidency*.

28. The details of Whitaker & Baxter's campaign are found in Mitchell, *Campaign of the Century*. Sinclair's use of professional publicity men is discussed generally in Sinclair, *I, Candidate for Governor*, 44.

29. For a broader discussion of how Coolidge maneuvered within the changing media environment of the 1920s and especially his relationship with public relations man Edward Bernays, see Greenberg, *Calvin Coolidge*. For specifics on Coolidge and Hollywood, see Leab, "Coolidge, Hays, and the 1920s Movies."

30. The film can be found on the Library of Congress website: http://memory.loc.gov/cgi-bin/query/r?ammem/coolbib:@field(NUMBER+@band(amrlv+coolidg1)).

31. Gould, *Modern American Presidency*, 66–76; Greenberg, *Calvin Coolidge*, 91–107; Leab, "Coolidge, Hays, and the 1920s Movies."

32. Ross, *Hollywood Left and Right*, 51–88.

33. For a discussion of the propaganda strategy and organization of the Committee of Public Information, see Vaughn, *Holding Fast the Inner Lines*.

34. Many journalists who had success in publicizing social problems and pushing for corporate and political reforms during the "muckraking era" joined the Committee of Public Information because they believed in the potential of the organization to educate and inform the American people about war aims. The propaganda organization, however, found greater success in constructing nationalistic support for the war through negative-based messaging about the dangers of the German "Hun," ultimately making many reformers lose faith in the public intellect and the value of public opinion. This analysis of public opinion theory is in Vaughn, *Holding Fast the Inner Lines*, 233–38.

35. Lippmann, *Public Opinion*.

36. Balogh, " 'Mirrors of Desire,' " 230; Skowronek, *Building a New American State*.

37. Rosten, *Hollywood*, 36–39.

38. After the Warner Bros. release of *The Jazz Singer* in 1927, the shift toward incorporating sound forced studios to partner with other corporations across the country, like General Electric, and to turn to Wall Street banks for investment funds. These changes intensified suspicion, not just from middle-class reformers and Catholic leaders but also from the ruling economic elites and the Federal Trade Commission, which during that same year charged Paramount Pictures Corporation with monopolistic operations in its ventures to link production, distribution, and exhibition. The commission charged the studio with "unfair methods of competition" and "intimidation," and while it did not force the breakup of the vertically integrated studio, the commission did keep such a close eye on its practices that Paramount and other studios abandoned early efforts to develop commercial radio stations. This process of litigation and the impact on Hollywood's decision to not get involved in radio broadcasting in 1927 is discussed in Hilmes, *Hollywood and Broadcasting*, 40–46.

39. Mayer planned his event for closer to Election Day, but it failed to generate the excitement and support that Warner's had received in September. See "Bourbon Allies to Be Studied," *Los Angeles Times*, November 3, 1932, A8.

40. Advertisement for the Motion Picture Electrical Parade and Sports Pageant, Franklin D. Roosevelt Scrapbook, JLWP.

41. News clipping, "Here Is Program of Big Film Pageant," n.d. [September 1932], ibid.

42. "Hollywood Stages Gala Pageant for Gov. Roosevelt," October 1, 1932, *Hearst Metrotone News* 4, no. 202, excerpt, Film and Television Library, University of California, Los Angeles.

43. News clipping, "Gov. Roosevelt Will Attend as Guest of Honor—Stupendous—Event to Be Benefit for Marion Davies Foundation," n.d. [September 1932], Franklin D. Roosevelt Scrapbook, JLWP.

44. Historians emphasize how radio and the turn to a more active government worked together to renegotiate the responsibilities of the federal government to the American people. For the connection between the new communications mediums prominently displayed by Hollywood and Roosevelt's turn toward new media strategies, see Muscio, *Hollywood's New Deal*. For a look at how radio ushered in these dramatic changes in communication via the mass media, see Brown, *Manipulating the Ether*; Craig, *Fireside Politics*; and Winfield, *FDR and the News Media*. For a consideration of how radio created a new realm of political activity for listeners, see Douglas, *Listening In*, 124–60; Hilmes, *Radio Voices*; and Levine and Levine, *The People and the President*. The landmark study on Roosevelt, the New Deal, and the transformation of federal government responsibilities is Kennedy, *Freedom from Fear*. See also Badger, *The New Deal*.

45. Muscio, *Hollywood's New Deal*.

46. Quoted in Eyman, *Lion of Hollywood*, 169.

47. Gabler, *An Empire of Their Own*, 120.

48. The film short appears as a special feature in *Gold Diggers of 1933*.

49. Standard Contract Agreement for the Cast of *42nd Street*, 42nd Street Picture File, folder 2872, Warner Brothers Archive, School of Cinematic Arts, University of Southern California, Los Angeles.

50. A more detailed description of the brothers' personalities and their frequently adversarial relationship can be found in Gable, *An Empire of Their Own*, 120–50.

51. Muscio, *Hollywood's New Deal*, explores the variety of ways in which the Warner brothers supported the New Deal through their short promotional films and themes in their theatrical productions. The film *The Road Is Open Again*, produced by Warner Bros. in 1933, supported the National Recovery Act and can be found at https://archive.org/details/gov.fdr.352.1.1.

52. Standard Contract Agreement for the Cast of *42nd Street*, 42nd Street Picture File, folder 2872, Warner Brothers Archive, School of Cinematic Arts, University of Southern California, Los Angeles.

53. Sklar, *City Boys*, 64.

54. Giovacchini, *Hollywood Modernism*. Another thorough exploration of the role of various shades of political ideology on the left in shaping Hollywood during this time can be found in Denning, *Cultural Front*. For a discussion of how the influx of stage stars influenced the politicization of Hollywood, see Ross, *Hollywood Left and Right*, 95–101.

55. Reagan and Hubler, *Where's the Rest of Me?*, 203.

56. A detailed assessment of the rising class consciousness among actors in the Screen Actors Guild and its implications in the 1940s can be found in Denning, *Cultural Front*, 3–114; and Lary May, *Big Tomorrow*, 175–213. Stephen Vaughn also explores how the Screen Actors Guild opened new opportunities for political leadership, in *Ronald Reagan in Hollywood*, 121–19.

57. Sklar, *Movie Made America*; Bergman, *We're in the Money*; Roddick, *A New Deal in Entertainment*.

58. Advertisement in *The Observer*, n.d. [September 1932], Franklin D. Roosevelt Scrapbook, JLWP.

59. Advertisement, "Saturday Night's the Night," ibid.

60. Letter, Jack Warner to Harry Warner, August 9, 1932, box 25, Correspondences, 1928–32, California before Election, DNCP, FDRL.

61. News clipping, Franklin D. Roosevelt Scrapbook, JLWP.

62. Letter, Jack Warner to William Wyler, January 19, 1940, box 58, file 743, Warner Bros., William Wyler Papers, MHL.

63. Barbas, *The First Lady of Hollywood*.

64. Telegram, M. H. McIntyre to Hugh Barrett Dobbs, January 17, 1934, Folder 310-B, President's Birthday Celebrations, 1934–43, PPF, FDRL.

65. "Capitol Presses Roosevelt Ball Preparations," *Washington Post*, January 14, 1934, R6.

66. "Nation Honors President Tonight; He Plans a Birthday Radio Talk," *New York Times*, January 30, 1934, 1.

67. For a deeper exploration of how mass consumer culture created a common terrain for the New Deal to succeed, among immigrant workers in particular, see Denning, *Cultural Front*; and Lizbeth Cohen, *Making a New Deal*. The newly created "mass media sphere," which radio helped to create, and how it impacted public perceptions of national events and linked Americans across the country is explored in Hilmes, *Radio Voices*.

68. "President Franklin D. Roosevelt's Birthday Song," lyrics and music by James A. Mundy, January 21, 1936, Folder 310-B, President's Birthday Ball Commission for Infantile Paralysis, 1936–43, PPF, FDRL.

69. Kennedy, *Freedom from Fear*, 284–87.

70. Rosten, *Hollywood*, 160.

71. Accounts of the pledges and donations are found in Rosten, *Hollywood*, 100.

72. "Movie and Radio Stars, Famous Orchestras to Help D.C. Observe Birthday Ball Tonight," *Washington Post*, January 30, 1937, 1.

73. Ibid.

74. Sklar, *Movie Made America*, 175–214.

75. For a look at the history of the Committee of Public Information, see Vaughn, *Holding Fast the Inner Lines*. A look at the role of Pickford and Douglas in selling liberty bonds can be found in Midkiff-DeBauche, "Reminiscences of the Past, Conditions of the Present," 129–39.

76. F. T. Birchallberlin, "Where Heroes Can Be Made to Order," *New York Times*, May 6, 1934, SM6.

77. "Washington Jams Birthday Balls to Aid in Nation's Fight against Infantile Paralysis," *Washington Post*, January 31, 1939, 4.

78. "D.C. Dances with Stars So 'Children May Walk Again,'" *Washington Post*, January 30, 1938, 12.

79. "President Wins $100 Naming Film," *Washington Post*, February 15, 1938, X1.

80. Hedley Donovan, "President's Birthday Balls Draw 20,000 Here," *Washington Post*, January 21, 1940, 1.

81. "Mickey Rooney to Join Stars at Parties Here," *Washington Post*, January 24, 1940, 1.

82. "Film Folk Steal Show at Capital," *New York Times*, January 30, 1940, 17.

83. "James Roosevelt Takes Film Post as Goldwyn Executive on Coast," *New York Times*, December 5, 1938, 1.

84. Muscio, *Hollywood's New Deal*, explores the personal relationships that developed between the Roosevelt family and various members of the new communications industry.

85. The quote from Will Hays and the analysis of this "quid pro quo" exchange is found in Welky, *The Moguls and the Dictators*, 68.

86. Harry Warner's exchange with Harry Hopkins can be found in Muscio, *Hollywood's New Deal*, 166. A broader discussion of the nuances of the negotiations between Will Hays, the Warner brothers, Hopkins, Arnold, and Roosevelt can be found in ibid, 154–81.

87. The quote from the trade press is from ibid., 187.

88. Welky, *The Moguls and the Dictators*, 238–39.

89. Details of the activities of the Hollywood for Roosevelt committee can be found in Hollywood for Roosevelt Committee, Folder 7024, PPF, FDRL.

90. Details concerning speeches, tours, radio broadcasts, and billboard announcements can be found in "Letter Reporting the Activities of the Hollywood for Roosevelt Organization in the 1940 Presidential Election," Hollywood for Roosevelt Committee, Folder 7024, PPF, FDRL.

91. Advertisement, "Why We of Hollywood Will Vote for Roosevelt," *New York Times*, ibid.

92. Wendell Willkie's campaign for the Republican nomination and his use of publicity to win the nomination are detailed in Kelley, *Professional Public Relations and Political Power*, 34–35.

93. Letter, Ralph Block to Miss Marguerite LeHand, Secretary to the President, November 16, 1940, Hollywood for Roosevelt Committee, Folder 7024, PPF, FDRL.

94. Rosten, *Hollywood*, 160.

95. Letter, Ralph Block to Miss Marguerite LeHand, Secretary to the President, November 16, 1940, Hollywood for Roosevelt Committee, Folder 7024, PPF, FDRL.

96. Letter, Franklin D. Roosevelt to Ralph Block, December 30, 1940, ibid.

97. Speech of Hon. James M. Mead, *Congressional Record*, February 14, 1941, Birthday Balls, Eleanor Roosevelt Pamphlet Collection, ibid.

98. Mark Sullivan, "Must All Candidates Have Political Glamor?," *Washington Post*, February 25, 1940, B6.

99. Ibid.

100. Testimony of J. Matthews, U.S. Congress, *Investigation of Un-American Propaganda Activities in the United States* (1939), 918–19.

101. Willard Edwards, "Witness Links Coast Radicals to Democrats," *Chicago Daily Tribune*, October 27, 1938, 4.

102. See, for example, "Reply of Dies to President," *New York Times*, October 27, 1938, 10. The role of the Hollywood trade press in perpetuating this image is also discussed in Welky, *The Moguls and the Dictators*, 142–44.

103. "Willard Edwards, New Deal Reds on Dies' List," *Chicago Daily Tribune*, October 27, 1938, 1.

104. "Dies Group to Investigate Hollywood," *Los Angeles Times*, February 16, 1940, 1; Thomas Brady, "Hollywood Heckles Its Hecklers," *New York Times*, August 25, 1940, 111.

105. Thomas Pryor, "Looking Back at It All," *New York Times*, December 29, 1940, 4.

106. Sally Reid, "Is Melvyn Douglas a Communist," *Photoplay*, September 1940, 88.

CHAPTER 2

1. Radio Address delivered by Hon. Gerald P. Nye, St. Louis, August 1, 1941, Folder, Speeches, September 1941, Wendell Willkie Papers, Lilly Library, Indiana University, Bloomington.

2. U.S. Congress, Senate Resolution 152, August 1, 1941, ibid.

3. Radio Address delivered by Hon. Gerald P. Nye, St. Louis Missouri, August 1, 1941, ibid.

4. Works that focus specifically on the silver screen message include Dick, *Star Spangled Screen*; Manvell, *Films and the Second World War*; and Sklar, *Movie Made America*, 249–85. Koppes and Black, *Hollywood Goes to War*, gives a detailed analysis of the organizational structure developed between Hollywood and the OWI in both domestic and overseas film branches.

5. More detail on the intervention debates can be found in Kennedy, *Freedom from Fear*, 381–464.

6. "Confessions of a Nazi Spy," New York Preview, *Motion Picture Daily*, April 28, 1939, Hollywood Production Code, Reel 15, MHL.

7. Ross, "*Confessions of a Nazi Spy*: Warner Bros., Anti-Fascism, and the Politicization of Hollywood," 49–59.

8. Welky, *The Moguls and the Dictators*.

9. "'Nazi Spy' Must Attraction Scoring Box Office Bulls Eye," *Hollywood Reporter*, April 28, 1939, Hollywood Production Code, Reel 15, MHL.

10. Letter, Walter Gaulke to Will Hays, August 15, 1939, MHL.

11. Testimony of Fredric March, U.S. Congress, *Investigation of Un-American Propaganda Activities in the United States*, August 17, 1940, vol. 3. This testimony points specifically to the Motion Picture Committee for Spanish Relief and how March went to dinner parties to support "humanitarian causes." For a list of all the other organizations, see Welky, *The Moguls and the Dictators*, 137–42.

12. Giovacchini, in *Hollywood Modernism*, discusses the vibrant Left community and its efforts to promote a democratic modernism on the screen and encourage political activism of the masses in Hollywood during the 1930s and the war effort. He examines how "Hollywood Europeans" and "Hollywood New Yorkers" brought realism to the screen in an effort to awaken the United States and the world to the dangers of totalitarian rule. But these intellectuals also saw, through film, the "possibility of molding a popular audience-oriented, and more democratic version of modernism" (35).

13. Nelson Bell, "The Screen Is Denied Freedom Guaranteed by Constitution," *Washington Post*, September 24, 1939, 3.

14. Giovacchini, *Hollywood Modernism*, 120.

15. Snow, "Confessions of a Hollywood Propagandist," 61–71.

16. Harry M. Warner, "United We Stand, Divided We Fall," pamphlet of address delivered June 5, 1940, Folder, Propaganda in Motion Pictures, Warner Brothers Archive, School of Cinematic Arts, University of Southern California, Los Angeles.

17. Douglas Fairbanks Jr., William Allen White Committee Speech, Chicago, September 18, 1940, Folder 4, Speeches, box 4, Douglas Fairbanks Jr. Collection, Boston University, Howard Gotlieb Library, Boston.

18. Fairbanks, *Salad Days*, 1988.

19. Address by Douglas Fairbanks Jr. before the Elementary School Principals' Division of the National Education Association, July 4, 1939, San Francisco; Speech by Douglas Fairbanks Jr., February 1942, Miami; Speech to the Rotary Club in favor of the Lend Lease Act by Douglas Fairbanks Jr., 1941; all in Folder 4, Speeches, box 4, Douglas Fairbanks Jr. Collection, Boston University, Howard Gotlieb Library, Boston. Speech by Douglas Fairbanks Jr. to the United Youth for Defense Rally, October 16, 1941, Folder 1, Speeches, box 5, ibid.

20. Fairbanks, *Salad Days*, 380–405.

21. Letter, Wendell Willkie to Senator D. Worth Clark, September 8, 1941 (also reprinted in the Senate hearings), Folder, Speeches, September 1941, Wendell Willkie Papers, Lilly Library, Indiana University, Bloomington.

22. A more detailed account of these hearings and the emergence of a "Hollywood Triumphant" can be found in Welky, *The Moguls and the Dictators*, 293–311.

23. Editorial, "F.D.R. Is Still the President," August 9, 1941, Folder, Franklin D. Roosevelt, 1930s-40s, box 60, JLWP.

24. The changes brought about from 1937 to 1945 in New Deal liberal ideology are discussed in Brinkley, *The End of Reform*. The New Deal liberalism the OWI and Hollywood advanced during the war was part of the "ideological adaptation" made by New Dealers, which Brinkley argues was a commitment to "consumer-oriented liberalism," a "Keynesian–welfare state approach to political economy," and a "fervent commitment to internationalism" (269).

25. Information on Lowell Mellett and his work with the Roosevelt administration can be found in Lowell Mellett Papers, FDRL.

26. For a discussion of Lowell Mellett pushing for Roosevelt to give the Academy Awards address, see Welky, *The Moguls and the Dictators*, 260–63.

27. Text of Roosevelt's Speech to Motion Picture Industry, *Washington Post*, February 28, 1941, 11.

28. An outline of the predecessors and successors of the OWI can be found in the overview/finding aid for the OWI. Koppes and Black, *Hollywood Goes to War*, 48–81, provides a detailed account of the background of the various agencies and individuals that ultimately composed the OWI.

29. Letter, Franklin D. Roosevelt to Lowell Mellett, December 18, 1941, Folder, Franklin D. Roosevelt, 1930s-40s, box 60, JLWP.

30. *Film Fact 1942: 20 Years of Self Government* (New York: Motion Picture Producers and Distributors of America), Folder, Motion Picture Bureau, misc., box 3, entry 6A, Records of the Historian Relating to the Domestic Branch, OWI.

31. Resolution Adopted by Coordinating Committee of War Activities Committee, transmitted by George J. Schaefer to President Roosevelt, December 12, 1941, Folder, Franklin D. Roosevelt, 1930-40s, box 60, JLWP.

32. Pamphlet, "HWM: Today and Tomorrow," Folder, Hollywood Writers' Mobilization, box 1535, entry 288, Correspondence Regarding Film Production, September 1943–October 1945, OWI.

33. Koppes and Black explore these divisions between the various domestic branches of the Bureau of Motion Pictures and the construction of its overseas branch in detail, in *Hollywood Goes to War.*

34. For a discussion of the "4-Minute Men" and the public education campaign, see Vaughn, *Holding Fast the Inner Lines*, 98–140. For a discussion of how film became one of many other "channels of communication" used to sell World War I, see ibid., 193–213.

35. For a discussion of how movie theaters became a "part of life on the home front, of a piece with tilling a victory garden, eating Liberty sandwiches (hamburgers), buying Thrift Stamps, and throwing rocks at Kaiser Bill's image," and a broader description of the place of movie theaters in Milwaukee during World War I, see Midkiff-DeBauche, "Reminiscences of the Past, Conditions of the Present," 129–39.

36. While many producers did film patriotically inspired films, the Committee of Public Information did not direct these; rather, they were voluntary efforts to show patriotism by individual producers. The collaboration between the motion picture industry and the Committee of Public Information centered mostly on recording aspects of the war and distributing these documentaries or "newsreels" to the public through their theater connections. See Vaughn, *Holding Fast the Inner Lines*, 203–8.

37. Letter, Ralph Block to Miss Marguerite LeHand, Secretary to the President, November 16, 1940, Hollywood for Roosevelt Committee, Folder 7024, PPF, FDRL.

38. All content of the ideology of the OWI manual can be found in "Government Informational Manual for the Motion Picture Industry," Folder, Government Informational Manual for the Motion Picture Industry, box 3, entry 6A, OWI.

39. A discussion of symbolic politics rooted in the mass media can be found in Farber, *Chicago '68*, 246–58.

40. This conflict involving "politics, propaganda, and profits" is explored extensively in Koppes and Black, *Hollywood Goes to War.*

41. Movie Summaries and Analyses, 1942, Folder, Bureau of Motion Pictures, box 3, entry 6A, OWI.

42. Memo from William Goetz to Producers, Directors, Writers, and Heads of All Departments, March 5, 1943, ibid.

43. Motion Picture Letter, vol. 1, no. 3, September 1942, Folder, Motion Picture Letter, box 1450, entry 265, General Correspondence of the Chief, Stanton Griffis, OWI.

44. Script, "OWI Food Short, Orson Welles, *Magic*," written by James Bloodworth, Folder, Food and Music, box 1532, entry 288, Correspondence Regarding Film Production, September 1943–October 1945, OWI.

45. "Bureau of Motion Pictures of the Office of War Information Defense Report," 1942, Folder, Bureau of Motion Pictures, box 3, entry 6A, OWI.

46. Examples of the polling chart and evaluation surveys conducted by Ohio State University and local theaters can be found in Folder, Evaluation Reports and Forms, box 1497, entry 275, Reference Files, April 1940–June 1943, OWI; information on the responsibilities of the Research, Reports, and Informational Division, as well as the breakdown of responsibilities within the Bureau of Motion Pictures as a whole, can be found in Memo from Elmer Davis to Branch Directors, Deputies, and Branch Chiefs, October 10, 1942, Folder, Criteria, Plans, and the Policy of the Bureau of Motion Pictures, box 1497, entry 275, Reference Files, April 1940–June 1941, OWI.

47. Outline of Research and Script Needs, Folder, Production Progress, Possibilities, etc., box 1497, entry 275, OWI.

48. Report, "The Need for a Coordinated Government War-Time Motion Picture Program," Folder, Bureau of Motion Pictures, box 3, entry 6A, OWI.

49. Letter, Taylor M. Mills to George Healy Jr., April 18, 1944, ibid.

50. Memo from Lowell Mellett to Elmer Davis, March 26, 1943, ibid.

51. Newsreels and OWI Campaigns and Programs, February 1943, Report No. 8, March 12, 1943, ibid.

52. These reports of newsreels and motion pictures are found in ibid.

53. Preliminary Motion Picture Survey, July 17, 1940, Folder, Publicity, box 1494, entry 273, Correspondence, July 1940–December 1941, OWI.

54. Report on Projects Being Photographed, Folder, Production Progress, Possibilities, etc., box 1497, entry 275, OWI.

55. Plans for the Promotion of Our Work, Folder, Bureau of Motion Pictures, box 3, entry 6A, OWI.

56. "Bureau of Motion Pictures of the Office of War Information Defense Report," 1942, ibid.

57. Evaluation of University Film Programs, by Edgar Dale, Folder, Evaluation Reports and Forms, box 1497, entry 275, OWI.

58. Letter, C. R. Reagan to Arch Mercey and Paul Reed, July 6, 1942, Folder, C. R. Reagan, box 1450, entry 265, OWI.

59. Letter, C. R. Reagan to Arch Mercey, May 4, 1942, Folder, C. R. Reagan, ibid.

60. Report on the Functions of the Educational Division of the Bureau of Motion Pictures, OWI, Folder, Criteria, Plans, and the Policy of the Bureau of Motion Pictures, box 1497, Reference File, entry 275, OWI.

61. Koppes and Black, *Hollywood Goes to War*, 110.

62. This "shakeout" is discussed in ibid., 113–41; and Weinberg, "What to Tell America," 73–89.

63. Wanger, "The OWI and Motion Pictures," 104.

64. Ibid., 107.

65. Ibid., 110.

66. The details of the budget cuts are found in Larson, "The Domestic Work of the Office of War Information," 442–43.

67. Although the OWI retained an official Domestic Bureau of Motion Pictures until October 6, 1945, the Hollywood War Activities Committee did not have government officials like Lowell Mellett comb through every theatrical film and oversee all propaganda structures. In fact, soon after the budget cuts, Mellett moved back to his administrative position in the Roosevelt administration, and the subsequent heads of the domestic branch of the Bureau of Motion Pictures were Hollywood insiders rather than government officials. The focus of government-sponsored film production moved toward war bonds as the Department of the Treasury financed films that war bond campaigns used. Treasury took advantage of the organization of the OWI to facilitate its communication with Hollywood writers, producers, actors, and directors. The relationship between the OWI and theatrical productions is described in detail in Koppes and Black, *Hollywood Goes to War*.

68. Letter, Taylor Mills to George Healy Jr., April 18, 1944, Folder, Bureau of Motion Pictures, box 3, entry 6A, OWI.

69. For discussion of the World War I liberty bond campaigns and the place of theaters and celebrities in this campaign, see Midkiff-DeBauche, "Reminiscences of the Past, Conditions of the Present," 129–39.

70. "Motion Picture Letter," September 1942, Folder, Motion Picture Letter, box 1450, entry 265, OWI.

71. Editorial, "Buy and Buy," Sybil Bruce Leach, *Photoplay Movie Mirror Magazine*, December 1942, 24.

72. "Dorothy Lamour, American," *Photoplay Movie Mirror Magazine*, December 1942, 27.

73. Kennedy, *Freedom from Fear*, 626; Blum, *V Was for Victory*, 16–21.

74. Wanger, "The OWI and Motion Pictures," 106.

75. Merton, *Mass Persuasion*.

76. Ibid., 76.

77. Ibid., 45–51.

78. "Motion Picture Letter," September 1942, Folder, Motion Picture Letter, box 1450, entry 265, OWI.

79. An example of this patriotically motivated individual can be found with a letter written by J. E. Morton to C. R. Reagan, January 23, 1945, Folder, Treasury 6th War Loan Drive, box 1665, 6th War Loan, entry 328, Correspondence Concerning Films for War Loans, OWI.

80. News clipping, "16mm Films to Aid Fifth War Loan Drive," *Educational Screen*, n.d. [1944], p. 266, Folder, Treasury 5th War Loan Drive, box 1663, entry 328, Correspondence Concerning Films for War Loans, OWI.

81. Letter, Treasury Department to All 16mm Projector Owners in America, May 26, 1944, Folder, Treasury 5th War Loan Drive (2), ibid.

82. Pamphlet, Nu-Art News, May 1944, New York, New York, Folder, Treasury 5th War Loan Drive (2), ibid.

83. Letter, Treasury Department to All 16mm Projector Owners in America, May 26, 1944, Folder, Treasury 5th War Loan Drive (2), ibid.

84. News clipping, "Rallies, Auctions, Special Stage Shows and Events Launch Bond Campaign," June 1944, Folder, Treasury 5th War Loan Drive, ibid.

85. Report, "Fifth War Loan Recognition of 16mm," Folder, Treasury 5th War Loan Drive, ibid.

86. Letter, William F. Gutwein to Twyman Films Inc., June 27, 1944, Folder, Treasury 5th War Loan Drive, ibid.

87. Multiple Correspondences, Folder, Treasury 5th War Loan Drive (2), ibid.

88. "A Report on the Distribution of 16mm Motion Pictures Prepared for the Fifth War Loan, June 12 to July 8, 1944," submitted to C. R. Reagan and compiled by the Princeton Film Center, July 1944, Folder, Treasury 5th War Loan Drive, ibid.

89. Letter, H. U. M. Higgins to C. R. Reagan, July 11, 1944, Folder, Treasury 5th War Loan Drive, ibid.

90. Letter, Ted Gamble to All Distributors of 16mm Film, September 28, 1944, Folder, Treasury Sixth War Loan Drive, box 1665, 6th War Loan, entry 328, OWI.

91. Informational Program for the 6th War Loan Drive, Folder, Treasury Sixth War Loan Drive, ibid.

92. Bulletin, "Flash," circulated by Merriman Holtz, February 9, 1945, Folder, Treasury Sixth War Loan Drive, ibid.

93. Letter, Tom Bailey to Francis Harmon, December 20, 1944, Folder, *All Star Bond Rally*, box 1532, entry 288, OWI. The *All Star Bond Rally* idea came after a successful Canadian war bond drive that featured parts of this production by Warner Bros. in 1943. When Ted Gamble recalled the success of this feature, he worked with Warner Bros. to cut references to Canada and use it as a staple for the 7th War Bond Campaign.

94. Letter, Tom Bailey to Ted Gamble, February 8, 1945, Folder, *All Star Bond Rally*, ibid.

95. Script, "All Star Bond Rally," written by Don Quinn, March 1, 1945, Folder, *All Star Bond Rally*, ibid. The film itself can be found at https://archive.org/details/AllStarBondRally.

96. Meeting notes for the Seventh War Loan 16mm film production and distribution, February 1, 1945, Folder, Treasury 6th War Loan References, box 1665, entry 328, OWI.

97. Newsletter, To All State 16mm Chairmen and Distributors, June 13, 1945, Folder, 7th War Loan References, box 1668, 7th War Loan, entry 328, OWI.

98. Publicity Manual for *All Star Bond Rally*, May 9, 1945, Folder, Treasury 7th War Loan References, box 1666, 6th and 7th War Loan, entry 328, OWI.

99. Ibid.

100. Letter, Bell & Howell Company, Chicago, December 18, 1944, Folder, Treasury 6th War Loan References, box 1665, entry 328, OWI.

CHAPTER 3

1. "H'wood Alliance Formed to Combat Alien Isms in Pix; Sam Wood Prexy," *Variety*, February 9, 1944, 8.

2. The statement of principles for the MPA appeared in various trade papers from February 9, 1944, through September 1944. Clippings of all these announcements are in Folder 6, Free World Association, Questionable Organizations, box 99, Walter Wanger Papers, WCFTR.

3. "Vice President Wallace Points Up Need for Vital, Imaginative Pix," *Variety*, February 9, 1944.

4. *Writers' Congress: Proceedings of the Conference Held in October 1943*. For the Roosevelt quote, see p. xi; for the Zanuck statement, see p. 5.

5. "Vice President Wallace Points Up Need for Vital, Imaginative Pix," *Variety*, February 9, 1944.

6. For a discussion of how L. B. Mayer "groomed" conservatives in his studio, see Ross, *Hollywood Left and Right*, 70–81.

7. "On the March," *Hollywood Reporter*, February 1944, 26, Walter Wanger Papers, WCFTR.

8. Most scholarly books on the communist hearings in Hollywood briefly acknowledge the MPA and its 1944 accusations of communist infiltration as the necessary congressional invitation to examine the industry but do not delve into any deeper analyses of the organization. See Ceplair and Englund, *The Inquisition in Hollywood*, 209–25; Sklar, *Movie Made*

America; 257–58; Lary May, *Big Tomorrow*, 203; Neve, *Film and Politics in America*, 87–92; and Giglio, *Here's Looking at You*, 101–5. The prominent exception to this trend appears in the most recent literature, especially in Critchlow, *When Hollywood Was Right*, 47–58. Critchlow examines how Hollywood conservatives seen as on the fringe in local and state politics during the 1930s and 1940s built connections with big businesses across the state and shaped the development of the modern conservative movement. Also, in *Hollywood Left and Right*, 89–130, Ross chronicles Edward G. Robinson's engagement with progressive politics during the 1930s and 1940s and the negative impact that it had on his career.

9. Script, Humphrey Bogart, October 28, 1944, CBS, Folder 4, Special Committee to Investigate Presidential Expenditures, box 7, HDCR.

10. "FDR Campaign Speech," Bette Davis, n.d. [1944?], Folder 1, box 4, #382, Bette Davis Papers, Boston University, Howard Gotlieb Library, Boston.

11. Advertisement, "Message to Washington," Folder 3, "Message to Washington," box 6, HDCR.

12. Script, "Message to Washington," April 28, 1943, Folder 3, "Message to Washington," 8–9, box 6, HDCR.

13. Ibid., 11.

14. In March, these protests continued in the aftermath of the Zoot Suit Riots, and the message was again reinforced about the need to eradicate white supremacist policies from across the country. See Report, "Hollywood Democratic Committee," Folder 1, History, box 1, HDCR.

15. "Government Informational Manual for the Motion Picture Industry," Folder, Government Informational Manual for the Motion Picture Industry, box 3, entry 6A, OWI.

16. Ibid.

17. Telegram, Mrs. Charles W. Tillett to Mrs. Henry Myers, April 27, 1943, Folder 3, "Message to Washington," box 6, HDCR.

18. The anger of liberals in the aftermath of the 1934 election and the widespread disbelief that studio executives could engage in such "dirty tricks" can be found in the epilogue of Mitchell, *Campaign of the Century*, 560–63.

19. Report, "Hollywood Democratic Committee," Folder 1, History, box 1, HDCR.

20. Ibid.

21. Letter, George Pepper to Mr. R. Isackmen, December 8, 1943, Folder, "United We Stand," HDCR. The meeting was originally planned for January, but over the course of the correspondence the rally was pushed back to February and then to March, so that references to the rally vary on which month is given for the event to take place.

22. Attendance Record for Meeting, November 30, 1943, Biltmore Hotel, Folder, "United We Stand," HDCR.

23. Report, "Hollywood Democratic Committee," Folder 1, History, box 1, HDCR.

24. Ibid.

25. Letter, E. C. Farnham to Friends, February 16, 1944, Folder, "United We Stand," HDCR.

26. Report, "Hollywood Democratic Committee," Folder 1, History, box 1, HDCR.

27. Script, "Let's Go Out and Ring Doorbells," March 24, 1944, NBC, Folder 17, "Let's Go Out and Ring Doorbells," 1944 Script, box 5, HDCR.

28. Ibid.

29. Letter, Clarence J. Novotny to Marc Connelly, September 1, 1944, Folder 9, California Democratic Party, box 2, HDCR.

30. Letter, Barbara Johnson to George Pepper, September 25, 1944, ibid.

31. News clipping, "No Make Believe in Hollywood's Democratic Group," October 6, 1944, Folder 12, HICCASP Publicity, box 7, HDCR.

32. Letter, Harry C. Huse to George Pepper, September 14, 1944, Folder 9, California Democratic Party, box 2, HDCR.

33. News clipping, "No Make Believe in Hollywood's Democratic Group," October 6, 1944, Folder 12, HICCASP Publicity, box 7, HDCR.

34. "Various New Devices to Capture the Votes," *New York Times*, November 2, 1944, 18.

35. "Model Campaign Methods," Folder 7, 1944 Election Misc., box 3, HDCR.

36. "Report of Campaign Activities of the Hollywood Democratic Committee as of October 27, 1944," Folder, 1944 Election, JLWP.

37. "Spot Announcement Forms Used for Democratic Candidates, Assistance to Democratic National Committee, General Election 1944," Folder 9, 1944 Radio Scripts, box 3, HDCR.

38. "Glamor Pusses," *Time* magazine, September 9, 1946, 24, Folder 20, Democratic National Committee, 1943–45, box 2, HDCR.

39. Telegram, Robert Newman to George Pepper, October 13, 1944, ibid.

40. Letter, Robert Newman to George Pepper, October 18, 1944, Folder 4, Special Committee to Investigate Presidential Expenditures, box 7, HDCR.

41. Script, "Typical Recorded Announcement Successfully Used in California Radio Campaign," Folder 1, box 572, 1944 General File, Misc. Speech Materials and Speech Drafts, Five Minute Spots, DNCP, FDRL.

42. Script for Orson Welles Broadcast, October 1, 1944, Folder 1, box 572, DNCP, FDRL.

43. Report, October 16, 1944, Folder, Transcripts, Misc. Billing, box 572, DNCP, FDRL.

44. Letter, J. Leonard Reinsch to Party Leaders Everywhere, October 16, 1944, Folder, Transcripts, Misc. Billing, box 572, DNCP, FDRL.

45. Letter, Hannah Dorner to George Pepper, August 24, 1944, Folder 3, box 1, Correspondence Re: HDC ICCASP Merger, 1944–45, HDCR.

46. Letter, Victor M. Ratner to Janice, August 10, 1944, Folder 20, Democratic National Committee, 1943–45, HDCR.

47. Notes on HDC Meeting, August 22, 1944, ibid.

48. For a more detailed discussion, see Blow, *Butting In*, 199–207.

49. Notes on HDC Meeting, August 22, 1944, Folder, Democratic National Committee, 1943–45, HDCR.

50. Ibid.

51. Balogh, "From Corn to Caviar."

52. Master Script, CBS Radio Script, Eve of the Election, November 6, 1944, Folder, Misc. Documents, Columbia Broadcasting System, DNCP, FDRL.

53. Telegram, Harry S. Truman to the Hollywood Democratic Committee, Folder 20, Democratic National Committee, 1943–45, box 2, HDCR.

54. Mark Sullivan, "Must All Candidates Have Political Glamor?," *Washington Post*, February 25, 1940, B6.

55. "The Swing Is On," *Washington Post*, October 9, 1944, 8.

56. Letter, Victor M. Ratner to Janice, August 10, 1944, Folder 20, Democratic National Committee, 1943–45, HDCR.

57. Milton Biow discusses how he sent catchy phrases to speechwriter Samuel Rosenman, which FDR frequently incorporated into wartime Fireside Chats. Biow, *Butting In*, 237.

58. Details of Warner's election activities can be found in Folder, 1944 Election, JLWP.

59. "M P Alliance Formed to Fight Subversive Forces," *Hollywood Reporter*, Folder 6, box 99, Walter Wanger Papers, WCFTR.

60. "On the March," *Motion Picture Herald*, February 19, 1944, ibid.

61. Member Letter of Invitation, October 5, 1944, Folder 3870, Motion Picture Alliance, Hedda Hopper Papers, MHL.

62. Statement of Policy, ibid.

63. For a more detailed discussion of how L. B. Mayer trained conservative actors, directors, and producers at MGM, see Ross, *Hollywood Left and Right*, 51–88.

64. Statement of Policy, Folder 3870, Motion Picture Alliance, Hedda Hopper Papers, MHL.

65. "Motion Picture Alliance States Its Principles," *Variety*, February 9, 1944, Folder 4, Motion Picture Alliance for the Preservation of American Ideals, box 81, CRCC.

66. A brief description of the failed efforts by conservatives in the 1944 election can be found in Farber, *Rise and Fall of Modern American Conservatism*, 25–34. Farber notes how "1944 was a bad time to be a conservative or a onetime 'isolationist'" (30). Critchlow also discusses the role of the MPA within the broader conservative movement in California. He argues that though Republican leaders in California were "chagrin[ed]" to see the hardline approach the MPA took to anticommunism, ultimately this "anticommunism forged the Hollywood Right." Critchlow, *When Hollywood Was Right*, 42–68.

67. "Faith" Editorial Comment, *Hollywood Citizen-News*, February 1944, Folder 4, Motion Picture Alliance for the Preservation of American Ideals, box 81, CRCC.

68. Ibid.

69. "Motion Picture Alliance States Its Principles," *Variety*, February 9, 1944, ibid.

70. "Americanize the Movies," February 9, 1944, ibid.

71. News clipping, *Script Magazine*, February 19, 1944, Folder 6, box 99, Walter Wanger Papers, WCFTR.

72. Red Kann, "On the March," *Motion Picture Herald*, February 19, 1944, 26, ibid.

73. "Hollywood Letter," March 7, 1944, Folder 4, box 81, part 2, CRCC.

74. Extension of Remarks of Hon. Robert R. Reynolds of North Carolina, March 7, 1944, *Congressional Record*, A1220, Folder 6, box 99, Walter Wanger Papers, WCFTR.

75. News clipping, "Reynolds Tieup with Film Group Exposed," Folder 4, box 81, CRCC.

76. Foreword, *The Truth about Hollywood*, pamphlet released by Council of Hollywood Guilds and Unions, 1944, Wisconsin State Historical Society, Madison.

77. Information on the debate within the Screen Writers Guild and the division between it and the Screen Playwrights Guild is found in Ceplair and Englund, *The Inquisition in Hollywood*, 32–41.

78. Extensive debate emerged about whether or not the Screen Playwrights Guild was orchestrated by Thalberg. Opponents claimed that Thalberg wrote the contracts and

McGuinness and the others were bribed with contracts to form the new union. Despite accusations of a conspiracy, no actual evidence exists. Ceplair and Englund discuss this in ibid. as well.

79. *Variety*, May 9, 1936.

80. Ceplair and Englund, *The Inquisition in Hollywood*, 44.

81. *The Truth about Hollywood*, 7, pamphlet released by Council of Hollywood Guilds and Unions, 1944, Wisconsin State Historical Society, Madison.

82. Ibid., 6.

83. Ibid., 17.

84. Ibid., 22.

85. "To the Members of the Motion Picture Alliance for the Preservation of American Ideals," *Hollywood Reporter*, June 27, 1944, Folder 3870, Motion Picture Alliance, Hedda Hopper Papers, MHL.

86. James Kevin McGuinness, "Double Cross in Hollywood," *New Leader*, July 15, 1944, Folder 6, box 99, Walter Wanger Papers, WCFTR.

87. "Mrs. Rogers Sued over Red Debate," *New York Times*, September 11, 1947, 30; "Inside Stuff—Pictures," *Variety*, October 8, 1947, 14.

88. First Annual Report of the Executive Committee to the Members of the Motion Picture Alliance for the Preservation of American Ideals, Folder 10, Motion Picture Alliance, box 1, Robert M. W. Vogel Papers, MHL.

89. Program, "We Speak for Freedom," Folder 17, Motion Picture Alliance for the Preservation of American Ideals, box 40, CRCC.

90. Oliver H. P. Garrett, "The MPA Exposes Itself," Folder 6, Motion Picture Alliance for the Preservation of American Ideals, July 1944–January 1945, box 81, CRCC.

91. Elmer Rice, "Strictly Personal . . . The MPA and American Ideals," *Saturday Review*, Folder 6, Motion Picture Alliance for the Preservation of American Ideals, July 1944–January 1945, ibid.

92. Nicknames appear in "Hollywood Letter," *New Masses*, March 7, 1944, Folder 4, Motion Picture Alliance for the Preservation of American Ideals, ibid.

93. Testimony of Lela Rogers, U.S. Congress, Committee on Un-American Activities, *Communist Infiltration of Hollywood Motion Picture Industry*, May 1947, 241.

94. Hopper, *Whole Truth and Nothing But*, 272–73.

95. The nuances of Hopper's anticommunism are explored in further detail in Frost, *Hedda Hopper's Hollywood*, 91–111.

96. Critchlow, *When Hollywood Was Right*, examines how anticommunist conservatives and members of the MPA shaped the development of the modern conservative movement first in California and then across the country. For specific discussion of the MPA, see 42–108.

97. "The MPA Exposes Itself," news clipping, Folder 6, Motion Picture Alliance for the Preservation of American Ideals, July 1944–January 1945, box 81, CRCC.

98. Editorial, "Americanize the Movies," Folder 6, box 99, Walter Wanger Papers, WCFTR.

99. "California: The Battle of Hollywood," *Time* magazine, February 14, 1944.

100. Editorial, Orson Welles, "Return to the Living," *Time* magazine, June 3, 1944, Folder 4, box 81, CRCC.

101. First Annual Report of the Executive Committee to the Members of the Motion Picture Alliance for the Preservation of American Ideals, Folder 10, Motion Picture Alliance, box 1, Robert M. W. Vogel Papers, MHL.

102. Editorial, "Name Your Man," *Variety*, March 8, 1944, Folder 4, box 81, CRCC.

103. Letter, George Pepper to Hannah Dorner, August 18, 1944, Folder 3, Correspondence Re: HDC ICCASP Merger, 1944–45, box 1, HDCR.

104. Terms of the merger appear in various statements and correspondences between the HDC and the ICCASP, in ibid.

105. Film historians have documented the postwar moment for liberalism in message films and how these films, written and directed by left-wing and radical writers, became the target of FBI and HUAC investigations into communist influence in Hollywood. For a look at the specific films, see Ceplair and Englund, *The Inquisition in Hollywood*; Neve, *Film and Politics in America*, especially 56–83; and Schwartz, *The Hollywood Writers' War*. Articles in Krutnik, *"Un-American" Hollywood: Politics and Film in the Blacklist Era*, explore the specific messages of movies deemed "potentially subversive" by HUAC investigators, including Krutnik, "A Living Part of the Class Struggle: Diego Rivera's *The Flower Carrier* and the Hollywood Left"; and Simon, "*The House I Live In*: Albert Maltz and the Fight against Anti-Semitism." For an exploration of the impact of the new documentary style of film, see Straw, "Documentary Realism and the Postwar Left." Stephen Vaughn, in "Political Censorship during the Cold War," highlights how, for the first time, censorship concerns focused not on sex and drugs but on the political purpose and potential of film and on where entertainment fit in with postwar education.

CHAPTER 4

1. Dorothy B. Jones, "Hollywood War Films, 1942–44," 1.

2. Telegram, Harry S. Truman to Dr. John R. Steelman, November 20, 1946, Folder, A White House Motion Picture Conference, Official Files, 73, HSTL.

3. Remarks of John R. Steelman, "Motion Pictures and the Government Program," Folder, A White House Motion Picture Conference, Official Files, 72, HSTL.

4. "Repubs Frown on Pix Bureau," *Variety*, November 20, 1946, 17.

5. Ibid.

6. Ibid.

7. "Hold On to Your Heads, Folks; Here Comes 80th Congress with Axes Out," *Variety*, January 1, 1947, 20.

8. Leo Rosten, "Movies and Propaganda," 116–24.

9. Scholarship on communism in Hollywood focuses on ten Hollywood producers, writers, and directors—John Howard Lawson, Dalton Trumbo, Albert Maltz, Edward Dmytryk, Ring Lardner Jr., Alvah Bessie, Herbert Biberman, Samuel Ornitz, Adrian Scott, and Lester Cole—whom HUAC called to Washington for questioning on communist loyalties and beliefs. Each of these men dramatically invoked First Amendment rights and refused to answer the question "Are you now, or have you ever been, a member of the Communist Party." These histories focus on the extent of the communist loyalties of these men and the implications of the "Hollywood Blacklist," which resulted when studio producers gathered at the New York Waldorf Astoria Hotel and issued the "Waldorf Statement"

that rebuked the "Hollywood Ten's" actions and vowed publically not to hire known communists. Debate over the impact of communism in Hollywood has spurred numerous insightful and compelling works, which reveal the partisan nature of the HUAC trials and the power-hungry politicians who used fears of communism to advance their own causes personally and politically and gain media attention in the process. Hollywood historians generally agree that while men like John Howard Lawson were active in the Communist Party, the studio system's vertical structure and box office focus made any attempt to insert communist propaganda essentially unrecognizable. For a discussion of the HUAC investigations in particular and the debate over the extent to which communism threatened motion picture productions, see Ceplair and Englund, *The Inquisition in Hollywood*; Gladchuk, *Hollywood and Anticommunism*; Freedland, *Hollywood on Trial*; and Billingsley, *Hollywood Party*. An exploration on those who cooperated with HUAC and the moral ramifications of these hearings can be found in Navasky, *Naming Names*. An overview of the antilabor and antiliberal impulses can be found in Giglio, *Here's Looking at You*, 95–118. Historiography on the blacklist shows these men to be victims of Red Scare politics and frequently highlights the bravery of their refusals to cooperate with HUAC and their standing up for their civil liberties. See, for example, Dmytryk, *Odd Man Out*; Horne, *Final Victim of the Blacklist*; and Humphries, *Hollywood's Blacklists*. A consideration of the personal ramifications of the blacklist in the lives of its victims, pointing to the deaths of John Garfield, J. Edward Bromberg, and Canada Lee as potentially linked to the blacklist, can be found in Giglio, *Here's Looking at You*, 110–18.

10. For a look at the Cold War constraints imposed on Hollywood, see Ceplair and Englund, *The Inquisition in Hollywood*; Neve, *Film and Politics in America*; Sklar, *Movie Made America*; Whitfield, *Culture of the Cold War*; and Wall, *Inventing the "American Way."* There is a great discussion of the reorientation of American values in postwar Hollywood in Lary May, *Big Tomorrow*, 175–213.

11. For an examination of how women began to challenge studio control over their work, see Carman, "Independent Stardom," 583–615. For a broader analysis of the de Havilland court case and its impact on the studio system, see Schatz, *The Genius of the System*.

12. Bruck, *When Hollywood Had a King*, 113–14.

13. Speech for Olivia de Havilland, April 14, 1946, Folder 4, Correspondence Re: ICCASP, 1946, box 1, HDCR.

14. Neve, *Film and Politics in America*, 56–83.

15. Reagan and Hubler, *Where's the Rest of Me?*, 192.

16. This account of the incident appears in Vaughn, *Ronald Reagan in Hollywood*, 128–29; and Billingsley, *Hollywood Party*, 123–25.

17. Details concerning the growing tensions between the United States, Great Britain, and democracy and the Soviet Union and communism and the impact on American politics and culture can be found in Diggins, *Proud Decades*, 54–86. The broader cultural impact of this rising anticommunism and how it transformed cultural values can be found in Whitfield, *Culture of the Cold War*.

18. This is Ronald Reagan's account of the event from his autobiography, 190–96. Vaughn addresses the events of the "Kilkenny brawl" in *Ronald Reagan in Hollywood*, 129–32; as does Billingsley in *Hollywood Party*, 122–26.

19. Reagan and Hubler, *Where's the Rest of Me?*, 193; see also Vaughn, *Ronald Reagan in Hollywood*, 129–32. The event is also referred to, but not described in as much detail, in Ceplair and Englund, *The Inquisition in Hollywood*, 228–32. Resignations of many members, in particular that of Jimmy Roosevelt, are noted in Folder 8, Executive Board and Council, 1946–47, Folder 18, Roosevelt, James, box 7, HDCR.

20. "That Commie Probe," October 22, 1947, *Variety*, 3.

21. Testimony of Richard Arlen, U.S. Congress, Committee on Un-American Activities, *Communist Infiltration of Hollywood Motion Picture Industry*, May 1947, 235.

22. Testimony of Adolphe Menjou, ibid., 316.

23. "The Original Statement of the Committee for the First Amendment and Its Original Signers," Folder, Hayden, Sterling, box 4, Hollywood Blacklist, HUAC Records.

24. Draft of comments on live television, October 26, 1947, file 596, Committee for the First Amendment, box 46, William Wyler Papers, MHL.

25. Telegram, Barley C. Crum to William Wyler, October 19, 1947, ibid.

26. Radio Advertisement, "They Do Not Speak for Us," n.d. [1947], ibid.

27. Chicago speech, February 1949, Folder 1701, Speeches, 1948–71, box 131, John Huston Papers, MHL.

28. A reprint of this statement appears in "Film Industry's Policy Defined," *Variety*, November 26, 1947, 3.

29. Humphrey Bogart, "I'm No Communist," *Photoplay*, May 1948, 53.

30. Ibid.

31. For a detailed exploration of Robinson and how he was persecuted by HUAC for his liberal political activities, see Ross, *Hollywood Left and Right*, 89–129.

32. "Johnston Deal for Important Spot with MPPDA Near Inking; Hays Stays," *Variety*, January 25, 1945, 3.

33. Pamphlet, Eric Johnston, "Utopia Is Production," an address to the convention of the International Alliance of Theatrical Stage Employees and Motion Picture Machine Operators, July 23, 1946, Folder 83, MPA Speeches, 1946–52, box 7, EAJP.

34. Reminiscences of Eric Johnston, 1959, 839–44, Oral History Collection, Columbia University, New York, New York.

35. In *America Unlimited*, Johnston articulates his economic ideas of a "peoples' capitalism," which fits into historical definitions of a "corporate liberalism" as outlined by scholars like Wall, in *Inventing the "American Way."*

36. Critchlow, *When Hollywood Was Right*, 65.

37. Testimony of Jack Warner, U.S. Congress, Committee on Un-American Activities, *Communist Infiltration of Hollywood Motion Picture Industry*, May 1947, 368. For a more thorough examination of the labor union conflict, see Ceplair and Englund, *The Inquisition in Hollywood*; and Lary May, *Big Tomorrow*, 180–89. Conflict would continue over the next three years, with similar jurisdictional disputes between the IATSE and the CSU, and the anticommunism campaign waged by Roy Brewer against Herb Sorrell derailed popular support for Sorrell. Brewer characterized Sorrell's 1945 strike as a "communist inspired and communist directed" attack on "American labor traditions," effectively pushing the ideals and rhetoric of the MPA to support corporate studios' stances. In reality, Herb Sorrell sought to establish a union that would work for laborers, not for corporate studio demands. Sorrell answered communist accusations by explaining that communists thrived

on poor working conditions, and he constantly sought to secure betterment through industry and to show the potential kindness of capitalism, an agenda that no true communist would ever pursue. Nevertheless, communists did support the increasingly militant tactics that Sorrell used during CSU strikes. For Brewer and Johnston, making labor American in Hollywood meant rejecting the militant radicalism and rhetoric of class conflict to pursue open cooperation between labor and management that would break the industry free from the union stranglehold Johnston saw as detrimental.

38. Reagan and Hubler, *Where's the Rest of Me?*, 160.

39. Ibid., 161.

40. Ibid., 194.

41. Johnston, *America Unlimited*, 49.

42. Pamphlet by Eric Drake Davison, "Eric Johnston Speaks," March 2, 1950, Folder 83, box 6, EAJP.

43. Pamphlet, Eric Johnston, "Utopia Is Production," 11, an address to the convention of the International Alliance of Theatrical Stage Employees and Motion Picture Machine Operators, July 23, 1946, Folder 83, MPA Speeches, 1946–52, box 7, EAJP.

44. "Statement by Eric Johnston, President of the Motion Picture Association of America, to the House Committee on Un-American Activities," Folder, Eric Johnston, box 4, Hollywood Blacklist, HUAC Records.

45. "Red Inquiry," *Variety*, June 4, 1947, 22; "Statement by Eric Johnston, President of the Motion Picture Association of America, to the House Committee on Un-American Activities," Folder, Eric Johnston, box 4, Hollywood Blacklist, HUAC Records.

46. This stance is discussed in Lary May, *Big Tomorrow*, 177.

47. Eric Johnston, "Finds Trade Barriers Impinge Screen Freedom: Eric Johnston Replies to Sir Alexander Korda's Charges against Hollywood," December 15, 1946, Folder 7, MPA Articles and Statements, 1946–58, box 6, EAJP.

48. "Statement by Eric Johnston, President of the Motion Picture Association of America, to the House Committee on Un-American Activities," Folder, Eric Johnston, box 4, Hollywood Blacklist, HUAC Records.

49. Cabell Phillips, "Un-American Committee Puts on Its 'Big Show,'" *New York Times*, October 26, 1947, E7.

50. Critchlow, *When Hollywood Was Right*, 85.

51. Testimony of James K. McGuinness, U.S. Congress, Committee on Un-American Activities, *Communist Infiltration of Hollywood Motion Picture Industry*, May 1947, 101–2.

52. Testimony of John C. Moffitt, ibid., 171.

53. Ibid., 155.

54. Testimony of Adolphe Menjou, ibid., 314.

55. Testimony of Jack Warner, ibid., 361.

56. A discussion of specifics in this coordination with government and Mellett appears as a correction of the record at the end of his testimony; see ibid., 376. Taylor discussed working with Mellett in the private hearings in May and was very angry when this information was leaked. Alexander, *Reluctant Witness*, examines Taylor's experiences. See also Critchlow, *When Hollywood Was Right*, 91.

57. Testimony of James K. McGuinness, U.S. Congress, Committee on Un-American Activities, *Communist Infiltration of Hollywood Motion Picture Industry*, May 1947, 103.

58. Ronald Reagan, HUAC testimony, October 23, 1947, in Bentley, *Thirty Years of Treason*, 147.

59. Testimony of Louis B. Mayer, U.S. Congress, Committee on Un-American Activities, *Communist Infiltration of Hollywood Motion Picture Industry*, October 20, 1947.

60. Statement by Eric Johnston, October 27, 1947, Folder, Eric Johnston, box 4, Hollywood Blacklist, HUAC Records.

61. Florence Lowe, "Probe Sidelights," *Variety*, October 29, 1947, 4.

62. Reminiscences of Eric Johnston, 1959, Columbia University, Oral History Collection, New York, New York.

63. For a discussion of the role of loyalty oaths, see James Patterson, *Grand Expectations*, 165–205; Whitfield, *Culture of the Cold War*; and Diggins, *Proud Decades*. For a consideration of the impact of the loyalty oaths in reinforcing domestic consensus in the home, see Elaine Tyler May, *Homeward Bound*.

64. Testimony of Gary Cooper, in Bentley, *Thirty Years of Treason*, 152.

65. Testimony of Robert Taylor, U.S. Congress, Committee on Un-American Activities, *Communist Infiltration of Hollywood Motion Picture Industry*, October 1947, 199.

66. Lillian Ross, "Onward and Upward with the Arts: Come in Lassie," *New Yorker*, February 21, 1948, 32.

67. Robert Sklar makes this argument in *Movie Made America*. A variety of other film histories also point to the breakdown of the studio system in the 1950s and how its struggle to produce profitable films at the box office stemmed from its uncreative production due to Cold War pressures to support consensus and the shifting economics because of the Paramount decision and television. See, for example, Biskind, *Easy Riders, Raging Bulls*; and Giglio, *Here's Looking at You*.

68. Sklar, *Movie Made America*, 279.

69. Letter, Samuel Goldwyn to President Harry Truman, September 16, 1947, Folder, British Tax, Official Files, 73, HSTL.

70. Jennifer Frost makes this argument about Hedda Hopper and her intense embrace of this conservative trend in Hollywood. She argues that in 1947 Hopper stood at the apex of her career, politically, socially, and economically, and that her alarm at the unstable postwar environment "fueled her conservatism." Frost, *Hedda Hopper's Hollywood*, 92.

71. Rand, *Screen Guide for Americans*. For a detailed history of Ayn Rand and her contributions to the American conservative movement in the postwar period, see Burns, *Goddess of the Market*.

72. Lillian Ross, "Onward and Upward with the Arts: Come in Lassie," *New Yorker*, February 21, 1948, 42.

73. Ibid., 46.

74. Sklar, *Movie Made America*; Whitefield, *Culture of the Cold War*.

75. For a look at how the HUAC hearings invigorated the New Right in Hollywood, see Critchlow, *When Hollywood Was Right*, 76–116.

76. Lillian Ross, "Onward and Upward with the Arts: Come in Lassie," *New Yorker*, February 21, 1948, 44.

77. Phillips-Fein, *Invisible Hands*, 53–70.

78. MPIC activities are briefly discussed in Vaughn, *Ronald Reagan in Hollywood*, 182–93.

79. MPIC Minutes, July 20, 1948, Folder 23, box 3, Walter Wanger Papers, WCFTR.

80. Proposed Charter of the MPIC, February 18, 1949, File 348, MPIC, 1948–50, AMPTPF, MHL.

81. "Hollywood Fights Back," *Kiplinger Magazine*, July 1950, Folder 23, MPIC, 1948–50, box 3, Walter Wanger Papers, WCFTR.

82. Chicago Conference, 1949, Notes of Public Relations, Folder 3, box 1, MPICR, MHL.

83. See Ronald Reagan, "A Guest Editorial," *Hartford Times*, December 11, 1951, Folder 352, MPIC Clippings and Reprints, box 36, AMPTPF, MHL. See also Rosalind Russell, "They Still Lie about Hollywood," *Look*, July 1951, Folder 13, box 24, Walter Wanger Papers, WCFTR.

84. Speech by Valentine Davies, "American Films: Ambassadors of Democracy," file 355, MPIC Speeches, AMPTPF, MHL.

85. A selection of these reports is found in Folder 23, General Reflections on the Constructive Influence of American Films Abroad in Behalf of Democracy, box 13, Walter Wanger Papers, WCFTR.

86. Remarks of Hon. Joseph F. Holt, "Films Building Good Will for America," April 27, 1953, *Congressional Record*, Folder 7, Congress, box 1, MPICR, MHL.

87. Block, "Propaganda and the Free Society," 677–86.

88. Critchlow, *When Hollywood Was Right*, examines the role of Hollywood conservatives in the rise of the New Right in Southern California and in shaping the modern conservative movement more broadly. For an examination of how grassroots suburban and evangelical mobilizations took root in other communities in Southern California, see McGirr, *Suburban Warriors*; and Dochuck, *From Bible Belt to Sunbelt*.

89. Block, "Propaganda and the Free Society," 678.

90. Wanger's response can be found in his letter to the MPA to then be publicized upon MPA approval, August 1950, file 3520, Walter Wanger File, Hedda Hopper Papers, MHL.

CHAPTER 5

1. "Homecoming to the Political Front," *New York Times*, June 1, 1952, E1.

2. Eisenhower served as president of Columbia University from 1948 to January 1953, when he was inaugurated as president of the United States. From 1951 through the first months of 1952, Eisenhower told Columbia's board of trustees that he needed to focus his attention on NATO in Europe and said that he would resign when his successor was found. For more details, see Smith, *Eisenhower in War and Peace*, 473–502.

3. C. B. Palmer, "Ike in Abilene and the Abilene in Ike," *New York Times*, June 1, 1951, SM11.

4. Allen, *Eisenhower and the Mass Media*, 24.

5. Detailed description of the Abilene campaign speech can be found in Edgerton, *Columbia History of American Television*, 208–9; Jamieson, *Packaging the Presidency*; and Allen, *Eisenhower and the Mass Media*.

6. Balogh, "From Corn to Caviar."

7. Lubell, *Future of American Politics*, 227.

8. Detailed discussion of Barton's advice to Eisenhower after the Abilene event can be found in Hollitz, "Eisenhower and the Admen." For a discussion of Montgomery's

reaction, see "Ike Has Improved on TV, Says Coach Montgomery," Folder, Eisenhower Aides, box 334, News Clippings and Publications, RNCF, DDEL.

9. Stanley Kelley Jr. uses the term "media consumers" to describe Eisenhower's successful strategy to attract the growing middle class to his Republican coalition with television advertising. Kelley, *Professional Public Relations and Political Power*, 155.

10. Diggins, *Proud Decades*.

11. Jamieson, *Packaging the Presidency*; Slaybaugh, "Adlai Stevenson, Television, and the Presidential Campaign of 1956."

12. For an analysis of cultural shifts that allowed for the president to be cast as a "leading man," see Peretti, *Leading Man*. From a political science perspective, Daniel Galvin examines how institutional shifts, especially in political party structures, increasingly made a priority of the promotion of the president, frequently at the expense of party building. He examines how, especially during the 1950s, Eisenhower attempted to remake the Republican Party into a more moderate party by using the strength of his personality and appeal. Galvin, *Presidential Party Building*.

13. The phrase "electoral politics" and the role of Louis B. Mayer in beginning this style of political activism during the 1920s come from Ross, *Hollywood Left and Right*.

14. "Report: The Influence of Television in the 1952 Election," coordinated by Dr. Joseph Seibert, Miami University, and funded by the Miami-Crosley Broadcasting Corporation, Folder, Television, Influence of in the 1952 Election, box 393, Television-Radio Division, DNCR, JFKL.

15. Craig Allen makes this argument in *Eisenhower and the Mass Media* and explores the process by which advertising executives transformed how the White House functioned.

16. Diamond and Bates, *The Spot*; Sabato, *Rise of Political Consultants*, 7–12; Jamieson, *Packaging the Presidency*; Gould, *Modern American Presidency*; Ansolabehere, Behr, and Iyengar, *The Media Game*. In his work on changes in political parties in *Why Parties*, Aldrich argues that during the 1950s, and especially in the 1960s, political parties assumed more organizational responsibilities to get candidates elected and took on the job of providing services, such as advertising, and figuring out strategies of dealing with television for the candidates.

17. Sabato, *Rise of Political Consultants*; Nimmo, *Political Persuaders*.

18. Steven Ross stands as a notable exception. His book *Hollywood Left and Right* explores the importance of George Murphy's work in Eisenhower's campaign, and he argues that Murphy paved the way for Reagan's success in the Republican Party.

19. Distribution of Durable Consumer Goods in American Families, in *Post-war Economic Trends in the United States*, ed. Ralph Freeman, in Diggins, *Proud Decades*, 186.

20. For a look at the anxieties surrounding television, and the use of mass media in politics specifically, in the aftermath of World War II and the triumph of the Nazi propaganda machine over the previous decade, see Greenberg, "A New Way of Campaigning."

21. Republican Associates News Letter, October 1956, Folder, Political, 1956, box 67, 10, JLWP.

22. Edgerton, *Columbia History of American Television*, 211.

23. Marchand, *Advertising the American Dream*.

24. Discussion of the history of the connection between BBD&O and the Republican Party, as well as the tensions in 1948 between party insiders and Barton, can be found in Hollitz, "Eisenhower and the Admen."

25. Murphy, *Say . . . Didn't You Used to Be George Murphy*, 313–15.

26. For an examination of the role of Murphy as liaison to Southern California money, see Critchlow, *When Hollywood Was Right*, 124–33.

27. Hollitz, "Eisenhower and the Admen," 29.

28. Ibid., 28.

29. Ibid.; Wood, "Television's First Political Spot Ad Campaign."

30. Wood, "Television's First Political Spot Ad Campaign," 269.

31. Pitchell, "Influence of Professional Campaign Management Firms in Partisan Elections in California"; Kelley, *Professional Public Relations and Political Power*. The *Western Political Quarterly* frequently chronicled the details of California campaigns and the implications in state and national politics during the 1950s and 1960s.

32. Letter, Darryl Zanuck to Cary Grant, Folder, Political, 1952, box 64:33, JLWP.

33. Letter, Samuel Goldwyn to President Harry Truman, September 16, 1947, Folder, British Tax, Official Files, 73, HSTL.

34. Letter, Darryl Zanuck to Sam Goldwyn, August 6, 1952, Folder, Political, 1952, box 64:32, JLWP.

35. "The Eisenhower Campaign" plan, January 8, 1952, Folder, Correspondence of Sig Narnon and Others Pertaining to the Nomination of General Eisenhower, box 1, Young & Rubicam, DDEL.

36. Letter, Darryl Zanuck to Sam Goldwyn, August 6, 1952, Folder, Political, 1952, box 64:32, JLWP.

37. Ibid.

38. Ibid.

39. Letter, Darryl Zanuck to Jack Warner, August 22, 1952, ibid.

40. Letter to Jack Warner and Samuel Goldwyn, October 15, 1952, Folder, Political, 1952, box 64:33, JLWP.

41. Ibid.

42. Letter, Jack Warner to Tex McCrary, October 10, 1952, ibid.

43. Kelley, *Professional Public Relations and Political Power*, 162–63.

44. Telegram, Corinne Griffith to Jack Warner, December 16, 1952, Folder, Political, 1952, box 64:32, JLWP.

45. Letter, George Murphy to the Ladies and Gentlemen of the Committee, December 16, 1952, Folder, Entertainment, Mr. George Murphy, box 7, Inaugural Committee of 1953 Records, DDEL.

46. Eric Johnston, speech, "Hollywood: America's Travelling Salesman," May 28, 1957, Folder, MPA Speeches, 1953–58, MS 118, box 7/84, EAJP.

47. Press release, January 23, 1952, File, International Development Advisory Board, Eric A. Johnston, box 83, Office of Budget and Accounting Records, 1953–61, WHCF, DDEL.

48. Coverage and details of the trip to the Soviet Union can also be found in File, Eric Johnston, January 1, 1949, box 355, News Clippings, RNCF, DDEL. More details of the specific agreements and exchanges Johnston made with Middle Eastern and African

countries can be found in cross reference sheet, February 16, 1960, Folder, Eric Johnston, box 1607, Alphabetical Files, WHCF, DDEL; Report to the President on Near East Mission, November 17, 1953, File, Eric Johnston, box 22, Administration Series, Eisenhower, Dwight D., Papers as President of the United States, 1953–61, Ann Whitman Files, DDEL; and Memo from J. S. Earman to L. Arthur Minnich, November 11, 1958, Folder, Eric Johnston, box 956, PPF 673, WHCF, DDEL.

49. References to Johnston's speaking tours for the Republican Party and Hollywood can all be found in the cross reference sheet, Eric Johnston, box 1607, Alphabetical Files, WHCF, DDEL.

50. News clipping, "Foreign Aid Rally Hailed by Johnston," March 16, 1958, File, Eric Johnston, January 1, 1949, box 355, News Clippings, RNCF, DDEL.

51. Mary Van Rensselaer Thayer, "Eric's Still in Show Biz," February 27, 1958, *Washington Post-Herald*, ibid.

52. News clipping, "Foreign Aid Rally Hailed By Johnston," March 16, 1958, ibid.

53. An Address by Robert Montgomery before the Republican Preparedness Dinner, Boston, November 13, 1951, File, Address by Robert Montgomery, box 1, Young & Rubicam, DDEL.

54. News clipping, "Ike Has Improved on TV, Says Coach Montgomery," Folder, Eisenhower Aides, box 334, News Clippings and Publications, RNCF, DDEL.

55. News clipping, Robert Lubeck, "Montgomery Denies He Tells Ike to Act for TV Talk," *Detroit News*, September 20, 1954, ibid.

56. News clipping, Isabelle Shelton, "Be Yourself on TV, Says Montgomery," *Washington Star*, February 16, 1957, ibid.

57. News clipping, Anthony Leviero, "Eisenhower's TV Speeches Are Major Productions," January 10, 1954, ibid.

58. Montgomery describes this work with Eisenhower and his "television education" in more depth in his book, *Open Letter from a Television Viewer*, 59–78.

59. News clipping, Terrence O'Flaherty, "TV at the White House—a Look at Ike's Studio," *San Francisco Chronicle*, March 29, 1954, Folder, Eisenhower Aides, box 334, News Clippings and Publications, RNCF, DDEL.

60. News clipping, Andrew Tully, "32 Persons Ran Around behind Ike Frantically," *Washington News*, August 24, 1954, ibid.

61. Montgomery, *Open Letter from a Television Viewer*, 60.

62. News clipping, Walker S. Buel, "Hollywood Touch Invades White House; Ike in Middle," January 31, 1954, Folder, Eisenhower Aides, box 334, News Clippings and Publications, RNCF, DDEL. Montgomery also discusses the popular criticism he received as a "latter-day Merlin," in *Open Letter from a Television Viewer*, 61–62.

63. News clipping, Harry Harris, "Montgomery Looks Ahead to GOP Convention," *Philadelphia Inquirer*, July 13, 1956, Folder, Eisenhower Aides, box 334, News Clippings and Publications, RNCF, DDEL.

64. John Fink, "TV Misses Heart of Convention," *Chicago Tribune*, August 21, 1956, A2; cross reference sheet, July 19, 1956, Folder, George Murphy, box 2192, WHCF, DDEL.

65. News clipping, Harry Harris, "Montgomery Looks Ahead to GOP Convention," *Philadelphia Inquirer*, July 13, 1956, Folder, Eisenhower Aides, box 334, News Clippings and Publications, RNCF, DDEL.

66. Discussion of the speech can be found in cross reference sheet, Folder, Robert Montgomery, box 2141, Alphabetical Files, WHCF, DDEL; and news clipping, Ruth Dean, "Robert Montgomery Claims Jefferson for Republicans," *Washington Star*, March 25, 1954, Folder, Eisenhower Aides, box 334, News Clippings and Publications, RNCF, DDEL.

67. Discussion of the details of the rally can be found in Letter, George Murphy to Thomas Stephens, Secretary to the President, September 10, 1954, Folder, George Murphy, box 934, PPF, 179, WHCF, DDEL.

68. Letter, Samuel Goldwyn, Jack Warner, and Darryl Zanuck to Mr. Jones, June 23, 1954, Folder, Political, 2950B, JLWP.

69. Galvin, *Presidential Party Building*, 45–46. In his research on Eisenhower, Galvin argues that the president did more to build the party than prey on it, contrary to dominant theories of presidential leadership in political science.

70. Ibid., 45.

71. Request for Speaker at Kansas City, Mo., rally, April 25, 1956, Folder, George Murphy, file 1904, box 26, Hedda Hopper Papers, MHL.

72. Newspaper clippings, "Film Stars Get Set for Eisenhower," *Los Angeles Examiner*, October 17, 1956, and "Parade of Stars to Greet President," *Los Angeles Examiner*, October 19, 1956, Folder, General Dwight Eisenhower, file 660, box 16, Hedda Hopper Papers, MHL.

73. Kelley, *Professional Public Relations and Political Power*, 199–200.

74. Ideas in Connection with Citizens TV Programming, August 28, 1956, General Program, #1, Folder, TV Scripts, box 6, Young & Rubicam, DDEL.

75. Thoughts and Ideas Re: Citizens TV, August 28, 1956, Folder, Talent, box 7, Proposed Budgets and Policies for TV, 1956 Campaign, Young & Rubicam, DDEL.

76. TV Plans for Citizens for Eisenhower-Nixon, September 13, 1956, #2, Folder, TV Scripts, box 6, Young & Rubicam, DDEL.

77. Letter, Preston Wood to David Levy, August 3, 1956, Folder, 1959 Lincoln Day Speech, box 9, Young & Rubicam, DDEL.

78. Network Television for National Citizens for Eisenhower-Nixon: The One Hour Program, September 14, 1956, Folder, Eisenhower-Nixon Present "Four More Years," box 8, Young & Rubicam, DDEL.

79. TV Plans for Citizens for Eisenhower-Nixon, September 13, 1956, #2, Folder, TV Scripts, box 6, Young & Rubicam, DDEL.

80. Ibid.

81. Message to Hander and Crider from David Levy, September 4, 1956, Folder, Talent, box 7, Young & Rubicam, DDEL.

82. Citizens TV, August 28, 1956, Folder, Talent, box 7, Young & Rubicam, DDEL.

83. Discussion of the efforts to bring in writers, directors, and editors can be found in Television Programming for Citizens TV, August 28, 1956, Folder, TV Scripts, box 6, Young & Rubicam, DDEL.

84. Thoughts and Ideas in Connection with Television Programming for Citizens for Eisenhower-Nixon, #1, ibid.

85. These requests can be found on pp. 3–4 in ibid.

86. TV Plans for Citizens for Eisenhower-Nixon TV, September 13, 1956, #2, ibid.

87. Proposed TV Programming for Citizens for Eisenhower-Nixon, September 5, 1956, ibid.

88. TV Plans for Citizens for Eisenhower-Nixon TV, September 13, 1956, #2, ibid.

89. Thoughts and Ideas in Connection with Television Programming for Citizens for Eisenhower-Nixon, #1, ibid.

90. Letter to All Citizens, State Chairmen, and Co-Chairmen from Richard Tobin, n.d. [September 1956], ibid.

91. Thoughts and Ideas in Connection with Television Programming for Citizens for Eisenhower-Nixon, #1, ibid.

92. Letter to All Citizens, State Chairmen, and Co-Chairmen from Richard Tobin, n.d. [September 1956], ibid.

93. Revised Program Plan for the TV Hour on Election Eve, September 28, 1956, Folder, TV Recommendations for 1956 Eisenhower-Nixon Campaign Made by Young and Rubicam, box 8, Young & Rubicam, DDEL.

94. Script, Citizens for Eisenhower Present "Four More Years," November 5, 1956, Folder, Transcript, "Citizens for Eisenhower-Nixon" Present "Four More Years," box 8, Young & Rubicam, DDEL.

95. Revised Program Plan for the TV Hour on Election Eve, September 28, 1956, Folder, TV Recommendations for 1956 Eisenhower-Nixon Campaign Made by Young and Rubicam, box 8, Young & Rubicam, DDEL.

96. Script, Citizens for Eisenhower Present "Four More Years," November 5, 1956, Folder, Transcript, "Citizens for Eisenhower-Nixon" Present "Four More Years," box 8, Young & Rubicam, DDEL.

97. For a discussion of Eisenhower's "Modern Republicanism," see Diggins, *Proud Decades*, 122–47; and James Patterson, *Grand Expectations*, 243–75. A critique by conservatives of this modern Republicanism can be found in Farber, *Rise and Fall of Modern Conservatism*, 9–76. For a broader discussion of the battles between conservative and liberal Republicans during the 1950s and the ultimate success of the conservatives in American politics, see Critchlow, *The Conservative Ascendency*.

98. Citizens TV Report, August 28, 1956, Folder, Talent, box 7, Young & Rubicam, DDEL.

99. TV Plans for Citizens for Eisenhower-Nixon TV, September 13, 1956, #2, Folder, TV Scripts, box 6, Young & Rubicam, DDEL.

100. Republican Associates News Letter, October 1956, Folder, Political, 1956, box 67, 10, JLWP. On the tradition of merchandising policies, see Balogh, "Mirrors of Desire."

101. Letter, Sam Ervin to Paul Butler, June 2, 1955, Folder, Television-Radio Division Correspondence Re: Creation of, box 393, Television-Radio Division, DNCR, JFKL.

102. Excerpt from Letter, Senator Lyndon Johnson to Paul Butler, ibid.

103. For example, see Letter, Senator Paul Douglas to Paul Butler, June 14, 1955, and Letter, Representative Hugh Alexander to Paul Butler, June 9, 1955, among several other letters found in ibid.

104. Edgerton, *Columbia History of American Television*, 218.

105. Democratic National Committee Publicity Plan for the 1956 Presidential Election Campaign, Folder, Norman, Craig & Kummel 5-Minute Spot Descriptions, box 384, Television-Radio Division, DNCR, JFKL.

106. Ibid.

107. Discussion of this decision to change advertising companies can be found in Slaybaugh, "Adlai Stevenson, Television, and the Presidential Campaign of 1956," 9.

108. "Report: The Influence of Television in the 1952 Election," Folder, Television, Influence of in the 1952 Election, box 393, Television-Radio Division, DNCR, JFKL.

109. Memo to Mr. Finnegan and Mr. McCloskey from Marciarose Shestack, Re: Programs for Five-Minute TV Network Spots Week of October 15–21, Folder, Television—5-Minute Campaign Spots, box 393, Television-Radio Division, DNCR. JFKL.

110. "Campaign Train—5 Minute Spots," Folder, Norman, Craig & Kummel, Five Minute Spot Descriptions, box 384, Television-Radio Division, DNCR, JFKL.

111. Slaybaugh, "Adlai Stevenson, Television, and the Presidential Campaign of 1956"; Jamieson, *Packaging the Presidency*, 39–121.

112. "This Is What I Believe" series, Folder, Norman, Craig & Kummel, 5 Minute Spot Descriptions, box 384, Television-Radio Division, DNCR, JFKL.

113. Ibid.

114. For more details on the "Stevenson Effect" on liberals in California and the media campaigns orchestrated by Democratic Clubs, including "Hollywood for Stevenson," see Bell, *California Crucible*, 55–82.

115. Letter, Allen Rivkin to Kenneth Fry, August 27, 1952, Folder, Hollywood for Stevenson Sparkman II, box 371, Television-Radio Division, DNCR, JFKL.

116. Memorandum Re: Hollywood Volunteer Effort, September 14, 1952, ibid.

117. Memorandum Re: Distribution, from Hollywood for Stevenson to Tom Durrance, September 22, 1952, ibid.

118. Ibid.

119. Balogh, "From Corn to Caviar."

120. Letter, Dore Schary to Adlai Stevenson, December 2, 1955, Folder, Correspondence, Adlai Stevenson, 1952, July 9–1961 February 24, box 20, Dore Schary Papers, WCFTR.

121. Slaybaugh, "Adlai Stevenson, Television, and the Presidential Campaign of 1956"; Jamieson, *Packaging the Presidency*, 39–121.

122. Book Review, W. H. Lawrence, "A Political Product to Market," *New York Times*, January 22, 1956, 226.

123. John G. Schneider, *The Golden Kazoo* (New York: Rinehart, 1956).

124. Stanley Kelley Jr., "P.R. Man: Political Mastermind," *New York Times*, September 2, 1956, 6.

125. Balogh, "From Corn to Caviar."

126. Kelley, *Professional Public Relations and Political Power*, 155.

127. Ibid., 222.

128. Ibid., 224–25.

CHAPTER 6

1. Austin C. Wehrwein, "Wisconsin Battle One of Contrasts," *New York Times*, February 21, 1960, 55.

2. White, *The Making of the President*, 91.

3. Media Strategy Outline, Folder, Media Campaign: Wisconsin Primary, 1/21/60–4/5/60, box 38, Political, Pre-Administration, RFKP, JFKL.

4. "High Hopes: 1960 Presidential Campaign Song," Frank Sinatra, 1960 Campaign On-line Exhibition, JFKL, http://www.jfklibrary.org/Asset-Viewer/Ugsn5uL3JEOaQG96CQx-tuQ.aspx.

5. Austin C. Wehrwein, "Wisconsin Battle One of Contrasts," *New York Times*, February 21, 1960, 55.

6. Gould, *Modern American Presidency*; Donaldson, *First Modern Campaign*.

7. Troy, *See How They Ran*. Diamond and Silverman, *White House to Your House*, points to television in the 1960 election as drastically changing the political landscape through media transformation. The memory of Kennedy the celebrity is explored in Hellman, *Kennedy Obsession*.

8. For a discussion of how Democratic presidents have veered toward party predation rather than party building, see Galvin, *Presidential Party Building*, 163–246.

9. "Truman Diamond Jubilee," Folder, Radio-TV arrangements, General, 9/15/1958–10/27/1959, box 395, Television-Radio Division, DNCR, JFKL.

10. See the program for the Truman Diamond Jubilee, in Folder, Dinners, Truman Diamond Jubilee, 5/8/1959, box 439, Chairman's File, 1960, DNCR, JFKL.

11. Memorandum Re: Truman Diamond Anniversary Closed-Circuit Program, Proposed Financial Program, February 18, 1959, ibid.

12. "Truman Diamond Jubilee," Folder, Radio-TV arrangements, General, 9/15/1958–10/27/1959, box 395, Television-Radio Division, DNCR, JFKL.

13. Truman Jubilee Organization Program, prepared by the Democratic National Committee, Folder, Dinners, Truman Diamond Jubilee, 5/8/1959, box 439, Chairman's File, 1960, DNCR, JFKL.

14. News clipping, *Cleveland Plain Dealer*, August 2, 1960, Folder, Eisenhower-Aides, box 334, News Clippings and Publications, Republican National Committee, DDEL.

15. Dallek, *An Unfinished Life*, 43–44.

16. Details of Joseph Kennedy's Hollywood years can be found in Beauchamp, *Joseph P. Kennedy Presents*.

17. This argument is expanded upon in ibid.

18. According to ibid., 325, Kennedy was key in the Roosevelt campaign, not only in donating money but also in convincing William Randolph Hearst to support Roosevelt, ultimately swinging the California delegation to Roosevelt's side in 1932. See Kennedy, *I'm for Roosevelt*.

19. Dallek, *An Unfinished Life*, 117–21.

20. Beauchamp, *Joseph P. Kennedy Presents*, 372–90.

21. Ibid., 372–403; Dallek, *An Unfinished Life*, 206–74.

22. Kennedy's advisers, in particular Arthur Schlesinger Jr., continued to remind him of the need to go on the offensive and win liberal support within the Democratic Party, which looked at him warily after the Draft Stevenson movement had failed. Letter, Arthur Schlesinger Jr. to John F. Kennedy, August 26, 1960, Folder, Special Correspondence, Arthur Schlesinger Jr., 1959, box 32, POF, JFKL. These disappointed liberals noted that failure at the convention came because "Kennedy supporters had been working for four years, and had many full-time people on their payroll, and had spent approximately 2 million dollars in their fight for the nomination." Newsletter, Joseph S. Smolen to Stevenson Supporters, ibid.

23. For a look at the role of Eleanor Roosevelt in the Democratic Party during the 1950s and the conflict she had with John F. Kennedy, see Black, *Casting Her Own Shadow.*

24. Transcript, College News Conference, December 7, 1958, box 25, Eleanor Roosevelt, Theodore Sorensen Papers, JFKL.

25. Letter, John F. Kennedy to Mrs. Franklin D. Roosevelt, December 11, 1958, Special Correspondence, box 32, Eleanor Roosevelt, POF, JFKL.

26. Letter, Mrs. Franklin D. Roosevelt to Senator John Kennedy, December 18, 1958, ibid.

27. Kelley, *Professional Public Relations and Political Power*, 199–200.

28. Jacobs and Shapiro, "Issues, Candidate Image, and Priming," 527–40.

29. Media Strategy Outline, Folder, Media Campaign: Wisconsin Primary, 1/21/60–4/5/60, box 38, Political, Pre-Administration, RFKP, JFKL.

30. *Primary*, directed by Robert Drew, 1960, New Video Group, released on DVD in 2003.

31. See, for example, "Campaign Contribution Kits," June 24, 1960, which contained pledge forms for supporting Kennedy's campaign; in exchange, one-dollar contributors received a complimentary recording of Sinatra's song. Campaigns by State, PPP, Presidential Campaign Files, 1960, JFKL.

32. Austin C. Wehrwein, "Wisconsin Battle One of Contrasts," *New York Times*, February 21, 1960, 55.

33. Statistics concerning the spending of each candidate can be found in Jamieson, *Packaging the Presidency*, 165–68. For a discussion of Lyndon Johnson and his authority within the Democratic Party and his efforts to win the party nomination, see Schulman, *Lyndon B. Johnson and American Liberalism*, 34–55.

34. See the description of Kennedy winning the Democratic presidential nomination in Dallek, *An Unfinished Life*, 229–66.

35. Seymour Korman, "Sinatra, Pals Singing Along with Kennedy," *Chicago Daily Tribune*, September 5, 1960, 13.

36. Dallek, *An Unfinished Life*, 258–66.

37. Conference Panel Discussion, "The Role of Broadcasting in Politics: The 1960 Conventions and Campaigns," Folder, Radio-TV Arrangements, General, 9/15/58–10/27/59, box 395, Television-Radio Division, DNCR, JFKL.

38. Details of these conflicts are outlined in Jamieson, *Packaging the Presidency*, 165–68.

39. Report, "The Problem of the Press Blackout and Dimout," Folder, Radio-TV Arrangements, General, box 395, Television-Radio Division, DNCR, JFKL.

40. Ross, *Hollywood Left and Right*, 214. Here Ross discusses how Belafonte demanded that Kennedy "establish close ties with Martin Luther King Jr." if he wanted to make a difference. Belafonte also could not stand Nixon, so these two factors motivated him to shoot the campaign spot.

41. "Television and the Voter," address by Sig Mickelson, president of CBS News, October 28, 1959, Folder, TV Arrangements, Media Plan Summary, box 395, Television-Radio Division, DNCR, JFKL.

42. For Denove's promotion of a "theme line" to link all spots, see memo from Jack Denove to Robert Kennedy, September 27, 1960, Folder, Media Campaign: Democratic

National Committee, 8/22/60–10/28/60, box 37, General Subject File, Pre-Administration Political File, RFKP, JFKL. For the quotation about the economical use of spot advertisements, see Alexander, *Money in Politics*, 257.

43. Immediately following the debates, scholars began to question the impact of these debates; see White, *The Making of the President*, 306–23; Lang and Lang, "Ordeal by Debate," 277–88; and Salant, "The Television Debates," 335–50. For a discussion of more current considerations and evaluations of the impact of these television debates, see Druckman, "Power of Television Images," 559–57, in which the author reviews the evidence and argues that television debates did make a difference in the election. On the other hand, in *Power of News*, Schudson argues that the Nixon-Kennedy debates have been remembered as influencing political decisions in 1960, but this memory stems from the perceived power of television. At the time, Schudson argues, television debates did not drastically change the way voters viewed the candidates—the significance that historians have placed on them reveals the power scholars attribute to television.

44. "Television and the Voter," an address by Sig Mickelson, president of CBS News, October 28, 1959, Folder, TV Arrangements, Media Plan Summary, box 395, Television-Radio Division, DNCR, JFKL.

45. Memo from J. Leonard Reinsch to Robert Kennedy, Re: TV, September 26, 1960, Folder, Media Campaign: Democratic National Committee, 8/22/60–10/28/60, box 37, General Subject File, Pre-Administration Political File, RFKP, JFKL.

46. Oral interview with Don Hewitt by Vicki Daitch, October 8, 2002, Oral History Files, JFKL.

47. "Television and the Voter," an address by Sig Mickelson, president of CBS News, October 28, 1959, Folder, TV Arrangements, Media Plan Summary, box 395, Television-Radio Division, DNCR, JFKL.

48. Gladwin Hill, "Election Pleases the Movie World," *New York Times*, November 11, 1960, 37.

49. Roscoe Drummond, "Hollywood and Politics," *Hartford Courant*, October 27, 1958, 10.

50. Murray Schumach, "Sinatra Dismisses Blacklisted Writer," *New York Times*, April 9, 1960, 1.

51. Hedda Hopper, "Columnist Tells of Her Travels," *Los Angeles Times*, April 1, 1960, 8.

52. For more details on the grassroots mobilization that started to take shape by the end of the 1950s in the Democratic Party, see Bell, *California Crucible*, 105–54.

53. Devine, *Henry Wallace's 1948 Presidential Campaign*.

54. Outline: Theatre Authority Inc., Folder, Benefits, General, 1956–65, box A44, series III, NAACPR, LC.

55. Raymond, *Stars for Freedom*.

56. For a terrific discussion of Belafonte's "movement politics," see Ross, *Hollywood Left and Right*, 185–226.

57. Letter, Marion R. Steward to Sammy Davis Jr., July 25, 1957, Folder, Benefits, Apollo Theater, 1957–58, box A44, series III, NAACPR, LC.

58. These requests appear in a letter to Sammy Davis Jr. from Mario Stewart. Davis's reply can be found in a subsequent letter in the same file, Davis to Stewart, October 30, 1957, ibid.

59. NAACP Press Release, "Sammy Davis and Trio in Benefit for NAACP," April 10, 1958, ibid.

60. Apollo Theater Benefit Total Income Return Figures, April 1958, ibid.

61. Letter, Sammy Davis Jr., n.d. [1958], ibid.

62. Telegraph from A. Philip Randolph, Harry Belafonte, and Rev. Gardner Taylor to Governor Rockefeller, March 18, 1960, Folder, Martin Luther King Jr., Committee to Defend, box 24, A. Philip Randolph Papers, LC.

63. Joe Hyams, "The Trouble with Being Frank Sinatra," *Los Angeles Times*, May 24, 1959, 20.

64. "Sinatra Gives Views on Race in July *Ebony*, July 3, 1958, *Los Angeles Sentinel*, 2.

65. Letter in support of the Tribute to Martin Luther King Jr. from A. Philip Randolph, December 8, 1960, Folder, Martin Luther King Jr. Tribute, box 24, A. Philip Randolph Papers, LC.

66. Letter in support of the Tribute to Martin Luther King Jr. from Harry Belafonte and A. Philip Randolph, January 3, 1961, ibid.

67. Letter in support of the Tribute to Martin Luther King Jr. from Sidney Poitier and Harry Emerson Fosdick, n.d. [December 1960–January 1961], ibid.

68. Financial Statement as of January 9, 1961, with net profit predictions, ibid.

69. "Let's Talk," *Los Angeles Sentinel*, October 5, 1961, A6.

70. Russell Baker, "Show People Help Democratic Coffers," *New York Times*, January 20, 1961, 1.

71. "There's No Business Like Show Business," *Hartford Courant*, December 13, 1960, 18.

72. The figures for Kennedy's campaign expenses and a breakdown of these figures appear in Alexander, *Money in Politics*, 53–78.

73. Ibid., 79.

74. An outline of the Dollars for Democrats programs, history, and goals can be found in the booklet by Bernard Hennessey, *Dollars for Democrats, 1959*, in Folder, Promotion and Fundraising, 1960, box 4, Kenneth Birkhead Personal Papers, JFKL.

75. Alexander, *Money in Politics*, 96.

76. Draft, "Fundraising Plan for the Democratic National Committee," 1955, Folder, Finance Committee—Fundraising, 1954–56, box 440, Chairman's File, 1960, DNCR, JFKL. See a description of the dinners in Alexander, *Money in Politics*, 113.

77. News clipping, Wilkerson, "Trade Views," *Hollywood Reporter*, January 26, 1956, Folder, Actors and Actresses in Politics, 1963, Core Collection, MHL.

78. Inaugural Activities Calendar and Information, Folder, 1961 Inaugural Invitations, box 3, Jerry Bruno Papers, JFKL.

79. Final Report of the Chairman, Inaugural Committee, 1961, Folder, 1961, Pre-Inaugural Committee Report, box 1, 1961 Inaugural Committee Report and Correspondence, Inaugural Committee Files, JFKL.

80. Maxine Cheshire, "Frankie Would Have Done the Same Thing for Nixon," *Washington Post*, January 7, 1961. D6.

81. "Democrats in Red to Tune of $3,000,000," *Hartford Courant*, January 8, 1961, A4.

82. Tom Wicker, "Weather Limits Crowds at Fetes," *New York Times*, January 20, 1961, 1.

83. Russell Baker, "Show People Help Democratic Coffers," *New York Times*, January 20, 1961, 1.

84. "John F. Kennedy Inaugural Gala," January 19, 1961, Washington Armory, Washington, D.C. (Michael Hirsh Productions), Audio Visual Archive, JFKL.

85. European political theorists traditionally refer to different estates in society as exerting authority and control in society. In pre-Revolution France, these estates were the Catholic clergy and the nobility, with the third estate being those not included in the first two. The idea of estates has frequently been applied to the American system of government, with the first estate being the judiciary, the second the federal government, the third the citizenry, and the fourth the press. While there is not a commonly acknowledged "fifth estate," the assertion of entertainment as the "sixth estate" emphasized the permanence and important civic duty of entertainment, the point I believe Bette Davis was attempting to express in her statement.

86. "Gala Set Inauguration Even Innovation in Fund-Raising," *Baltimore Sun*, January 13, 1961, 6.

87. Details on the establishment of the President's Club can be found in Alexander, *Money in Politics*, 96–116. A discussion of the President's Club in terms of the broader debate about campaign finance can be found in Zelizer, "Seeds of Cynicism."

88. Galvin, *Presidential Party Building*, 163–81.

89. Ibid., 165–74.

90. Alexander, *Money in Politics*, 98.

91. Zelizer, "Seeds of Cynicism," touches on the post-Watergate effort of Democrats to turn to "new private fundraising techniques." See also Giglio, *Here's Looking at You*.

92. Draft, "Fundraising Plan for the Democratic National Committee," 1955, Folder, Finance Committee—Fundraising, 1954–56, box 440, Chairman's File, 1960, DNCR, JFKL.

93. Alexander, *Money in Politics*, 169.

94. The rise of the Sunbelt as an economic and political force in American politics and a shaper of the modern Republican Party has recently received extensive scholarly attention. Bruce Schulman broke ground in studying the economic transition of the South, in *From Cotton Belt to Sunbelt*. Recent scholarship has also focused on how these economic developments shaped the Sunbelt's political landscape. See Lassiter, *Silent Majority*; Kruse, *White Flight*; and Farber, *Rise and Fall of Modern American Conservatism*, 77–258.

95. Galvin, *Presidential Party Building*, 41–159.

96. "The What and Why of the Action Program of Republican Associates," Folder, Political, 1956, file 2951A, JLWP. Critchlow, *When Hollywood Was Right*, offers a more detailed analysis of Republican Associates and the connections forged by big businesses and Hollywood conservatives during the 1950s and 1960s.

97. "Our Need: A Businesslike Approach," A Report Prepared by Republican Associates at the Direction of Homer M. Preston, Chairman, Folder, Political, 1959, box 70, JLWP.

98. Letter to Alphonzo Bell from Richard Nixon, May 30, 1959, ibid.

99. For an example of the public sentiment against Kennedy's association with Sinatra, see Letter, Pierre Salinger to Joseph C. Healy, January 31, 1961, WHCNF, box 2577, Sinatra, Frank, JFKL.

100. Discussion of Kennedy and the DNC's treatment of Sammy Davis Jr. can be found in Early, "Sammy Davis Jr.," 19.

101. "The Hollywood Set and the Kennedy Family," *U.S. News and World Report*, October 16, 1961, 60.

102. Telegraph, E. Otimm to President, September 25, 1961, WHCNF, box 2577, Frank Sinatra, JFKL.

103. Press Release, Editors of *Private Affairs Magazine*, n.d. [November or December 1961], ibid.

104. Edward T. Folliard, "GOP 'Rough' Drive Opens against JFK," *Washington Post*, October 16, 1963, A1.

105. "Mr. Sinatra's Civil Rights," *Chicago Daily Tribune*, September 16, 1963, 11.

106. Letter to Hedda Hopper from Les Kaufman, May 19, 1964, regarding participation on the panel Hollywood and Politics, Folder 3806, Hollywood Press Club Debate, Actors in Politics, Subject File, Awards and Events, Hedda Hopper Papers, MHL. See also news clipping, "Should Pix and Politix Mix? Consensus of Press Club Panel: Could, and Should," *Variety*, June 11, 1964, Folder, Actors and Actresses in Politics, 1964–67, COREC, MHL.

107. See, for example, Letter Re: Stars for Freedom, from Pauline Marshall, Secretary for Stars for Freedom, to Lew Wasserman, November 4, 1963, Folder, MCA Artists, Subject File 1, Howard W. Flemming Collection, MHL. See also news clippings regarding civil rights activities in Hollywood, in Folder, Actors and Actresses in Politics, 1963–67, COREC, MHL; and Raymond, *Stars for Freedom*.

108. News clipping, "Some Celebrities Share the Scene," Folder, Actors and Actresses in Politics, through 1963, COREC, MHL.

109. For a look at how the civil rights movement used television to promote awareness and influence public opinion, see Torres, *Black, White, and in Color*; Ward, *Culture and the Modern African American Freedom Struggle*; and Graham, *Framing the South*.

110. For a discussion of the use of media and symbolic protests, see Gitlin, *The Whole World Is Watching*; and Farber, *Chicago '68*.

111. News clipping, "Many Showfolk to Protest Viet Policy When LBJ Visits Here," *Variety*, June 12, 1967, Folder, Actors and Actresses in Politics, 1963–67, COREC, MHL.

112. Ross, *Hollywood Left and Right*, 227–69; Weiner, *Gimme Some Truth*; Martin, *The Theater Is in the Street*.

CHAPTER 7

1. Gladwin Hill, "Nixon Denounces the Press as Biased," *New York Times*, November 8, 1962, 1.

2. Joan Barthel, "Hilarious, Brash, Flat, Peppery, Repetitious, Topical, and in Borderline Taste," *New York Times*, October 6, 1968, SM32.

3. Galvin, *Presidential Party Building*, 70–98.

4. A description of the election eve telethons and the broader electoral struggle between Nixon and Humphrey in 1968 can be found in Jamieson, *Packaging the Presidency*, 221–75.

5. McGinniss, *Selling of the President*, 151.

6. Ibid., 158.

7. Ibid., 155.

8. A more detailed description of the tensions between Eisenhower and Nixon because of Nixon's lack of media organizational experience can be found in Allen, *Eisenhower and the Mass Media*, 150–89.

9. Quotation from Eisenhower and his ideological view of the party can be found in Galvin, *Presidential Party Building*, 50–51.

10. Critchlow, *When Hollywood Was Right*, 142.

11. For discussion of the 1962 campaign, see Anderson and Lee, "The 1962 Election in California," 396–420. Throughout this analysis of the 1962 campaign, a key theme emerges that Nixon made a priority of negotiating ideological cleavages in the Republican Party in California. Anderson and Lee even discuss how Nixon's opponent, Pat Brown, used his advantage as an incumbent to focus more of the campaign on his image by working with consultants "in creating a 'new image' for [himself] of a forceful, decisive leader."

12. Greenberg, *Nixon's Shadow*, 40–54. Here Greenberg discusses the "Checkers speech"; more broadly, he also discusses how intellectual liberals like Lippmann viewed the embrace of the mass media as downright dangerous. They pointed to the Holocaust and the Red Scare as evidence of the ability of demagoguery to manipulate the public through emotional appeals in the media. Greenberg argues that "in an era when analysts decried the personalization of politics, Nixon seemed hateful not just as a politician, but as a person." Greenberg expands on this argument about the anxiety surrounding decisions concerning television, in "A New Way of Campaigning."

13. Discussion of the various stages of the "New Nixon" can be found in Greenberg, *Nixon's Shadow*. His look specifically at the New Nixon of the 1950s can be found on pp. 36–72.

14. Allen, *Eisenhower and the Mass Media*, 179–80.

15. Ibid., 180.

16. For a discussion of Richard Nixon and his role in the California Republican Party, as well as party leaders' support for him, see Critchlow, *When Hollywood Was Right*, 127–45. As Critchlow shows, with its personal connection to Nixon, Republican Associates would become an important financial contributor to the GOP; however, in 1960, this organization focused on the local Republican Party structures in Southern California and on financial contributions and not necessarily on coming up with publicity strategies for the national campaign.

17. Critchlow, *When Hollywood Was Right*, 130.

18. Art Buchwald, "Stars Turn Noses Up, Aid Campaign," *Los Angeles Times*, October 22, 1960, B6. For the formation of the Celebrities for Nixon group, see news clipping, "To Match Kennedy's Hollywood Aids, Celebrities Group to Support Nixon," *New York Herald Tribune*, n.d., Folder, Nixon Celebrity Group, box 4, Campaign to Civil Rights, 1960 Campaign Papers, RMNL.

19. News clipping, "Helen Hayes Stands to Be Counted, Too," local paper in Dayton, Ohio, August 22, 1960, ibid.

20. Critchlow, *When Hollywood Was Right*, 140.

21. A more detailed description of Nixon's lack of media organizational experience can be found in Allen, *Eisenhower and the Mass Media*, 150–89. For analysis of how the "savvy expert" had become "flatfooted and [had] fallen behind the times," see Greenberg, *Nixon's Shadow*, 71.

22. Media strategies to make Kennedy appear as the aggressor in the television appearances and debates were part of this effort to present Nixon as the respectable, clean candidate. See discussions of debate strategy, in Presidential Debate Preparations, PPS 61, 1960 Campaign Papers, RMNL. For an example of the use of this strategy in other television presentations, see Joe Cesida, "Sponsor Backstage," September 5, 1960, Folder, News Clippings, Campaign 1960, box 1, Alan Wallace Collection, RMNL.

23. Art Buchwald, "Stars Turn Noses Up, Aid Campaign," *Los Angeles Times*, October 22, 1960, B6.

24. James Reston, "Richard Nixon's Farewell: A Tragic Story," *New York Times*, November 9, 1962, 34.

25. Greenberg, *Nixon's Shadow*.

26. Bell, *California Crucible*, 2.

27. Details of this campaign can be found in Ross, *Hollywood Left and Right*, 163–75.

28. This is a continuation of how he spoke to audiences with the MPIC, which became a staple of how he addressed Republican audiences in the 1960s. See, for an example, "Great Speech by Ronald Reagan Thrills Capacity Ladies' Day Meeting at the Hilton," *Executive Club News*, March 26, 1965, Folder, Ronald Reagan, 1965–67, box 1, PPS 501, Ronald Reagan, Special Files, Research Files, 1968 Campaign Materials, RMNL.

29. For a discussion of how the Hollywood Right mobilized for Goldwater in 1964, see Critchlow, *When Hollywood Was Right*, 169–76.

30. Anderson and Lee, "The 1966 Election in California," 539.

31. Ibid., 550.

32. Letter in support of Reagan for President, n.d. [1967], Folder, Ronald Reagan, 1967–68, box 1, PPS 501, Ronald Reagan, Special Files, Research Files, Campaign 1968 Collection, PPP, RMNL.

33. Handwritten note by Richard Nixon in direct response to the memo from Pat Buchanan to Richard Nixon, n.d. [1968], Folder, Reagan, Speech Files III, ibid.

34. Michael Miles, "Reagan and the Respectable Right," Folder, Reagan, Articles Re: California Politics and Government, ibid.

35. Ibid.

36. "Ronald Reagan: Here's the Rest of Him," *Ripon Forum*, June 1968, Folder, Reagan and California Politics and Government, box 1, PPS 501, Ronald Reagan Special Files, Research Files, Campaign 1968 Collection, PPP, RNPL; Michael Miles, "Reagan and the Respectable Right," ibid. For a discussion of Nixon's "southern strategy" and its origins and details, see Lassiter, *Silent Majority*, 223–75; Schulman, *The Seventies*, 102–17; and Farber, *Rise and Fall of Modern American Conservatism*, 77–118.

37. Notes from Paul Keyes, 1963, Folder, Paul W. Keyes, box 409, WHCF, RMNL.

38. Memorandum from Len Garment to Richard Nixon, Re: Meet the Press, October 22, 1966, Folder, RMN, General, box 92, Cabinet box 26 or 29, Len Garment, WHCF, RMNL.

39. Memorandum for Mr. Garment, Re: 1968 Presidential Election, Folder, Misc. #2, box 69, Name File box 3 of 29, 1968 Political Campaign, Len Garment, WHCF, RMNL.

40. Letter, Bill Gavin to Richard Nixon, n.d. [1967], Folder, Bill Gavin (2 of 3), box 69, Name File box 3 of 29, 1968 Campaign File, Len Garment, WHCF, RMNL.

41. Klapper, *Effects of Mass Communication*. Discussion of Gavin's knowledge of communication theory comes from letter from Gavin to Len Garment, n.d. [1967], Folder, Bill

Gavin, 2 of 3, box 69, Name File box 3 of 29, 1968 Campaign File, Len Garment, WHCF, RMNL. Gavin's push for Nixon to connect to the soul of American voters comes in a memo to Garment from Gavin, Re: Soul, ibid.

42. Background on Harry Treleaven, his work with George Bush, and his advertising philosophy can be found in McGinniss, *Selling of the President*, 41–45.

43. This interaction between Nixon and Ailes is described in ibid., 63.

44. For a look at Goldwater and his relationship to the Republican Party, see Perlstein, *Before the Storm*; and Farber, *Rise and Fall of Modern American Conservatism*. Discussion of the grassroots campaign of Goldwater specifically can be found in McGirr, *Suburban Warriors*; and Critchlow, *The Conservative Ascendency*.

45. Memorandum from Ellsworth to DC, Mitchell, Stans, Haldeman, Flanigan, Kleindienst, and Garment, June 9, 1968, Folder, Strategy, box 81, Topical File box 15 of 29, Len Garment, WHCF, RMNL.

46. Memorandum from Bill Gavin to Len Garment, January 19, 1968, Folder, Bill Gavin, 2 of 3, box 69, Name File box 3 of 29, 1968 Campaign File, Len Garment, WHCF, RMNL.

47. Ibid.

48. For a discussion of the "Daisy" advertisement and its impact on political advertising, see Mann, *Daisy Petals and Mushroom Clouds*. Critchlow examines how in 1964 the use of stars on both sides of the campaign "was by no means unique." Critchlow, *When Hollywood Was Right*, 174.

49. Memo from Bess Abell to President Lyndon Johnson, March 3, 1965, in Critchlow and Raymond, *Hollywood and Politics*, 41–43.

50. For a discussion of Johnson's behind-the-scenes political tactics, see Schulman, *Lyndon B. Johnson and American Liberalism*.

51. Letter to Len Garment from Bill Gavin, n.d. [1968], Folder, Bill Gavin, 2 of 3, box 69, Name File box 3 of 29, 1968 Campaign File, Len Garment, WHCF, RMNL.

52. Memo from Bill Gavin to Len Garment, Re: Nixon notes, ibid.

53. Memo from Bill Gavin to Len Garment, Re: RN and the teachers, n.d. [1968], ibid.

54. Memorandum from Ray Price, Re: Recommendation for the General Strategy for Now through Wisconsin, in Appendix, McGinness, *Selling of the President*, 195.

55. See also Report by Richard Melville Bernstein, public relations advertiser from New York City, "Public Relations Analysis of Particular Areas," Folder, Public Relations, General, box 79, Topical File 13 of 29, 1968 Campaign File, Len Garment, WHCF, RMNL.

56. Report, "Nixon and His Image as a Loser," Folder, Bill Gavin, 2 of 3, box 69, Name File box 3 of 29, 1968 Campaign File, Len Garment, WHCF, RMNL.

57. Memorandum from Bill Gavin to Len Garment and Pat Buchanan, Re: Slogans and Other Things, Folder, Bill Gavin, 1 of 3, ibid.

58. Memorandum from Harry Treleaven, Re: Nixon for President Advertising in the Primary Campaigns, in Appendix, McGinniss, *Selling of the President*, 171–80.

59. Kelley, *Professional Public Relations and Political Power*, 199–200.

60. Memo from Bill Gavin, Re: Analysis, in Appendix, McGinniss, *Selling of the President*, 187–89.

61. See memorandum from Bill Gavin to Len Garment, December 1, 1967, Folder, Bill Gavin, 3 of 3, box 69, Name File box 3 of 29, 1968 Campaign File, Len Garment, WHCF,

RMNL. For a look at the types of slogans, music, and media montages, see Letter, Bill Gavin to Len Garment, Re: Nixon Now, September 25, 1968, ibid.

62. Memo from Roger Ailes to Len Garment and Frank Shakespeare, July 6, 1968, Folder, Roger Ailes, box 67, Name File box 1 of 29, ibid.

63. Memo from Bill Gavin to Len Garment, Re: The Campaign, n.d. [summer 1968], Folder, Bill Gavin, box 69, Name File box 3 of 29, ibid.

64. Greenberg's *Nixon's Shadow* focuses in depth on how Nixon adapted to the changing media environment from the 1950s to the 1970s. He examines the broader 1968 media campaign and mentions the *Laugh-In* appearance (136). Perlstein's *Nixonland* also briefly mentions *Laugh-In* as a small part of the broader campaign (332–33).

65. "Verrry Interesting . . . but Wild," *Time* magazine, October 11, 1968, http://www .time.com/tim/printout/0,8816902389,00.html.

66. Joan Barthel, "Hilarious, Brash, Flat, Peppery, Repetitious, Topical, and in Borderline Taste," *New York Times*, October 6, 1968, SM32.

67. Ibid.

68. See memo on nonverbal communication, Folder, Bill Gavin, 2 of 3, box 69, Name File box 3 of 29, 1968 Campaign File, Len Garment, WHCF, RMNL.

69. "G.O.P. TV Commercial Evokes Protests on Image of Humphrey," *New York Times*, October 29, 1968, 35.

70. Memo from Bill Gavin to Len Garment, Folder, Bill Gavin, 1 of 3, box 69, Name File box 3 of 29, 1968 Campaign File, Len Garment, WHCF, RMNL.

71. Sabato, *Rise of Political Consultants*.

72. Outline of the event can be found in President Nixon's daily diary, August 22, 1972, Presidential Daily Diary, RMNL. The quote comes from "What Makes Him Run," *Chicago Daily Defender*, August 26, 1972, 5. This article also contains a description of the rally and Sammy Davis Jr.'s motivations for supporting President Nixon.

73. Letter, Richard Nixon to Sammy Davis Jr., September 14, 1972, Folder 1, box 27, WHSF, RMNL.

74. Roger Ailes, Confidential Report: Television for Nixon, November 1968, Folder, 1968 Television Strategy, Len Garment Files, 1968 Campaign File, WHCF, RMNL.

75. John Wayne endorsements, Folder, Endorsements, box 74, box 7 of 29, Len Garment Files, 1968 Campaign File, WHCF, RMNL.

76. See a description of this in McGinniss, *Selling of the President*, 151.

77. For a look at how Nixon ran a continuous campaign, which has since become a staple of the modern American presidency, see Gould, *Modern American Presidency*.

78. There are many studies exploring Watergate, Nixon's "dark" character, and his illegal activities. Among landmark books are Kutler, *Wars of Watergate*; Schulman, *The Seventies*; and Olson, *Watergate: The Presidential Scandal That Shook America*. Three books stand as important chronicles of the events and the Committee to Re-elect the President organization. For an account of the investigation of the Watergate scandal, see Woodward and Bernstein, *All the President's Men*. For a look at the organization of the Committee to Re-elect the President, see *The Presidential Transcripts*, with commentary by the staff of the *Washington Post*; and Safire, *Before the Fall*.

79. Haynes Johnson, "Watergate Seemed to Be a Simple Public Relations Crisis," in *The Presidential Transcripts*, xxxi–xxxv.

80. Memo for H. R. Haldeman from Charles Colson, Re: Celebrities, October 12, 1971, Folder, Celebrities, 3 of 3, box 9, HHRHC, RMNL.

81. The role of late-night movies in generating political support for Murphy and Reagan is explored in Ross, *Hollywood Left and Right*, 167–83. The statement by Murphy is quoted on p. 168.

82. A discussion of the Republican strategy to use these studio actors to gain publicity and promote a particular image can be found in Hal Humphrey, "Grand Old Party Raids Hollywood," *Los Angeles Times*, June 10, 1965, 14, Folder, Actors and Actresses in Politics, 1964–67, COREC, MHL.

83. Memo from Jeb Stuart Magruder to H. R. Haldeman, December 6, 1971, Folder, Celebrities, 4 of 4, box 14, Subseries B: Alphabetical, series II: Subject Files, Jeb Stuart Magruder, CRPC, RMNL.

84. Memo from Herbert Porter to John Mitchell, November 8, 1971, Re: Administration Initiative Affecting the Movie Industry, ibid.

85. Suggested Agenda, "Opening Remarks by the Attorney General," ibid.

86. Memo from Herbert Porter to John Mitchell, Re: Funding Celebrities Committee, April 11, 1972, Folder, Celebrities, 2 of 4, box 14, Jeb Stuart Magruder, CRPC, RMNL. On the budget and mobilizing "prime movers" in the industry, see Memo to H. R. Haldeman from Jeb Stuart Magruder, December 6, 1971, Folder, Celebrities, 4 of 4, box 14, Subseries B: Alphabetical, series II: Subject Files, Jeb Stuart Magruder, CRPC, RMNL.

87. Memo for Jeb Stuart Magruder (author unknown), January 26, 1972, Folder, Celebrities, 3 of 4, box 14, Jeb Stuart Magruder, CRPC, RMNL. See also memo to Jeb Stuart Magruder and H. R. Haldeman from Herbert Porter, January 31, 1972, ibid.

88. James Conaway, "Instead of Fighting for a Place on It, Sammy Davis Has Bought the Bus," *New York Times*, October 15, 1972, 32.

89. Memo for the President from Robert Brown, June 20, 1972, Folder, Celebrities, 2 of 3, box 9, HHRHC, RMNL.

90. Memo to John Mitchell and Jeb Stuart Magruder from Herbert Porter, April 13, 1972, Folder, Celebrities, 3 of 3, ibid.

91. Memo to John Mitchell and Jeb Stuart Magruder from Herbert Porter, April 13, 1972, ibid.

92. James Conaway, "Instead of Fighting for a Place on It, Sammy Davis Jr. Has Bought the Bus," *New York Times*, October 15, 1972, 32.

93. Letter to the Editor, "Embarrassed by Sammy Davis," *Washington Post*, August 31, 1972, 23.

94. Discussion of the "black blitz" can be found in Monrow W. Karmin, "The Black Blitz: A Small Group of Blacks Work Hard to Convince Others That the President Should Get Their Vote," *Wall Street Journal*, October 27, 1972, 32. For a discussion of Nixon's attempt to court African Americans for the Republican Party, see Wright, "Loneliness of the Black Conservative."

95. Report, "Celebrities for the President," Folder, Celebrities, 3 of 4, box 14, Jeb Stuart Magruder, CRPC, RMNL.

96. Memo to John Mitchell from John Foust, May 5, 1972, Folder, Celebrities, 2 of 3, box 9, HRHC, RMNL.

97. Memo to H. R. Haldeman from Herbert Porter, Re: Briefing for Confirmed Celebrities, April 24, 1972, ibid.

98. Memo to H. R. Haldeman and John Mitchell from Jeb Stuart Magruder, March 10, 1972, Folder, Celebrities, 1 of 4, box 14, Jeb Stuart Magruder, CRPC, RMNL.

99. Memo to H. R. Haldeman and Jeb Stuart Magruder from Herbert Porter, January 31, 1972, Folder, Celebrities, 4 of 4, ibid.

100. Memo to Jeb Stuart Magruder from H. R. Haldeman, Re: Celebrities, March 21, 1972, Folder, Celebrities, 1 of 4, ibid.

101. Memo to H. R. Haldeman from Stephen Bull, Re: Celebrity Reception, July 4, 1972, Folder, Celebrities, 1 of 3, box 8, HRHC, RMNL.

102. Robert Semple Jr., "Nixons Entertain Their Hollywood Backers," *New York Times*, August 28, 1972, 30.

103. Memo to Herbert Porter from Raymond Caldiero, June 26, 1972, Folder, Celebrities II, 2 of 2, box 9, HRHC, RMNL.

104. Memo to Larry Higby and Alexander Butterfield from Gordon Strachan, June 29, 1972, Folder, Celebrities, 1 of 3, box 8, HRHC, RMNL.

105. Memo to H. R. Haldeman from Charles Colson, October 12, 1971, Folder, Celebrities, 3 of 3, box 9, HHRHC, RMNL.

106. Memo to Herbert Porter from Raymond Caldiero, June 26, 1972, Folder, Celebrities II, 2 of 2, box 9, HRHC, RMNL.

107. Letter to the Editor of *Newsweek* from Raymond Caldiero, September 20, 1972, Folder, Celebrities II, 1 of 2, box 9, Subseries A: Working Files, series II Presidential Administration Files, HRHC, RMNL.

108. Quoted in Biskind, *Easy Riders, Raging Bulls*, 14.

109. For a look at the violence that erupted between protestors and Mayor Richard Daley and the clash between traditional political style and the new political outlook that valued media and symbolic politics, see Farber, *Chicago '68*.

110. McGovern's analysis of the changes begot by his commission and a broader exploration of the changes in the primary campaign over the course of the twentieth century and the ramifications of this new primary structure can be found in Walker, "Primary Game," 64–78.

111. William Rentschler, "McGovern Mimics Nixon '68 Campaign Techniques," *Chicago Tribune*, September 24, 1972, 7.

112. Ibid.

113. The following description of the role of celebrities in the McGovern campaign can be found in Letter, Eden Lispon to R. H. Nolte, Institute of Current World Affairs, September 22, 1972, Folder, Sparklies, Theodore White Papers, JFKL.

114. Ibid.

115. Gary Hart's description of celebrities as "sparklies" can be found in ibid. See also news clipping, Leroy Aarons, "Singing and Ushering for McGovern," *Washington Post*, April 17, 1972, Folder, Celebrities I, 2 of 3, box 9, HRHC, RMNL.

116. News clipping, Leroy Aarons, "Singing and Ushering for McGovern," *Washington Post*, April 17, 1972, Folder, Celebrities I, 2 of 3, box 9, HRHC, RMNL.

117. MacLaine, *My Lucky Stars*, 211.

118. For more of a discussion on the role of Beatty in the McGovern campaign, see Ross, *Hollywood Left and Right*, 324–41.

119. Ibid., 329.

120. Frustration felt by disappointed fans was articulated in Chris Chase, "Love Is Hell, Warren," *New York Times*, June 25, 1972, 1.

121. Letter, Eden Lispon to R. H. Nolte, Institute of Current World Affairs, September 22, 1972, Folder, Sparklies, Theodore White Papers, JFKL.

122. Wolfe, *Radical Chic*.

123. Letter to the Editor of *Newsweek* from Raymond Caldiero, September 20, 1972, Folder, Celebrities II, 1 of 2, box 9, Subseries A: Working Files, series II, Presidential Administration Files, HHRHC, RMNL.

124. This appears throughout the account of the campaign in Gary Hart, *Right from the Start*.

125. McCandlish Phillips, "Rock'n'Rhetoric Rally in the Garden Aids McGovern," *New York Times*, June 15, 1972, 1.

126. Letter, Eden Lispon to R. H. Nolte, Institute of Current World Affairs, September 22, 1972, Folder, Sparklies, Theodore White Papers, JFKL.

127. Canon, *Actors, Athletes, and Astronauts*.

CONCLUSION

1. For a history of D. A. Pennebaker and the circumstances surrounding the production of *The War Room*, see Menand, "Being There."

2. *The War Room*.

3. *The Return of the War Room*.

4. Alan Schroeder also discusses the Clinton performance in *Final Days* as an embodiment of what he calls "The Showbiz Presidency." Clinton's performance here, Schroeder argues, embodied how the president became "celebrity-in-chief" over the course of the twentieth century. Schroeder, *Celebrity-in-Chief*, 1–5.

5. For a discussion of how Reagan cultivated these connections in California and then during the national campaign, see Critchlow, *When Hollywood Was Right*, 205–13. Critchlow argues that the Hollywood Right lost cultural power by 1980 but won political power with Reagan's election.

6. Troy, *Morning in America*, 27.

7. Rogin, *Ronald Reagan*. For a discussion of how Reagan used popular culture icons to communicate with the American people, see Troy, *Morning in America*.

8. For example, Reagan's press secretary, Larry Speakes, prominently and proudly had a sign on his desk that stated: "You don't tell us how to stage the news and we don't tell you how to cover it." See Kurtz, *Spin Cycle*, xxii.

9. Schudson, *The Power of News*, argues that the political and journalism elites succumbed to this belief more than the electorate itself (124–41).

10. Ibid., 137.

11. For more details on the movie *Final Days* and the Clinton White House's connections with Hollywood, see Schroeder, *Celebrity-in-Chief*, 1–5. The film itself can be accessed via the William J. Clinton Presidential Library YouTube channel: https://www.youtube.com/watch?v=PbbUYhyoWz8.

12. Robinson, *Dance of the Comedians*.

13. Leslie Wayne, "A Hollywood Production: Political Money," *New York Times*, September 12, 1996, 1.

14. Footage of the White House Correspondents' Dinner, April 29, 2000, can be accessed on the William J. Clinton Presidential Library YouTube feed: https://www.youtube.com/watch?v=OsxgsofXiEg. Reuters also released a story of the event and the film *Final Days*, on May 1, 2000.

15. Postman, *Amusing Ourselves to Death*.

16. These questions were tackled by sociologists and political scientists. See, for example, essays in Skocpol and Fiorina, *Civic Engagement in American Democracy*. See also Gitlin, especially *The Whole World Is Watching* and *Media Unlimited*. Putnam's *Bowling Alone* also advances this argument and generated much debate about the historical decline in civic identity and arguments about changing conceptions of community as well.

17. Quotation from Norman Nie, in Jeffrey Jones, *Entertaining Politics*, 21.

18. See, for example, ibid.; Street, *Politics and Popular Culture*; and Street, Inthorn, and Scott, *From Entertainment to Citizenship*.

19. Thomas Patterson, *Out of Order*, has examined ways in which the political process in the post-Watergate era has resembled the values of a newsroom, with journalists focused on scandal and negativity in their coverage of American politics. Fallows, *Breaking the News*, also points to how contemporary media coverage undermines democracy in its efforts to show American politics as a game and to increase ratings through polarizing talking heads. A recent critique of the undemocratic implications of the contemporary role of mass media in the politics of incivility was presented by Roderick P. Hart in a lecture, "C-SPAN Archives Distinguished Lecture."

20. Gould, *Modern American Presidency*; Troy, *See How They Ran*.

21. Gabler, *Life: The Movie*.

22. Political scientists and historians have debated extensively the nature of popular participation in American politics during the nineteenth century. A terrific discussion of this debate and the limits of popular engagement can be found in Altschuler and Blumin, "Limits of Political Engagement in Antebellum America." For a discussion of participation and expansion of corruption in American political machines after the Civil War, see Summers, *Party Games*.

23. Heale, *Presidential Quest*.

24. McGerr, *Decline of Popular Politics*.

Bibliography

GOVERNMENT RECORDS

Dwight D. Eisenhower Presidential Library, Abilene, Kansas
    Ann Whitman Files
    Files of Young & Rubicam, Citizens for Eisenhower, Staff Files
    Inaugural Committee of 1953 Records
    President's Personal Files
    Republican National Committee Files
    White House Central Files
Franklin D. Roosevelt Presidential Library, Hyde Park, New York
    Democratic National Committee Papers
    President's Personal Files
Harry S. Truman Presidential Library, Independence, Missouri
    Official Files
John F. Kennedy Presidential Library, Boston, Massachusetts
    Audio Visual Archive
    Democratic National Committee Records
    Inaugural Committee Files
    Jerry Bruno Papers
    Kenneth Birkhead Personal Papers
    Oral History Files
    President's Official File
    Robert F. Kennedy Papers
    Theodore Sorensen Papers
    Theodore White Papers
    White House Central Name File
National Archives and Records Administration
    Center for Legislative Archives, Washington, D.C.
        RG233, Records of the U.S. House of Representatives, House Committee on
            Internal Security, Committee on Un-American Activities
    Archives II, College Park, Maryland
        RG6, Office of War Information
Richard M. Nixon Presidential Library, Yorba Linda, California
    Alan Wallace Collection
    Committee for the Re-election of the President Collection
    Harold Robbins (H.R.) Haldeman Collection
    Pre-Presidential Papers

President's Daily Dairy
President's Office File
President's Personal File
White House Central Files
    Alphabetical Name Files
    Subject Files
White House Special Files

ARCHIVES AND MANUSCRIPT COLLECTIONS

Academy of Motion Picture Arts and Sciences, Margaret Herrick Library, Beverly Hills, California
    American Motion Picture and Television Production Files
    CORE Collection
    Hedda Hopper Papers
    Howard W. Flemming Collection
    John Huston Papers
    Motion Picture Industry Council Records
    Robert M. W. Vogel Papers
    William Wyler Papers
Boston University, Howard Gotlieb Library, Boston, Massachusetts
    Bette Davis Papers
    Douglas Fairbanks Jr. Collection
California State University, Oviatt Library, Northridge
    Jewish Federation Council of Greater Los Angeles, Community Relations Committee Collection
Columbia University, Oral History Collection, New York, New York
    Reminiscences of Eric Johnston
Indiana University, Lilly Library, Bloomington
    Wendell Willkie Papers
Joel E. Ferris Research Library, Spokane, Washington
    Eric A. Johnston Papers
Library of Congress, Washington, D.C.
    A. Philip Randolph Papers
    National Association for the Advancement of Colored People Records
University of Southern California, Los Angeles
    School of Cinematic Arts
        Jack L. Warner Papers
    Warner Brothers Archive
Wisconsin Center for Film and Theater Research, Madison
    Dore Schary Papers
    Historical Pamphlet Collection
    Hollywood Democratic Committee Records
    Melvyn Douglas Papers
    Walter Wanger Papers

VIDEO/TELEVISION SOURCES

Gold Diggers of 1933. Directed by Mervyn LeRoy. 1933. Warner Home Video, DVD, 2006.

Primary. Directed by Robert Drew. 1960. New Video Group, DVD, 2003.

The War Room. Directed by Chris Hegedus and D. A. Pennebaker. 1993. Criterion Collection, DVD, 2012.

The Return of the War Room. Panel discussion courtesy of the William J. Clinton Foundation and Pennebaker-Hegedus Films. Criterion Collection, DVD, 2012.

Note on audiovisual sources: Digital archives contain a wealth of audiovisual sources, making it easier for scholars to incorporate film, television, and advertisements into their work. The Library of Congress maintains a digital collection of early motion picture films, including *Visitin' round at Coolidge Corners*, [Pathe?], 1924. Library of Congress Motion Picture, Broadcasting and Recorded Sound Division, Washington D.C. http://memory.loc.gov/cgi-bin/query/r?ammem/coolbib:@field(NUMBER+@band(amrlv+coolidg1))

Archive.org is a database for radio, newsreels, and government propaganda productions; it is keyword searchable and holds a variety of New Deal promotional films, including: *The Road is Open Again*, an N.R.A. Official Featurette. Directed by Alfred E. Green. Warner Bros., 1933. https://archive.org/details/gov.fdr.352.1.1. It also holds the Universal Newsreels, which Universal City Studios put in the public domain and for which it gave materials to the National Archives. This collection has newsreel coverage of major political and international events from 1929 to 1967. Finally, this database also holds promotional government films, including the World War II propaganda films referenced in the text, among them *All Star Bond Rally*. Directed by Michael Audley. 20th Century Fox, 1945. https://archive.org/details/AllStarBondRally

Archived by the Museum of the Moving Image, www.livingroomcandidate.org documents political television advertisements for campaigns since the 1952 presidential election, including those referenced in the text through the 1968 campaign.

NEWSPAPERS AND MAGAZINES

Baltimore Sun

Chicago Defender

Chicago Tribune

Congressional Record

Hartford Courant

Hollywood Citizen-News

Hollywood Reporter

Los Angeles Examiner

Los Angeles Sentinel

Los Angeles Times

Motion Picture Daily

Motion Picture Herald

New Yorker

New York Herald Tribune

New York Times

Photoplay

Photoplay Movie Mirror Magazine

Time Magazine

U.S. News and World Report

Variety

Washington Post

PUBLISHED PRIMARY SOURCES, MEMOIRS, AND BIOGRAPHIES

Alexander, Herbert. *Money in Politics*. New York: Public Affairs Press, 1972.

Bentley, Eric. *Thirty Years of Treason: Excerpts from Hearings before the House Committee on Un-American Activities, 1938–1968*. 2nd ed. New York: Thunder's Mouth Press/Nation's Books, 2002.

Biow, Milton H. *Butting In: An Ad Man Speaks Out*. New York: Doubleday, 1964.

Dmytryk, Edward. *Odd Man Out: A Memoir of the Hollywood Ten*. Carbondale: Southern Illinois University Press, 1996.

Fairbanks, Douglas, Jr. *The Salad Days*. New York: Doubleday, 1988.

Hart, Gary. *Right from the Start: A Chronicle of the McGovern Campaign*. New York: Quadrangle/New York Times Book Company, 1973.

Hays, Will H. *The Memoirs of Will Hays*. New York: Doubleday, 1955.

Hopper, Hedda. *Whole Truth and Nothing But*. New York: Doubleday, 1963.

Johnston, Eric. *America Unlimited*. New York: Doubleday, Doran, 1944.

Kennedy, Joseph P. *I'm for Roosevelt*. New York: Reynal and Hitchcock, 1936.

Klapper, Joseph T. *The Effects of Mass Communication: An Analysis of Research on the Effectiveness and Limitations of Mass Media in Influencing Opinions, Values, and Behavior of Their Audiences*. New York: Free Press, 1960.

Lippmann, Walter. *Public Opinion*. New York: Macmillan, 1922.

MacLaine, Shirley. *My Lucky Stars: A Hollywood Memoir*. New York: Bantam, 1995.

McGinniss, Joe. *The Selling of the President, 1968*. New York: Pocket Publishing, 1970.

Montgomery, Robert. *Open Letter from a Television Viewer*. New York: Heineman, 1968.

Murphy, George. *Say . . . Didn't You Used to Be George Murphy?* New York: Bartholomew House, 1970.

The Presidential Transcripts. New York: Dell, 1974.

Rand, Ayn. *Screen Guide for Americans*. Beverly Hills, Calif.: Motion Picture Alliance for the Preservation of American Ideals, 1948.

Reagan, Ronald, and Richard Hubler. *Where's the Rest of Me?* New York: Dell, 1965.

Safire, William. *Before the Fall: An Inside View of the Pre-Watergate White House*. New York: Doubleday, 1975.

Sinclair, Upton. *I, Candidate for Governor, and How I Got Licked*. Pasadena, Calif.: Upton Sinclair, 1935.

———. *I, Governor of California, and How I Ended Poverty: A True Story of the Future*. Pasadena, Calif.: Upton Sinclair, 1933.

U.S. Congress. House of Representatives. *Investigation of Communist Propaganda, Report 2290*. 71st Cong., 1st sess., 1931. Washington, D.C.: Government Printing Office, 1931.

———. House of Representatives. Committee on Un-American Activities. *Communist Infiltration of Hollywood Motion Picture Industry*. 1947, unpublished. Accessed via LexisNexis Congressional Hearings Digital Collection, Hearing ID: HRG-1947-UAH-0015.

———. House of Representatives. Committee on Un-American Activities. *Investigation of Un-American Activities and Propaganda*. 75th Cong., 1st sess., 193. Washington, D.C.: Government Printing Office, 1939.

———. Senate. Committee on Interstate Commerce. *Hearings before a Subcommittee on Interstate Commerce: Propaganda in Motion Pictures.* 77th Cong., 1st sess., 1941. Washington, D.C.: Government Printing Office, 1924.

White, Theodore. *The Making of the President, 1960.* New York: Atheneum, 1961.

Wolfe, Tom. *Radical Chic and Mau-Mauing the Flak Catchers.* New York: Picador, 1971.

Woodward, Bob, and Carl Bernstein. *All the President's Men.* New York: Simon and Schuster, 1974.

Writers Congress: The Proceedings of the Conference Held in October 1943 under the Sponsorship of the Hollywood Writers' Mobilization and the University of California. Berkeley: University of California Press, 1944.

Zukor, Adolph, with Dale Kramer. *The Public Is Never Wrong.* New York: Putnam, 1953.

SECONDARY SOURCES: JOURNAL ARTICLES

Altschuler, Glenn C., and Stuart M. Blumin. "Limits of Political Engagement in Antebellum America: A New Look at the Golden Age of Participatory Democracy." *Journal of American History* 84 (1997): 855–85.

Anderson, Totton J., and Eugene C. Lee. "The 1962 Election in California." *Western Political Quarterly* 16 (1963): 396–420.

———. "The 1966 Election in California." *Western Political Quarterly* 20 (1967): 535–54.

Block, Ralph. "Propaganda and the Free Society." *Public Opinion Quarterly* (Winter 1948–49): 677–86.

Carman, Emily Susan. "Independent Stardom: Female Film Stars and the Studio System in the 1930s." *Women's Studies: An Interdisciplinary Journal* (2008): 583–15.

"Conservatism: A Roundtable." *Journal of American History* 98 (2011): 723–73.

Druckman, James N. "The Power of Television Images: The First Kennedy-Nixon Debate Revisited." *Journal of Politics* 65 (2003): 559–71.

Hichborn, Franklin, and Herbert C. Jones. "The Party, the Machine, and the Vote: The Story of Cross-Filing in California Politics." *California Historical Society Quarterly* (1959): 349–57.

Hollitz, John E. "Eisenhower and the Admen: The Television Spot Campaign of 1952." *Wisconsin Magazine of History* 66 (1982): 25–39.

Jacobs, Lawrence R., and Robert Y. Shapiro. "Issues, Candidate Image, and Priming: The Use of Private Polls in Kennedy's 1960 Presidential Campaign." *American Political Science Review* 88 (1994): 527–40.

Jones, Dorothy B. "Hollywood War Films, 1942–44." *Hollywood Quarterly* 1 (1945): 1–19.

Lang, Kurt, and Gladys Engel Lang. "Ordeal by Debate: Viewer Reactions." *Public Opinion Quarterly* 26 (1962): 277–88.

Larson, Cedric. "The Domestic Work of the Office of War Information." *Hollywood Quarterly* 3 (1948): 434–43.

Pitchell, Robert J. "The Electoral System and Voting Behavior." *Western Political Quarterly* (1959): 459–84.

———. "The Influence of Professional Campaign Management Firms in Partisan Elections in California." *Western Political Quarterly* (1958): 278–300.

Rosten, Leo. "Movies and Propaganda." *Annals of the American Academy of Political and Social Science* 254 (1947): 116–24.

Salant, Richard S. "The Television Debates: A Revolution That Deserves a Future." *Public Opinion Quarterly* 26 (1962): 335–50.

Slaybaugh, Douglas. "Adlai Stevenson, Television, and the Presidential Campaign of 1956." *Illinois Historical Journal* 89 (1996): 2–16.

Walker, Jack. "The Primary Game." *Wilson Quarterly* 12 (1988): 64–78.

Wanger, Walter. "The OWI and Motion Pictures." *Public Opinion Quarterly* (1943): 100–110.

Weinberg, Sydney. "What to Tell America: The Writers' Quarrel in the Office of War Information." *Journal of American History* 55 (1968): 73–89.

Wood, Stephen C. "Television's First Political Spot Ad Campaign: Eisenhower Answers America." *Presidential Quarterly* 20 (1990): 265–83.

Zelizer, Julian. "Seeds of Cynicism: The Struggle over Campaign Finance Reform, 1956–1974." *Journal of Policy History* 14 (2002): 73–111.

SECONDARY SOURCES: BOOKS, ESSAYS IN BOOKS, DISSERTATIONS, AND PAPERS

Aldrich, John H. *Why Parties? The Origin and Transformation of Political Parties in America.* Chicago: University of Chicago Press, 1995.

Alexander, Linda. *Reluctant Witness: Robert Taylor, Hollywood, and Communism.* Swansboro, N.C.: Tease Publishing, 2008.

Allen, Craig. *Eisenhower and the Mass Media: Peace, Prosperity, and Prime-Time TV.* Chapel Hill: University of North Carolina Press, 1993.

Anderson, Terry. *The Movement and the Sixties: Protest in America from Greensboro to Wounded Knee.* New York: Oxford University Press, 1995.

Ansolabehere, Stephen, Roy Behr, and Shanto Iyengar. *The Media Game: American Politics in the Television Age.* New York: Macmillan, 1993.

Badger, Anthony. *The New Deal: The Depression Years.* New York: Ivan R. Dee, 2002.

Baker, Jean. *Affairs of Party: The Political Culture of Northern Democrats in the Mid-Nineteenth Century.* Ithaca: Cornell University Press, 1983.

Balogh, Brian. "From Corn to Caviar: The Evolution of Presidential Electoral Communications, 1960 to 2000." In *Elections and American Political History*, edited by Gareth Davies and Julian Zelizer. Philadelphia: University of Pennsylvania Press, forthcoming.

———. " 'Mirrors of Desire': Interest Groups, Elections, and the Targeted Style in Twentieth Century America." In *The Democratic Experiment: New Directions in American Political History*, edited by Meg Jacobs, William Novak, and Julian Zelizer. Princeton: Princeton University Press, 2003.

Barbas, Samantha. *The First Lady of Hollywood: A Biography of Louella Parsons.* Berkeley: University of California Press, 2005.

———. *Movie Crazy: Fans, Stars, and the Cult of Celebrity.* New York: Palgrave, 2002.

Beauchamp, Carl. *Joseph P. Kennedy Presents: His Hollywood Years.* New York: Knopf, 2009.

Bell, Jonathan. *California Crucible: The Forging of Modern American Liberalism.* Philadelphia: University of Pennsylvania Press, 2012.

Bergman, Andrew. *We're in the Money: Depression America and Its Films*. New York: New York University Press, 1971.

Berkowitz, Edward. *Something Happened: A Political and Cultural Overview of the Seventies*. New York: Columbia University Press, 2006.

Billingsley, Kenneth Lloyd. *Hollywood Party: How Communism Seduced the American Film Industry in the 1930s and 1940s*. Roseville, Calif.: Forum, 1998.

Biskind, Peter. *Easy Riders, Raging Bulls: How the Sex-Drugs-and-Rock'n'Roll Generation Saved Hollywood*. New York: Simon and Schuster, 1998.

———. *Seeing Is Believing: How Hollywood Taught Us to Stop Worrying and Love the Fifties*. New York: Pantheon, 1993.

Black, Allida. *Casting Her Own Shadow: Eleanor Roosevelt and the Shaping of Postwar Liberalism*. New York: Columbia University Press, 1996.

Blum, John Morton. *V Was for Victory: Politics and American Culture during World War II*. New York: Harcourt Brace Jovanovich, 1976.

Bodnar, John. *Blue Collar Hollywood: Liberalism, Democracy, and Working People in American Film*. Baltimore: Johns Hopkins University Press, 2003.

Boorstin, Daniel J. *The Image: Or What Happened to the American Dream*. New York: Atheneum, 1961.

Brinkley, Alan. *The End of Reform: New Deal Liberalism in Recession and War*. New York: Knopf, 1995.

———. *Franklin Delano Roosevelt*. New York: Oxford University Press, 2010.

Brown, Robert J. *Manipulating the Ether: The Power of Broadcast Radio in Thirties America*. Baltimore: Johns Hopkins University Press, 2005.

Brownstein, Ronald. *The Power and the Glitter: The Hollywood-Washington Connection*. New York: Pantheon, 1991.

Bruck, Connie. *When Hollywood Had a King: The Reign of Lew Wasserman, Who Leveraged Talent into Power and Influence*. New York: Random House, 2003.

Burns, Jennifer. *Goddess of the Market: Ayn Rand and the American Right*. New York: Oxford University Press, 2009.

Cannon, Lou. *President Reagan: The Role of a Lifetime*. New York: Simon and Schuster, 1991.

Canon, David. *Actors, Athletes, and Astronauts: Political Amateurs in the United States Congress*. Chicago: University of Chicago Press, 1990.

Ceplair, Larry, and Steven Englund. *The Inquisition in Hollywood: Politics in the Film Community, 1930–1960*. 2nd ed. Chicago: University of Illinois Press, 2003.

Cohen, Lizbeth. *A Consumer's Republic: The Politics of Mass Consumption in Postwar America*. New York: Vintage Books, 2003.

———. *Making a New Deal: Industrial Workers in Chicago, 1919–1939*. New York: Cambridge University Press, 1990.

Cohen, Paula Marantz. *Silent Film and the Triumph of the American Myth*. New York: Oxford University Press, 2001.

Couvares, Francis G., ed. *Movie Censorship and American Culture*. Washington, D.C.: Smithsonian Institution Press, 1996.

Craig, Douglas B. *Fireside Politics: Radio and Political Culture in the United States*. Baltimore: Johns Hopkins University Press, 2005.

Critchlow, Donald. *The Conservative Ascendency: How the GOP Right Made Political History*. Cambridge: Harvard University Press, 2007.

———. *When Hollywood Was Right: How Movie Stars, Studio Moguls, and Big Business Remade American Politics*. New York: Cambridge University Press, 2013.

Critchlow, Donald, and Emilie Raymond. *Hollywood and Politics: A Sourcebook*. London: Routledge, 2009.

Cruikshank, Jeffrey L., and Arthur W. Schultz. *The Man Who Sold America: The Amazing but True Story of Albert D. Lasker and the Creation of the Advertising Century*. Boston: Harvard Business Review Press, 2010.

Dallek, Robert. *An Unfinished Life: John F. Kennedy, 1917–1963*. New York: Back Bay Books, 2003.

Denning, Michael. *The Cultural Front: The Laboring of American Culture in the Twentieth Century*. 2nd ed. New York: Verso, 2011.

Deverell, William. *Whitewashed Adobe: The Rise of Los Angeles and the Remaking of Its Mexican Past*. Berkeley: University of California Press, 2005.

Devine, Thomas. *Henry Wallace's 1948 Presidential Campaign and the Future of Postwar Liberalism*. Chapel Hill: University of North Carolina Press, 2013.

Diamond, Edwin, and Stephen Bates. *The Spot: The Rise of Political Advertising on Television*. 3rd ed. Cambridge: MIT Press, 1992.

Diamond, Edwin, and Robert Silverman. *White House to Your House: Media and Politics in Virtual America*. Cambridge: MIT Press, 1995.

Dick, Bernard. *The Star Spangled Screen: The American World War II Film*. Louisville: University Press of Kentucky, 1985.

Didion, Joan. *Political Fictions*. New York: Knopf, 2001.

Diggins, John Patrick. *The Proud Decades: America in War and Peace, 1941–1960*. New York: W. W. Norton, 1988.

Dochuck, Darren. *From Bible Belt to Sunbelt: Plain-Fold Religion, Grassroots Politics, and the Rise of Evangelical Conservatism*. New York: W. W. Norton, 2011.

Doherty, Thomas Patrick. *Pre-Code Hollywood: Sex, Immorality, and Insurrection in American Cinema, 1930–1934*. New York: Columbia University Press, 1999.

Donaldson, Gary A. *The First Modern Campaign: Kennedy, Nixon, and the Election of 1960*. Lanham, Md.: Rowman and Littlefield, 2007.

Douglas, Susan J. *Listening In: Radio and the American Imagination*. Minneapolis: University of Minnesota Press, 1997.

———. "The Presidency, Media Affordances, and Media Aptitudes." Paper presented at the Recasting Presidential History conference, Miller Center for Public Affairs, Charlottesville, Va., 2012.

Early, Gerald. "Sammy Davis Jr." In *The Sammy Davis Jr. Reader*, edited by Gerald Early and Sammy Davis Jr. New York: Farrar, Straus, and Giroux, 2001.

Edgerton, Gary. *The Columbia History of American Television*. New York: Columbia University Press, 2007.

Erenberg, Lewis. *Steppin' Out: New York Nightlife and the Transformation of American Culture, 1890–1930*. Chicago: University of Chicago Press, 1981.

Eyman, Scott. *The Lion of Hollywood: The Life and Legend of Louis B. Mayer*. New York: Simon and Schuster, 2005.

Fallows, James. *Breaking the News: How the Media Undermine Democracy.* New York: Pantheon, 1996.

Farber, David. *Chicago '68.* Chicago: University of Chicago Press, 1987.

———. *The Rise and Fall of Modern American Conservatism.* Princeton: Princeton University Press, 2010.

———, ed. *The Sixties: From Memory to History.* Chapel Hill: University of North Carolina Press, 1994.

Feeney, Mark. *Nixon at the Movies: A Book about Belief.* Chicago: University of Chicago Press, 2004.

Fones-Wolf, Elizabeth A. *Selling Free Enterprise: The Business Assault on Labor and Liberalism.* Chicago: University of Chicago Press, 1994.

Frank, Thomas. *The Conquest of Cool: Business Culture, Counterculture, and the Rise of Hip Consumerism.* Chicago: University of Chicago Press, 1997.

Fraser, Steve, and Gary Gerstle, eds. *The Rise and Fall of the New Deal Order, 1930–1980.* Princeton: Princeton University Press, 1990.

Freedland, Michael. *Hollywood on Trial: McCarthyism's War against the Movies.* London: Anova Books, 2007.

Frost, Jennifer. *Hedda Hopper's Hollywood: Celebrity Gossip and American Conservatism.* New York: New York University Press, 2011.

Gabler, Neal. *An Empire of Their Own: How the Jews Invented Hollywood.* New York: Doubleday, 1988.

———. *Life: The Movie; How Entertainment Conquered Reality.* New York: Knopf, 1998.

Galvin, Daniel. *Presidential Party Building: Dwight D. Eisenhower to George W. Bush.* Princeton: Princeton University Press, 2009.

Giglio, Ernest. *Here's Looking at You: Hollywood, Film, and Politics.* New York: Peter Lang, 2005.

Giovacchini, Saverio. *Hollywood Modernism: Film and Politics in the Age of the New Deal.* Philadelphia: Temple University Press, 2001.

Gitlin, Todd. *Media Unlimited: How the Torrent of Images and Sounds Overwhelms Our Lives.* Rev. ed. New York: Metropolitan Books, 2001.

———. *The Whole World Is Watching: Mass Media in the Making and Un-making of the New Left.* Berkeley: University of California Press, 1980.

Gladchuk, John Joseph. *Hollywood and Anticommunism: HUAC and the Evolution of the Red Menace, 1935–1950.* New York: Routledge, 2007.

Gould, Lewis L. *The Modern American Presidency.* Lawrence: University Press of Kansas, 2004.

Graham, Allison. *Framing the South: Hollywood, Television, and Race during the Civil Rights Struggle.* Baltimore: Johns Hopkins University Press, 2001.

Greenberg, David. *Calvin Coolidge.* New York: Times Books, 2007.

———. "A New Way of Campaigning: Eisenhower, Stevenson, and the Anxieties of Television Politics." In *Liberty and Justice for All? Rethinking Politics in Cold War America,* edited by Kathleen G. Donohue. Boston: University of Massachusetts Press, 2012.

———. *Nixon's Shadow: The History of an Image.* New York: W. W. Norton, 2003.

Grieveson, Lee. *Policing Cinema: Movies and Censorship in Early-Twentieth-Century America.* Berkeley: University of California Press, 2004.

Harris, Mark. *Pictures at a Revolution: Five Movies and the Birth of a New Hollywood.* New York: Penguin, 2008.

Hart, Roderick P. "C-SPAN Archives Distinguished Lecture." In *The C-SPAN Archives: An Interdisciplinary Resource for Discovery, Learning, and Engagement,* edited by Robert Browning and Patrice Buzzanell. West Lafayette, Ind.: Purdue University Press, 2014.

Heale, M. J. *The Presidential Quest: Candidates and Images in American Political Culture, 1787–1852.* New York: Longman Press, 1982.

Hellman, John. *The Kennedy Obsession: The Myth of JFK.* New York: Columbia University Press, 1997.

Hilmes, Michele. *Hollywood and Broadcasting: From Radio to Cable.* Urbana: University of Illinois Press, 1990.

———. *Radio Voices: American Broadcasting, 1922–1952.* Minneapolis: University of Minnesota Press, 1999.

Horne, Gerald. *The Final Victim of the Blacklist: John Howard Lawson, Dean of the Hollywood Ten.* Berkeley: University of California Press, 2006.

Humphries, Reynold. *Hollywood's Blacklists: A Political and Cultural History.* Edinburgh: Edinburgh University Press, 2008.

Irwin, Will. *The House That Shadows Built: The Story of Adolph Zukor and His Circle.* New York: Doubleday, 1928.

Jamieson, Kathleen Hall. *Packaging the Presidency: A History and Criticism of Presidential Campaign Advertising.* New York: Oxford University Press, 1996.

———. *The Press Effect: Politicians, Journalists, and the Stories That Shape the Political World.* New York: Oxford University Press, 2003.

Jones, Jeffrey. *Entertaining Politics: Satiric Television and Political Engagement.* 2nd ed. Lanham, Md.: Rowman and Littlefield, 2010.

Kelley, Stanley. *Professional Public Relations and Political Power.* Baltimore: Johns Hopkins University Press, 1956.

Kennedy, David. *Freedom from Fear: The American People in Depression and War, 1929–1945.* New York: Oxford University Press, 1999.

Kernell, Samuel. *Going Public: New Strategies of Presidential Leadership.* 4th ed. Washington, D.C.: CQ Press, 2007.

Koppes, Clayton, and Gregory Black. *Hollywood Goes to War: How Politics, Profits, and Propaganda Shaped World War II Movies.* New York: Free Press, 1987.

Kovarik, Bill. *Revolution in Communications: Media History from Gutenberg to the Digital Age.* New York: Continuum, 2011.

Kruse, Kevin. *White Flight: Atlanta and the Making of Modern Conservatism.* Princeton: Princeton University Press, 2005.

Krutkik, Frank. "A Lifting Part of the Class Struggle: Diego Rivera's *The Flower Carrier* and the Hollywood Left." In *Un-American Hollywood: Politics and Film in the Blacklist Era,* edited by Frank Krutkik et al. New Brunswick: Rutgers University Press, 2008.

Kurtz, Howard. *Spin Cycle: Inside the Clinton Propaganda Machine.* New York: Pan Books, 1998.

Kutler, Stanley. *The Wars of Watergate: The Last Crisis of Richard Nixon.* New York: Knopf, 1990.

Langdon, Jennifer. *Caught in the Crossfire: Adrian Scott and the Politics of Americanism in 1940s Hollywood.* New York: Columbia University Press, 2008.

Lassiter, Matthew. *The Silent Majority: Suburban Politics in the Sunbelt South.* Princeton: Princeton University Press, 2006.

Leab, Daniel J. "Coolidge, Hays, and the 1920s Movies: Some Aspects of Image and Reality." In *Calvin Coolidge and the Coolidge Era: Essays on the History of the 1920s,* edited by John Earl Haynes. Washington, D.C.: Library of Congress, 1998.

Leuchtenburg, William E. *In the Shadow of FDR: From Harry Truman to George W. Bush.* New York: Cornell University Press, 2001.

Levine, Lawrence W. *Highbrow/Lowbrow: The Emergence of Cultural Hierarchy in America.* Cambridge: Harvard University Press, 1988.

Levine, Lawrence W., and Cornelia R. Levine. *The People and the President: America's Conversation with FDR.* Boston: Beacon, 2002.

Lubell, Samuel. *The Future of American Politics.* New York: Harper, 1951.

Mann, Robert. *Daisy Petals and Mushroom Clouds: LBJ, Barry Goldwater, and the Ad That Changed American Politics.* Baton Rouge: Louisiana State University Press, 2011.

Manvell, Roger. *Films and the Second World War.* New York: Dell, 1974.

Martin, Bradford. *The Theater Is in the Street: Politics and Public Performance in Sixties America.* Boston: University of Massachusetts Press, 2004.

May, Elaine Tyler. *Homeward Bound: American Families in the Cold War Era.* New York: Basic Books, 1988.

May, Lary. *The Big Tomorrow: Hollywood and the Politics of the American Way.* Chicago: University of Chicago Press, 2000.

———. *Recasting America: Culture and Politics in the Age of the Cold War.* Chicago: University of Chicago Press, 1989.

———. *Screening Out the Past: The Birth of Mass Culture and the Motion Picture Industry.* Chicago: University of Chicago Press, 1980.

McGerr, Michael E. *The Decline of Popular Politics: The American North, 1865–1928.* New York: Oxford University Press, 1986.

McGirr, Lisa. *Suburban Warriors: The Origin of the New American Right.* Princeton: Princeton University Press, 2001.

McGovern, Charles. *Sold American: Consumption and Citizenship, 1890–1945.* Chapel Hill: University of North Carolina Press, 2006.

McLuhan, Marshall. *Understanding Media: The Extensions of Man.* New York: McGraw-Hill, 1964.

Menand, Louis. "Being There." Article accompanying *The War Room,* directed by Chris Hegedus and D. A. Pennebaker. 1993. Criterion Collection, DVD, 2012.

Merton, Robert K. *Mass Persuasion: The Social Psychology of the War Bond Drive.* 3rd ed. New York: Howard Fertig, 2004.

Midkiff-DeBauche, Leslie. "Reminiscences of the Past, Conditions of the Present: At the Movies in Milwaukee in 1918." In *American Movie Audiences: From the Turn of the Century to the Early Sound Era,* edited by Melvyn Stokes and Richard Maltby. London: British Film Institute, 1999.

Miller, James. *Flowers in the Dustbin: The Rise of Rock and Roll, 1947–1977.* New York: Simon and Schuster, 1999.

Mitchell, Greg. *The Campaign of the Century: Upton Sinclair's Race for Governor of California and the Birth of Media Politics*. New York: Random House, 1992.

Muscio, Giuliana. *Hollywood's New Deal*: Philadelphia: Temple University Press, 1997.

Navasky, Victor. *Naming Names*. New York: Viking, 1980.

Neve, Brian. *Film and Politics in America: A Social Tradition*. New York: Routledge, 1992.

Nimmo, Dan. *Political Persuaders: The Techniques of Modern Election Campaigns*. Englewood Cliffs, N.J.: Prentice-Hall, 1970.

Olson, Keith W. *Watergate: The Presidential Scandal That Shook America*. Lawrence: University Press of Kansas, 2003.

Owens, John R., Edmond Costantini, and Louis Weschler. *California Politics and Parties*. New York: Macmillan, 1970.

Parenti, Michael. *Make Believe Media: The Politics of Entertainment*. New York: St. Martin's, 1992.

Parker, Allison M. *Purifying America: Women, Cultural Reform, and Pro-Censorship Activism, 1873–1933*. Urbana: University of Illinois Press, 1997.

Patterson, James. *Grand Expectations: The United States, 1945–1974*. New York: Oxford University Press, 1996.

Patterson, Thomas. *Out of Order*. New York: Random House, 1994.

Peretti, Burton W. *The Leading Man: Hollywood and the Presidential Image*. New Brunswick: Rutgers University Press, 2012.

Perlstein, Rick. *Before the Storm: Barry Goldwater and the Unmaking of American Consensus*. New York: Nation Books, 2009.

———. *Nixonland: The Rise of a President and the Fracturing of America*. New York: Simon and Schuster, 2008.

Phillips-Fein, Kim. *Invisible Hands: The Businessmen's Crusade against the New Deal*. New York: W. W. Norton, 2009.

Pizzitola, Louis. *Hearst over Hollywood: Power, Passion, and Propaganda in the Movies*. New York: Columbia University Press, 2002.

Ponce de Leon, Charles. *Self-Exposure: Human Interest Journalism and the Emergence of Celebrity in America, 1980–1940*. Chapel Hill: University of North Carolina Press, 2002.

Postman, Neil. *Amusing Ourselves to Death: Public Discourse in the Age of Show Business*. New York: Penguin, 1986.

Powers, Stephen. *Hollywood's America: Social and Political Themes in Motion Pictures*. Boulder: Westview, 1996.

Putnam, Robert. *Bowling Alone: The Collapse and Revival of American Community*. New York: Simon and Schuster, 2000.

Raymond, Emilie. *From My Dead Cold Hands: Charlton Heston and American Politics*. Lexington: University of Kentucky Press, 2006.

———. *Stars for Freedom*. Seattle: University of Washington Press, forthcoming.

Robinson, Peter M. *The Dance of the Comedians: The People, the President, and the Performance of Political Standup Comedy in America*. Boston: University of Massachusetts Press, 2010.

Roddick, Nick. *A New Deal in Entertainment: Warner Brothers in the 1930s*. London: British Film Institute, 1983.

Rogin, Michael. *Ronald Reagan: "The Movie" and Other Episodes in Political Demonology*. Berkeley: University of California Press, 1987.

Ross, Steven. "*Confessions of a Nazi Spy*: Warner Bros., Anti-Fascism, and the Politicization of Hollywood." In *Warners' War: Politics, Pop Culture, and Propaganda in Wartime Hollywood*, edited by Martin Kaplan and Johanna Blakley. Los Angeles: Norman Lear Center Press, University of Southern California, 2004.

———. *Hollywood Left and Right: How Movie Stars Shape American Politics*. New York: Oxford University Press, 2011.

———. "The Revolt of the Audience: Reconsidering Audiences and Reception during the Silent Era." In *American Movie Audiences: From the Turn of the Century to the Early Sound Era*, edited by Melvyn Stokes and Richard Maltby. London: British Film Institute, 1999.

———. *Working Class Hollywood*. Princeton: Princeton University Press, 1999.

Rosten, Leo. *Hollywood: The Movie Colony, the Movie Makers*. New York: Harcourt Brace, 1941.

Sabato, Larry. *The Rise of Political Consultants: New Ways of Winning Elections*. New York: Basic Books, 1981.

Schlesinger, Arthur M., Jr. *History of United States Political Parties*. New York: Chelsea House, 1973.

Schroeder, Alan. *Celebrity-in-Chief: How Show Business Took over the White House*. Boulder: Westview, 2004.

Schudson, Michael. *The Power of the News*. Cambridge: Harvard University Press, 1995.

Schulman, Bruce. *From Cotton Belt to Sunbelt: Federal Policy, Economic Development, and the Transformation of the South, 1938–1980*. New York: Oxford University Press, 1991.

———. *Lyndon B. Johnson* and *American Liberalism*. 2nd ed. Boston: Bedford/ St. Martin's, 2010.

———. *The Seventies: The Great Shift in American Culture, Society, and Politics*. New York: Free Press, 2001.

Schwartz, Sheila. *The Hollywood Writers' War*. New York: Knopf, 1982.

Scott, Ian. *American Politics in Hollywood Film*. Chicago: Fitzroy Dearborn, 2000.

Simon, Art. "*The House I Live In*: Albert Maltz and the Fight against Anti-Semitism." In *Un-American Hollywood: Politics and Film in the Blacklist Era*, edited by Frank Krutkik. New Brunswick: Rutgers University Press, 2008.

Sklar, Robert. *City Boys: Cagney, Bogart, Garfield*. Princeton: Princeton University Press, 1992.

———. *Movie Made America: A Cultural History of the American Movies*. 2nd ed. New York: Vintage Books, 1994.

Skocpol, Theda, and Morris P. Riorina, eds. *Civic Engagement in American Democracy*. Washington, D.C.: Brookings Institution Press, 1999.

Skowronek, Stephen. *Building a New American State: The Expansion of National Administrative Capacities, 1877–1920*. New York: Cambridge University Press, 1982.

Smith, Jean Edward. *Eisenhower in War and Peace*. New York: Random House, 2012.

Snow, Nancy. "Confessions of a Hollywood Propagandist: Harry Warner, FDR, and Celluloid Persuasion." In *Warners' War: Politics, Pop Culture, and Propaganda in*

Wartime Hollywood, edited by Martin Kaplan and Johanna Blakley. Los Angeles: Norman Lear Center Press, University of Southern California, 2004.

Starr, Paul. *The Creation of the Media: Political Origins in Modern Communications*. New York: Basic Books, 2004.

Stokes, Melvyn, and Richard Maltby, eds. *American Movie Audiences: From the Turn of the Century to the Early Sound Era*. London: British Film Institute, 1999.

Straw, Will. "Documentary Realism and the Postwar Left." In *Un-American Hollywood: Politics and Film in the Blacklist Era*, edited by Frank Krutkik. New Brunswick: Rutgers University Press, 2008.

Street, John. *Politics and Popular Culture*. Cambridge: Polity Press, 1997.

Street, John, Sanna Inthorn, and Martin Scott. *From Entertainment to Citizenship: Politics and Popular Culture*. Manchester, UK: University of Manchester Press, 2013.

Summers, Mark W. *Party Games: Getting, Keeping, and Using Power in Gilded Age Politics*. Chapel Hill: University of North Carolina Press, 2003.

Susman, Warren. *Culture as History: The Transformation of American Society in the Twentieth Century*. New York: Pantheon, 1985.

Torres, Sasha. *Black, White, and in Color: Television and Black Civil Rights*. Princeton: Princeton University Press, 2003.

Troy, Gil. *Morning in America: How Ronald Reagan Invented the 1980s*. Princeton: Princeton University Press, 2005.

———. *See How They Ran: The Changing Role of the Presidential Candidate*. Cambridge: Harvard University Press, 1996.

Vaughn, Stephen L. *Holding Fast the Inner Lines: Democracy, Nationalism, and the Committee on Public Information*. Chapel Hill: University of North Carolina Press, 1980.

———. "Political Censorship during the Cold War." In *Movie Censorship and American Culture*, edited by Francis G. Couvares. Boston: University of Massachusetts Press, 2006.

———. *Ronald Reagan in Hollywood*. New York: Cambridge University Press, 1994.

Wall, Wendy. *Inventing the "American Way": The Politics of Consensus from the New Deal to the Civil Rights Movement*. New York: Oxford University Press, 2008.

Ward, Brian. *Just My Soul Responding: Rhythm and Blues, Black Consciousness, and Race Relations*. Berkeley: University of California Press, 1998.

———, ed. *Culture and the Modern African American Freedom Struggle*. Gainesville: University Press of Florida, 2001.

Weiner, Jon. *Gimme Some Truth: The John Lennon FBI Files*. Berkeley: University of California Press, 2000.

Welky, David. *The Moguls and the Dictators: Hollywood and the Coming of WWII*. Baltimore: Johns Hopkins University Press, 2008.

Whitfield, Stephen. *The Culture of the Cold War*. Baltimore: Johns Hopkins University Press, 1991.

Winfield, Betty Houchin. *FDR and the News Media*. New York: Columbia University Press, 1994.

Wright, Leah. "The Loneliness of the Black Conservative: Black Republicans and the Grand Old Party." Ph.D. diss., Princeton University, 2009.

Index

Abell, Bess, 200, 215

Actors Equity Association, 172

Actors' Refugee Committee, 46

Adamson, Harold, 71

Advertising: and entertainment, 4, 9; and political process, 6, 7, 8, 15, 19, 131–34, 155, 156, 235 (n. 27); and presidential election of 1952, 9, 139, 155, 156, 258 (n. 15); and Eisenhower, 10, 131–32, 134–35, 147–49, 160, 163; and Hoover, 15, 19, 20, 134, 237 (n. 13); and war bond campaign, 68, 70, 72, 73; and celebrity political activism, 88; and presidential election of 1944, 88, 90; and television, 131, 133, 135, 177; and public opinion polls, 131, 170, 190, 205; and presidential election of 1956, 132, 133, 147–49, 151, 152; and celebrity political culture, 160; and John F. Kennedy, 160, 165, 168, 170; and presidential election of 1960, 168, 170, 194; and Nixon, 193, 194, 199, 201, 205–6, 210; and Lyndon Johnson, 200

Affordable Health Care Act, 232

Africa, 140, 259–60 (n. 48)

African Americans: and Office of War Information, 56–57, 64; and 16mm films, 70; and presidential election of 1960, 168. *See also* Civil rights

Agnew, Spiro, 212

Ailes, Roger, 190, 191–92, 199, 202, 203, 209–10

The Alamo (film), 194

Alexander, Herbert, 168, 177

Alger, Horatio, 5

Alger Hiss hearings, 206

Allen, James, 63

All Star Bond Rally (film), 71, 72, 247 (n. 93)

America First, 42, 96, 97

American Farm Bureau Federation, 88

American Federation of Labor, 88, 237 (n. 15)

American Federation of Television and Radio Artists, 172

American Guild of Musical Artists, 172

American Guild of Variety Artists, 172

Americanism: and war bond campaign, 67; rhetoric of, 78, 91–92, 99–100, 120, 122, 123, 128; politics of, 104, 109, 110, 112, 138, 141, 197; and Eisenhower, 136

Americanism Defense League, 97

American Legion, 92, 226

American way of life: and Motion Picture Alliance, 75, 77, 91, 92, 98; and anticommunism, 112

Anticommunism: and California politics, 4; and conservatism, 51, 104, 123; and Motion Picture Alliance, 75, 92, 93, 98, 250 (n. 66); in postwar years, 78; and House Un-American Activities Committee, 101, 111, 120; and Murphy, 104, 112, 115; and Wanger, 104, 124, 128; and liberalism, 107, 110, 154, 173; and Johnston, 112–13; and motion picture industry, 126–27, 128, 136, 138

Anti-Semitism, 26, 43, 56–57, 93, 96, 128

Arbuckle, Fatty, 111

Arnold, Thurman, 34

Authors League of America, 94

Authors League Fund, 172

Autry, Gene, 33

Bacall, Lauren, 109, 116, 154

Ball, Lucille, 35, 211

Barrymore, Ethel, 12

Barrymore, Lionel, 12

Barton, Bruce, 130, 133, 134, 135

Basie, Count, 175, 186

Batten, Barton, Durstine & Osborn (BBD&O), 130, 131, 133, 134, 139, 146, 193

Baxter, Leone, 2, 6, 8

Beatty, Warren, 218, 221–22, 223

Belafonte, Harry, 168, 173–77, 179, 186, 265 (n. 40)

Bendix, William, 84

Bennett, Constance, 89

Bennett, Joan, 35, 84, 87

The Bennetts (radio show), 2, 6

Benny, Jack, 161

Berg, Gertrude, 89

Bergen, Candice, 222

Berle, Milton, 89

Berlin, Irving, 37, 144

Bernays, Edward, 19, 237 (n. 13)

Bernstein, Leonard, 176, 180

Bessie, Alvah, 252 (n. 9)

The Best Years of Our Lives (film), 101, 109, 117–18

Beyoncé, 232

Biberman, Herbert, 252 (n. 9)

Bilbo, Theodore G., 80, 81

Biograph, 17

Biow, Milton, 88, 90, 250 (n. 57)

Bishop, Joey, 175, 180

Black Panthers, 222

Block, Ralph, 37, 54, 56, 126, 127

Boettiger, Anna Roosevelt, 33–34

Boettiger, John, 34

Bogart, Humphrey: and studio contract system, 25; and New Deal, 26; and Roosevelt, 35, 78–79, 84, 87, 88–91, 110; and Dies, 40; political involvement of, 48, 92, 110–11, 138; and House Un-American Activities Committee, 109, 116, 171; and Stevenson, 154, 155

Bonnie and Clyde (film), 219

Bracken, Eddie, 70

Brewer, Roy, 114, 124, 254–55 (n. 37)

Britt, May, 184

Bromberg, J. Edward, 253 (n. 9)

Brown, Pat, 188, 196, 270 (n. 11)

Bryan, William Jennings, 51

Bureau of Motion Pictures, 55–56, 58–61, 62, 63, 64, 65, 244 (n. 33), 245 (n. 67)

Bush, George H. W., 198

Butler, Paul, 152

Cagney, James, 39, 40, 83, 88

Caldiero, Ray, 217, 218–19, 223

California: gubernatorial election of 1934, 1–3, 5–7, 9, 10, 14, 19, 32, 36, 82, 91, 101, 135, 161, 232, 234 (n. 9); and celebrity political activism, 4–5, 13; weakness of partisan identification in, 6, 8; and direct legislation, 8; open party system of, 8, 14, 18–19, 20; open primary system of, 15; and cross-filing system, 18–19; gubernatorial election of 1938, 82; and presidential election of 1948, 134; and political role of television, 136, 150, 160, 161; and presidential election of 1952, 137, 138–39; gubernatorial election of 1962, 188, 195, 196, 270 (n. 11); gubernatorial election of 1966, 196

California Supreme Court, 105

Campaign Associates, 193

Campaign finance reform, 182

Cantor, Eddie, 154

Capitalism, 99, 106, 110, 112, 114, 117, 122, 140, 213, 215. *See also* Democracy

Capone, Al, 113

Capra, Frank, 54

Carne, Judy, 189

Carrillo, Leo, 23

Carville, James, 226

Catholic Church, 6, 21, 238 (n. 38)

Catholic Legion of Decency, 6, 110

Celebrities for Nixon, 194, 212, 215, 216, 217

Celebrity, public role of, 9, 13, 14, 17, 20, 23, 123, 196

Celebrity political activism: role in political process, 10, 13, 19–20, 23, 41; and presidential election of 1940, 34–35, 37; and communism, 39–40; and World War II propaganda effort, 44, 48–49, 53, 59, 65; and war bond campaigns, 67, 68,

72; and presidential election of 1944, 77, 78–80, 84–90, 227; Dies's characterization of, 79, 104; and civil rights, 79–82, 83, 86, 90, 168, 173–76, 177, 184, 186–87; "Message to Washington" event, 80–82; and "United We Stand" rally, 83, 248 (n. 21); and voter registration, 84; and spot endorsements, 85; credibility of, 90, 99; and Motion Picture Alliance, 93; and House Un-American Activities Committee, 104, 111, 119, 170, 171; and democracy, 105; and box office support, 105–6; debates on, 108; and presidential election of 1952, 139, 152; and presidential election of 1956, 145, 146–48; and Democratic Party, 161, 162, 173, 178, 179–80, 184; and presidential election of 1960, 161–62, 166, 176, 179–80; and Nixon, 184, 186, 190, 197–98, 201, 210–18, 221–24, 229; opportunities and limitations of, 184–87; and Stars for Freedom, 187; and Lyndon Johnson, 200–201; and McGovern, 218–23

Celebrity political culture: and political legitimacy, 4, 157, 159, 164, 165, 189, 194, 231; foundation of, 9, 19, 23; growth of, 10, 157; and philanthropic efforts, 28, 29–34; and John F. Kennedy, 158–59, 160, 161, 164, 165, 182, 185, 186, 189, 192, 194, 226–27; and voter attitudes, 187, 227; and Nixon, 188, 189, 198–99, 205, 206; and William J. Clinton, 225–26, 228–29; and Reagan, 227–28

Chamber of Commerce, 20, 112

Champion, Gower, 147

Champion, Marge, 147

Chapin, Dwight, 215

Chaplin, Charlie, 37, 42, 65, 113

Chase, Chevy, 229

Churchill, Winston, 106

Citizens for Eisenhower Committee, 129, 132, 136, 137, 145–51, 155, 183, 192, 194

Citizens' Research Foundation, 177

Civic culture: and political participation, 9; role of Hollywood entertainment

industry in, 9, 14, 23, 26, 28, 41, 44; and Office of War Information, 58, 59; and war bond campaigns, 66, 73

Civil rights: and Hollywood entertainment industry, 28, 57; and Hollywood Free World Association, 76; and celebrity political activism, 79–82, 83, 86, 90, 168, 173–76, 177, 184, 186–87; and Hollywood Democratic Committee, 99, 100, 173; and Democratic Party, 171, 173, 184, 186; and Sammy Davis Jr., 173–75, 176, 177, 184, 186, 213, 215; and McGovern, 221

Civil Rights Act (1964), 187

Clark, Bennet "Champ," 42

Clark, D. Worth, 50

Clinton, Hillary, 229

Clinton, William J., 225–29, 230, 232

Clooney, George, 227, 228

Cold War: and Hollywood entertainment industry, 10, 98, 103, 104, 110, 112, 120, 122, 126–27, 128, 137, 139, 140; propaganda of, 104, 127, 131; and Eisenhower, 127, 140–41

Cole, Lester, 252 (n. 9)

Cole, Nat King, 168, 174, 179

College News Conference (television show), 164

Colson, Charles, 211

Committee for the First Amendment, 109–10, 115, 116, 127

Committee of Public Information, 13, 20, 32, 50, 55–56, 63, 238 (n. 34), 244 (n. 36)

Committee to Defend America by Aiding the Allies, 48, 49

Committee to Re-elect the President (CREEP), 190, 210–13, 215–18, 220, 223

Communism: Motion Picture Alliance against, 75, 92, 93, 94, 97, 98, 250 (n. 66), 251 (n. 96); and liberalism, 106–7. *See also* Anticommunism

Communist Party, 39, 40, 46–47, 97, 108, 117

Communist political activities: Fish's assessment of, 14–15; and artists and writers on Left, 25, 46; and Dies, 39, 40; and Office of War Information, 57;

and House Un-American Activities
Committee investigation, 103, 104, 108,
119, 252–53 (n. 9)
Community Chest, 28
Conference of Studio Unions (CSU),
113–14, 115, 254–55 (n. 37)
Confessions of a Nazi (film), 37, 42, 43,
45–46, 47
Congress of Industrial Organizations, 88
Conservative movement: and military-
industrial complex, 4; and critique of
liberal political activism, 47, 91; and
anticommunism, 51, 105, 123; ideology
of, 75, 77, 103, 136, 248 (n. 8), 257 (n. 88);
and presidential election of 1944, 78,
101; and congressional elections of
1942, 82; and Motion Picture Alliance,
93, 98, 250 (n. 66), 251 (n. 96)
Consumer culture, 15, 18, 30, 51, 62, 232,
243 (n. 24)
Coolidge, Calvin, 19–20, 92, 133, 237 (n. 13)
Cooper, Gary, 91, 93, 120, 147–48, 163
Corey, Wendell, 144
Corwin, Norman, 83, 109
Cotten, Joseph, 59
Council of Hollywood Unions and Guilds, 96
Cowles, Gardner "Mike," Jr., 63
Crawford, Joan, 25
Creel, George, 20
Crisis (film), 225
Crosby, Bing, 63, 71, 186
Crossfire (film), 101
Curtis, Tony, 176, 180

The Daily Show (television show), 4, 232
Daley, Richard, 166, 219
Davies, Marion, 27, 163
Davis, Bette: and John F. Kennedy, 10,
176, 180; on sixth estate, 10, 180, 268
(n. 85); and Roosevelt, 23, 79, 91; and
Screen Actors Guild, 25; and League of
Women Shoppers, 39; and war bond
campaign, 65, 67, 71; and Democratic
Party, 171; and McGovern, 222

Davis, Elmer, 54, 60
Davis, Sammy, Jr.: and John F. Kennedy,
166; and civil rights, 173–75, 176, 177,
184, 186, 213, 215; marriage to Britt, 184;
and Republican Party, 184, 186, 209,
213; and *Laugh-In*, 189; and Nixon,
207–9, 211, 213–16
Defilement of Race (Nazi publication), 47
De Havilland, Olivia, 79, 83, 84, 85, 86,
105–7, 111, 163
Democracy: Office of War Information's
promotion of, 56–57, 58, 63, 64; and war
bond campaigns, 66; Motion Picture
Alliance on, 77, 98; and celebrity political activism, 105; and communism,
106; and Hollywood entertainment
industry, 112–13, 122, 124, 140
Democratic National Committee (DNC):
and Hollywood for Roosevelt, 37; and
Hollywood Democratic Committee, 77,
81–82, 85, 87–88, 90, 100; and celebrity
political activism, 78–79, 128, 162, 169,
177, 194; and Office of War Information,
101; and television, 166, 168, 169; and
House Un-American Activities Committee, 170; and presidential election
of 1960, 177–79; and President's Club,
181–82, 227; and presidential election of
1968, 191; Watergate offices, 210
Democratic Party: and Sinclair, 2; and
Hollywood entertainment industry, 9,
15, 22, 74, 79, 82, 85, 87, 89, 90, 110–11,
138, 145, 166, 179, 181, 186, 190; and
presidential election of 1932, 22; and
New Deal programs, 30; and presidential election of 1940, 35, 36–37; allegations of communist infiltration of, 40,
111; and World War II, 44; and Mellett,
51; and Office of War Information, 64;
economic policies of, 77; racial policies
of, 77; and presidential election of 1944,
87; and House Un-American Activities
Committee, 104, 145, 162; and presidential election of 1956, 133, 151, 159; and

presidential election of 1952, 152–55; and presidential election of 1960, 158–59, 161–62, 165–66, 169, 176–78; and media image of candidates, 160; Truman Diamond Jubilee production, 161, 162; and John F. Kennedy, 164, 165–66, 264 (n. 22); fund-raising of, 177–82; and presidential election of 1972, 190, 218–23; and presidential election of 1968, 219–20

Denove, Jack, 168, 169, 226

Dewey, Thomas, 116, 130, 134

DiCaprio, Leonardo, 228

Dies, Martin, 38–39, 40, 78, 79, 98, 104, 116

Direct referendum voting, 235 (n. 29)

Disney, Walt, 91, 93, 137

Dmytryk, Edward, 252 (n. 9)

Documentary filmmaking, introduction of, 101

Dodd, Claire, 23

Dollars for Democrats campaign, 177–78, 181–82

Don't Look Back (documentary), 225

Douglas, Helen Gahagan, 86

Douglas, Kirk, 189, 211

Douglas, Melvyn, 7, 35, 40–41, 46, 82, 161

Douglas Edwards with the News (television program), 169

Dramatists Guild, 94

Drew, Robert, 165, 225

Duffy, Ben, 134, 135

Dunne, Irene, 194

Dunne, Phillip, 7, 82, 109

Durante, Jimmy, 85, 86, 161

Durrance, Thomas, 154

Dylan, Bob, 222, 225

Easy Rider (film), 219

Eddy, Nelson, 63

The Effect of Mass Media (Klapper), 198

Ehrlichman, John, 215

Eisenhower, Dwight: television campaigns of, 8, 10, 133, 134–35, 138–39, 141, 145, 151, 159, 160, 163, 168, 193–94, 227; and Cold War, 127, 140–41; and Hollywood entertainment industry, 128, 136, 139–44, 185, 211, 230; as president of Columbia University, 129, 257 (n. 2); and presidential election of 1952, 129–32, 137, 138–39, 145, 153, 155, 258 (n. 9); and Montgomery, 130, 131, 133, 134, 141–44, 148, 149, 156, 162, 163, 193–94, 206, 227; and presidential election of 1956, 132, 133, 144, 145–51, 178; and Republican Party, 139, 144–45, 146, 150, 151, 156–57, 192, 195, 199, 210, 258 (n. 12), 261 (n. 69); foreign policy of, 140–41; and Reagan, 196

Eisenhower, Mamie, 149

Eisenstein, Sergei, 15

"Election Eve" radio special, 35

Ellington, Duke, 174, 175

"End Poverty in California" (EPIC), 2, 3, 5, 6

Entertainment: role in political communication, 3–4, 6, 7, 8, 9, 10, 12, 13, 14, 15, 22, 41, 43–44, 53, 76–77, 78, 82, 86, 88, 89–90, 95, 98, 104, 113, 118, 147, 154, 159, 160, 202; debates on meaning of, 9, 16–17, 43–51, 77, 78, 90, 93, 97–98, 99, 101, 102, 104, 110, 115, 118, 123, 127–28, 230, 237 (n. 18); and Office of War Information, 59–60, 61, 63–64; and war bond campaign, 65, 66, 67, 71, 72, 73; patriotic, 83–84; manipulative power of, 101. *See also* Hollywood entertainment industry

Entertainment Industry Joint Committee for Eisenhower-Nixon, 137–38, 139

Establishing Anzio Beachhead (film), 69

The Execution of Private Slovik (film), 171

Executive Reorganization Act of 1939, 52

Face the Nation (television program), 169

Fairbanks, Douglas, Jr., 26, 35, 37, 43, 48–49, 52, 56, 230

Fairbanks, Douglas, Sr., 32, 65, 113

Fallon, Jimmy, 232

Farmer, Frances, 17

Fascism: and Hollywood entertainment industry, 28, 127; and Roosevelt, 33, 38; Harry Warner's speech on, 47; and Office of War Information, 55, 56; and Motion Picture Alliance, 75, 93, 94, 97

Faye, Alice, 205

FBI: Harry Warner on, 47; and communist influence investigations, 97; and House Un-American Activities Committee, 116, 171, 176; and message films, 252 (n. 105)

Federal Deposit Insurance Corporation, 31

Federal government: and Hollywood entertainment industry, 10, 17, 19–20, 34, 42–43, 102; and New Deal programs, 30; and motion picture industry, 51, 52–53, 64, 102, 123; and radio, 239 (n. 44)

Federal Theatre Project, 40

Federal Trade Commission, 21, 238 (n. 38)

Fifth War Loan Drive, 68–69, 70

"Film Fact, 1942" (Motion Picture Producers and Distributors of America), 53

Final Days (short film), 229–30

First Amendment rights, and House Un-American Activities Committee, 252 (n. 9)

Fish, Hamilton, Jr., 14–15, 43–44

Fitzgerald, Ella, 168, 175, 176, 177, 179

Flynn, John T., 42

Fonda, Henry, 35, 179

Fonda, Jane, 187

Fontaine, Joan, 107

Ford, Gerald, 229

Ford, Henry, 17

42nd Street (film), 24

42nd Street Special, 23, 24, 28

Foundation for Economic Education, 123

Four Full Years (film), 147, 148

Fox, William, 17, 18

France, 37, 47

Franco, Francisco, 46

Freedom Riders, 176

Free market: and California politics, 4; and Motion Picture Alliance, 77, 123; and Johnston, 121, 123, 140, 144; and

Hollywood entertainment industry, 126, 137; and Montgomery, 141

Gable, Clark, 39, 54, 91, 93

Galifianakis, Zach, 232

Gamble, Theodore "Ted," 69, 70, 72, 247 (n. 93)

Gardner, Eva, 154

Garfield, John, 84, 253 (n. 9)

Garland, Judy, 71, 88

Garment, Leonard (Len), 198, 199, 201, 202

Garner, John Nance, 27

Gavin, Bill, 198, 200, 201, 202–3, 204, 205

Gaynor, Janet, 29, 33

General Electric, 196, 238 (n. 38)

Gentleman's Agreement (film), 101

Giancana, Sam, 186

Gilbert, Price, 63

Gleason, Jackie, 191, 210

Goldwater, Barry, 196, 199, 200

Goldwyn, Samuel: and censorship of Hollywood entertainment industry, 17; and business interests of Hollywood entertainment industry, 18, 121; and New Deal, 26; and James Roosevelt, 33; and anti-Semitism, 56–57; and Republican Party, 128, 132, 136–38, 144, 145; and Eisenhower, 156; and studio contract system, 187

Grable, Betty, 71

Grant, Cary, 84

Grapes of Wrath (film), 115

Great Britain, 48, 121, 137, 163

Great Depression, 21, 26–27, 28, 32, 121, 122. *See also* New Deal

The Great Dictator (film), 42

Guild, Bascom & Bonfigli, 168

Gutwein, William, 69

Haldeman, H. R., 211, 216

Hall, Arsenio, 227

Harding, Warren, 13, 15, 237 (n. 13)

Harris, Lou, 165

Hart, Gary, 221

Hawn, Goldie, 221, 222

Hayes, Helen, 194

Hays, Will H., 13–14, 17–18, 21, 34, 54, 111

Hayworth, Rita, 59, 96

Hearst, William Randolph, 2, 12, 17, 92, 164, 264 (n. 18)

Hearst, William Randolph, Jr., 164

Hepburn, Katharine, 109

Heston, Charlton, 216

Hewitt, Don, 169, 170

Higgins, H. U. M., 70

Hitler, Adolf: propaganda of, 32–33, 48, 49, 155; and France, 37; dangers for European Jews under, 45; threat of expansion, 47; and Hollywood entertainment industry efforts against, 50; white supremacist world view of, 56; and Office of War Information, 57

Hoffman, Dustin, 190, 222

Hollywood Anti-Nazi League, 46, 117

Hollywood Blacklist, 104, 252–53 (n. 9)

Hollywood Committee for Polish Relief, 46

Hollywood Democratic Committee (HDC): and Democratic National Committee, 77, 81–82, 85, 87–88, 90, 100; and presidential election of 1944, 83–90, 230; and Republican Party, 89, 90, 222; and Motion Picture Alliance, 92, 93, 96, 103; and civil rights, 99, 100, 173; and Roosevelt, 106; and New Deal liberalism, 111; and grassroots mobilization, 171–72

Hollywood Dream Machine: political potential of, 1, 5, 8, 10; and media exploitation, 5; and presidential election of 1940, 36; and World War II, 44, 50; and presidential election of 1952, 154; and presidential election of 1960, 159–60, 163

Hollywood entertainment industry: and political communication, 4, 7, 8, 37; and publicity, 5, 17, 49–50, 73, 87, 90, 98, 165; business interests of, 6–7, 14, 16–17, 18, 21, 22, 26–27, 33, 34, 41, 57, 58, 101, 124–25, 126, 138, 140, 156–57, 238 (n. 38); self-censorship code, 6–7, 119;

and moral values, 7, 9–10, 14, 15, 17, 43, 236 (n. 9); role in political process, 8–10, 12–13, 14, 15–16, 18, 21–22, 27, 38, 41, 44–45, 79, 99, 103, 135–36; and meaning of "celebrity," 9; and philanthropic efforts, 9, 10, 26–27, 28, 29–34, 41, 67, 74, 172–75; and engagement in "industry politics," 10, 14, 21, 37, 41, 44, 163, 172, 211; and engagement in "patriotic politics," 10, 37, 41, 136; and engagement in "electoral politics," 10, 131, 160, 185, 258 (n. 13); and social respectability, 13, 236 (n. 9); and censorship policies, 14, 17, 19–20, 26, 28, 32, 43, 47, 54, 119, 123, 238 (n. 38), 252 (n. 105); and presidential politics, 22, 34–38, 131, 189, 192; and labor unions, 25–26, 79, 90, 94–95, 113–15, 128; and communist activity allegations, 40; and war bond campaigns, 44, 50, 53, 54, 61, 62, 65–74; and World War II propaganda efforts, 44, 47, 48, 49–50, 59, 65, 76, 78, 99, 109; and Office of War Information, 44, 76, 81, 82, 101, 106, 110, 123; and engagement in "ideological politics," 76, 107, 111; and engagement in "politics of Americanism," 104, 112, 138, 197

Hollywood for Roosevelt, 34, 35–37, 54, 79, 82, 84, 126

Hollywood for Stevenson, 154–55

Hollywood Free World Association (HFWA): inaugural dinner of, 75; and New Deal ideology, 75–76, 77, 99; and use of film to promote ideology, 76; Motion Picture Alliance challenging recognition of, 94, 96; and Wanger, 95–96

Hollywood Independent Citizens Committee of the Arts, Sciences, and Professions (HICCASP), 100–101, 106–7, 127, 171

Hollywood Press Club, 186

Hollywood Republican Club, 137–38

Hollywood Technical Directors League, 15

Hollywood Ten, 110, 119, 171, 252–53 (n. 9)

Hollywood Victory Committee, 54, 95

Hollywood War Activities Committee, 60, 64, 70, 245 (n. 67)

Hollywood Writers' Mobilization, 54, 94, 99

Holt, Joseph F., 126

Hoover, Herbert: and Mayer, 12–13, 15, 21, 23, 131, 150, 230, 238 (n. 39); and media advice of advertising executives, 15, 19, 20, 134, 237 (n. 13); public image of, 19, 38; and Motion Picture Alliance, 92; and Republican Party, 139

Hoover, J. Edgar, 164, 175, 176

Hope, Bob, 70, 71, 148, 218

Hopkins, Harry, 34, 45

Hopkins, Miriam, 39

Hopper, Hedda, 28, 97–98, 145, 198, 256 (n. 70)

Horacek, Joe, 212

House Un-American Activities Committee (HUAC): and Dies, 39; and Motion Picture Alliance, 94, 98, 101, 108, 116, 120; investigations of, 97, 103, 104, 108, 109, 116–20, 123, 126, 136, 145, 152, 162, 176, 252–53 (n. 9); and message films, 104, 108, 252 (n. 105); criticism of, 109, 116, 119, 127; repercussions of, 120, 121; legacy of, 171, 172

Hudson, Rock, 205

Hughes, Rupert, 94, 95

Humphrey, Hubert: and presidential election of 1960, 158, 159, 165, 177, 225; and mass media, 166, 193; and presidential election of 1968, 189, 190–92, 204, 205, 219–20; and media politics, 190–91, 192; and presidential election of 1972, 216

Huston, John, 109–10

Huston, Walter, 84, 85

I, Candidate for Governor (Sinclair), 7, 234 (n. 5)

I, Governor of California (Sinclair), 2

Independent Citizens Committee of the Arts, Sciences, and Professions, Inc. (ICCASP), 100

Industrial Workers of the World, 237 (n. 15)

Interest groups, 16, 22, 161, 237 (n. 14)

International Alliance of Theatrical Stage Employees (IATSE), 113, 115, 254 (n. 37)

International Development Advisory Board, 140

Internet, 232

Invasion of the Marshall Islands (film), 69

Irwin, William, 13, 236 (n. 5)

Jack Denove Productions, 165, 168, 226

Jackie Gleason Show (television show), 153

Jack Paar Show (television show), 169, 198

Jackson, Andrew, 179, 196

Japanese Americans, 57

Japanese militarism, 57

Jay-Z, 232

The Jazz Singer (film), 23, 24, 238 (n. 38)

Jefferson, Thomas, 118, 181

Jefferson-Jackson Day Dinners, 177, 178

Jennifer Jones Speaks for the "Fighting Generation" (short film), 70–71

Jewish Americans: in Hollywood entertainment industry, 9, 11, 16, 20–21, 24, 231–32; political involvement of, 12, 23, 24, 26, 45, 206; Nye's accusations against, 42; European exiles as, 46; and anti-Semitism, 56–57; and Motion Picture Alliance, 96

Johnson, Hiram W., 18

Johnson, Lady Bird, 200

Johnson, Lyndon, 152, 161, 166, 181, 187, 200–201, 215, 229

Johnston, Eric: and Hollywood entertainment industry, 111–13, 115, 118–19, 123–24, 125, 254–55 (n. 37); and doctrine of production, 112–13; and corporate liberalism, 113, 254 (n. 35); and labor unions, 114–15; and House Un-American Activities Committee, 115–16, 126, 134; and free market, 121, 123, 140, 144; and Truman, 137; and Eisenhower, 139–41, 143–44, 156, 163

Joint Anti-Fascist Refugee League, 117

Jolson, Al, 12, 19

Jones, Dorothy, 102, 103

Jones, Jennifer, 70–71

Kann, Maurice, 51

Kann, Red, 93

Kelley, Stanley, Jr., 8, 145, 156–57, 164, 202, 230, 235 (n. 29), 258 (n. 9)

Kelly, Gene, 85, 86, 109, 116, 176, 179

Kennedy, John F.: and media politics, 8, 10, 84, 158, 160–61, 162, 163, 164, 165, 166, 181, 184, 185, 191, 192, 194, 205, 206, 207, 228, 230–31; inaugural gala of, 10, 176–81, 182; and celebrity political culture, 158–59, 160, 161, 164, 165, 182, 185, 186, 189, 192, 194, 226–27; and presidential election of 1960, 158–59, 164–70, 171, 177, 188, 190–91, 191, 195, 199, 202, 213, 220, 225, 226, 229, 266 (n. 43); and television, 160, 164, 165, 168, 169–70, 193, 195; and William J. Clinton, 226–27

Kennedy, Joseph, 158, 159, 160, 162–64, 264 (n. 18)

Kennedy, Robert, 160, 184, 186, 202, 205, 213

Keyes, Paul, 191, 197–98, 202, 204

King, Martin Luther, Jr., 168, 173, 174, 175, 187, 265 (n. 40)

Kissinger, Henry, 212, 215

Klapper, Joseph, 198

Koverman, Ida, 12–13

Kraft Theater (television show), 153

Labor unions: and Hollywood entertainment industry, 25–26, 79, 90, 94–95, 113–15, 128; Motion Picture Alliance against, 97, 113; and House Un-American Activities Committee, 108; and Democratic Party, 152, 154, 158, 166

Laemmle, Carl, 17, 18

Lamour, Dorothy, 17, 29, 33, 65, 71

Lancaster, Burt, 221, 223

Lang, Fritz, 46

Lardner, Ring, Jr., 114, 252 (n. 9)

Lasker, Albert, 2, 6, 237 (n. 13)

Latin America, 49

Lavery, Emmet, 97

Lawford, Patricia, 162

Lawford, Peter, 162, 165, 166, 170–71, 175, 176, 178, 179

Lawson, John Howard, 26, 46, 91, 94, 107, 252–53 (n. 9)

Leach, Sybil Bruce, 65

League of Decency, 43

League of New York Theaters, 172

League of Women Shoppers, 39

Lee, Canada, 253 (n. 9)

Left: and movement politics, 4, 187; and Hollywood entertainment industry, 16, 41, 46; artists and writers of, 25, 46; and World War II, 46–47, 97; ideology of, 76, 99; and political language of entertainment, 104; splintering of, 105–11, 113; party structures of, 186; New Left, 186, 187; and democratic modernism, 242 (n. 12)

Leigh, Janet, 176, 180

Lend-Lease Act, 48

Lennon, John, 187

"Let's Go Out and Ring Door Bells" entertainment campaign, 84

Levy, David, 147–48

Lewis, William, 63

Liberalism: and California politics, 4, 7; and presidential election of 1940, 34–35, 36; Dies on, 40; and Popular Front, 46; conservatives' critique of, 47; and New Deal, 51, 78, 243 (n. 24); ideology of, 75, 77, 90, 106, 107, 110, 111, 114, 120, 154, 171; and political communication, 77; and presidential election of 1944, 77, 78–79, 82, 90, 101; and freedom of the screen, 91; and message films, 104, 120, 252 (n. 105); and House Un-American Activities Committee, 108–9, 111, 170–71, 173, 176

Lincoln, Abraham, 181

Lippmann, Walter, 20, 38, 193, 270 (n. 12)

Lodge, Henry Cabot, 163

Lord & Thomas advertising agency, 2, 6, 7

Los Angeles Council for Civic Unity, 83

Lubell, Samuel, 130, 144

MacLaine, Shirley, 179, 218–19, 221–22, 223

MacLeish, Archibald, 63

Magic (short film), 59

Magnuson, Warren G., 85

Magruder, Jeb Stuart, 211, 212

Maltz, Albert, 117, 171, 252 (n. 9)

March, Frederic, 7, 40, 48, 171, 176, 179, 181, 242 (n. 11)

March on Washington (1963), 187

Marion Davies Foundation, 27

Market crash of 1929, 21, 24, 163

Martin, Dean, 175, 186

Martin, Dick, 189

Martin, Joseph, 103, 116

Martin, Tony, 154

Marx, Groucho, 35

Marx, Harpo, 71

Massey, Raymond, 37

Mass media: political system dominated by, 1, 3, 9, 10, 133, 235 (n. 27); and publicity, 5; power of, 8, 143, 156; early attitudes toward, 13; and Office of War Information, 55, 58, 62; and celebrity political activism, 79, 87, 88, 224; and presidential election of 1952, 130, 131, 139, 258 (n. 9); and Roosevelt, 133, 143, 159, 193, 230; and Republican Party, 144, 150, 151, 152, 156; and presidential election of 1956, 151; and Democratic Party, 152, 162, 164, 166; and presidential election of 1960, 159; liberal bias in, 188; expansion of, 190, 232; Lippmann on, 193, 270 (n. 12); technology of, 232. *See also* Media politics

Mass-mediated politics, 3, 4, 5, 9

Master of Emergencies (film), 13

Matthews, J. B., 39–40

Mayer, Louis B.: and California gubernatorial election of 1934, 2; and Republican Party, 2, 6, 12, 13, 14, 15, 18, 22, 133, 134; political involvement of, 8, 12–13, 14, 20, 21, 22, 23, 38, 77, 165, 238 (n. 39), 258 (n. 13); and Hoover, 12–13, 15, 21, 23, 131, 150, 230, 238 (n. 39); and business potential of Hollywood entertainment industry, 16, 17, 18, 21; and Vitagraph, 24; and anti-Semitism, 57; and Motion Picture Alliance, 92; and House

Un-American Activities Committee, 110, 118–19; and Johnston, 112; and studio contract system, 187

McCarthy, Eugene, 220

McCarthy, Joe, 173, 192

McCloskey, Matthew, 179

McDowell, John, 108, 118

McGinniss, Joe, 205

McGovern, George, 190, 207, 218–23

McGovern-Fraser Commission, 220, 230

McGuinness, James K., 94, 95, 96, 117, 251 (n. 78)

McHugh, Jimmy, 71

McLuhan, Marshall, 3

Mead, James M., 38

Meany, George, 155

Media-driven performative politics, 4, 5, 10, 195, 224, 235 (nn. 15, 32)

Media image: and publicity, 5, 19, 85; and studio contract system, 24; and Office of War Information, 59; and John F. Kennedy, 160, 161, 170, 271 (n. 22); and Nixon, 189, 193, 195, 197–99, 201, 203, 271 (n. 22); and Reagan, 197

Media politics: and political mudslinging, 1; and California gubernatorial election of 1934, 3, 5, 6–7, 234 (n. 9); and grassroots mobilization, 4; strategies of, 5, 6, 9; and John F. Kennedy, 8, 10, 84, 158, 160–61, 162, 163, 164, 165, 166, 181, 184, 185, 191, 192, 194, 205, 206, 207, 228, 230–31; and Reagan, 8, 10, 195, 196–97, 201, 211, 228, 230, 271 (n. 28); and Nixon, 8, 11, 188–90, 191, 192–95, 197–207, 209, 210–17, 227, 270 (n. 12), 273 (n. 64); development of, 12–13, 133; and primary races, 84; and fund-raising, 161, 165, 173, 176–77, 186; and campaign costs, 177–84; and Humphrey, 190–91, 192; and scandals, 231, 277 (n. 19)

Meet the Press (television show), 169, 198, 203

Mellett, Lowell, 51–55, 58, 60, 61, 64, 118, 127, 245 (n. 67), 255 (n. 56)

Menjou, Adolphe, 117–18

Merriam, Frank, 2, 5, 19

Merton, Robert K., 67

Merv Griffin Show (television show), 191

Mexican Americans, and civil rights, 83

MGM studio: and political participation, 2; and Republican Party, 12; and censorship, 20; and Bureau of Motion Pictures, 58, 59; and war bond campaign, 72; and Sam Wood, 75, 91; and Motion Picture Alliance, 75, 91, 92, 93, 94; and conservatives, 77; and Screen Playwrights Guild, 95

Mickelson, Sig, 168, 169, 170

Middle class, 16, 237 (n. 18), 238 (n. 38)

Military-industrial complex, 4

Mission to Moscow (film), 93, 118

Mr. Blabbermouth (short film), 59

Mitchell, John, 212, 215

Moffitt, John C., 117

Monroe, Lucy, 63

Monterey Pop (documentary), 225

Montgomery, Robert: and presidential electoral politics, 10, 132, 144, 222; and Screen Actors Guild, 25; and Dies, 40; and World War II efforts, 54; on communism, 115, 134; and Eisenhower, 130, 131, 133, 134, 141–44, 148, 149, 156, 162, 163, 193–94, 206, 227; and Republican Party, 134, 135, 141, 144

Moore, Victor, 84

Moral values, and Hollywood entertainment industry, 7, 9–10, 14, 15, 17, 43, 236 (n. 9)

Morgenthau, Henry, Jr., 69

Morris, Chester, 59

Motion Picture Alliance for the Preservation of American Ideals (MPA): statement of principles, 75, 92, 93; on dangers of "message films," 76–77, 98; and rhetoric of Americanism, 78, 91–92, 99–100; and accusations of communist infiltration, 93, 95, 96, 97, 98, 103, 128, 247 (n. 8); and conservative movement, 93, 98, 250 (n. 66), 251 (n. 96); and House Un-American Activities Committee, 94, 98, 101, 108, 116, 120;

ideology of, 95, 99, 101, 113, 115, 123, 127, 254 (n. 37); and isolationist groups, 96; membership as controversial, 97; and Rand, 122; and Wanger, 128, 257 (n. 90); and presidential election of 1952, 137

Motion Picture Committee Co-Operating for National Defense (War Activities Committee), 53, 54, 71

Motion Picture Committee for Polish Relief, 46

Motion Picture Democratic Committee, 82

Motion Picture Electrical Parade and Sports Pageant, 21–22, 26–28, 32

Motion picture industry: and Sinclair's proposed tax and economic system, 2, 6; economic power of, 15, 17, 140; development of, 16–17; vertical structure of, 18, 34, 53, 60, 62, 121, 137, 253 (n. 9); and labor unions, 25–26; and philanthropic efforts, 26, 27, 28, 29, 46, 74, 172; Nye's investigation of propaganda efforts, 42–44; and federal government, 51, 52–53, 64, 102, 123; and Office of War Information guidelines, 55–58; and House Un-American Activities Committee investigation, 103, 108, 109; role of, 124–26, 140–41; and Joseph Kennedy, 162–64. *See also* Hollywood entertainment industry; Studio contract system

Motion Picture Industry Council (MPIC), 123–26, 128, 172, 196, 271 (n. 28)

Motion Picture Producers and Distributors of America (MPPDA), 14, 18, 53, 96, 112; Production Code Administration, 7, 45

Motion Picture Relief Fund, 27, 28

Movie stars: media image of, 20, 24; wealth and fame of, 21; and production process, 24; and Screen Actors Guild, 25; and World War II war effort participation, 53–54, 56, 61; in newsreels, 61; and war bond campaigns, 65–66, 68, 69–71. *See also* Studio contract system

Muckraking era, 20, 238 (n. 34)

Mullendore, W. C., 123

Mundy, James A., 30

Murphy, George: and presidential electoral politics, 10, 132, 134, 138, 139, 145, 161, 222; and anticommunism, 104, 112, 115; and Movietime U.S.A. offensive, 125; and Republican Party, 134, 135, 136, 137–38, 144, 183, 258 (n. 18); and Eisenhower, 148, 156, 162, 163, 178, 195, 206; and Nixon, 194; and media politics, 195–96, 197, 201, 211

Music Corporation of America (MCA), 212

Muskie, Edmund, 216

National Association for the Advancement of Colored People (NAACP), 173–74, 175, 176, 186

National Association of Visual Education Dealers, 64, 69, 70

National Committee for the Birthday Ball for the President, 29

National Emergency Council, 51

National Industrial Recovery Act, 24

National Infantile Paralysis Foundation, 172

National Labor Relations Board, 40, 114

National School Service program, 55

National Service Corps, 200

Nazarro, Cliff, 88

Nazism: and anti-Nazi motion pictures, 37, 42, 43, 45–46, 47, 52; and France, 37, 47; and conquest of Poland, 47; Harry Warner on, 47–48; Jack Warner on, 47–48; Fairbanks on, 48, 49; and Hollywood entertainment industry efforts against, 50; and Office of War Information, 57; and Motion Picture Alliance, 94, 96, 97

Nazi-Soviet Nonaggression Pact, 46–47

Negro Actors Guild, 172

The Negro Soldier (film), 64, 70

Neutrality Act, 45

New Deal: challenges to, 4; and Roosevelt's coalition, 22, 24, 26, 41, 45, 82, 87, 133; and Hollywood entertainment industry, 23, 24, 25, 41, 46, 51, 81, 102–3,

104, 113, 123, 132; and philanthropic efforts, 29–34; promotion of, 30; conservative critics of, 38; as communist threat, 40; ideology of, 51, 56, 58, 75–76, 87, 91, 92, 99, 105, 111, 113, 114, 116, 122, 123, 141, 151, 243 (n. 24)

Newman, Paul, 187, 222

Newspapers Guild, 94

Newsreels, 23, 27, 55, 56, 60–61

New York Waldorf Astoria Hotel, 110, 252–53 (n. 9)

Nicholson, Jack, 221

Nickelodeons, 16

Nitti, Frank, 113

Nixon, Pat, 149, 193

Nixon, Richard: and media politics, 8, 11, 188–90, 191, 192–95, 197–207, 209, 210–17, 227, 270 (n. 12), 273 (n. 64); and House Un-American Activities Committee, 116; and presidential election of 1952, 138, 193, 206; and presidential election of 1956, 146, 149, 151; and presidential election of 1960, 157, 160, 166, 169, 181, 188, 191, 193, 195, 199, 205, 206, 207, 209, 266 (n. 43); and fund-raising, 184; and celebrity political activism, 184, 186, 190, 197–98, 201, 210–18, 221–24, 229; and gubernatorial election of 1962, 188, 192, 195, 196, 270 (n. 11); and presidential election of 1968, 188–89, 197, 198, 199–207, 209, 220, 228; and media image, 189, 193, 195, 197–99, 201, 203, 271 (n. 22); and television, 193, 198–99, 203, 205; and presidential election of 1972, 207–18, 222–23; and permanent campaign, 210; resignation of, 229–30

Norman, Craig & Kummel (NC&K), 152, 153

North Star (film), 118

Nye, Gerald, 42–44, 45, 50, 78, 79, 96, 97–98, 103–4, 116

Obama, Barack, 232

O'Brien, Pat, 35

Oceans 11 (film), 165

Office of Censor, 58

Office of Facts and Figures, 52

Office of Governmental Reports, 52

Office of the Coordinator of Inter-American Affairs, 49, 52

Office of War Information (OWI): Hollywood entertainment industry's collaboration with, 44, 76, 81, 82, 101, 106, 110, 123; agencies of, 52, 243 (n. 28), 245 (n. 67); creation of, 54–55; overseas branch of, 55, 64; guidelines for motion picture industry, 55–57, 81, 83; budget cuts of, 67; and war bond films, 70, 71, 73; Motion Picture Alliance against, 92; and liberalism, 96, 106; and New Deal ideology, 243 (n. 24)

Office of War Mobilization and Reconversion, 102, 103, 123

On the Waterfront (film), 205

Ornitz, Samuel, 252 (n. 9)

Paley, William, 149

Paramount Pictures, 18, 238 (n. 38)

Parsons, Louella, 28

Party machines: and political participation, 3, 9, 10, 15–16, 18–19, 231; and Democratic Party, 152

Patriotism: and Hollywood entertainment industry's World War II efforts, 44, 50, 51, 52, 53, 54, 76, 109; and short films, 47, 56, 58, 59; and Office of War Information, 55; and war bond campaign, 66, 67, 68, 71; and Motion Picture Alliance, 91, 93; Hollywood entertainment industry's Cold War efforts, 105, 112, 126, 128; and Eisenhower, 136

Peace Corps, 200

Pearl Harbor, Japanese attack on, 51

Pease, Frank, 15

Pedagogical films, 58, 61, 62

Pennebaker, D. A., 225–26, 228

Pepper, Claude, 80

Pepper, George, 85, 87

Person to Person (television show), 169

Peter, Paul, and Mary, 222

Peters, Ralph, 59

Philanthropic efforts: and Hollywood entertainment industry, 9, 10, 26–27, 28, 29–34, 41, 67, 74, 172–75; and New Deal, 29–34; and partisan activities, 47; and World War II mobilization, 53, 54

Pickford, Mary, 32, 65, 113

Poitier, Sidney, 174, 175, 176, 177, 179, 186

Poland, 47

Political apathy, role of media politics in, 235 (n. 27)

Political communication: role of entertainment in, 3–4, 6, 7, 8, 9, 10, 12, 13, 14, 15, 22, 41, 43–44, 53, 76–77, 78, 82, 86, 88, 89–90, 95, 98, 104, 113, 118, 147, 154, 159, 160, 202; and television, 143; and radio, 239 (n. 44)

Political consultants: and Hollywood entertainment industry, 4, 6, 7; in California, 6; and television, 8; and presidential election of 1956, 14; and presidential election of 1952, 131, 139, 156, 157; and presidential election of 1972, 190; and presidential election of 1968, 199–207

Political legitimacy, and politicians as celebrities, 4, 157, 159, 164, 165, 189, 194, 231. *See also* Celebrity political culture

Political mudslinging, and media politics, 1

Political process: and advertising, 6, 7, 8, 15, 19, 131–34, 155, 156, 235 (n. 27); role of Hollywood entertainment industry in, 8–10, 12–13, 14, 15–16, 18, 21–22, 27, 38, 41, 44–45, 79, 99, 103, 135–36; and celebrity political activism, 10, 13, 19–20, 23, 41; commodification of, 235 (n. 27)

Poll tax, 80, 81

Popular Front alliance, 46, 107

Powell, Pamela, 207, 209, 218

Power, Tyrone, 70

Poynter, Nelson, 55, 58, 60

Presidential Countdown (television show), 169

Presley, Elvis, 216

Price, Ray, 199, 201, 202

Pride of the Marines (film), 117
Primary (documentary), 165, 225, 226, 227
Primary Colors (film), 229
Production Division, Bureau of Motion Pictures, 60
Prowse, Juliet, 180
Publicity: and Hollywood entertainment industry, 5, 17, 49–50, 73, 87, 90, 98, 165; and war bond campaign, 72, 73–74; and Motion Picture Alliance, 93
Public opinion: and Hollywood entertainment industry, 10, 22, 33, 37, 123; and mass media, 20; value of, 20, 238 (n. 34); and New Deal programs, 30; and pollsters, 131, 170, 190, 205
Public Opinion (Lippmann), 20
Public relations campaigns, 9, 16, 22–23, 41, 72–73, 124, 126, 138, 141, 196

Quinn, Anthony, 83

Radio: political role of, 8, 133; Roosevelt's use of, 23, 29–30, 250 (n. 57); and presidential election of 1940, 35; and Nye's investigation of propaganda efforts, 42–43; and Office of War Information, 55; and war bond campaign, 68, 69, 72; and presidential election of 1944, 79, 86, 89, 91; "Hollywood for Roosevelt" broadcast, 84; celebrity activists' spot radio endorsements, 85, 86, 87, 91, 135; "Hollywood Fights Back" broadcast, 109; and presidential election of 1952, 138; and Hollywood entertainment industry, 238 (n. 38); and federal government's role, 239 (n. 44); and public opinion, 240 (n. 67)
Radio Writers Guild, 94
Rambo (film), 227–28
Rand, Ayn, 121–22, 123
Randolph, A. Philip, 174
Rankin, John E., 80
Rat Pack, 175, 186, 211
Rayburn, Sam, 161
Read, Leonard, 123

Reagan, C. R., 62–63, 64, 66, 68, 69, 70, 73
Reagan, Ronald: and presidential election of 1980, 1, 161, 227–28; and media politics, 8, 10, 195, 196–97, 201, 211, 228, 230, 271 (n. 28); and Screen Actors Guild, 25, 114, 118; and World War II efforts, 54; and anticommunism, 104; and message films, 106; on communism, 106–7, 115, 126, 134, 253 (n. 18); and House Un-American Activities Committee, 116, 118, 134; and Movietime U.S.A. offensive, 125; and Republican Party, 128, 132, 183, 258 (n. 18); and Eisenhower, 196; and gubernatorial election of 1966, 196–97; and presidential election of 1968, 197
Red Cross, 28, 59, 61
Reeves, Rosser, 135
Reinsch, J. Leonard, 87, 168, 169
Republican Associates (RA), 183–84, 270 (n. 16)
Republican National Committee (RNC), 13, 135, 144, 145, 193
Republican Party: and Mayer, 2, 6, 12, 13, 14, 15, 18, 22, 133, 134; and Hollywood entertainment industry, 9, 12–13, 15, 18, 111, 123, 128, 136, 156, 157, 183, 184, 185, 190; and Hays, 13–14; and presidential election of 1932, 22; and philanthropic efforts, 27–28; and presidential election of 1940, 35, 36; and World War II, 44; and New Deal, 45, 102–3; and Office of War Information, 64; and Hollywood Democratic Committee, 89, 90, 222; and political language of entertainment, 104; and presidential election of 1952, 129, 131, 135, 136, 141, 145, 153, 155; and presidential election of 1956, 133, 144, 145–46; and presidential election of 1948, 134; and Eisenhower, 139, 144–45, 146, 150, 151, 156–57, 192, 195, 199, 210, 258 (n. 12), 261 (n. 69); and media image of candidates, 160; fund-raising of, 182–84; ideological cleavages in, 192, 270 (n. 11)

Republican Sustaining Fund, 183
Research, Reports, and Information Division, Bureau of Motion Pictures, 60
Reston, James, 195
Reynolds, Robert R., 93–94
Rice, Elmer, 89, 97
Right: and movement politics, 4; and Hollywood entertainment industry, 41, 76, 99, 250 (n. 66); ideology of, 76, 99, 113; and political language of entertainment, 76–77, 104; New Right, 184, 257 (n. 88)
RKO studio, 53
Robert Montgomery Presents Television Show (television show), 149
Robinson, Edward G., 85, 88, 91, 111, 248 (n. 8)
Rockefeller, Nelson, 189, 199
Rogers, Ginger, 97, 194, 206
Rogers, Howard Emmett, 94, 95
Rogers, Lela, 97, 98, 123
Rogers, Will, 22, 25
Rogers, Will, Jr., 81
Rooney, Mickey, 29, 33
Roosevelt, Eleanor, 23, 31, 32, 39, 164, 165, 166
Roosevelt, Franklin Delano: and California gubernatorial election of 1934, 2, 7; and Jack Warner, 14, 22, 23, 24, 26, 27, 32, 34, 37, 43, 49, 91, 114; and presidential election of 1932, 14, 22, 27; public relations campaigns of, 22–23; and "forgotten man" icon, 24; birthday ball celebrations of, 29–33, 38, 43, 61; and presidential election of 1936, 31–32; and presidential election of 1940, 34–35, 36, 37–38, 40–41, 49; Nye's accusations against, 43, 50, 103; and World War II policies, 45, 48–49, 51, 80, 86; Four Freedoms, 51, 56; and motion picture industry, 52–53, 102, 120; and Office of War Information, 54–55, 64; State of the Union address of 1942, 56; and Japanese American internment camps, 57; in newsreels, 60–61; and Fifth War Loan Drive, 69; and

Hollywood entertainment industry's World War II efforts, 76, 95; and presidential election of 1944, 77, 78, 79–81, 82, 86–91, 92, 100, 101, 105, 107, 110, 136, 168; and Democratic networks, 84, 154; death of, 87, 101, 103, 105, 106, 111, 114, 128; Motion Picture Alliance against principles of, 92; influence of, 103, 144, 172; and Reagan, 107; Rand on, 122; and Wanger, 127; and mass media, 133, 143, 159, 193, 230; Eisenhower's service under, 151; and Joseph Kennedy, 163, 264 (n. 18); Fireside Chats of, 250 (n. 57). *See also* New Deal
Roosevelt, James (Jimmy), 33, 35, 106–7, 254 (n. 19)
Rosenman, Samuel, 250 (n. 57)
Rosenthal, Philip, 229
Ross, Lillian, 120, 122
Rosten, Leo, 21, 36, 103, 108
Rourke, Jack, 191
Rowan, Dan, 189, 204
Rowan & Martin's Laugh-In (television show), 188–89, 191, 203–5, 210, 273 (n. 64)
Rubinstein, Arthur, 89
Rubirosa, Porfirio, 185
Rumsfeld, Donald, 215
Russell, Louis, 108

Sahl, Mort, 161
Salinger, Pierre, 195
"Salute to Roosevelt" radio event, 35
Saturday Night Live (television show), 4, 229, 230
Schaefer, George J., 53
Schary, Dore, 96, 106, 107, 124, 138, 155, 161
Schenck, Joseph, 6
Schlatter, George, 204
Schlesinger, Arthur, Jr., 63, 264 (n. 22)
Schneider, John, 155
Schreiber, Taft, 212, 216
Schwarzenegger, Arnold, 1
Scott, Adrian, 252 (n. 9)
Scott, Martha, 84

Screen Actors Guild (SAG), 25–26, 106, 114, 118, 172, 239 (n. 56)

Screen Directors Guild, 25

Screen Playwrights Guild, 93, 94–95, 250–51 (n. 78)

Screen Producers Guild, 25

Screen Writers Guild, 25, 93, 94–95, 97

Selma voting rights campaign, 187

Selznick, David O., 56–57, 97

Selznick International Studio, 33

Seventh War Loan Drive, 71, 72, 247 (n. 93)

Shakespeare, Frank, 199, 202

Shearer, Norma, 32

Sherwood, Robert, 48, 55

Shirley Temple fabrication, 40

Shore, Dinah, 84

Short films: and anti-Sinclair forces in California gubernatorial election of 1934, 2–3; and Hollywood entertainment industry's World War II efforts, 47, 51; and Office of War Information, 56, 58, 59, 70

Simon and Garfunkel, 222

Sinatra, Frank: and war bond campaign, 71; and presidential election of 1944, 87, 89; and House Un-American Activities Committee, 109, 170, 176; and presidential election of 1952, 138, 154, 155; and John F. Kennedy, 158, 160, 165, 166, 170, 171, 176, 178, 179, 180, 181, 184, 185–86, 225, 226, 265 (n. 31); and Rat Pack, 175; and civil rights, 176, 177, 186; and Republican Party, 186, 211, 213; and Nixon, 186, 211, 215–16

Sinclair, Upton: and California gubernatorial election of 1934, 1–3, 5–8, 10, 19, 32, 36, 82, 91, 101; and political involvement of Hollywood entertainment industry, 26, 28

16mm films, 61–63, 64, 65, 66–73, 101

Sixth estate, and role of Hollywood entertainment industry, 10, 180, 181, 268 (n. 85)

Sixth War Loan Drive, 70

Skelton, Red, 179

Skouras, Spyros, 147

Smith, Kate, 67

Social class, 15, 16, 18, 20, 95, 117–20, 237 (n. 18), 238 (n. 38)

Socialism, 46, 141

Social media, 232

Social Security, 30

Song of Russia (film), 118

Sorrell, Herb, 113, 114, 254–55 (n. 37)

Southern California Crusade for Freedom, 128

Southern California Republican Party, 183

Southern Christian Leadership Conference (SCLC), 173, 174, 175, 186

Southern evangelicals, migration to Southern California, 4

Southern Pacific Railroad, 18

Soviet Union: and World War II, 46–47; and Hollywood Free World Association, 76; Motion Picture Alliance against, 93; postwar tensions with, 106; and Hollywood entertainment industry, 113; and Johnston, 140; and Nixon, 192

Spacey, Kevin, 229

Spanish Civil War (1936), 40, 46, 117, 127, 172

Spielberg, Steven, 219

Stalin, Joseph, 106, 118

Star Wars (film), 228

Steelman, John R., 102, 123

Stephanopoulos, George, 226

Stevens, George, 109

Stevenson, Adlai, 133, 138, 151–55, 158, 159, 161, 166, 193, 194, 195, 264 (n. 22)

Stewart, James, 218

Stewart, Jon, 232

Streisand, Barbra, 190, 221, 227

Stripling, Robert, 108, 119

Studio contract system: and support for political candidates, 5, 24, 32, 47, 86, 224, 232; political influence of, 7, 24, 26, 28, 29; conditions of, 24–25; and labor unions, 25; and de Havilland, 105; and Hollywood Ten, 110, 119; collapse of, 121, 187, 256 (n. 67). *See also* Hollywood entertainment industry; Motion picture industry

Sullivan, Ed, 148
Sullivan, Mark, 38, 89
Swayze, John Cameron, 149

Taft, Robert A., 103, 130, 137
Taylor, Robert, 29, 39, 118, 120, 255 (n. 56)
Technological determinism, effects of, 3, 234 (n. 11)
Ted Bates Company, 135
Television: political role of, 3–4, 8, 131, 133, 135, 136, 138–39, 143, 144, 160, 162, 230, 235 (n. 27), 258 (n. 16); and Eisenhower, 8, 10, 133, 134–35, 138–39, 141, 145, 151, 159, 160, 163, 168, 193–94, 227; and presidential election of 1952, 9, 129–30, 131, 134–35, 138–39, 145, 154, 155; and motion picture industry, 121, 128, 137; and advertising, 131, 133, 135, 177; growth of, 133; and presidential election of 1956, 133, 144, 145, 146–50, 151, 152; and John F. Kennedy, 160, 164, 165, 168, 169–70, 193, 195; and presidential election of 1960, 160, 166, 168, 169, 177, 264 (n. 7); and Nixon, 193, 198–99, 203, 205
Temple, Shirley, 39, 40
Tenney, Jack, 93
Texas Visual Education Company, 62–63
Thalberg, Irving, 95, 250–51 (n. 78)
Theaters: as central area for community engagement, 55, 89–90; and war bond events, 65, 68
Theatre Authority, 172–74
Thomas, J. Parnell, 108, 116, 119–20
Tobin, Richard, 149
Tolan-Kilgore-Pepper bill, 81
Tonight Show (television show), 1
Tracy, Spencer, 109
Traditional family values, and California politics, 4
Treleaven, Harry, 198–99, 202
Truman, Harry S.: and presidential election of 1944, 89; and motion picture industry, 102, 103, 105, 123, 137, 230; as president, 111, 144; and Cold War, 124, 127; and presidential election of 1948, 135; and Democratic Party, 136, 161, 162; Eisenhower's service under, 151; Truman Diamond Jubilee production, 161, 162
Trumbo, Dalton, 106, 252 (n. 9)
Turrou, Leon G., 45
Twentieth Century Fox, 71
Twenty-sixth Amendment, 190, 219, 230

Understanding Media (McLuhan), 3
"United for California" campaign, 2
United Nations, and Office of War Information, 57
United Service Organization (USO), 50, 54, 71, 78, 91, 110
U.S. Agriculture Department, 61
U.S. Coast Guard, 61
U.S. Commerce Department, 61
U.S. Commission of Inter-American Development, 113
U.S. Defense Department, 37
U.S. Interior Department, 61
U.S. Justice Department, 34, 61, 121, 182
U.S. Labor Department, 40
U.S. Signal Corps, 61
U.S. State Department, 37, 126
U.S. Supreme Court, 33
U.S. Treasury Department, 44, 61, 65, 66–72, 245 (n. 67)
United States v. Paramount Pictures, 121
U.S. War Department, 61
"United We Survive, Divided We Fall" (Harry Warner), 47
Upper class, and entertainment, 16, 20

Valenti, Jack, 229
Victory War Loan Drive, 70
Vietnam War, 187, 200, 221
The View (television show), 232
Visitin' Round at Coolidge Corner (campaign film), 19
Vitagraph, 17, 23–24
Voice of America, 55
Volunteerism, 28, 29, 32, 54, 60, 64, 77
Volunteers for Nixon, 192–93, 194

Voter attitudes: perceptions of, 15–16, 237 (n. 14); and influence of Hollywood entertainment industry, 99, 147, 160, 202; and television, 143, 147; and public opinion polls, 165; and celebrity political culture, 187, 227

Voter turnout: and patriotic entertainment, 83–84; and celebrity political activism, 87, 90, 162; role of media politics in, 132–33, 235 (n. 27); decline in, 230; history of, 231, 277 (n. 22)

Voting Rights Act (1965), 187

Wag the Dog (film), 229

Wallace, Henry, 35, 75, 76, 171

Wanger, Walter: on entertainment, 46, 63–64, 127–28; and Roosevelt, 52; on war bond campaign, 67; and Hollywood Free World Association, 95–96; and anticommunism, 104, 124, 128; on motion picture industry, 124; and Movietime U.S.A. offensive, 125; and Motion Picture Alliance, 128, 257 (n. 90)

War Activities Committee (Motion Picture Committee Co-Operating for National Defense), 53, 54, 71

Warm Springs Foundation for Infantile Paralysis, 29–30, 32, 41

Warner, Harry: and Roosevelt, 23, 27, 43, 49; family background of, 24; on Hollywood entertainment industry's role in international markets, 34; political involvement of, 45, 46, 47–48; and Johnston, 112

Warner, Jack L.: and California gubernatorial election of 1934, 2, 6; and presidential electoral politics, 10, 138–39; political involvement of, 14, 21–24, 27–28, 45, 46, 47–48, 92, 114, 238 (n. 39); and Roosevelt, 14, 22, 23, 24, 26, 27, 32, 34, 37, 43, 49, 91, 114; family background of, 24; and philanthropic efforts, 27, 28; and World War II efforts, 54, 118; and anti-Semitism, 56–57; and

anticommunism, 104, 115; and House Un-American Activities Committee, 110, 115, 116, 118; and Johnston, 112; and Hollywood Ten, 119; and Republican Party, 128, 132, 135, 136–38, 144, 145, 183; and Eisenhower, 156, 163; and studio contract system, 187

Warner Bros. Studio: motto of, 23; growth of, 23–24; and New Deal promotional films, 24; and studio contract system, 25; political involvement of, 26–27, 47; training films for U.S. Department of Commerce, 61; Motion Picture Alliance against, 93; and de Havilland, 105; and labor union strikes, 114; and war bond campaign, 247 (n. 93)

The War Room (documentary), 226, 227, 228–29

Washington, Dinah, 175

Washington, George, 231

Wasserman, Lew, 105

Wayne, John, 189, 194, 206, 210, 218

Welch, Raquel, 222

Welles, Orson, 59, 70, 79, 84, 85, 87, 92, 96, 99

Welles Wonder Show (short film), 59

The West Wing (television show), 229

Whistling in Dixie (film), 58

Whitaker, Clem, 2, 6, 8

Whitaker & Baxter, 2, 3, 6, 7, 8, 235 (n. 29)

Whitaker & Baxter's Campaigns, Inc., 8

White, Theodore, 158

White, William Allen, 48, 49

White House Correspondents' Dinner, 229

Wilder, Billy, 109

Willkie, Wendell, 35–36, 43, 50, 134

Will Mastin Trio, 174

Wilson, Woodrow, 32

Wolfe, Tom, 222

Wood, John, 108

Wood, Sam, 75, 91

Working class, and entertainment, 16, 20

Works Progress Administration, 31, 40

World War I, 13, 20, 32, 55–56, 161, 238 (n. 34)

World War II: and Hollywood entertainment industry, 37, 49–50, 76, 99, 109; and isolationists, 42, 45, 48, 49, 50, 78, 97; and Hollywood-inspired propaganda, 44, 47, 48, 49–50, 59, 65, 76, 78, 99, 109; and patriotism, 44, 50, 51, 52, 53, 54, 76, 109; Roosevelt's policies during, 45, 48–49, 51, 80, 86; and Japanese attack on Pearl Harbor, 51; and war films, 54

Writers' Congress, 76, 101, 127

Wyler, William, 28, 109

Young & Rubicam (Y&R), 131, 146–49, 163

Youngstein, Max, 71, 72

Your Hit Parade (radio show), 78, 87

Zanuck, Darryl, 54, 76, 101, 136–38, 144, 145, 156, 215

Zanuck, Richard, 215

Zoot Suit Riots, 83, 248 (n. 14)

Zukor, Adolph, 13, 17, 18, 24